The Qur'an

Compiled by
M.H. Shakir

Published by

Tahrike Tarsile Qur'an, Inc.

Publishers and Distributors of the Holy Qur'an
80-08 51st Avenue
Elmhurst, New York 11373
E-Mail: read@koranusa.org
http://www.koranusa.org

Published by
Tahrike Tarsile Qur'an, Inc.

Publishers and Distributors of the Holy Qur'an
80-08 51st Avenue
Elmhurst, New York 11373
E-Mail: read@koranusa.org
http://www.koranusa.org

Seventeenth U.S. Edition 2011

Library of Congress Catalog Number: 84-060213

British Library Cataloguing in Publication Data

ISBN: 978-0-94036818-7 (racksize) English

Printed in Canada

Publisher's Introduction

The Qur'an is a divine message revealed by God to Prophet Muhammad (Peace be upon him - PBUH) over a period of 23 years. In 610 AD while Prophet Muhammad (PBUH) was meditating in the cave of Hira, outside the city of Mecca, Angel Gabriel visited Muhammad commanding him to *"Read"* (Chapter 96: Verse 1). This was the first verse revealed to Muhammad from God (Glorified is He). Over the next several years, Prophet Muhammad (PBUH) continued to receive revelations from God, which were ultimately compiled into 114 chapters.

The revelation of the Qur'an came over a period of time. The chapters of the Qur'an tend to be arranged by the place of revelation; generally, chapters revealed in Madina are longer and are placed in the first half of the Qur'an while chapters revealed in Mecca tend to be shorter and are placed in the latter half. Although some verses and chapters can be read on their own, the Qur'an is best understood in the light of the times and the culture in which it was revealed and of course, some background knowledge of the Arabic language.

There are three qualities which are particularly strongly emphasized in the Qur'an: forgiveness, justice and the value of human life. In chapter 5, verse 32 of the Qur'an, we are told: *"If anyone slew a person, unless it be for murder or for spreading mischief in the land – it would be as if he slew the whole people: and if anyone saved a life, it would be as though he saved the life of the whole people."*

Forgiveness is another core message of the Qur'an. Not only is God infinitely merciful and compassionate, but He enjoins these qualities on Muslims, just as he does on all humanity. As we see in chapter 5, verse 45 of the Qur'an: *"We ordained therein for them: life for life, eye for eye, nose for nose, ear for ear, tooth for tooth and wounds equal for equal; but if anyone remits the retaliation by way of charity, it is an act of atonement for himself. And if any fail to judge by (the light of) what God has revealed, they are (no better than) wrongdoers."* The message of forgiveness is repeated often throughout the Qur'an; readers familiar with the New Testament will recognize the similarity of the Qur'an's message of forgiveness to that taught by Jesus.

Justice is one of the cornerstones of the Qur'an; throughout this Revelation, Muhammad exhorted believers and non-believers alike to treat one another justly and with fairness. In chapter 4, verse 135 of the Qur'an, we are told: *"O you who believe! Stand out firmly for justice as witnesses to God; even against yourself, or your parents or your kin and whether it is against rich or poor: for God can best protect both. Follow not the lusts (of your hearts) lest you swerve and if you distort (justice) or decline to do justice, verily God is well acquainted with all you do."* The Qur'an teaches that every one of us is to treat others with justice as well as kindness.

The Qur'an is a continuation of the revelation that came to Abraham in the Book of Abraham upon Papyri, to Moses as the Torah (Taurat), to Jesus as the Bible (Injeel) and to David in the Psalms (Zabur):

"The same religion He has established for you as that which He enjoined on Noah— that which We have sent by inspiration to you—and that which We enjoined on Abraham, Moses, and Jesus; namely, that you should remain steadfast in religion, and make no divisions therein ..." (The Qur'an, 42:13)

The stories of prophets of the Torah and the Bible, as many readers may know, are also found in the Qur'an; indeed, many of these prophets have a place of prominence in Islam. Abraham is regarded as the patriarch of all three of the great monotheistic faiths.

In Islamic tradition, Abraham and Isma'il (Ishmael) built the Kaaba in Mecca: "And remember Abraham and Isma'il raised the foundations of the House (with this prayer): *'Our Lord! Accept this service from us; for you are the All-Hearing, the All-Knowing.'"* (The Qur'an, 2:127). The valley in which Mecca is located is known as the Valley of Abraham in commemoration of this event.

linguistic complexity, which makes it somewhat difficult to translate. As such, translations of the Qur'an, such as is presented here, should be regarded as a simple interpretation of its meaning – in order to truly understand and to experience the Qur'an as it was originally revealed, it is essential that it be read in the original Arabic.

Tahrike Tarsile Qur'an, Inc., February 2011

PREFACE

The Qur'an is the final conclusion of all divine revelations especially the family of Abrahamic faith: of the Torah revealed to Moses and the Bible revealed to Jesus, peace be upon both of them. Islam's first and most significant tenet is *Tawhid,* the belief in the one and only God Who reveals the same truth to various nations, addressing each of them in its own language, according to its own understanding, culture and traditions. Muslims believe that since there is only one God, there is likewise only one truth, one human race that descended from one couple, Adam and Eve, one heaven, one hell, and one way to achieve salvation and eternal bliss.

While inviting the faithful to lead a pious and righteous life, the Holy Qur'an also contains many observations on natural phenomena and explanatory details in total agreement with modern scientific discoveries. Read in it about the creation of planets in the universe, referred to as "worlds" (1:2), about the earth splitting from the sun then getting cooled in preparation for life (21:30), about the creation of everything in pairs (36:36), about the succession of the night and the day (36:37), about the numerous earthly and celestial phenomena ... Read in it about the galaxies, the stars, the planetary systems, and the orbiting of the sun and the moon (36:38-40), the creation of which, the Holy Qur'an asserts, is greater and more complex than that of our human species. The Holy Qur'an refers to the heavenly strata (84:18-25) and to the "heavenly bodies," the asteroids and the comets. It informs us that water is the origin of life (21:30). Read in the Holy Qur'an about the stages through which the human embryo passes till it develops a living being (23:12-15); it is in complete agreement with modern science. And the Holy Qur'an refers to the gradual evolution, the six periods of aeons culminating in the life as we know it (7:54).

While he is mentioned in the Qur'an numerous times, the importance of Abraham (and his descendants) to the Islamic faith can perhaps best be summed up in the following verses: *"We gave him (Abraham) Isaac and Jacob: all (three) We guided: and before him We guided Noah, and among his progeny, David, Solomon, Job, Joseph, Moses, and Aaron: thus do We reward those who do good: and Zakariya and John and Jesus and Elias: all in the ranks of the Righteous: and Ismail and Elisha and Jonah and Lut: and to all We gave favor above the nations: (To them) and to their fathers, and progeny and brethren: We chose them. And We guided them to a straight way."* The Qur'an, 6:83-86

The story of Noah and the Flood is told in the Qur'an as well; Noah is considered a prophet in Islam, just as he is in Judaism and Christianity and the accounts in the Qur'an and the Old Testament (Gen. 6:9 – 8:19) are remarkably similar; in the Qur'an, we read: *"So we inspired him (with this message): 'Construct the Ark within Our sight and under our guidance; then when comes Our command and the fountains of the earth gush forth, take on board pairs of every species, male and female; and your family – except those of them against whom the Word has already gone forth: and address me not in favor of the wrongdoers, for they shall be drowned (in the flood)."* The Qur'an, 23:27

Mary, the mother of Prophet Jesus, has a chapter dedicated in her name and is one of the few women to be mentioned by name. As we read in the Qur'an: *"Behold! The angels said: 'O Mary! God has chosen you and purified you – chosen you above the women of all nations.'"* (The Qur'an 3:42) Mary is in fact mentioned more times in the Qur'an than she is in the Bible.

The Qur'an was revealed not to distinguish Islam as a separate religion, but the revelation of God came as the final message that embodies a universal message for people of all times. Arabic is the language that was used for the revelation of this divine message and was also the language of the people that the Qur'an was initially revealed to. The Arabic language is known for its poetic qualities and its

Is there any description of our creation more eloquent than this? Is there anyone who can alter this sequence in our creation? If all human beings are unable to come into this world in any way other than the one stated in these verses, then it is the speech of the Almighty, the Creator of everything and everyone, the Lord of the Worlds. So Praise be to God and Exalted is He above what they describe.

The Holy Qur'an contains a vast wealth of knowledge relevant to the science of astronomy; it enjoins the faithful to contemplate upon the creation of the heavens and the earth, encouraging them to look above to witness the wonders of the heavenly kingdom so that they may realize the Greatness and Omnipotence of their Creator.

No human being can ever be acquainted with all the knowledge embedded in the Holy Qur'an, for it is the speech of the Almighty, the Praised and the Glorified One, Who has said, "Say: If the sea were ink for the words of my Lord, the sea would surely be consumed before the words of my Lord are exhausted even if We were to bring the like of it to add thereto" (Qur'an, 18:109).

Yasin T. al-Jibouri
Falls Church, Virginia, U.S.A.
August 1999

NAMES

The following list shows the Arabic names and their English equivalents.

ARABIC NAMES:	ENGLISH EQUIVALENTS
Allah	God
Adam	Adam
Ayyub	Job
Dawood	David
Firon	Pharaoh
Habeel	Abel
Haroun	Aaron
Ibrahim	Abraham
Ilyas	Elias
Imrān	Amran
Injeel	Gospel
Ishāq	Isaac
Ismail	Ishmael
Isa	Jesus
Jalut	Goliath
Jibreel	Gabriel
Qabeel	Cain
Lut	Lot
Majuj	Magog
Maryam	Mary
Masjid	Mosque
Mikaeel	Michael
Misr	Egypt
Musa	Moses
Nasrani	Christian
Nuh	Noah
Qarun	Korah
Saba	Sheba
Sulaiman	Solomon
Talut	Saul
Taurat	Torah
Uzair	Ezra
Yahudi	Jew
Yahya	John the Baptist

NAMES

ARABIC NAMES:	ENGLISH EQUIVALENTS
Yajuj	Gog
Yaqoub	Jacob
Yunus	Jonah
Yusuf	Joseph
Zakariya	Zacharias

CONTENTS

CONTENTS

CONTENTS

THE OPENING

1. **In the name of Allah, the Beneficent, the Merciful.**
2. All praise is due to Allah, the Lord of the Worlds.
3. The Beneficent, the Merciful.
4. Master of the Day of Judgment.
5. Thee do we serve and Thee do we beseech for help.
6. Keep us on the right path.
7. The path of those upon whom Thou hast bestowed favors. Not (the path) of those upon whom Thy wrath is brought down, nor of those who go astray.

THE COW

In the name of Allah, the Beneficent, the Merciful.

1. Alif Lam Mim.
2. This Book, there is no doubt in it, is a guide to those who guard (against evil).
3. Those who believe in the unseen and keep up prayer and spend out of what We have given them.
4. And who believe in that which has been revealed to you and that which was revealed before you and they are sure of the hereafter.
5. These are on a right course from their Lord and these it is that shall be successful.
6. Surely those who disbelieve, it being alike to them whether you warn them, or do not warn them, will not believe.
7. Allah has set a seal upon their hearts and upon their hearing and there is a covering over their eyes, and there is a great punishment for them.
8. And there are some people who say: We believe in Allah and the last day; and they are not at all believers.
9. They desire to deceive Allah and those who believe, and they deceive only themselves and they do not perceive.
10. There is a disease in their hearts, so Allah added to their disease and they shall have a painful chastisement because they lied.

11. And when it is said to them, Do not make mischief in the land, they say: We are but peace-makers.

12. Now surely they themselves are the mischief makers, but they do not perceive.

13. And when it is said to them: Believe as the people believe, they say: Shall we believe as the fools believe? Now surely they themselves are the fools, but they do not know.

14. And when they meet those who believe, they say: We believe; and when they are alone with their evil ones, they say: Surely we are with you, we were only mocking.

15. Allah shall pay them back their mockery, and He leaves them alone in their inordinacy, blindly wandering on.

16. These are they who buy error for the right direction, so their bargain shall bring no gain, nor are they the followers of the right direction.

17. Their parable is like the parable of one who kindled a fire, but when it had illumined all around him, Allah took away their light, and left them in utter darkness—they do not see.

18. Deaf, dumb (and) blind, so they will not turn back.

19. Or like abundant rain from the cloud in which is utter darkness and thunder and lightning; they put their fingers into their ears because of the thunder peal, for fear of death, and Allah encompasses the unbelievers.

20. The lightning almost takes away their sight; whenever it shines on them they walk in it, and when it becomes dark to them they stand still; and if Allah had pleased He would certainly have taken away their hearing and their sight; surely Allah has power over all things.

21. O men! serve your Lord Who created you and those before you so that you may guard (against evil).

22. Who made the earth a resting place for you and the heaven a canopy and (Who) sends down rain from the cloud, then brings forth with it subsistence for you of the fruits; therefore do not set up rivals to Allah while you know.

23. And if you are in doubt as to that which We have revealed to Our servant, then produce a chapter like it and call on your witnesses besides Allah if you are truthful.

24. But if you do (it) not and never shall you do (it), then be on your guard against the fire of which men and stones are the fuel; it is prepared for the unbelievers.

25. And convey good news to those who believe and do good

deeds, that they shall have gardens in which rivers flow; whenever they shall be given a portion of the fruit thereof, they shall say: This is what was given to us before; and they shall be given the like of it, and they shall have pure mates in them, and in them, they shall abide.

26. Surely Allah is not ashamed to set forth any parable—(that of) a lowest or any thing above that; then as for those who believe, they know that it is the truth from their Lord, and as for those who disbelieve, they say: What is it that Allah means by this parable: He causes many to err by it and many He leads aright by it! but He does not cause to err by it (any) except the transgressors,

27. Who break the covenant of Allah after its confirmation and cut asunder what Allah has ordered to be joined, and make mischief in the land; these it is that are the losers.

28. How do you deny Allah and you were dead and He gave you life? Again He will cause you to die and again bring you to life; then you shall be brought back to Him.

29. He it is Who created for you all that is in the earth, and He directed Himself to the heaven, so He made them complete seven heavens, and He knows all things.

30. And when your Lord said to the angels, I am going to place in the earth a vicegerent, they said: What! wilt Thou place in it such as shall make mischief in it and shed blood, and we celebrate Thy praise and extol Thy holiness? He said: Surely I know what you do not know.

31. And He taught Adam all the names, then presented them to the angels; then He said: Tell me the names of those if you are right.

32. They said: Glory be to Thee! we have no knowledge but that which Thou hast taught us; surely Thou art the Knowing, the Wise.

33. He said: O Adam! inform them of their names. Then when he had informed them of their names, He said: Did I not say to you that I surely know what is secrets in the heavens and the earth and (that) I know what you manifest and what you hide?

34. And when We said to the angels: Make obeisance to Adam they did obeisance, but Satan (did it not). He refused and he was proud, and he was one of the unbelievers.

35. And We said: O Adam! Dwell you and your wife in the

garden and eat from it a plenteous (food) wherever you wish and do not approach this tree, for then you will be of the unjust.

36. But the Shaitan made them both fall from it, and caused them to depart from that (state) in which they were; and We said: Get forth, some of you being the enemies of others, and there is for you in the earth an abode and a provision for a time.

37. Then Adam received (some) words from his Lord, so He turned to him mercifully; surely He is Oft-returning (to mercy), the Merciful.

38. We said: Go forth from this (state) all; so surely there will come to you a guidance from Me, then whoever follows My guidance, no fear shall come upon them, nor shall they grieve.

39. And (as to) those who disbelieve in and reject My communications, they are the inmates of the fire, in it they shall abide.

40. O children of Israel! call to mind My favor which I bestowed on you and be faithful to (your) covenant with Me, I will fulfill (My) covenant with you; and of Me, Me alone, should you be afraid.

41. And believe in what I have revealed, verifying that which is with you, and be not the first to deny it, neither take a mean price in exchange for My communications; and Me, Me alone should you fear.

42. And do not mix up the truth with the falsehood, nor hide the truth while you know (it).

43. And keep up prayer and pay the poor-rate and bow down with those who bow down.

44. What! do you enjoin men to be good and neglect your own souls while you read the Book; have you then no sense?

45. And seek assistance through patience and prayer, and most surely it is a hard thing except for the humble ones,

46. Who know that they shall meet their Lord and that they shall return to Him.

47. O children of Israel! call to mind My favor which I bestowed on you and that I made you excel the nations.

48. And be on your guard against a day when one soul shall not avail another in the least, neither shall intercession on its behalf be accepted, nor shall any compensation be taken from it, nor shall they be helped.

49. And when We delivered you from Firon's people, who subjected you to severe torment, killing your sons and sparing your women, and in this there was a great trial from your Lord.

50. And when We parted the sea for you, so We saved you and drowned the followers of Firon and you watched by.

51. And when We appointed a time of forty nights with Musa, then you took the calf (for a god) after him and you were unjust.

52. Then We pardoned you after that so that you might give thanks.

53. And when We gave Musa the Book and the distinction that you might walk aright.

54. And when Musa said to his people: O my people! you have surely been unjust to yourselves by taking the calf (for a god), therefore turn to your Creator (penitently), so kill your people, that is best for you with your Creator: so He turned to you (mercifully), for surely He is the Oft-returning (to mercy), the Merciful.

55. And when you said: O Musa! we will not believe in you until we see Allah manifestly, so the punishment overtook you while you looked on.

56. Then We raised you up after your death that you may give thanks.

57. And We made the clouds to give shade over you and We sent to you manna and quails: Eat of the good things that We have given you; and they did not do Us any harm, but they made their own souls suffer the loss.

58. And when We said: Enter this city, then eat from it a plenteous (food) wherever you wish, and enter the gate making obeisance, and say, forgiveness. We will forgive you your wrongs and give more to those who do good (to others).

59. But those who were unjust changed it for a saying other than that which had been spoken to them, so We sent upon those who were unjust a pestilence from heaven, because they transgressed.

60. And when Musa prayed for drink for his people, We said: Strike the rock with your staff. So there gushed from it twelve springs; each tribe knew its drinking place: Eat and drink of the provisions of Allah and do not act corruptly in the land, making mischief.

61. And when you said: O Musa! we cannot bear with one food, therefore pray Lord on our behalf to bring forth for us out of what the earth grows, of its herbs and its cucumbers and its garlic and its lentils and its onions. He said: Will you exchange that which is better for that which is worse? Enter a city, so you

will have what you ask for. And abasement and humiliation were brought down upon them, and they became deserving of Allah's wrath; this was so because they disbelieved in the communications of Allah and killed the prophets unjustly; this was so because they disobeyed and exceeded the limits.

62. Surely those who believe, and those who are Jews, and the Christians, and the Sabians, whoever believes in Allah and the Last day and does good, they shall have their reward from their Lord, and there is no fear for them, nor shall they grieve.

63. And when We took a promise from you and lifted the mountain over you: Take hold of the law (Torah) We have given you with firmness and bear in mind what is in it, so that you may guard (against evil).

64. Then you turned back after that; so were it not for the grace of Allah and His mercy on you, you would certainly have been among the losers.

65. And certainly you have known those among you who exceeded the limits of the Sabbath, so We said to them: Be (as) apes, despised and hated.

66. So We made them an example to those who witnessed it and those who came after it, and an admonition to those who guard (against evil).

67. And when Musa said to his people: Surely Allah commands you that you should sacrifice a cow; they said: Do you ridicule us? He said: I seek the protection of Allah from being one of the ignorant.

68. They said: Call on your Lord for our sake to make it plain to us what she is. Musa said: He says, Surely she is a cow neither advanced in age nor too young, of middle age between that (and this); do therefore what you are commanded.

69. They said: Call on your Lord for our sake to make it plain to us what her color is. Musa said: He says, Surely she is a yellow cow; her color is intensely yellow, giving delight to the beholders.

70. They said: Call on your Lord for our sake to make it plain to us what she is, for surely to us the cows are all alike, and if Allah please we shall surely be guided aright.

71. Musa said: He says, Surely she is a cow not made submissive that she should plough the land, nor does she irrigate the tilth; sound, without a blemish in her. They said: Now you have brought the truth; so they sacrificed her, though they had not the mind to do (it).

72. And when you killed a man, then you disagreed with

respect to that, and Allah was to bring forth that which you were going to hide.

73. So We said: Strike the (dead body) with part of the (sacrificed cow), thus Allah brings the dead to life, and He shows you His signs so that you may understand.

74. Then your hearts hardened after that, so that they were like rocks, rather worse in hardness; and surely there are some rocks from which streams burst forth, and surely there are some of them which split asunder so water issues out of them, and surely there are some of them which fall down for fear of Allah, and Allah is not at all heedless of what you do.

75. Do you then hope that they would believe in you, and a party from among them indeed used to hear the Word of Allah, then altered it after they had understood it, and they know (this).

76. And when they meet those who believe they say: We believe, and when they are alone one with another they say: Do you talk to them of what Allah has disclosed to you that they may contend with you by this before your Lord? Do you not then understand?

77. Do they not know that Allah knows what they keep secret and what they make known?

78. And there are among them illiterates who know not the Book but only lies, and they do but conjecture.

79. Woe, then, to those who write the book with their hands and then say: This is from Allah, so that they may take for it a small price; therefore woe to them for what their hands have written and woe to them for what they earn.

80. And they say: Fire shall not touch us but for a few days. Say: Have you received a promise from Allah, then Allah will not fail to perform His promise, or do you speak against Allah what you do not know?

81. Yea! whoever earns evil and his sins beset him on every side, these are the inmates of the fire; in it they shall abide.

82. And (as for) those who believe and do good deeds, these are the dwellers of the garden; in it they shall abide.

83. And when We made a covenant with the children of Israel: You shall not serve any but Allah and (you shall do) good to (your) parents, and to the near of kin and to the orphans and the needy, and you shall speak to men good words and keep up prayer and pay the poor-rate. Then you turned back except a few of you and (now too) you turn aside.

84. And when We made a covenant with you: You shall not

shed your blood and you shall not turn your people out of your cities; then you gave a promise while you witnessed.

85. Yet you it is who slay your people and turn a party from among you out of their homes, backing each other up against them unlawfully and exceeding the limits; and if they should come to you, as captives you would ransom them—while their very turning out was unlawful for you. Do you then believe in a part of the Book and disbelieve in the other? What then is the reward of such among you as do this but disgrace in the life of this world, and on the day of resurrection they shall be sent back to the most grievous chastisement, and Allah is not at all heedless of what you do.

86. These are they who buy the life of this world for the hereafter, so their chastisement shall not be lightened nor shall they be helped.

87. And most certainly We gave Musa the Book and We sent apostles after him one after another; and We gave Isa, the son of Marium, clear arguments and strengthened him with the holy spirit, What! whenever then an apostle came to you with that which your souls did not desire, you were insolent so you called some liars and some you slew.

88. And they say: Our hearts are covered. Nay, Allah has cursed them on account of their unbelief; so little it is that they believe.

89. And when there came to them a Book from Allah verifying that which they have, and aforetime they used to pray for victory against those who disbelieve, but when there came to them (Prophet) that which they did not recognize, they disbelieved in him; so Allah's curse is on the unbelievers.

90. Evil is that for which they have sold their souls—that they should deny what Allah has revealed, out of envy that Allah should send down of His grace on whomsoever of His servants He pleases; so they have made themselves deserving of wrath upon wrath, and there is a disgraceful punishment for the unbelievers.

91. And when it is said to them, Believe in what Allah has revealed, they say: We believe in that which was revealed to us; and they deny what is besides that, while it is the truth verifying that which they have. Say: Why then did you kill Allah's Prophets before if you were indeed believers?

92. And most certainly Musa came to you with clear argu-

ments, then you took the calf (for a god) in his absence and you were unjust.

93. And when We made a covenant with you and raised the mountain over you: Take hold of what We have given you with firmness and be obedient. They said: We hear and disobey. And they were made to imbibe (the love of) the calf into their hearts on account of their unbelief. Say: Evil is that which your belief bids you if you are believers.

94. Say: If the future abode with Allah is specially for you to the exclusion of the people, then invoke death if you are truthful.

95. And they will never invoke it on account of what their hands have sent before, and Allah knows the unjust.

96. And you will most certainly find them the greediest of men for life (greedier) than even those who are polytheists; every one of them loves that he should be granted a life of a thousand years, and his being granted a long life will in no way remove him further off from the chastisement, and Allah sees what they do.

97. Say: Whoever is the enemy of Jibreel—for surely he revealed it to your heart by Allah's command, verifying that which is before it and guidance and good news for the believers.

98. Whoever is the enemy of Allah and His angels and His apostles and Jibreel and Meekaeel, so surely Allah is the enemy of the unbelievers.

99. And certainly We have revealed to you clear communications and none disbelieve in them except the transgressors.

100. What! whenever they make a covenant, a party of them cast it aside? Nay, most of them do not believe.

101. And when there came to them an Apostle from Allah verifying that which they have, a party of those who were given the Book threw the Book of Allah behind their backs as if they knew nothing.

102. And they followed what the Shaitans chanted of sorcery in the reign of Sulaiman, and Sulaiman was not an unbeliever, but the Shaitans disbelieved, they taught men sorcery and that was sent down to the two angels at Babylon, Harut and Marut, yet these two taught no man until they had said, "Surely we are only a trial, therefore do not be a disbeliever." Even then men learned from these two, magic by which they might cause a separation between a man and his wife; and they cannot hurt with it any one except with Allah's permission, and they learned what harmed

them and did not profit them, and certainly they know that he who bought it should have no share of good in the hereafter and evil was the price for which they sold their souls; had they but known this.

103. And if they had believed and guarded themselves (against evil), reward from Allah would certainly have been better; had they but known (this).

104. O you who believe! do not say "Herd us,"; and say (instead): "Watch over us," and (then) "Listen!", and for the unbelievers there is a painful chastisement.

105. Those who disbelieve from among the followers of the Book do not like, nor do the polytheists, that the good should be sent down to you from your Lord, and Allah chooses especially whom He pleases for His mercy, and Allah is the Lord of mighty grace.

106. Whatever communications We abrogate or cause to be forgotten, We bring one better than it or like it. Do you not know that Allah has power over all things?

107. Do you not know that Allah's is the kingdom of the heavens and the earth, and that besides Allah you have no guardian or helper?

108. Rather you wish to put questions to your Apostle, as Musa was questioned before; and whoever adopts unbelief instead of faith, he indeed has lost the right direction of the way.

109. Many of the followers of the Book wish that they could turn you back into unbelievers after your faith, out of envy from themselves, (even) after the truth has become manifest to them; but pardon and forgive, so that Allah should bring about His command; surely Allah has power over all things.

110. And keep up prayer and pay the poor-rate and whatever good you send before for yourselves, you shall find it with Allah; surely Allah sees what you do.

111. And they say: None shall enter the garden (or paradise) except he who is a Jew or a Christian. These are their vain desires. Say: Bring your proof if you are truthful.

112. Yes! whoever submits himself entirely to Allah and he is the doer of good (to others) he has his reward from his Lord, and there is no fear for him nor shall he grieve.

113. And the Jews say: The Christians do not follow anything (good) and the Christians say: The Jews do not follow anything (good) while they recite the (same) Book. Even thus say those who have no knowledge, like to what they say; so Allah shall

judge between them on the day of resurrection in what they differ.

114. And who is more unjust than he who prevents (men) from the masjids of Allah, that His name should be remembered in them, and strives to ruin them? (As for) these, it was not proper for them that they should have entered them except in fear; they shall meet with disgrace in this world, and they shall have great chastisement in the hereafter.

115. And Allah's is the East and the West, therefore, whither you turn, thither is Allah's purpose; surely Allah is Amplegiving, Knowing.

116. And they say: Allah has taken to himself a son. Glory be to Him; rather, whatever is in the heavens and the earth is His; all are obedient to Him.

117. Wonderful Originator of the heavens and the earth, and when He decrees an affair, He only says to it, Be, so there it is.

118. And those who have no knowledge say: Why does not Allah speak to us or a sign come to us? Even thus said those before them, the like of what they say; their hearts are all alike. Indeed We have made the communications clear for a people who are sure.

119. Surely We have sent you with the truth as a bearer of good news and as a warner, and you shall not be called upon to answer for the companions of the flaming fire.

120. And the Jews will not be pleased with you, nor the Christians until you follow their religion. Say: Surely Allah's guidance, that is the (true) guidance. And if you follow their desires after the knowledge that has come to you, you shall have no guardian from Allah, nor any helper.

121. Those to whom We have given the Book read it as it ought to be read. These believe in it; and whoever disbelieves in it, these it is that are the losers.

122. O children of Israel, call to mind My favor which I bestowed on you and that I made you excel the nations.

123. And be on your guard against a day when no soul shall avail another in the least neither shall any compensation be accepted from it, nor shall intercession profit it, nor shall they be helped.

124. And when his Lord tried Ibrahim with certain words, he fulfilled them. He said: Surely I will make you an Imam of men. Ibrahim said: And of my offspring? My covenant does not include the unjust, said He.

125. And when We made the House a pilgrimage for men and a (place of) security, and: Appoint for yourselves a place of prayer on the standing-place of Ibrahim. And We enjoined Ibrahim and Ismail saying: Purify My House for those who visit (it) and those who abide (in it) for devotion and those who bow down (and) those who prostrate themselves.

126. And when Ibrahim said: My Lord, make it a secure town and provide its people with fruits, such of them as believe in Allah and the last day. He said: And whoever disbelieves, I will grant him enjoyment for a short while, then I will drive him to the chastisement of the fire; and it is an evil destination.

127. And when Ibrahim and Ismail raised the foundations of the House: Our Lord! accept from us; surely Thou art the Hearing, the Knowing:

128. Our Lord! and make us both submissive to Thee and (raise) from our offspring a nation submitting to Thee, and show us our ways of devotion and turn to us (mercifully), surely Thou art the Oft-returning (to mercy), the Merciful.

129. Our Lord! and raise up in them an Apostle from among them who shall recite to them Thy communications and teach them the Book and the wisdom, and purify them; surely Thou art the Mighty, the Wise.

130. And who forsakes the religion of Ibrahim but he who makes himself a fool, and most certainly We chose him in this world, and in the hereafter he is most surely among the righteous.

131. When his Lord said to him, Be a Muslim, he said: I submit myself to the Lord of the worlds.

132. And the same did Ibrahim enjoin on his sons and (so did) Yaqoub. O my sons! surely Allah has chosen for you (this) faith, therefore die not unless you are Muslims.

133. Nay! were you witnesses when death visited Yaqoub, when he said to his sons: What will you serve after me? They said: We will serve your God and the God of your fathers, Ibrahim and Ismail and Ishaq, one God only, and to Him do we submit.

134. This is a people that have passed away; they shall have what they earned and you shall have what you earn, and you shall not be called upon to answer for what they did.

135. And they say: Be Jews or Christians, you will be on the right course. Say: Nay! (we follow) the religion of Ibrahim, the Hanif, and he was not one of the polytheists.

136. Say: We believe in Allah and (in) that which had been

revealed to us, and (in) that which was revealed to Ibrahim and Ismail and Ishaq and Yaqoub and the tribes, and (in) that which was given to Musa and Isa, and (in) that which was given to the prophets from their Lord, we do not make any distinction between any of them, and to Him do we submit.

137. If then they believe as you believe in Him, they are indeed on the right course, and if they turn back, then they are only in great opposition, so Allah will suffice you against them, and He is the Hearing, the Knowing.

138. (Receive) the baptism of Allah, and who is better than Allah in baptising? and Him do we serve.

139. Say: Do you dispute with us about Allah, and He is our Lord and your Lord, and we shall have our deeds and you shall have your deeds, and we are sincere to Him.

140. Nay! do you say that Ibrahim and Ismail and Yaqoub and the tribes were Jews or Christians? Say: Are you better knowing or Allah? And who is more unjust than he who conceals a testimony that he has from Allah? And Allah is not at all heedless of what you do.

141. This is a people that have passed away; they shall have what they earned and you shall have what you earn, and you shall not be called upon to answer for what they did.

142. The fools among the people will say: What has turned them from their Direction (of Prayer) which they had? Say: The East and the West belong only to Allah; He guides whom He likes to the right path.

143. And thus We have made you a medium (just) nation that you may be the bearers of witness to the people and (that) the Apostle may be a bearer of witness to you; and We did not make that which you would have to be the qiblah but that We might distinguish him who follows the Apostle from him who turns back upon his heels, and this was surely hard except for those whom Allah has guided aright; and Allah was not going to make your faith to be fruitless; most surely Allah is Affectionate, Merciful to the people.

144. Indeed We see the turning of your face to heaven, so We shall surely turn you to a qiblah which you shall like; turn then your face towards the Sacred Mosque, and wherever you are, turn your face towards it, and those who have been given the Book most surely know that it is the truth from their Lord; and Allah is not at all heedless of what they do.

145. And even if you bring to those who have been given the

Book every sign they would not follow your qiblah, nor can you be a follower of their qiblah, neither are they the followers of each other's qiblah, and if you follow their desires after the knowledge that has come to you, then you shall most surely be among the unjust.

146. Those whom We have given the Book recognize him as they recognize their sons, and a party of them most surely conceal the truth while they know (it).

147. The truth is from your Lord, therefore you should not be of the doubters.

148. And every one has a direction to which he should turn, therefore hasten to (do) good works; wherever you are, Allah will bring you all together; surely Allah has power over all things.

149. And from whatsoever place you come forth, turn your face towards the Sacred Mosque; and surely it is the very truth from your Lord, and Allah is not at all heedless of what you do.

150. And from whatsoever place you come forth, turn your face towards the Sacred Mosque; and wherever you are turn your faces towards it, so that people shall have no accusation against you, except such of them as are unjust; so do not fear them, and fear Me, that I may complete My favor on you and that you may walk on the right course.

151. Even as We have sent among you an Apostle from among you who recites to you Our communications and purifies you and teaches you the Book and the wisdom and teaches you that which you did not know.

152. Therefore remember Me, I will remember you, and be thankful to Me, and do not be ungrateful to Me.

153. O you who believe! seek assistance through patience and prayer; surely Allah is with the patient.

154. And do not speak of those who are slain in Allah's way as dead; nay, (they are) alive, but you do not perceive.

155. And We will most certainly try you with somewhat of fear and hunger and loss of property and lives and fruits; and give good news to the patient,

156. Who, when a misfortune befalls them, say: Surely we are Allah's and to Him we shall surely return.

157. Those are they on whom are blessings and mercy from their Lord, and those are the followers of the right course.

158. Surely the Safa and the Marwa are among the signs appointed by Allah; so whoever makes a pilgrimage to the House or pays a visit (to it), there is no blame on him if he goes

round them both; and whoever does good spontaneously, then surely Allah is Grateful, Knowing.

159. Surely those who conceal the clear proofs and the guidance that We revealed after We made it clear in the Book for men, these it is whom Allah shall curse, and those who curse shall curse them (too).

160. Except those who repent and amend and make manifest (the truth), these it is to whom I turn (mercifully); and I am the Oft-returning (to mercy), the Merciful.

161. Surely those who disbelieve and die while they are disbelievers, these it is on whom is the curse of Allah and the angels and men all;

162. Abiding in it; their chastisement shall not be lightened nor shall they be given respite.

163. And your God is one God! there is no god but He; He is the Beneficent, the Merciful.

164. Most surely in the creation of the heavens and the earth and the alternation of the night and the day, and the ships that run in the sea with that which profits men, and the water that Allah sends down from the cloud, then gives life with it to the earth after its death and spreads in it all (kinds of) animals, and the changing of the winds and the clouds made subservient between the heaven and the earth, there are signs for a people who understand.

165. And there are some among men who take for themselves objects of worship besides Allah, whom they love as they love Allah, and those who believe are stronger in love for Allah and O, that those who are unjust had seen, when they see the chastisement, that the power is wholly Allah's and that Allah is severe in requiting (evil).

166. When those who were followed shall renounce those who followed (them), and they see the chastisement and their ties are cut asunder.

167. And those who followed shall say: Had there been for us a return, then we would renounce them as they have renounced us. Thus will Allah show them their deeds to be intense regret to them, and they shall not come forth from the fire.

168. O men! eat the lawful and good things out of what is in the earth, and do not follow the footsteps of the Shaitan; surely he is your open enemy.

169. He only enjoins you evil and indecency, and that you may speak against Allah what you do not know.

170. And when it is said to them, Follow what Allah has

revealed, they say: Nay! we follow what we found our fathers upon. What! and though their fathers had no sense at all, nor did they follow the right way.

171. And the parable of those who disbelieve is as the parable of one who calls out to that which hears no more than a call and a cry; deaf, dumb (and) blind, so they do not understand.

172. O you who believe! eat of the good things that We have provided you with, and give thanks to Allah if Him it is that you serve.

173. He has only forbidden you what dies of itself, and blood, and flesh of swine, and that over which any other (name) than (that of) Allah has been invoked; but whoever is driven to necessity, not desiring, nor exceeding the limit, no sin shall be upon him; surely Allah is Forgiving, Merciful.

174. Surely those who conceal any part of the Book that Allah has revealed and take for it a small price, they eat nothing but fire into their bellies, and Allah will not speak to them on the day of resurrection, nor will He purify them, and they shall have a painful chastisement.

175. These are they who buy error for the right direction and chastisement for forgiveness; how bold they are to encounter fire.

176. This is because Allah has revealed the Book with the truth; and surely those who go against the Book are in a great opposition.

177. It is not righteousness that you turn your faces towards the East and the West, but righteousness is this that one should believe in Allah and the last day and the angels and the Book and the prophets, and give away wealth out of love for Him to the near of kin and the orphans and the needy and the wayfarer and the beggars and for (the emancipation of) the captives, and keep up prayer and pay the poor-rate; and the performers of their promise when they make a promise, and the patient in distress and affliction and in time of conflicts—these are they who are true (to themselves) and these are they who guard (against evil).

178. O you who believe! retaliation is prescribed for you in the matter of the slain; the free for the free, and the slave for the slave, and the female for the female, but if any remission is made to any one by his (aggrieved) brother, then prosecution (for the bloodwit) should be made according to usage, and payment should be made to him in a good manner; this is an alleviation

from your Lord and a mercy; so whoever exceeds the limit after this, he shall have a painful chastisement.

179. And there is life for you in (the law of) retaliation, O men of understanding, that you may guard yourselves.

180. Bequest is prescribed for you when death approaches one of you, if he leaves behind wealth for parents and near relatives, according to usage, a duty (incumbent) upon those who guard (against evil).

181. Whoever then alters it after he has heard it, the sin of it then is only upon those who alter it; surely Allah is Hearing, Knowing.

182. But he who fears an inclination to a wrong course or an act of disobedience on the part of the testator, and effects an agreement between the parties, there is no blame on him. Surely Allah is Forgiving, Merciful.

183. O you who believe! fasting is prescribed for you, as it was prescribed for those before you, so that you may guard (against evil).

184. For a certain number of days; but whoever among you is sick or on a journey, then (he shall fast) a (like) number of other days; and those who are not able to do it may effect a redemption by feeding a poor man; so whoever does good spontaneously it is better for him; and that you fast is better for you if you know.

185. The month of Ramazan is that in which the Quran was revealed, a guidance to men and clear proofs of the guidance and the distinction; therefore whoever of you is present in the month, he shall fast therein, and whoever is sick or upon a journey, then (he shall fast) a (like) number of other days; Allah desires ease for you, and He does not desire for you difficulty, and (He desires) that you should complete the number and that you should exalt the greatness of Allah for His having guided you and that you may give thanks.

186. And when My servants ask you concerning Me, then surely I am very near; I answer the prayer of the suppliant when he calls on Me, so they should answer My call and believe in Me that they may walk in the right way.

187. It is made lawful to you to go into your wives on the night of the fast; they are an apparel for you and you are an apparel for them; Allah knew that you acted unfaithfully to yourselves, so He has turned to you (mercifully) and removed from you (this burden); so now be in contact with them and seek

what Allah has ordained for you, and eat and drink until the whiteness of the day becomes distinct from the blackness of the night at dawn, then complete the fast till night, and have not contact with them while you keep to the mosques; these are the limits of Allah, so do not go near them. Thus does Allah make clear His communications for men that they may guard (against evil).

188. And do not swallow up your property among yourselves by false means, neither seek to gain access thereby to the judges, so that you may swallow up a part of the property of men wrongfully while you know.

189. They ask you concerning the new moon. Say: They are times appointed for (the benefit of) men, and (for) the pilgrimage; and it is not righteousness that you should enter the houses at their backs, but righteousness is this that one should g ard (against evil); and go into the houses by their doors and be careful (of your duty) to Allah, that you may be successful.

190. And fight in the way of Allah with those who fight with you, and do not exceed the limits, surely Allah does not love those who exceed the limits.

191. And kill them wherever you find them, and drive them out from whence they drove you out, and persecution is severer than slaughter, and do not fight with them at the Sacred Mosque until they fight with you in it, but if they do fight you, then slay them; such is the recompense of the unbelievers.

192. But if they desist, then surely Allah is Forgiving, Merciful.

193. And fight with them until there is no persecution, and religion should be only for Allah, but if they desist, then there should be no hostility except against the oppressors.

194. The Sacred month for the sacred month and all sacred things are (under the law of) retaliation; whoever then acts aggressively against you, inflict injury on him according to the injury he has inflicted on you and be careful (of your duty) to Allah and know that Allah is with those who guard (against evil).

195. And spend in the way of Allah and cast not yourselves to perdition with your own hands, and do good (to others); surely Allah loves the doers of good.

196. And accomplish the pilgrimage and the visit for Allah, but if you are prevented, (send) whatever offering is easy to obtain, and do not shave your heads until the offering reaches its

destination; but whoever among you is sick or has an ailment of the head, he (should effect) a compensation by fasting or alms or sacrificing; then when you are secure, whoever profits by combining the visit with the pilgrimage (should take) what offering is easy to obtain; but he who cannot find (any offering) should fast for three days during the pilgrimage and for seven days when you return; these (make) ten (days) complete; this is for him whose family is not present in the Sacred Mosque, and be careful (of your duty) to Allah, and know that Allah is severe in requiting (evil).

197. The pilgrimage is (performed in) the well-known months; so whoever determines the performance of the pilgrimage therein, there shall be no intercourse nor fornication nor quarrelling amongst one another; and whatever good you do, Allah knows it; and make provision, for surely the provision is the guarding of oneself, and be careful (of your duty) to Me, O men of understanding.

198. There is no blame on you in seeking bounty from your Lord, so when you hasten on from (Mount) "Arafat", then remember Allah near the Holy Monument, and remember Him as He has guided you, though before that you were certainly of the erring ones.

199. Then hasten on from the Place from which the people hasten on and ask the forgiveness of Allah; surely Allah is Forgiving, Merciful.

200. So when you have performed your devotions, then laud Allah as you lauded your fathers, rather a greater lauding. But there are some people who say, Our Lord! give us in the world, and they shall have no resting place.

201. And there are some among them who say: Our Lord! grant us good in this world and good in the hereafter, and save us from the chastisement of the fire.

202. They shall have (their) portion of what they have earned, and Allah is swift in reckoning.

203 And laud Allah during the numbered days; then whoever hastens off in two days, there is no blame on him, and whoever remains behind, there is no blame on him, (this is) for him who guards (against evil), and be careful (of your duty) to Allah, and know that you shall be gathered together to Him.

204. And among men is he whose speech about the life of this world causes you to wonder, and he calls on Allah to witness as to what is in his heart, yet he is the most violent of adversaries.

205. And when he turns back, he runs along in the land that he may cause mischief in it and destroy the tilth and the stock, and Allah does not love mischief-making.

206. And when it is said to him, guard against (the punishment of) Allah; pride carries him off to sin; therefore hell is sufficient for him; and certainly it is an evil resting place.

207. And among men is he who sells himself to seek the pleasure of Allah; and Allah is Affectionate to the servants.

208. O you who believe! enter into submission one and all, and do not follow the footsteps of Shaitan; surely he is your open enemy.

209. But if you slip after clear arguments have come to you, then know that Allah is Mighty, Wise.

210. They do not wait aught but that Allah should come to them in the shadows of the clouds along with the angels, and the matter has (already) been decided; and (all) matters are returned to Allah.

211. Ask the Israelites how many a clear sign have We given them; and whoever changes the favor of Allah after it has come to him, then surely Allah is severe in requiting (evil).

212. The life of this world is made to seem fair to those who disbelieve, and they mock those who believe, and those who guard (against evil) shall be above them on the day of resurrection; and Allah gives means of subsistence to whom he pleases without measure.

213. (All) people are a single nation; so Allah raised prophets as bearers of good news and as warners, and He revealed with them the Book with truth, that it might judge between people in that in which they differed; and none but the very people who were given it differed about it after clear arguments had come to them, revolting among themselves; so Allah has guided by His will those who believe to the truth about which they differed; and Allah guides whom He pleases to the right path.

214. Or do you think that you would enter the garden while yet the state of those who have passed away before you has not come upon you; distress and affliction befell them and they were shaken violently, so that the Apostle and those who believed with him said: When will the help of Allah come? Now surely the help of Allah is nigh!

215. They ask you as to what they should spend. Say: Whatever wealth you spend, it is for the parents and the near of kin and the orphans and the needy and the wayfarer, and whatever good you do, Allah surely knows it.

216. Fighting is enjoined on you, and it is an object of dislike to you; and it may be that you dislike a thing while it is good for you, and it may be that you love a thing while it is evil for you, and Allah knows, while you do not know.

217. They ask you concerning the sacred month about fighting in it. Say: Fighting in it is a grave matter, and hindering (men) from Allah's way and denying Him, and (hindering men from) the Sacred Mosque and turning its people out of it, are still graver with Allah, and persecution is graver than slaughter; and they will not cease fighting with you until they turn you back from your religion, if they can; and whoever of you turns back from his religion, then he dies while an unbeliever—these it is whose works shall go for nothing in this world and the hereafter, and they are the inmates of the fire; therein they shall abide.

218. Surely those who believed and those who fled (their home) and strove hard in the way of Allah these hope for the mercy of Allah and Allah is Forgiving, Merciful.

219. They ask you about intoxicants and games of chance. Say: In both of them there is a great sin and means of profit for men, and their sin is greater than their profit. And they ask you as to what they should spend. Say: What you can spare. Thus does Allah make clear to you the communications, that you may ponder,

220. On this world and the hereafter. And they ask you concerning the orphans Say: To set right for them (their affairs) is good, and if you become co-partners with them, they are your brethren; and Allah knows the mischief-maker and the peace-maker; and if Allah had pleased, He would certainly have caused you to fall into a difficulty; surely Allah is Mighty, Wise.

221. And do not marry the idolatresses until they believe, and certainly a believing maid is better than an idolatress woman, even though she should please you; and do not give (believing women) in marriage to idolaters until they believe, and certainly a believing servant is better than an idolater, even though he should please you; these invite to the fire, and Allah invites to the garden and to forgiveness by His will, and makes clear His communications to men, that they may be mindful.

222. And they ask you about menstruation. Say: It is a discomfort; therefore keep aloof from the women during the menstrual discharge and do not go near them until they have become clean; then when they have cleansed themselves, go in to them as Allah has commanded you; surely Allah loves those who turn much (to Him), and He loves those who purify themselves.

223. Your wives are a tilth for you, so go into your tilth when you like, and do good beforehand for yourselves; and be careful (of your duty) to Allah, and know that you will meet Him, and give good news to the believers.

224. And make not Allah because of your swearing (by Him) an obstacle to your doing good and guarding (against evil) and making peace between men, and Allah is Hearing, Knowing.

225. Allah does not call you to account for what is vain in your oaths, but He will call you to account for what your hearts have earned, and Allah is Forgiving, Forbearing.

226. Those who swear that they will not go in to their wives should wait four months; so if they go back, then Allah is surely Forgiving, Merciful.

227. And if they have resolved on a divorce, then Allah is surely Hearing, Knowing.

228. And the divorced women should keep themselves in waiting for three courses; and it is not lawful for them that they should conceal what Allah has created in their wombs, if they believe in Allah and the last day; and their husbands have a better right to take them back in the meanwhile if they wish for reconciliation; and they have rights similar to those against them in a just manner, and the men are a degree above them, and Allah is Mighty, Wise.

229. Divorce may be (pronounced) twice; then keep (them) in good fellowship or let (them) go with kindness; and it is not lawful for you to take any part of what you have given them, unless both fear that they cannot keep within the limits of Allah; then if you fear that they cannot keep within the limits of Allah, there is no blame on them for what she gives up to become free thereby. These are the limits of Allah, so do not exceed them, and whoever exceeds the limits of Allah these it is that are the unjust.

230. So if he divorces her she shall not be lawful to him afterwards until she marries another husband; then if he divorces her there is no blame on them both if they return to each other (by marriage), if they think that they can keep within the limits of Allah, and these are the limits of Allah which He makes clear for a people who know.

231. And when you divorce women and they reach their prescribed time, then either retain them in good fellowship or set them free with liberality, and do not retain them for injury, so that you exceed the limits, and whoever does this, he indeed is unjust to his own soul; and do not take Allah's communications

for a mockery, and remember the favor of Allah upon you, and that which He has revealed to you of the Book and the Wisdom, admonishing you thereby; and be careful (of your duty to) Allah, and know that Allah is the Knower of all things.

232. And when you have divorced women and they have ended their term (of waiting), then do not prevent them from marrying their husbands when they agree among themselves in a lawful manner; with this is admonished he among you who believes in Allah and the last day, this is more profitable and purer for you; and Allah knows while you do not know.

233. And the mothers should suckle their children for two whole years for him who desires to make complete the time of suckling; and their maintenance and their clothing must be borne by the father according to usage; no soul shall have imposed upon it a duty but to the extent of its capacity; neither shall a mother be made to suffer harm on account of her child, nor a father on account of his child, and a similar duty (devolves) on the (father's) heir; but if both desire weaning by mutual consent and counsel, there is no blame on them, and if you wish to engage a wet-nurse for your children, there is no blame on you so long as you pay what you promised for according to usage; and be careful of (your duty to) Allah and know that Allah sees what you do.

234. And (as for) those of you who die and leave wives behind, they should keep themselves in waiting for four months and ten days; then when they have fully attained their term, there is no blame on you for what they do for themselves in a lawful manner; and Allah is aware of what you do.

235. And there is no blame on you respecting that which you speak indirectly in the asking of (such) women in marriage or keep (the proposal) concealed within your minds; Allah knows that you will mention them, but do not give them a promise in secret unless you speak in a lawful manner, and do not confirm the marriage tie until the writing is fulfilled, and know that Allah knows what is in your minds, therefore beware of Him, and know that Allah is Forgiving, Forbearing.

236. There is no blame on you if you divorce women when you have not touched them or appointed for them a portion, and make provision for them, the wealthy according to his means and the straitened in circumstances according to his means, a provision according to usage; (this is) a duty on the doers of good (to others).

237. And if you divorce them before you have touched them

and you have appointed for them a portion, then (pay to them) half of what you have appointed, unless they relinquish or he should relinquish in whose hand is the marriage tie; and it is nearer to righteousness that you should relinquish; and do not neglect the giving of free gifts between you; surely Allah sees what you do.

238. Attend constantly to prayers and to the middle prayer and stand up truly obedient to Allah.

239. But if you are in danger, then (say your prayers) on foot or on horseback; and when you are secure, then remember Allah, as He has taught you what you did not know.

240. And those of you who die and leave wives behind, (make) a bequest in favor of their wives of maintenance for a year without turning (them) out, then if they themselves go away, there is no blame on you for what they do of lawful deeds by themselves, and Allah is Mighty, Wise.

241. And for the divorced women (too) provision (must be made) according to usage; (this is) a duty on those who guard (against evil).

242. Allah thus makes clear to you His communications that you may understand.

243. Have you not considered those who went forth from their homes, for fear of death, and they were thousands, then Allah said to them, Die; again He gave them life; most surely Allah is Gracious to people, but most people are not grateful.

244. And fight in the way of Allah, and know that Allah is Hearing, Knowing.

245. Who is it that will offer of Allah a goodly gift, so He will multiply it to him manifold, and Allah straitens and amplifies, and you shall be returned to Him.

246. Have you not considered the chiefs of the children of Israel after Musa, when they said to a prophet of theirs: Raise up for us a king, (that) we may fight in the way of Allah. He said: May it not be that you would not fight if fighting is ordained for you? They said: And what reason have we that we should not fight in the way of Allah, and we have indeed been compelled to abandon our homes and our children. But when fighting was ordained for them, they turned back, except a few of them, and Allah knows the unjust.

247. And their prophet said to them: Surely Allah has raised Talut to be a king over you. They said: How can he hold kingship over us while we have a greater right to kingship than

he, and he has not been granted an abundance of wealth? He said: Surely Allah has chosen him in preference to you, and He has increased him abundantly in knowledge and physique, and Allah grants His kingdom to whom He pleases, and Allah is Amplegiving, Knowing.

248. And the prophet said to them: Surely the sign of His kingdom is, that there shall come to you the chest in which there is tranquillity from your Lord and residue of the relics of what the children of Musa and the children of Haroun have left, the angels bearing it; most surely there is a sign in this for those who believe.

249. So when Talut departed with the forces, he said: Surely Allah will try you with a river; whoever then drinks from it, he is not of me, and whoever does not taste of it, he is surely of me, except he who takes with his hand as much of it as fills the hand; but with the exception of a few of them they drank from it. So when he had crossed it, he and those who believed with him, they said: We have today no power against Jalut and his forces. Those who were sure that they would meet their Lord said: How often has a small party vanquished a numerous host by Allah's permission, and Allah is with the patient.

250. And when they went out against Jalut and his forces they said: Our Lord, pour down upon us patience, and make our steps firm and assist us against the unbelieving people.

251. So they put them to flight by Allah's permission. And Dawood slew Jalut, and Allah gave him kingdom and wisdom, and taught him of what He pleased. And were it not for Allah's repelling some men with others, the earth would certainly be in a state of disorder; but Allah is Gracious to the creatures.

252. These are the communications of Allah: We recite them to you with truth; and most surely you are (one) of the apostles.

253. We have made some of these apostles to excel the others; among them are they to whom Allah spoke, and some of them He exalted by (many degrees of) rank; and We gave clear miracles to Isa son of Marium, and strengthened him with the holy spirit. And if Allah had pleased, those after them would not have fought one with another after clear arguments had come to them, but they disagreed; so there were some of them who believed and others who denied; and if Allah had pleased they would not have fought one with another, but Allah brings about what He intends.

254. O you who believe! spend out of what We have given you

before the day comes in which there is no bargaining, neither any friendship nor intercession, and the unbelievers—they are the unjust.

255. Allah is He besides Whom there is no god, the Ever-living, the Self-subsisting by Whom all subsist; slumber does not overtake Him nor sleep; whatever is in the heavens and whatever is in the earth is His; who is he that can intercede with Him but by His permission? He knows what is before them and what is behind them, and they cannot comprehend anything out of His knowledge except what He pleases, His knowledge extends over the heavens and the earth, and the preservation of them both tires Him not, and He is the Most High, the Great.

256. There is no compulsion in religion; truly the right way has become clearly distinct from error; therefore, whoever disbelieves in the Shaitan and believes in Allah, he indeed has laid hold on the firmest handle, which shall not break off, and Allah is Hearing, Knowing.

257. Allah is the guardian of those who believe. He brings them out of the darkness into the light; and (as to) those who disbelieve, their guardians are Shaitans who take them out of the light into the darkness; they are the inmates of the fire, in it they shall abide.

258. Have you not considered him (Namrud) who disputed with Ibrahim about his Lord, because Allah had given him the kingdom? When Ibrahim said: My Lord is He who gives life and causes to die, he said: I give life and cause death. Ibrahim said: So surely Allah causes the sun to rise from the east, then make it rise from the west; thus he who disbelieved was confounded; and Allah does not guide aright the unjust people.

259. Or the like of him (Uzair) who passed by a town, and it had fallen down upon its roofs; he said: When will Allah give it life after its death? So Allah caused him to die for a hundred years, then raised him to life. He said: How long have you tarried? He said: I have tarried a day, or a part of a day. Said He: Nay! you have tarried a hundred years; then look at your food and drink—years have not passed over it; and look at your ass; and that We may make you a sign to men, and look at the bones, how We set them together, then clothed them with flesh; so when it became clear to him, he said: I know that Allah has power over all things.

260. And when Ibrahim said: My Lord! show me how Thou

givest life to the dead, He said: What! and do you not believe? He said: Yes, but that my heart may be at ease. He said: Then take four of the birds, then train them to follow you, then place on every mountain a part of them, then call them, they will come to you flying; and know that Allah is Mighty, Wise.

261. The parable of those who spend their property in the way of Allah is as the parable of a grain growing seven ears (with) a hundred grains in every ear; and Allah multiplies for whom He pleases; and Allah is Ample-giving, Knowing.

262. (As for) those who spend their property in the way of Allah, then do not follow up what they have spent with reproach or injury, they shall have their reward from their Lord, and they shall have no fear nor shall they grieve.

263. Kind speech and forgiveness is better than charity followed by injury; and Allah is Self-sufficient, Forbearing.

264. O you who believe! do not make your charity worthless by reproach and injury, like him who spends his property to be seen of men and does not believe in Allah and the last day; so his parable is as the parable of a smooth rock with earth upon it, then a heavy rain falls upon it, so it leaves it bare; they shall not be able to gain anything of what they have earned; and Allah does not guide the unbelieving people.

265. And the parable of those who spend their property to seek the pleasure of Allah and for the certainty of their souls is as the parable of a garden on an elevated ground, upon which heavy rain falls so it brings forth its fruit twofold but if heavy rain does not fall upon it, then light rain (is sufficient); and Allah sees what you do.

266. Does one of you like that he should have a garden of palms and vines with streams flowing beneath it; he has in it all kinds of fruits; and old age has overtaken him and he has weak offspring, when, (lo!) a whirlwind with fire in it smites it so it becomes blasted; thus Allah makes the communications clear to you, that you may reflect.

267. O you who believe! spend (benevolently) of the good things that you earn and or what We have brought forth for you out of the earth, and do not aim at what is bad that you may spend (in alms) of it, while you would not take it yourselves unless you have its price lowered, and know that Allah is Self-sufficient, Praiseworthy.

268. Shaitan threatens you with poverty and enjoins you to be

niggardly, and Allah promises you forgiveness from Himself and abundance; and Allah is Ample-giving, Knowing.

269. He grants wisdom to whom He pleases, and whoever is granted wisdom, he indeed is given a great good and none but men of understanding mind.

270. And whatever alms you give or (whatever) vow you vow, surely Allah knows it; and the unjust shall have no helpers.

271. If you give alms openly, it is well, and if you hide it and give it to the poor, it is better for you; and this will do away with some of your evil deeds; and Allah is aware of what you do.

272. To make them walk in the right way is not incumbent on you, but Allah guides aright whom He pleases; and whatever good thing you spend, it is to your own good; and you do not spend but to seek Allah's pleasure; and whatever good things you spend shall be paid back to you in full, and you shall not be wronged.

273. (Alms are) for the poor who are confined in the way of Allah—they cannot go about in the land; the ignorant man thinks them to be rich on account of (their) abstaining (from begging); you can recognise them by their mark; they do not beg from men importunately; and whatever good thing you spend, surely Allah knows it.

274. (As for) those who spend their property by night and by day, secretly and openly, they shall have their reward from their Lord and they shall have no fear, nor shall they grieve.

275. Those who swallow down usury cannot arise except as one whom Shaitan has prostrated by (his) touch does rise. That is because they say, trading is only like usury; and Allah has allowed trading and forbidden usury. To whomsoever then the admonition has come from his Lord, then he desists, he shall have what has already passed, and his affair is in the hands of Allah; and whoever returns (to it)—these are the inmates of the fire; they shall abide in it.

276. Allah does not bless usury, and He causes charitable deeds to prosper, and Allah does not love any ungrateful sinner.

277. Surely they who believe and do good deeds and keep up prayer and pay the poor-rate they shall have their reward from their Lord, and they shall have no fear, nor shall they grieve.

278. O you who believe! Be careful of (your duty to) Allah and relinquish what remains (due) from usury, if you are believers.

279. But if you do (it) not, then be apprised of war from Allah

and His Apostle; and if you repent, then you shall have your capital; neither shall you make (the debtor) suffer loss, nor shall you be made to suffer loss.

280. And if (the debtor) is in straitness, then let there be postponement until (he is in) ease; and that you remit (it) as alms is better for you, if you knew.

281. And guard yourselves against a day in which you shall be returned to Allah; then every soul shall be paid back in full what it has earned, and they shall not be dealt with unjustly.

282. O you who believe! when you deal with each other in contracting a debt for a fixed time, then write it down; and let a scribe write it down between you with fairness; and the scribe should not refuse to write as Allah has taught him, so he should write; and let him who owes the debt dictate, and he should be careful of (his duty to) Allah, his Lord, and not diminish anything from it; but if he who owes the debt is unsound in understanding, or weak, or (if) he is not able to dictate himself, let his guardian dictate with fairness; and call in to witness from among your men two witnesses; but if there are not two men, then one man and two women from among those whom you choose to be witnesses, so that if one of the two errs, the second of the two may remind the other; and the witnesses should not refuse when they are summoned; and be not averse to writing it (whether it is) small or large, with the time of its falling due; this is more equitable in the sight of Allah and assures greater accuracy in testimony, and the nearest (way) that you may not entertain doubts (afterwards), except when it is ready merchandise which you give and take among yourselves from hand to hand, then there is no blame on you in not writing it down; and have witnesses when you barter with one another, and let no harm be done to the scribe or to the witness; and if you do (it) then surely it will be a transgression in you, and be careful of (your duty) to Allah, Allah teaches you, and Allah knows all things.

283. And if you are upon a journey and you do not find a scribe, then (there may be) a security taken into possession; but if one of you trusts another, then he who is trusted should deliver his trust, and let him be careful (of his duty to) Allah, his Lord; and do not conceal testimony, and whoever conceals it, his heart is surely sinful; and Allah knows what you do.

284. Whatever is in the heavens and whatever is in the earth is Allah's; and whether you manifest what is in your minds or hide it, Allah will call you to account according to it; then He will

forgive whom He pleases and chastise whom He pleases, and Allah has power over all things.

285. The apostle believes in what has been revealed to him from his Lord, and (so do) the believers; they all believe in Allah and His angels and His books and His apostles; We make no difference between any of His apostles; and they say: We hear and obey, our Lord! Thy forgiveness (do we crave), and to Thee is the eventual course.

286. Allah does not impose upon any soul a duty but to the extent of its ability; for it is (the benefit of) what it has earned, and upon it (the evil of) what it has wrought: Our Lord! do not punish us if we forget or make a mistake; Our Lord! do not lay on us a burden as Thou didst lay on those before us; Our Lord! do not impose upon us that which we have not the strength to bear; and pardon us and grant us protection and have mercy on us, Thou art our Patron, so help us against the unbelieving people.

THE FAMILY OF IMRAN

In the name of Allah, the Beneficent, the Merciful.

1. Alif Lam Mim.
2. Allah, (there is) no god but He, the Everliving, the Self-subsisting by Whom all things subsist.
3. He has revealed to you the Book with truth, verifying that which is before it, and He revealed the Torah and the Gospel aforetime, a guidance for the people, and He sent the Qur'an.
4. Surely they who disbelieve in the communications of Allah —they shall have a severe chastisement; and Allah is Mighty, the Lord of retribution.
5. Allah—surely nothing is hidden from Him in the earth or in the heaven.
6. He it is Who shapes you in the wombs as He likes; there is no god but He, the Mighty, the Wise.
7. He it is Who has revealed the Book to you; some of its verses are decisive, they are the basis of the Book, and others are allegorical; then as for those in whose hearts there is perversity, they follow the part of it which is allegorical, seeking to mislead, and seeking to give it (their own) interpretation, but none knows

its interpretation except Allah, and those who are firmly rooted in knowledge say: We believe in it, it is all from our Lord; and none do mind except those having understanding.

8. Our Lord! make not our hearts to deviate after Thou hast guided us aright, and grant us from Thee mercy; surely Thou art the most liberal Giver.

9. Our Lord! surely Thou art the Gatherer of men on a day about which there is no doubt; surely Allah will not fail (His) promise.

10. (As for) those who disbelieve, surely neither their wealth nor their children shall avail them in the least against Allah, and these it is who are the fuel of the fire.

11. Like the striving of the people of Firon and those before them; they rejected Our communications, so Allah destroyed them on account of their faults; and Allah is severe in requiting (evil).

12. Say to those who disbelieve: You shall be vanquished, and driven together to hell; and evil is the resting-place.

13. Indeed there was a sign for you in the two hosts (which) met together in encounter; one party fighting in the way of Allah and the other unbelieving, whom they saw twice as many as themselves with the sight of the eye; and Allah strengthens with His aid whom He pleases; most surely there is a lesson in this for those who have sight.

14. The love of desires, of women and sons and hoarded treasures of gold and silver and well bred horses and cattle and tilth, is made to seem fair to men; this is the provision of the life of this world; and Allah is He with Whom is the good goal (of life).

15. Say: Shall I tell you of what is better than these? For those who guard (against evil) are gardens with their Lord, beneath which rivers flow, to abide in them, and pure mates and Allah's pleasure; and Allah sees the servants.

16. Those who say: Our Lord! surely we believe, therefore forgive us our faults and save us from the chastisement of the fire.

17. The patient, and the truthful, and the obedient, and those who spend (benevolently) and those who ask forgiveness in the morning times.

18. Allah bears witness that there is no god but He, and (so do) the angels and those possessed of knowledge, maintaining His creation with justice; there is no god but He, the Mighty, the Wise.

19. Surely the (true) religion with Allah is Islam, and those to whom the Book had been given did not show opposition but after knowledge had come to them, out of envy among themselves; and whoever disbelieves in the communications of Allah then surely Allah is quick in reckoning.

20. But if they dispute with you, say: I have submitted myself entirely to Allah and (so) every one who follows me; and say to those who have been given the Book and the unlearned people: Do you submit yourselves? So if they submit then indeed they follow the right way; and if they turn back, then upon you is only the delivery of the message and Allah sees the servants.

21. Surely (as for) those who disbelieve in the communications of Allah and slay the prophets unjustly and slay those among men who enjoin justice, announce to them a painful chastisement.

22. Those are they whose works shall become null in this world as well as the hereafter, and they shall have no helpers.

23. Have you not considered those (Jews) who are given a portion of the Book? They are invited to the Book of Allah that it might decide between them, then a part of them turn back and they withdraw.

24. This is because they say: The fire shall not touch us but for a few days; and what they have forged deceives them in the matter of their religion.

25. Then how will it be when We shall gather them together on a day about which there is no doubt, and every soul shall be fully paid what it has earned, and they shall not be dealt with unjustly?

26. Say: O Allah, Master of the Kingdom! Thou givest the kingdom to whomsoever Thou pleasest and takest away the kingdom from whomsoever Thou pleasest, and Thou exaltest whom Thou pleasest and abasest whom Thou pleasest; in Thine hand is the good; surely, Thou hast power over all things.

27. Thou makest the night to pass into the day and Thou makest the day to pass into the night, and Thou bringest forth the living from the dead and Thou bringest forth the dead from the living, and Thou givest sustenance to whom Thou pleasest without measure.

28. Let not the believers take the unbelievers for friends rather than believers; and whoever does this, he shall have nothing of (the guardianship of) Allah, but you should guard yourselves against them, guarding carefully; and Allah makes you cautious

of (retribution from) Himself; and to Allah is the eventual coming.

29. Say: Whether you hide what is in your hearts or manifest it, Allah knows it, and He knows whatever is in the heavens and whatever is in the earth, and Allah has power over all things.

30. On the day that every soul shall find present what it has done of good and what it has done of evil, it shall wish that between it and that (evil) there were a long duration of time; and Allah makes you to be cautious of (retribution from) Himself; and Allah is Compassionate to the servants.

31. Say: If you love Allah, then follow me, Allah will love you and forgive you your faults, and Allah is Forgiving, Merciful.

32. Say: Obey Allah and the Apostle; but if they turn back, then surely Allah does not love the unbelievers.

33. Surely Allah chose Adam and Nuh and the descendants of Ibrahim and the descendants of Imran above the nations.

34. Offspring, one of the other; and Allah is Hearing, Knowing.

35. When a woman of Imran said: My Lord! surely I vow to Thee what is in my womb, to be devoted (to Thy service); accept therefore from me, surely Thou art the Hearing, the Knowing.

36. So when she brought forth, she said: My Lord! Surely I have brought it forth a female—and Allah knew best what she brought forth—and the male is not like the female, and I have named it Marium, and I commend her and her offspring into Thy protection from the accursed Shaitan.

37. So her Lord accepted her with a good acceptance and made her grow up a good growing, and gave her into the charge of Zakariya; whenever Zakariya entered the sanctuary to (see) her, he found with her food. He said: O Marium! whence comes this to you? She said: It is from Allah. Surely Allah gives to whom He pleases without measure.

38. There did Zakariya pray to his Lord; he said: My Lord! grant me from Thee good offspring; surely Thou art the Hearer of prayer.

39. Then the angels called to him as he stood praying in the sanctuary: That Allah gives you the good news of Yahya verifying a Word from Allah, and honorable and chaste and a prophet from among the good ones.

40. He said: My Lord! when shall there be a son (born) to me, and old age has already come upon me, and my wife is barren? He said: Even thus does Allah what He pleases.

41. He said: My Lord! appoint a sign for me. Said He: Your sign is that you should not speak to men for three days except by signs; and remember your Lord much and glorify Him in the evening and the morning.

42. And when the angels said: O Marium! surely Allah has chosen you and purified you and chosen you above the women of the world.

43. O Marium! keep to obedience to your Lord and humble yourself, and bow down with those who bow.

44. This is of the announcements relating to the unseen which We reveal to you; and you were not with them when they cast their pens (to decide) which of them should have Marium in his charge, and you were not with them when they contended one with another.

45. When the angels said: O Marium, surely Allah gives you good news with a Word from Him (of one) whose name is the Messiah, Isa son of Marium, worthy of regard in this world and the hereafter and of those who are made near (to Allah).

46. And he shall speak to the people when in the cradle and when of old age, and (he shall be) one of the good ones.

47. She said: My Lord! when shall there be a son (born) to me, and man has not touched me? He said: Even so, Allah creates what He pleases; when He has decreed a matter, He only says to it, Be, and it is.

48. And He will teach him the Book and the wisdom and the Tavrat and the Injeel.

49. And (make him) an apostle to the children of Israel: That I have come to you with a sign from your Lord, that I determine for you out of dust like the form of a bird, then I breathe into it and it becomes a bird with Allah's permission and I heal the blind and the leprous, and bring the dead to life with Allah's permission and I inform you of what you should eat and what you should store in your houses; most surely there is a sign in this for you, if you are believers.

50. And a verifier of that which is before me of the Taurat, and that I may allow you part of that which has been forbidden you, and I have come to you with a sign from your Lord, therefore be careful of (your duty to) Allah and obey me.

51. Surely Allah is my Lord and your Lord, therefore serve Him; this is the right path.

52. But when Isa perceived unbelief on their part, he said: Who will be my helpers in Allah's way? The disciples said: We

are helpers (in the way) of Allah: We believe in Allah and bear witness that we are submitting ones.

53. Our Lord! we believe in what Thou hast revealed and we follow the apostle, so write us down with those who bear witness.

54. And they planned and Allah (also) planned, and Allah is the best of planners.

55. And when Allah said: O Isa, I am going to terminate the period of your stay (on earth) and cause you to ascend unto Me and purify you of those who disbelieve and make those who follow you above those who disbelieve to the day of resurrection; then to Me shall be your return, so I will decide between you concerning that in which you differed.

56. Then as to those who disbelieve, I will chastise them with severe chastisement in this world and the hereafter, and they shall have no helpers.

57. And as to those who believe and do good deeds, He will pay them fully their rewards; and Allah does not love the unjust.

58. This We recite to you of the communications and the wise reminder.

59. Surely the likeness of Isa is with Allah as the likeness of Adam; He created him from dust, then said to him, Be, and he was.

60. (This is) the truth from your Lord, so be not of the disputers.

61. But whoever disputes with you in this matter after what has come to you of knowledge, then say: Come let us call our sons and your sons and our women and your women and our near people and your near people, then let us be earnest in prayer, and pray for the curse of Allah on the liars.

62. Most surely this is the true explanation, and there is no god but Allah; and most surely Allah—He is the Mighty, the Wise.

63. But if they turn back, then surely Allah knows the mischief-makers.

64. Say: O followers of the Book! come to an equitable proposition between us and you that we shall not serve any but Allah and (that) we shall not associate aught with Him, and (that) some of us shall not take others for lords besides Allah; but if they turn back, then say: Bear witness that we are Muslims.

65. O followers of the Book! why do you dispute about Ibrahim, when the Taurat and the Injeel were not revealed till after him; do you not then understand?

66. Behold! you are they who disputed about that of which you had knowledge; why then do you dispute about that of which you have no knowledge? And Allah knows while you do not know.

67. Ibrahim was not a Jew nor a Christian but he was (an) upright (man), a Muslim, and he was not one of the polytheists.

68. Most surely the nearest of people to Ibrahim are those who followed him and this Prophet and those who believe and Allah is the guardian of the believers.

69. A party of the followers of the Book desire that they should lead you astray, and they lead not astray but themselves, and they do not perceive.

70. O followers of the Book! Why do you disbelieve in the communications of Allah while you witness (them)?

71. O followers of the Book! Why do you confound the truth with the falsehood and hide the truth while you know?

72. And a party of the followers of the Book say: Avow belief in that which has been revealed to those who believe, in the first part of the day, and disbelieve at the end of it, perhaps they go back on their religion.

73. And do not believe but in him who follows your religion. Say: Surely the (true) guidance is the guidance of Allah—that one may be given (by Him) the like of what you were given; or they would contend with you by an argument before your Lord. Say: Surely grace is in the hand of Allah, He gives it to whom He pleases; and Allah is Ample-giving, Knowing.

74. He specially chooses for His mercy whom He pleases; and Allah is the Lord of mighty grace.

75. And among the followers of the Book there are some such that if you entrust one (of them) with a heap of wealth, he shall pay it back to you; and among them there are some such that if you entrust one (of them) with a dinar he shall not pay it back to you except so long as you remain firm in demanding it; this is because they say: There is not upon us in the matter of the unlearned people any way (to reproach); and they tell a lie against Allah while they know.

76. Yea, whoever fulfills his promise and guards (against evil)—then surely Allah loves those who guard (against evil).

77. (As for) those who take a small price for the covenant of Allah and their own oaths—surely they shall have no portion in the hereafter, and Allah will not speak to them, nor will He look upon them on the day of resurrection nor will He purify them, and they shall have a painful chastisement.

78. Most surely there is a party amongst those who distort the Book with their tongue that you may consider it to be (a part) of the Book, and they say, It is from Allah, while it is not from Allah; and they tell a lie against Allah whilst they know.

79. It is not meet for a mortal that Allah should give him the Book and the wisdom and prophethood, then he should say to men: Be my servants rather than Allah's; but rather (he would say): Be worshippers of the Lord because of your teaching the Book and your reading (it yourselves).

80. And neither would he enjoin you that you should take the angels and the prophets for lords; what! would he enjoin you with unbelief after you are Muslims?

81. And when Allah made a covenant through the prophets: Certainly what I have given you of Book and wisdom—then an apostle comes to you verifying that which is with you, you must believe in him, and you must aid him. He said: Do you affirm and accept My compact in this (matter)? They said: We do affirm. He said: Then bear witness, and I (too) am of the bearers of witness with you.

82. Whoever therefore turns back after this, these it is that are the transgressors.

83. Is it then other than Allah's religion that they seek (to follow), and to Him submits whoever is in the heavens and the earth, willingly or unwillingly, and to Him shall they be returned.

84. Say: We believe in Allah and what has been revealed to us, and what was revealed to Ibrahim and Ismail and Ishaq and Yaqoub and the tribes, and what was given to Musa and Isa and to the prophets from their Lord; we do not make any distinction between any of them, and to Him do we submit.

85. And whoever desires a religion other than Islam, it shall not be accepted from him, and in the hereafter he shall be one of the losers.

86. How shall Allah guide a people who disbelieved after their believing and (after) they had borne witness that the Apostle was true and clear arguments had come to them; and Allah does not guide the unjust people.

87. (As for) these, their reward is that upon them is the curse of Allah and the angels and of men, all together.

88. Abiding in it; their chastisement shall not be lightened nor shall they be respited.

89. Except those who repent after that and amend, then surely Allah is Forgiving, Merciful.

90. Surely, those who disbelieve after their believing, then

increase in unbelief, their repentance shall not be accepted, and these are they that go astray.

91. Surely, those who disbelieve and die while they are unbelievers, the earth full of gold shall not be accepted from one of them, though he should offer to ransom himself with it; these it is who shall have a painful chastisement, and they shall have no helpers.

92. By no means shall you attain to righteousness until you spend (benevolently) out of what you love; and whatever thing you spend, Allah surely knows it.

93. All food was lawful to the children of Israel except that which Israel had forbidden to himself, before the Taurat was revealed. Say: Bring then the Taurat and read it, if you are truthful.

94. Then whoever fabricates a lie against Allah after this, these it is that are the unjust.

95. Say: Allah has spoken the truth, therefore follow the religion of Ibrahim, the upright one; and he was not one of the polytheists.

96. Most surely the first house appointed for men is the one at Mecca, blessed and a guidance for the nations.

97. In it are clear signs, the standing place of Ibrahim, and whoever enters it shall be secure, and pilgrimage to the House is incumbent upon men for the sake of Allah, (upon) every one who is able to undertake the journey to it; and whoever disbelieves, then surely Allah is Self-sufficient, above any need of the worlds.

98. Say: O followers of the Book! why do you disbelieve in the communications of Allah? And Allah is a witness of what you do.

99. Say: O followers of the Book! why do you hinder him who believes from the way of Allah? You seek (to make) it crooked, while you are witness, and Allah is not heedless of what you do.

100. O you who believe! if you obey a party from among those who have been given the Book, they will turn you back as unbelievers after you have believed.

101. But how can you disbelieve while it is you to whom the communications of Allah are recited, and among you is His Apostle? And whoever holds fast to Allah, he indeed is guided to the right path.

102. O you who believe! be careful of (your duty to) Allah with the care which is due to Him, and do not die unless you are Muslims.

103. And hold fast by the covenant of Allah all together and be not disunited, and remember the favor of Allah on you when you were enemies, then He united your hearts so by His favor you became brethren; and you were on the brink of a pit of fire, then He saved you from it; thus does Allah make clear to you His communications that you may follow the right way.

104. And from among you there should be a party who invite to good and enjoin what is right and forbid the wrong, and these it is that shall be successful.

105. And be not like those who became divided and disagreed after clear arguments had come to them, and these it is that shall have a grievous chastisement.

106. On the day when (some) faces shall turn white and (some) faces shall turn black; then as to those whose faces turn black: Did you disbelieve after your believing? Taste therefore the chastisement because you disbelieved.

107. And as to those whose faces turn white, they shall be in Allah's mercy; in it they shall abide.

108. These are the communications of Allah which We recite to you with truth, and Allah does not desire any injustice to the creatures.

109. And whatever is in the heavens and whatever is in the earth is Allah's; and to Allah all things return.

110. You are the best of the nations raised up for (the benefit of) men; you enjoin what is right and forbid the wrong and believe in Allah; and if the followers of the Book had believed it would have been better for them; of them (some) are believers and most of them are transgressors.

111. They shall by no means harm you but with a slight evil; and if they fight with you they shall turn (their) backs to you, then shall they not be helped.

112. Abasement is made to cleave to them wherever they are found, except under a covenant with Allah and a covenant with men, and they have become deserving of wrath from Allah, and humiliation is made to cleave to them; this is because they disbelieved in the communications of Allah and slew the prophets unjustly; this is because they disobeyed and exceeded the limits.

113. They are not all alike; of the followers of the Book there is an upright party; they recite Allah's communications in the nighttime and they adore (Him).

114. They believe in Allah and the last day, and they enjoin what is right and forbid the wrong, and they strive with one

another in hastening to good deeds, and those are among the good.

115. And whatever good they do, they shall not be denied it, and Allah knows those who guard (against evil).

116. (As for) those who disbelieve, surely neither their wealth nor their children shall avail them in the least against Allah; and these are the inmates of the fire; therein they shall abide.

117. The likeness of what they spend in the life of this world is as the likeness of wind in which is intense cold (that) smites the seed produce of a people who have done injustice to their souls and destroys it; and Allah is not unjust to them, but they are unjust to themselves.

118. O you who believe! do not take for intimate friends from among others than your own people; they do not fall short of inflicting loss upon you; they love what distresses you; vehement hatred has already appeared from out of their mouths, and what their breasts conceal is greater still; indeed, We have made the communications clear to you, if you will understand.

119. Lo! you are they who will love them while they do not love you, and you believe in the Book (in) the whole of it; and when they meet you they say: We believe, and when they are alone, they bite the ends of their fingers in rage against you. Say: Die in your rage; surely Allah knows what is in the breasts.

120. If good befalls you, it grieves them, and if an evil afflicts you, they rejoice at it; and if you are patient and guard yourselves, their scheme will not injure you in any way; surely Allah comprehends what they do.

121. And when you did go forth early in the morning from your family to lodge the believers in encampments for war and Allah is Hearing, Knowing.

122. When two parties from among you had determined that they should show cowardice, and Allah was the guardian of them both, and in Allah should the believers trust.

123. And Allah did certainly assist you at battle of Badr when you were weak; be careful of (your duty to) Allah then, that you may give thanks.

124. When you said to the believers: Does it not suffice you that your Lord should assist you with three thousand of the angels sent down?

125. Yea! if you remain patient and are on your guard, and they come upon you in a headlong manner, your Lord will assist you with five thousand of the havoc-making angels.

126. And Allah did not make it but as good news for you, and that your hearts might be at ease thereby, and victory is only from Al'ah, the Mighty, the Wise.

127. That He may cut off a portion from among those who disbelieve, or abase them so that they should return disappointed of attaining what they desired.

128. You have no concern in the affair whether He turns to them (mercifully) or chastises them, for surely they are unjust.

129. And whatever is in the heavens and whatever is in the earth is Allah's; He forgives whom He pleases and chastises whom He pleases; and Allah is Forgiving, Merciful.

130. O you who believe! do not devour usury, making it double and redouble, and be careful of (your duty to) Allah, that you may be successful.

131. And guard yourselves against the fire which has been prepared for the unbelievers.

132. And obey Allah and the Apostle, that you may be shown mercy.

133. And hasten to forgiveness from your Lord; and a Garden, the extensiveness of which is (as) the heavens and the earth, it is prepared for those who guard (against evil).

134. Those who spend (benevolently) in ease as well as in straitness, and those who restrain (their) anger and pardon men; and Allah loves the doers of good (to others).

135. And those who when they commit an indecency or do injustice to their souls remember Allah and ask forgiveness for their faults—and who forgives the faults but Allah, and (who) do not knowingly persist in what they have done.

136. (As for) these—their reward is forgiveness from their Lord, and gardens beneath which rivers flow, to abide in them, and excellent is the reward of the laborers.

137. Indeed there have been examples before you; therefore travel in the earth and see what was the end of the rejecters.

138. This is a clear statement for men, and a guidance and an admonition to those who guard (against evil).

139. And be not infirm, and be not grieving, and you shall have the upper hand if you are believers.

140. If a wound has afflicted you (at battle of Ohud), a wound like it has also afflicted the (unbelieving) people; and We bring these days to men by turns, and that Allah may know those who believe and take witnesses from among you; and Allah does not love the unjust.

141. And that He may purge those who believe and deprive the unbelievers of blessings.

142. Do you think that you will enter the garden while Allah has not yet known those who strive hard from among you, and (He has not) known the patient.

143. And certainly you desired death before you met it; so indeed you have seen it and you look (at it).

144. And Muhammad is no more than an apostle; the apostles have already passed away before him; if then he dies or is killed, will you turn back upon your heels? And whoever turns back upon his heels, he will by no means do harm to Allah in the least; and Allah will reward the grateful.

145. And a soul will not die but with the permission of Allah; the term is fixed; and whoever desires the reward of this world, I shall give him of it, and whoever desires the reward of the hereafter I shall give him of it; and I will reward the grateful.

146. And how many a prophet has fought with whom were many worshippers of the Lord; so they did not become weak-hearted on account of what befell them in Allah's way, nor did they weaken, nor did they abase themselves; and Allah loves the patient.

147. And their saying was no other than that they said: Our Lord! forgive us our faults and our extravagance in our affair, and make firm our feet and help us against the unbelieving people.

148. So Allah gave them the reward of this world and better reward of the hereafter and Allah loves those who do good (to others).

149. O you who believe! if you obey those who disbelieve, they will turn you back upon your heels, so you will turn back losers.

150. Nay! Allah is your Patron and He is the best of the helpers.

151. We will cast terror into the hearts of those who disbelieve, because they set up with Allah that for which He has sent down no authority, and their abode is the fire; and evil is the abode of the unjust.

152. And certainly Allah made good to you His promise, when you slew them by His permission, until when you became weak-hearted and disputed about the affair and disobeyed after He had shown you that which you loved; of you were some who desired this world and of you were some who desired the hereafter; then He turned you away from them that He might try

you; and He has certainly pardoned you, and Allah is Gracious to the believers.

153. When you ran off precipitately and did not wait for any one, and the Apostle was calling you from your rear, so He gave you another sorrow instead of (your) sorrow, so that you might not grieve at what had escaped you, nor (at) what befell you; and Allah is aware of what you do.

154. Then after sorrow He sent down security upon you, a calm coming upon a party of you, and (there was) another party whom their own souls had rendered anxious; they entertained about Allah thoughts of ignorance quite unjustly, saying: We have no hand in the affair. Say: Surely the affair is wholly (in the hands) of Allah. They conceal within their souls what they would not reveal to you. They say: Had we any hand in the affair, we would not have been slain here. Say: Had you remained in your houses, those for whom slaughter was ordained would certainly have gone forth to the places where they would be slain, and that Allah might test what was in your breasts and that He might purge what was in your hearts; and Allah knows what is in the breasts.

155. (As for) those of you who turned back on the day when the two armies met, only the Shaitan sought to cause them to make a slip on account of some deeds they had done, and certainly Allah has pardoned them; surely Allah is Forgiving, Forbearing.

156. O you who believe! be not like those who disbelieve and say of their brethren when they travel in the earth or engage in fighting: Had they been with us, they would not have died and they would not have been slain; so Allah makes this to be an intense regret in their hearts; and Allah gives life and causes death, and Allah sees what you do.

157. And if you are slain in the way of Allah or you die, certainly forgiveness from Allah and mercy is better than what they amass.

158. And if indeed you die or you are slain, certainly to Allah shall you be gathered together.

159. Thus it is due to mercy from Allah that you deal with them gently, and had you been rough, hard hearted, they would certainly have dispersed from around you; pardon them therefore and ask pardon for them, and take counsel with them in the affair; so when you have decided, then place your trust in Allah; surely Allah loves those who trust.

160. If Allah assists you, then there is none that can overcome

you, and if He forsakes you, who is there then that can assist you after Him? And on Allah should the believers rely.

161. And it is not attributable to a prophet that he should act unfaithfully; and he who acts unfaithfully shall bring that in respect of which he has acted unfaithfully on the day of resurrection; then shall every soul be paid back fully what it has earned, and they shall not be dealt with unjustly.

162. Is then he who follows the pleasure of Allah like him who has made himself deserving of displeasure from Allah, and his abode is hell; and it is an evil destination.

163. There are (varying) grades with Allah, and Allah sees what they do.

164. Certainly Allah conferred a benefit upon the believers when He raised among them an Apostle from among themselves, reciting to them His communications and purifying them, and teaching them the Book and the wisdom, although before that they were surely in manifest error.

165. What! when a misfortune befell you, and you had certainly afflicted (the unbelievers) with twice as much, you began to say: Whence is this? Say: It is from yourselves; surely Allah has power over all things.

166. And what befell you on the day when the two armies met (at Ohud) was with Allah's knowledge, and that He might know the believers.

167. And that He might know the hypocrites; and it was said to them: Come, fight in Allah's way, or defend yourselves. They said: If we knew fighting, we would certainly have followed you. They were on that day much nearer to unbelief than to belief. They say with their mouths what is not in their hearts; and Allah best knows what they conceal.

168. Those who said of their brethren whilst they (themselves) held back: Had they obeyed us, they would not have been killed. Say: Then avert death from yourselves if you speak the truth.

169. And reckon not those who are killed in Allah's way as dead; nay, they are alive (and) are provided sustenance from their Lord;

170. Rejoicing in what Allah has given them out of His grace, and they rejoice for the sake of those who, (being left) behind them, have not yet joined them, that they shall have no fear, nor shall they grieve.

171. They rejoice on account of favor from Allah and (His) grace, and that Allah will not waste the reward of the believers.

172. (As for) those who responded (at Ohud) to the call of Allah and the Apostle after the wound had befallen them, those among them who do good (to others) and guard (against evil) shall have a great reward.

173. Those to whom the people said: Surely men have gathered against you, therefore fear them, but this increased their faith, and they said: Allah is sufficient for us and most excellent is the Protector.

174. So they returned with favor from Allah and (His) grace; no evil touched them and they followed the pleasure of Allah; and Allah is the Lord of mighty grace.

175. It is only the Shaitan that causes you to fear from his friends, but do not fear them, and fear Me if you are believers.

176. And let not those grieve you who fall into unbelief hastily; surely they can do no harm to Allah at all; Allah intends that He should not give them any portion in the hereafter, and they shall have a grievous chastisement.

177. Surely those who have bought unbelief at the price of faith shall do no harm at all to Allah, and they shall have a painful chastisement.

178. And let not those who disbelieve think that Our granting them respite is better for their souls; We grant them respite only that they may add to their sins; and they shall have a disgraceful chastisement.

179. On no account will Allah leave the believers in the condition which you are in until He separates the evil from the good; nor is Allah going to make you acquainted with the unseen, but Allah chooses of His apostles whom He pleases; therefore believe in Allah and His apostles; and if you believe and guard (against evil), then you shall have a great reward.

180. And let not those deem, who are niggardly in giving away that which Allah has granted them out of His grace, that it is good for them; nay, it is worse for them; they shall have that whereof they were niggardly made to cleave to their necks on the resurrection day; and Allah's is the heritage of the heavens and the earth; and Allah is aware of what you do.

181. Allah has certainly heard the saying of those who said: Surely Allah is poor and we are rich. I will record what they say, and their killing the prophets unjustly, and I will say: Taste the chastisement of burning.

182. This is for what your own hands have sent before and because Allah is not in the least unjust to the servants.

183. (Those are they) who said: Surely Allah has enjoined us
that we should not believe in any apostle until he brings us an
offering which the fire consumes. Say: Indeed, there came to you
apostles before me with clear arguments and with that which you
demand; why then did you kill them if you are truthful?

184. But if they reject you, so indeed were rejected before you
apostles who came with clear arguments and scriptures and the
illuminating book.

185. Every soul shall taste of death, and you shall only be
paid fully your reward on the resurrection day; then whoever is
removed far away from the fire and is made to enter the garden,
he indeed has attained the object; and the life of this world is
nothing but a provision of vanities.

186. You shall certainly be tried respecting your wealth and
your souls, and you shall certainly hear from those who have
been given the Book before you and from those who are polytheists much annoying talk; and if you are patient and guard
(against evil), surely this is one of the affairs (which should be)
determined upon.

187. And when Allah made a covenant with those who were
given the Book: You shall certainly make it known to men and
you shall not hide it; but they cast it behind their backs and took
a small price for it; so evil is that which they buy.

188. Do not think those who rejoice for what they have done
and love that they should be praised for what they have not
done—so do by no means think them to be safe from the
chastisement, and they shall have a painful chastisement.

189. And Allah's is the kingdom of the heavens and the earth,
and Allah has power over all things.

190. Most surely in the creation of the heavens and the earth
and the alternation of the night and the day there are signs for
men who understand.

191. Those who remember Allah standing and sitting and
lying on their sides and reflect on the creation of the heavens and
the earth: Our Lord! Thou hast not created this in vain! Glory be
to Thee; save us then from the chastisement of the fire:

192. Our Lord! surely whomsoever Thou makest enter the
fire, him Thou hast indeed brought to disgrace, and there shall
be no helpers for the unjust:

193. Our Lord! surely we have heard a preacher calling to the
faith, saying: Believe in your Lord, so we did believe; Our Lord!

forgive us therefore our faults, and cover our evil deeds and make us die with the righteous.

194. Our Lord! and grant us what Thou hast promised us by Thy apostles and disgrace us not on the day of resurrection; surely Thou dost not fail to perform the promise.

195. So their Lord accepted their prayer: That I will not waste the work of a worker among you, whether male or female, the one of you being from the other; they, therefore, who fled and were turned out of their homes and persecuted in My way and who fought and were slain, I will most certainly cover their evil deeds, and I will most certainly make them enter gardens beneath which rivers flow; a reward from Allah, and with Allah is yet better reward.

196. Let it not deceive you that those who disbelieve go to and fro in the cities fearlessly.

197. A brief enjoyment! then their abode is hell, and evil is the resting-place.

198. But as to those who are careful of (their duty to) their Lord, they shall have gardens beneath which rivers flow, abiding in them; an entertainment from their Lord, and that which is with Allah is best for the righteous.

199. And most surely of the followers of the Book there are those who believe in Allah and (in) that which has been revealed to you and (in) that which has been revealed to them, being lowly before Allah; they do not take a small price for the communications of Allah; these it is that have their reward with their Lord; surely Allah is quick in reckoning.

200. O you who believe! be patient and excel in patience and remain steadfast, and be careful of (your duty to) Allah, that you may be successful.

WOMEN

In the name of Allah, the Beneficent, the Merciful.

1. O people! be careful of (your duty to) your Lord, Who created you from a single being and created its mate of the same (kind) and spread from these two, many men and women; and be

careful of (your duty to) Allah, by Whom you demand one of another (your rights), and (to) the ties of relationship; surely Allah ever watches over you.

2. And give to the orphans their property, and do not substitute worthless (things) for (their) good (ones), and do not devour their property (as an addition) to your own property; this is surely a great crime.

3. And if you fear that you cannot act equitably towards orphans, then marry such women as seem good to you, two and three and four; but if you fear that you will not do justice (between them), then (marry) only one or what your right hands possess; this is more proper, that you may not deviate from the right course.

4. And give women their dowries as a free gift, but if they of themselves be pleased to give up to you a portion of it, then eat it with enjoyment and with wholesome result.

5. And do not give away your property which Allah has made for you a (means of) support to the weak of understanding, and maintain them out of (the profits of) it, and clothe them and speak to them words of honest advice.

6. And test the orphans until they attain puberty; then if you find in them maturity of intellect, make over to them their property, and do not consume it extravagantly and hastily, lest they attain to full age; and whoever is rich, let him abstain altogether, and whoever is poor, let him eat reasonably; then when you make over to them their property, call witnesses in their presence; and Allah is enough as a Reckoner.

7. Men shall have a portion of what the parents and the near relatives leave, and women shall have a portion of what the parents and the near relatives leave, whether there is little or much of it; a stated portion.

8. And when there are present at the division the relatives and the orphans and the needy, give them (something) out of it and speak to them kind words.

9. And let those fear who, should they leave behind them weakly offspring, would fear on their account; so let them be careful of (their duty to) Allah, and let them speak right words.

10. (As for) those who swallow the property of the orphans unjustly, surely they only swallow fire into their bellies and they shall enter burning fire.

11. Allah enjoins you concerning your children: The male shall have the equal of the portion of two females; then if they

are more than two females, they shall have two-thirds of what the deceased has left, and if there is one, she shall have the half; and as for his parents, each of them shall have the sixth of what he has left if he has a child, but if he has no child and (only) his two parents inherit him, then his mother shall have the third; but if he has brothers, then his mother shall have the sixth after (the payment of) a bequest he may have bequeathed or a debt; your parents and your children, you know not which of them is the nearer to you in usefulness; this is an ordinance from Allah: Surely Allah is Knowing, Wise.

12. And you shall have half of what your wives leave if they have no child, but if they have a child, then you shall have a fourth of what they leave after (payment of) any bequest they may have bequeathed or a debt; and they shall have the fourth of what you leave if you have no child, but if you have a child then they shall have the eighth of what you leave after (payment of) a bequest you may have bequeathed or a debt; and if a man or a woman leaves property to be inherited by neither parents nor offspring, and he (or she) has a brother or a sister, then each of them two shall have the sixth, but if they are more than that, they shall be sharers in the third after (payment of) any bequest that may have been bequeathed or a debt that does not harm (others); this is an ordinance from Allah: and Allah is Knowing, Forbearing.

13. These are Allah's limits; and whoever obeys Allah and His Apostle, He will cause him to enter gardens beneath which rivers flow, to abide in them; and this is the great achievement.

14. And whoever disobeys Allah and His Apostle and goes beyond His limits, He will cause him to enter fire to abide in it, and he shall have an abasing chastisement.

15. And as for those who are guilty of an indecency from among your women, call to witnesses against them four (witnesses) from among you; then if they bear witness confine them to the houses until death takes them away or Allah opens some way for them.

16. And as for the two who are guilty of indecency from among you, give them both a punishment; then if they repent and amend, turn aside from them; surely Allah is Oft-returning (to mercy), the Merciful.

17. Repentance with Allah is only for those who do evil in ignorance, then turn (to Allah) soon, so these it is to whom Allah turns (mercifully), and Allah is ever Knowing, Wise.

18. And repentance is not for those who go on doing evil deeds, until when death comes to one of them, he says: Surely now I repent; nor (for) those who die while they are unbelievers. These are they for whom We have prepared a painful chastisement.

19. O you who believe! it is not lawful for you that you should take women as heritage against (their) will, and do not straiten them in order that you may take part of what you have given them, unless they are guilty of manifest indecency, and treat them kindly; then if you hate them, it may be that you dislike a thing while Allah has placed abundant good in it.

20. And if you wish to have (one) wife in place of another and you have given one of them a heap of gold, then take not from it anything; would you take it by slandering (her) and (doing her) manifest wrong?

21. And how can you take it when one of you has already gone in to the other and they have made with you a firm covenant?

22. And marry not woman whom your fathers married, except what has already passed; this surely is indecent and hateful, and it is an evil way.

23. Forbidden to you are your mothers and your daughters and your sisters and your paternal aunts and your maternal aunts and brothers' daughters and sisters' daughters and your mothers that have suckled you and your foster-sisters and mothers of your wives and your step-daughters who are in your guardianship, (born) of your wives to whom you have gone in; but if you have not gone in to them, there is no blame on you (in marrying them), and the wives of your sons who are of your own loins, and that you should have two sisters together, except what has already passed; surely Allah is Forgiving, Merciful.

24. And all married women except those whom your right hands possess (this is) Allah's ordinance to you; and lawful for you are (all women) besides those, provided that you seek (them) with your property, taking (them) in marriage not committing fornication. Then as to those whom you profit by, give them their dowries as appointed; and there is no blame on you about what you mutually agree after what is appointed; surely Allah is Knowing, Wise.

25. And whoever among you has not within his power ampleness of means to marry free believing women, then (he may marry) of those whom your right hands possess from among

your believing maidens; and Allah knows best your faith: you are (sprung) the one from the other; so marry them with the permission of their masters, and give them their dowries justly, they being chaste, not fornicating, nor receiving paramours; and when they are taken in marriage, then if they are guilty of indecency, they shall suffer half the punishment which is (inflicted) upon free women. This is for him among you who fears falling into evil; and that you abstain is better for you, and Allah is Forgiving, Merciful.

26. Allah desires to explain to you, and to guide you into the ways of those before you, and to turn to you (mercifully), and Allah is Knowing, Wise.

27. And Allah desires that He should turn to you (mercifully), and those who follow (their) lusts desire that you should deviate (with) a great deviation.

28. Allah desires that He should make light your burdens, and man is created weak.

29. O you who believe! do not devour your property among yourselves falsely, except that it be trading by your mutual consent; and do not kill your people; surely Allah is Merciful to you.

30. And whoever does this aggressively and unjustly, We will soon cast him into fire; and this is easy to Allah.

31. If you shun the great sins which you are forbidden, We will do away with your small sins and cause you to enter an honorable place of entering.

32. And do not covet that by which Allah has made some of you excel others; men shall have the benefit of what they earn and women shall have the benefit of what they earn; and ask Allah of His grace; surely Allah knows all things.

33. And to every one We have appointed heirs of what parents and near relatives leave; and as to those with whom your right hands have ratified agreements, give them their portion; surely Allah is a witness over all things.

34. Men are the maintainers of women because Allah has made some of them to excel others and because they spend out of their property; the good women are therefore obedient, guarding the unseen as Allah has guarded; and (as to) those on whose part you fear desertion, admonish them, and leave them alone in the sleeping-places and beat them; then if they obey you, do not seek a way against them; surely Allah is High, Great.

35. And if you fear a breach between the two, then appoint a

judge from his people and a judge from her people; if they both desire agreement, Allah will effect harmony between them; surely Allah is Knowing, Aware.

36. And serve Allah and do not associate any thing with Him, and be good to the parents and to the near of kin and the orphans and the needy and the neighbor of (your) kin and the alien neighbor, and the companion in a journey and the wayfarer and those whom your right hands possess; surely Allah does not love him who is proud, boastful;

37. Those who are stingy and bid people to be stingy and hide what Allah has given them out of His grace; and We have prepared for the unbelievers a disgraceful chastisement.

38. And those who spend their property (in alms) to be seen of the people and do not believe in Allah nor in the last day; and as for him whose associate is the Shaitan, an evil associate is he!

39. And what (harm) would it have done them if they had believed in Allah and the last day and spent (benevolently) of what Allah had given them? And Allah knows them.

40. Surely Allah does not do injustice to the weight of an atom, and if it is a good deed He multiplies it and gives from Himself a great reward.

41. How will it be, then, when We bring from every people a witness and bring you as a witness against these?

42. On that day will those who disbelieve and disobey the Apostle desire that the earth were levelled with them, and they shall not hide any word from Allah.

43. O you who believe! do not go near prayer when you are intoxicated until you know (well) what you say, nor when you are under an obligation to perform a bath—unless (you are) travelling on the road—until you have washed yourselves; and if you are sick, or on a journey, or one of you come from the privy or you have touched the women, and you cannot find water, betake yourselves to pure earth, then wipe your faces and your hands; surely Allah is Pardoning, Forgiving.

44. Have you not considered those to whom a portion of the Book has been given? They buy error and desire that you should go astray from the way.

45. And Allah best knows your enemies; and Allah suffices as a Guardian, and Allah suffices as a Helper.

46. Of those who are Jews (there are those who) alter words from their places and say: We have heard and we disobey and: Hear, may you not be made to hear! and: "Listen to us", distort-

ing (the word) with their tongues and taunting about religion; and if they had said (instead): We have heard and we obey, and hearken, and "Look at us", it would have been better for them and more upright; but Allah has cursed them on account of their unbelief, so they do not believe but a little.

47. O you who have been given the Book! believe that which We have revealed, verifying what you have, before We alter faces then turn them on their backs, or curse them as We cursed the violaters of the Sabbath, and the command of Allah shall be executed.

48. Surely Allah does not forgive that anything should be associated with Him, and forgives what is besides that to whomsoever He pleases; and whoever associates anything with Allah, he devises indeed a great sin.

49. Have you not considered those who attribute purity to themselves? Nay, Allah purifies whom He pleases; and they shall not be wronged the husk of a date stone.

50. See how they forge the lie against Allah, and this is sufficient as a manifest sin.

51. Have you not seen those to whom a portion of the Book has been given? They believe in idols and false deities and say of those who disbelieve: These are better guided in the path than those who believe.

52. Those are they whom Allah has cursed, and whomever Allah curses you shall not find any helper for him.

53. Or have they a share in the kingdom? But then they would not give to people even the speck in the date stone.

54. Or do they envy the people for what Allah has given them of His grace? But indeed We have given to Ibrahim's children the Book and the wisdom, and We have given them a grand kingdom.

55. So of them is he who believes in him, and of them is he who turns away from him, and hell is sufficient to burn.

56. (As for) those who disbelieve in Our communications, We shall make them enter fire; so oft as their skins are thoroughly burned, We will change them for other skins, that they may taste the chastisement; surely Allah is Mighty, Wise.

57. And (as for) those who believe and do good deeds, We will make them enter gardens beneath which rivers flow, to abide in them for ever; they shall have therein pure mates, and We shall make them enter a dense shade.

58. Surely Allah commands you to make over trusts to their

owners and that when you judge between people you judge with justice; surely Allah admonishes you with what is excellent; surely Allah is Seeing, Hearing.

59. O you who believe! obey Allah and obey the Apostle and those in authority from among you; then if you quarrel about anything, refer it to Allah and the Apostle, if you believe in Allah and the last day; this is better and very good in the end.

60. Have you not seen those who assert that they believe in what has been revealed to you and what was revealed before you? They desire to summon one another to the judgment of the Shaitan, though they were commanded to deny him, and the Shaitan desires to lead them astray into a remote error.

61. And when it is said to them: Come to what Allah has revealed and to the Apostle, you will see the hypocrites turning away from you with (utter) aversion.

62. But how will it be when misfortune befalls them on account of what their hands have sent before? Then they will come to you swearing by Allah: We did not desire (anything) but good and concord.

63. These are they of whom Allah knows what is in their hearts; therefore turn aside from them and admonish them, and speak to them effectual words concerning themselves.

64. And We did not send any apostle but that he should be obeyed by Allah's permission; and had they, when they were unjust to themselves, come to you and asked forgiveness of Allah and the Apostle had (also) asked forgiveness for them, they would have found Allah Oft-returning (to mercy), Merciful.

65. But no! by your Lord! they do not believe (in reality) until they make you a judge of that which has become a matter of disagreement among them, and then do not find any straitness in their hearts as to what you have decided and submit with entire submission.

66. And if We had prescribed for them: Lay down your lives or go forth from your homes, they would not have done it except a few of them; and if they had done what they were admonished, it would have certainly been better for them and best in strengthening (them);

67. And then We would certainly have given them from Ourselves a great reward.

68. And We would certainly have guided them in the right path.

69. And whoever obeys Allah and the Apostle, these are with

those upon whom Allah has bestowed favors from among the prophets and the truthful and the martyrs and the good, and a goodly company are they!

70. This is grace from Allah, and sufficient is Allah as the Knower.

71. O you who believe! take your precaution, then go forth in detachments or go forth in a body.

72. And surely among you is he who would certainly hang back! If then a misfortune befalls you he says: Surely Allah conferred a benefit on me that I was not present with them.

73. And if grace from Allah come to you, he would certainly cry out, as if there had not been any friendship between you and him: Would that I had been with them, then I should have attained a mighty good fortune.

74. Therefore let those fight in the way of Allah, who sell this world's life for the hereafter; and whoever fights in the way of Allah, then be he slain or be he victorious, We shall grant him a mighty reward.

75. And what reason have you that you should not fight in the way of Allah and of the weak among the men and the women and the children, (of) those who say: Our Lord! cause us to go forth from this town, whose people are oppressors, and give us from Thee a guardian and give us from Thee a helper.

76. Those who believe fight in the way of Allah, and those who disbelieve fight in the way of the Shaitan. Fight therefore against the friends of the Shaitan; surely the strategy of the Shaitan is weak.

77. Have you not seen those to whom it was said: Withhold your hands, and keep up prayer and pay the poor-rate; but when fighting is prescribed for them, lo! a party of them fear men as they ought to have feared Allah, or (even) with a greater fear, and say: Our Lord! why hast Thou ordained fighting for us? Wherefore didst Thou not grant us a delay to a near end? Say: The provision of this world is short, and the hereafter is better for him who guards (against evil); and you shall not be wronged the husk of a date stone.

78. Wherever you are, death will overtake you, though you are in lofty towers, and if a benefit comes to them, they say: This is from Allah; and if a misfortune befalls them, they say: This is from you. Say: All is from Allah, but what is the matter with these people that they do not make approach to understanding what is told (them)?

79. Whatever benefit comes to you (O man!), it is from Allah, and whatever misfortune befalls you, it is from yourself; and We have sent you (O Prophet!), to mankind as an apostle; and Allah is sufficient as a witness.

80. Whoever obeys the Apostle, he indeed obeys Allah; and whoever turns back, so We have not sent you as a keeper over them.

81. And they say: Obedience. But when they go out from your presence, a party of them decide by night upon doing otherwise than what you say; and Allah writes down what they decide by night, therefore turn aside from them and trust in Allah, and Allah is sufficient as a protector.

82. Do they not then meditate on the Quran? And if it were from any other than Allah, they would have found in it many a discrepancy.

83. And when there comes to them news of security or fear, they spread it abroad; and if they had referred it to the Apostle and to those in authority among them, those among them who can search out the knowledge of it would have known it, and were it not for the grace of Allah upon you and His mercy, you would have certainly followed the Shaitan save a few.

84. Fight then in Allah's way; this is not imposed on you except in relation to yourself, and rouse the believers to ardor; maybe Allah will restrain the fighting of those who disbelieve, and Allah is strongest in prowess and strongest to give an exemplary punishment.

85. Whoever joins himself (to another) in a good cause shall have a share of it, and whoever joins himself (to another) in an evil cause shall have the responsibility of it; and Allah controls all things.

86. And when you are greeted with a greeting, greet with a better (greeting) than it or return it; surely Allah takes account of all things.

87. Allah, there is no god but He—He will most certainly gather you together on the resurrection day, there is no doubt in it; and who is more true in word than Allah?

88. What is the matter with you, then, that you have become two parties about the hypocrites, while Allah has made them return (to unbelief) for what they have earned? Do you wish to guide him whom Allah has caused to err? And whomsoever Allah causes to err, you shall by no means find a way for him.

89. They desire that you should disbelieve as they have disbelieved, so that you might be (all) alike; therefore take not from among them friends until they fly (their homes) in Allah's way; but if they turn back, then seize them and kill them wherever you find them, and take not from among them a friend or a helper.

90. Except those who reach a people between whom and you there is an alliance, or who come to you, their hearts shrinking from fighting you or fighting their own people; and if Allah had pleased, He would have given them power over you, so that they should have certainly fought you; therefore if they withdraw from you and do not fight you and offer you peace, then Allah has not given you a way against them.

91. You will find others who desire that they should be safe from you and secure from their own people; as often as they are sent back to the mischief they get thrown into it headlong; therefore if they do not withdraw from you, and (do not) offer you peace and restrain their hands, then seize them and kill them wherever you find them; and against these We have given you a clear authority.

92. And it does not behoove a believer to kill a believer except by mistake, and whoever kills a believer by mistake, he should free a believing slave, and blood-money should be paid to his people unless they remit it as alms; but if he be from a tribe hostile to you and he is a believer, the freeing of a believing slave (suffices), and if he is from a tribe between whom and you there is a convenant, the blood-money should be paid to his people along with the freeing of a believing slave; but he who cannot find (a slave) should fast for two months successively: a penance from Allah, and Allah is Knowing, Wise.

93. And whoever kills a believer intentionally, his punishment is hell; he shall abide in it, and Allah will send His wrath on him and curse him and prepare for him a painful chastisement.

94. O you who believe! when you go to war in Allah's way, make investigation, and do not say to any one who offers you peace: You are not a believer. Do you seek goods of this world's life! But with Allah there are abundant gains; you too were such before, then Allah conferred a benefit on you; therefore make investigation; surely Allah is aware of what you do.

95. The holders back from among the believers, not having any injury, and those who strive hard in Allah's way with their property and their persons are not equal; Allah has made the

strivers with their property and their persons to excel the holders back a (high) degree, and to each (class) Allah has promised good; and Allah shall grant to the strivers above the holders back a mighty reward:

96. (High) degrees from Him and protection and mercy, and Allah is Forgiving, Merciful.

97. Surely (as for) those whom the angels cause to die while they are unjust to their souls, they shall say: In what state were you? They shall say: We were weak in the earth. They shall say: Was not Allah's earth spacious, so that you should have migrated therein? So these it is whose abode is hell, and it is an evil resort;

98. Except the weak from among the men and the children who have not in their power the means nor can they find a way (to escape);

99. So these, it may be, Allah will pardon them, and Allah is Pardoning, Forgiving.

100. And whoever flies in Allah's way, he will find in the earth many a place of refuge and abundant resources; and whoever goes forth from his house flying to Allah and His Apostle, and then death overtakes him, his reward is indeed with Allah and Allah is Forgiving, Merciful.

101. And when you journey in the earth, there is no blame on you if you shorten the prayer, if you fear that those who disbelieve will cause you distress; surely the unbelievers are your open enemy.

102. And when you are among them and keep up the prayer for them, let a party of them stand up with you, and let them take their arms; then when they have prostrated themselves let them go to your rear, and let another party who have not prayed come forward and pray with you, and let them take their precautions and their arms; (for) those who disbelieve desire that you may be careless of your arms and your luggage, so that they may then turn upon you with a sudden united attack; and there is no blame on you, if you are annoyed with rain or if you are sick, that you lay down your arms, and take your precautions; surely Allah has prepared a disgraceful chastisement for the unbelievers.

103. Then when you have finished the prayer, remember Allah standing and sitting and reclining; but when you are secure (from danger) keep up prayer; surely prayer is a timed ordinance for the believers.

104. And be not weak hearted in pursuit of the enemy; if you

suffer pain, then surely they (too) suffer pain as you suffer pain, and you hope from Allah what they do not hope; and Allah is Knowing, Wise.

105. Surely We have revealed the Book to you with the truth that you may judge between people by means of that which Allah has taught you; and be not an advocate on behalf of the treacherous.

106. And ask forgiveness of Allah; surely Allah is Forgiving, Merciful.

107. And do not plead on behalf of those who act unfaithfully to their souls; surely Allah does not love him who is treacherous, sinful;

108. They hide themselves from men and do not hide themselves from Allah, and He is with them when they meditate by night words which please Him not, and Allah encompasses what they do.

109. Behold! you are they who (may) plead for them in this world's life, but who will plead for them with Allah on the resurrection day, or who shall be their protector?

110. And whoever does evil or acts unjustly to his soul, then asks forgiveness of Allah, he shall find Allah Forgiving, Merciful.

111. And whoever commits a sin, he only commits it against his own soul; and Allah is Knowing, Wise.

112. And whoever commits a fault or a sin, then accuses of it one innocent, he indeed takes upon himself the burden of a calumny and a manifest sin.

113. And were it not for Allah's grace upon you and His mercy, a party of them had certainly designed to bring you to perdition, and they do not bring (aught) to perdition but their own souls, and they shall not harm you in any way, and Allah has revealed to you the Book and the wisdom, and He has taught you what you did not know, and Allah's grace on you is very great.

114. There is no good in most of their secret counsels except (in his) who enjoins charity or goodness or reconciliation between people; and whoever does this seeking Allah's pleasure, We will give him a mighty reward.

115. And whoever acts hostilely to the Apostle after that guidance has become manifest to him, and follows other than the way of the believers, We will turn him to that to which he has (himself) turned and make him enter hell; and it is an evil resort.

116. Surely Allah does not forgive that anything should be associated with Him, and He forgives what is besides this to

whom He pleases; and whoever associates anything with Allah, he indeed strays off into a remote error.

117. They do not call besides Him on anything but idols, and they do not call on anything but a rebellious Shaitan.

118. Allah has cursed him; and he said: Most certainly I will take of Thy servants an appointed portion:

119. And most certainly I will lead them astray and excite in them vain desires, and bid them so that they shall slit the ears of the cattle, and most certainly I will bid them so that they shall alter Allah's creation; and whoever takes the Shaitan for a guardian rather than Allah he indeed shall suffer a manifest loss.

120. He gives them promises and excites vain desires in them; and the Shaitan does not promise them but to deceive.

121. These are they whose abode is hell, and they shall not find any refuge from it.

122. And (as for) those who believe and do good, We will make them enter into gardens beneath which rivers flow, to abide therein for ever; (it is) a promise of Allah, true (indeed); and who is truer of word than Allah?

123. (This) shall not be in accordance with your vain desires nor in accordance with the vain desires of the followers of the Book; whoever does evil, he shall be requited with it, and besides Allah he will find for himself neither a guardian nor a helper.

124. And whoever does good deeds whether male or female and he (or she) is a believer—these shall enter the garden, and they shall not be dealt with a jot unjustly.

125. And who has a better religion than he who submits himself entirely to Allah? And he is the doer of good (to others) and follows the faith of Ibrahim, the upright one, and Allah took Ibrahim as a friend.

126. And whatever is in the heavens and whatever is in the earth is Allah's; and Allah encompasses all things.

127. And they ask you a decision about women. Say: Allah makes known to you His decision concerning them, and that which is recited to you in the Book concerning female orphans whom you do not give what is appointed for them while you desire to marry them, and concerning the weak among children, and that you should deal towards orphans with equity; and whatever good you do, Allah surely knows it.

128. And if a woman fears ill usage or desertion on the part of her husband, there is no blame on them, if they effect a reconciliation between them, and reconciliation is better, and avarice has been made to be present in the (people's) minds; and if you do

good (to others) and guard (against evil), then surely Allah is aware of what you do.

129. And you have it not in your power to do justice between wives, even though you may wish (it), but be not disinclined (from one) with total disinclination, so that you leave her as it were in suspense; and if you effect a reconciliation and guard (against evil), then surely Allah is Forgiving, Merciful.

130. And if they separate, Allah will render them both free from want out of His ampleness, and Allah is Ample-giving, Wise.

131. And whatever is in the heavens and whatever is in the earth is Allah's and certainly We enjoined those who were given the Book before you and (We enjoin) you too that you should be careful of (your duty to) Allah; and if you disbelieve, then surely whatever is in the heavens and whatever is in the earth is Allah's and Allah is Self-sufficient, Praise-worthy.

132. And whatever is in the heavens and whatever is in the earth is Allah's, and Allah is sufficient as a Protector.

133. If He please, He can make you pass away, O people! and bring others; and Allah has the power to do this.

134. Whoever desires the reward of this world, then with Allah is the reward of this world and the hereafter; and Allah is Hearing, Seeing.

135. O you who believe! be maintainers of justice, bearers of witness of Allah's sake, though it may be against your own selves or (your) parents or near relatives; if he be rich or poor, Allah is nearer to them both in compassion; therefore do not follow (your) low desires, lest you deviate; and if you swerve or turn aside, then surely Allah is aware of what you do.

136. O you who believe! believe in Allah and His Apostle and the Book which He has revealed to His Apostle and the Book which He revealed before; and whoever disbelieves in Allah and His angels and His apostles and the last day, he indeed strays off into a remote error.

137. Surely (as for) those who believe then disbelieve, again believe and again disbelieve, then increase in disbelief, Allah will not forgive them nor guide them in the (right) path.

138. Announce to the hypocrites that they shall have a painful chastisement:

139. Those who take the unbelievers for guardians rather than believers. Do they seek honor from them? Then surely all honor is for Allah.

140. And indeed He has revealed to you in the Book that when

you hear Allah's communications disbelieved in and mocked at, do not sit with them until they enter into some other discourse; surely then you would be like them; surely Allah will gather together the hypocrites and the unbelievers all in hell.

141. Those who wait for (some misfortune to befall) you; then if you have a victory from Allah they say: Were we not with you? And if there is a chance for the unbelievers, they say: Did we not acquire the mastery over you and defend you from the believers? So Allah shall judge between you on the day of resurrection; and Allah will by no means give the unbelievers a way against the believers.

142. Surely the hypocrites strive to deceive Allah, and He shall requite their deceit to them, and when they stand up to prayer, they stand up sluggishly; they do it only to be seen of men and do not remember Allah save a little.

143. Wavering between that (and this), (belonging) neither to these nor to those; and whomsoever Allah causes to err, you shall not find a way for him.

144. O you who believe! do not take the unbelievers for friends rather than the believers; do you desire that you should give to Allah a manifest proof against yourselves?

145. Surely the hypocrites are in the lowest stage of the fire, and you shall not find a helper for them.

146. Except those who repent and amend and hold fast to Allah and are sincere in their religion to Allah; these are with the believers, and Allah will grant the believers a mighty reward.

147. Why should Allah chastise you if you are grateful and believe? And Allah is the Multiplier of rewards, Knowing.

148. Allah does not love the public utterance of hurtful speech, unless (it be) by one to whom injustice has been done; and Allah is Hearing, Knowing.

149. If you do good openly or do it in secret or pardon an evil, then surely Allah is Pardoning, Powerful.

150. Surely those who disbelieve in Allah and His apostles and (those who) desire to make a distinction between Allah and His apostles and say: We believe in some and disbelieve in others; and desire to take a course between (this and) that.

151. These it is that are truly unbelievers, and We have prepared for the unbelievers a disgraceful chastisement.

152. And those who believe in Allah and His apostles and do not make a distinction between any of them—Allah will grant them their rewards; and Allah is Forgiving, Merciful.

153. The followers of the Book ask you to bring down to them a book from heaven; so indeed they demanded of Musa a greater thing than that, for they said: Show us Allah manifestly; so the lightning overtook them on account of their injustice. Then they took the calf (for a god), after clear signs had come to them, but We pardoned this; and We gave to Musa clear authority.

154. And We lifted the mountain (Sainai) over them at (the taking of the covenant) and We said to them: Enter the door making obeisance; and We said to them: Do not exceed the limits of the Sabbath; and We made with them a firm covenant.

155. Therefore, for their breaking their covenant and their disbelief in the communications of Allah and their killing the prophets wrongfully and their saying: Our hearts are covered; nay! Allah set a seal upon them owing to their unbelief, so they shall not believe except a few.

156. And for their unbelief and for their having uttered against Marium a grievous calumny.

157. And their saying: Surely we have killed the Messiah, Isa son of Marium, the apostle of Allah; and they did not kill him nor did they crucify him, but it appeared to them so (like Isa) and most surely those who differ therein are only in a doubt about it; they have no knowledge respecting it, but only follow a conjecture, and they killed him not for sure.

158. Nay! Allah took him up to Himself; and Allah is Mighty, Wise.

159. And there is not one of the followers of the Book but most certainly believes in this before his death, and on the day of resurrection he (Isa) shall be a witness against them.

160. Wherefore for the iniquity of those who are Jews did We disallow to them the good things which had been made lawful for them, and for their hindering many (people) from Allah's way.

161. And their taking usury though indeed they were forbidden it and their devouring the property of people falsely; and We have prepared for the unbelievers from among them a painful chastisement.

162. But the firm in knowledge among them and the believers believe in what has been revealed to you and what was revealed before you, and those who keep up prayers and those who give the poor-rate and the believers in Allah and the last day, these it is whom We will give a mighty reward.

163. Surely We have revealed to you as We revealed to Nuh, and the prophets after him, and We revealed to Ibrahim and

Ismail and Ishaq and Yaqoob and the tribes, and Isa and Ayub and Yunus and Haroun and Sulaiman and We gave to Dawood Psalms.

164. And (We sent) apostles We have mentioned to you before and apostles we have not mentioned to you; and to Musa, Allah addressed His Word, speaking (to him):

165. (We sent) apostles as the givers of good news and as warners, so that people should not have a plea against Allah after the (coming of) apostles; and Allah is Mighty, Wise.

166. But Allah bears witness by what He has revealed to you that He has revealed it with His knowledge, and the angels bear witness (also); and Allah is sufficient as a witness.

167. Surely (as for) those who disbelieve and hinder (men) from Allah's way, they indeed have strayed off into a remote error.

168. Surely (as for) those who disbelieve and act unjustly, Allah will not forgive them nor guide them to a path,

169. Except the path of hell, to abide in it for ever, and this is easy to Allah.

170. O people! surely the Apostle has come to you with the truth from your Lord, therefore believe, (it shall be) good for you; and if you disbelieve, then surely whatever is in the heavens and the earth is Allah's; and Allah is Knowing, Wise.

171. O followers of the Book! do not exceed the limits in your religion, and do not speak (lies) against Allah, but (speak) the truth; the Messiah, Isa son of Marium is only an apostle of Allah and His Word which He communicated to Marium and a spirit from Him; believe therefore in Allah and His apostles, and say not, Three. Desist, it is better for you; Allah is only one God: far be it from His glory that He should have a son; whatever is in the heavens and whatever is in the earth is His; and Allah is sufficient for a Protector.

172. The Messiah does by no means disdain that he should be a servant of Allah, nor do the angels who are near to Him, and whoever disdains His service and is proud, He will gather them all together to Himself.

173. Then as for those who believe and do good, He will pay them fully their rewards and give them more out of His grace; and as for those who disdain and are proud, He will chastise them with a painful chastisement. And they shall not find for themselves besides Allah a guardian or a helper.

174. O people! surely there has come to you manifest proof from your Lord and We have sent to you clear light.

175. Then as for those who believe in Allah and hold fast by Him, He will cause them to enter into His mercy and grace and guide them to Himself on a right path.

176. They ask you for a decision of the law. Say: Allah gives you a decision concerning the person who has neither parents nor offspring; if a man dies (and) he has no son and he has a sister, she shall have half of what he leaves, and he shall be her heir if she has no son; but if there be two (sisters), they shall have two-thirds of what he leaves; and if there are brethren, men and women, then the male shall have the like of the portion of two females; Allah makes clear to you, lest you err; and Allah knows all things.

THE FOOD

In the name of Allah, the Beneficent, the Merciful.

1. O you who believe! fulfill the obligations. The cattle quadrupeds are allowed to you except that which is recited to you, not violating the prohibition against game when you are entering upon the performance of the pilgrimage; surely Allah orders what He desires.

2. O you who believe! do not violate the signs appointed by Allah nor the sacred month, nor (interfere with) the offerings, nor the sacrificial animals with garlands, nor those going to the sacred house seeking the grace and pleasure of their Lord; and when you are free from the obligations of the pilgrimage, then hunt, and let not hatred of a people—because they hindered you from the Sacred Masjid—incite you to exceed the limits, and help one another in goodness and piety, and do not help one another in sin and aggression; and be careful of (your duty to) Allah; surely Allah is severe in requiting (evil).

3. Forbidden to you is that which dies of itself, and blood, and flesh of swine, and that on which any other name than that of Allah has been invoked, and the strangled (animal) and that beaten to death, and that killed by a fall and that killed by being smitten with the horn, and that which wild beasts have eaten, except what you slaughter, and what is sacrificed on stones set up (for idols) and that you divide by the arrows; that is a transgression. This day have those who disbelieve despaired of your religion, so fear them not, and fear Me. This day have I perfected

for you your religion and completed My favor on you and chosen for you Islam as a religion; but whoever is compelled by hunger, not inclining willfully to sin, then surely Allah is Forgiving, Merciful.

4. They ask you as to what is allowed to them. Say: The good things are allowed to you, and what you have taught the beasts and birds of prey, training them to hunt—you teach them of what Allah has taught you—so eat of that which they catch for you and mention the name of Allah over it; and be careful of (your duty to) Allah; surely Allah is swift in reckoning.

5. This day (all) the good things are allowed to you; and the food of those who have been given the Book is lawful for you and your food is lawful for them; and the chaste from among the believing women and the chaste from among those who have been given the Book before you (are lawful for you); when you have given them their dowries, taking (them) in marriage, not fornicating nor taking them for paramours in secret; and whoever denies faith, his work indeed is of no account, and in the hereafter he shall be one of the losers.

6. O you who believe! when you rise up to prayer, wash your faces and your hands as far as the elbows, and wipe your heads and your feet to the ankles; and if you are under an obligation to perform a total ablution, then wash (yourselves) and if you are sick or on a journey, or one of you come from the privy, or you have touched the women, and you cannot find water, betake yourselves to pure earth and wipe your faces and your hands therewith, Allah does not desire to put on you any difficulty, but He wishes to purify you and that He may complete His favor on you, so that you may be grateful.

7. And remember the favor of Allah on you and His covenant with which He bound you firmly, when you said: We have heard and we obey, and be careful of (your duty to) Allah, surely Allah knows what is in the breasts.

8. O you who believe! Be upright for Allah, bearers of witness with justice, and let not hatred of a people incite you not to act equitably; act equitably, that is nearer to piety, and be careful of (your duty to) Allah; surely Allah is Aware of what you do.

9. Allah has promised to those who believe and do good deeds (that) they shall have forgiveness and a mighty reward.

10. And (as for) those who disbelieve and reject our communications, these are the companions of the flame.

11. O you who believe! remember Allah's favor on you when a people had determined to stretch forth their hands towards

you, but He withheld their hands from you, and be careful of (your duty to) Allah; and on Allah let the believers rely.

12. And certainly Allah made a covenant with the children of Israel, and We raised up among them twelve chieftains; and Allah said: Surely I am with you; if you keep up prayer and pay the poor-rate and believe in My apostles and assist them and offer to Allah a goodly gift, I will most certainly cover your evil deeds, and I will most certainly cause you to enter into gardens beneath which rivers flow, but whoever disbelieves from among you after that, he indeed shall lose the right way.

13. But on account of their breaking their covenant We cursed them and made their hearts hard; they altered the words from their places and they neglected a portion of what they were reminded of; and you shall always discover treachery in them excepting a few of them; so pardon them and turn away; surely Allah loves those who do good (to others).

14. And with those who say, We are Christians, We made a covenant, but they neglected a portion of what they were reminded of, therefore We excited among them enmity and hatred to the day of resurrection; and Allah will inform them of what they did.

15. O followers of the Book! indeed Our Apostle has come to you making clear to you much of what you concealed of the Book and passing over much; indeed, there has come to you light and a clear Book from Allah;

16. With it Allah guides him who will follow His pleasure into the ways of safety and brings them out of utter darkness into light by His will and guides them to the right path.

17. Certainly they disbelieve who say: Surely, Allah—He is the Messiah, son of Marium. Say: Who then could control anything as against Allah when He wished to destroy the Messiah son of Marium and his mother and all those on the earth? And Allah's is the kingdom of the heavens and the earth and what is between them; He creates what He pleases; and Allah has power over all things.

18. And the Jews and the Christians say: We are the sons of Allah and His beloved ones. Say: Why does He then chastise you for your faults? Nay, you are mortals from among those whom He has created; He forgives whom He pleases and chastises whom He pleases; and Allah's is the kingdom of the heavens and the earth and what is between them, and to Him is the eventual coming.

19. O followers of the Book! indeed Our Apostle has come to

you explaining to you after a cessation of the (mission of the) apostles, lest you say: There came not to us a giver of good news or a warner, so indeed there has come to you a giver of good news and a warner; and Allah has power over all things.

20. And when Musa said to his people: O my people! remember the favor of Allah upon you when He raised prophets among you and made you kings and gave you what He had not given to any other among the nations.

21. O my people! enter the holy land which Allah has prescribed for you and turn not on your backs for then you will turn back losers.

22. They said: O Musa! surely there is a strong race in it, and we will on no account enter it until they go out from it, so if they go out from it, then surely we will enter.

23. Two men of those who feared, upon both of whom Allah had bestowed a favor, said: Enter upon them by the gate, for when you have entered it you shall surely be victorious, and on Allah should you rely if you are believers.

24. They said: O Musa! we shall never enter it so long as they are in it; go therefore you and your Lord, then fight you both, surely we will here sit down.

25. He said: My Lord! Surely I have no control (upon any) but my own self and my brother; therefore make a separation between us and the nation of transgressors.

26. He said: So it shall surely be forbidden to them for forty years, they shall wander about in the land, therefore do not grieve for the nation of transgressors.

27. And relate to them the story of the two sons of Adam with truth when they both offered an offering, but it was accepted from one of them and was not accepted from the other. He said: I will most certainly slay you. (The other) said: Allah only accepts from those who guard (against evil).

28. If you will stretch forth your hand towards me to slay me, I am not one to stretch forth my hand towards you to slay you; surely I fear Allah, the Lord of the worlds:

29. Surely I wish that you should bear the sin committed against me and your own sin, and so you would be of the inmates of the fire, and this is the recompense of the unjust.

30. Then his mind facilitated to him the slaying of his brother, so he slew him; then he became one of the losers.

31. Then Allah sent a crow digging up the earth so that he might show him how he should cover the dead body of his

brother. He said: Woe me! do I lack the strength that I should be like this crow and cover the dead body of my brother? So he became of those who regret.

32. For this reason did We prescribe to the children of Israel that whoever slays a soul, unless it be for manslaughter or for mischief in the land, it is as though he slew all men; and whoever keeps it alive, it is as though he kept alive all men; and certainly Our apostles came to them with clear arguments, but even after that many of them certainly act extravagantly in the land.

33. The punishment of those who wage war against Allah and His apostle and strive to make mischief in the land is only this, that they should be murdered or crucified or their hands and their feet should be cut off on opposite sides or they should be imprisoned; this shall be as a disgrace for them in this world, and in the hereafter they shall have a grievous chastisement,

34. Except those who repent before you have them in your power; so know that Allah is Forgiving, Merciful.

35. O you who believe! be careful of (your duty to) Allah and seek means of nearness to Him and strive hard in His way that you may be successful.

36. Surely (as for) those who disbelieve, even if they had what is in the earth, all of it, and the like of it with it, that they might ransom themselves with it from the punishment of the day of resurrection, it shall not be accepted from them, and they shall have a painful punishment.

37. They would desire to go forth from the fire, and they shall not go forth from it, and they shall have a lasting punishment.

38. And (as for) the man who steals and the woman who steals, cut off their hands as a punishment for what they have earned, an exemplary punishment from Allah; and Allah is Mighty, Wise.

39. But whoever repents after his iniquity and reforms (himself), then surely Allah will turn to him (mercifully); surely Allah is Forgiving, Merciful.

40. Do you not know that Allah—His is the kingdom of the heavens and the earth; He chastises whom He pleases; and forgives whom He pleases and Allah has power over all things.

41. O Apostle! let not those grieve you who strive together in hastening to unbelief from among those who say with their mouths: We believe, and their hearts do not believe, and from among those who are Jews; they are listeners for the sake of a lie, listeners for another people who have not come to you; they alter

the words from their places, saying: If you are given this, take it, and if you are not given this, be cautious; and as for him whose temptation Allah desires, you cannot control anything for him with Allah. Those are they for whom Allah does not desire that He should purify their hearts; they shall have disgrace in this world, and they shall have a grievous chastisement in the hereafter.

42. (They are) listeners of a lie, devourers of what is forbidden; therefore if they come to you, judge between them or turn aside from them, and if you turn aside from them, they shall not harm you in any way; and if you judge, judge between them with equity; surely Allah loves those who judge equitably.

43. And how do they make you a judge and they have the Taurat wherein is Allah's judgment? Yet they turn back after that, and these are not the believers.

44. Surely We revealed the Taurat in which was guidance and light; with it the prophets who submitted themselves (to Allah) judged (matters) for those who were Jews, and the masters of Divine knowledge and the doctors, because they were required to guard (part) of the Book of Allah, and they were witnesses thereof; therefore fear not the people and fear Me, and do not take a small price for My communications; and whoever did not judge by what Allah revealed, those are they that are the unbelievers.

45. And We prescribed to them in it that life is for life, and eye for eye, and nose for nose, and ear for ear, and tooth for tooth, and (that there is) reprisal in wounds; but he who foregoes it, it shall be an expiation for him; and whoever did not judge by what Allah revealed, those are they that are the unjust.

46. And We sent after them in their footsteps Isa, son of Marium, verifying what was before him of the Taurat and We gave him the Injeel in which was guidance and light, and verifying what was before it of Taurat and a guidance and an admonition for those who guard (against evil).

47. And the followers of the Injeel should have judged by what Allah revealed in it; and whoever did not judge by what Allah revealed, those are they that are the transgressors.

48. And We have revealed to you the Book with the truth, verifying what is before it of the Book and a guardian over it, therefore judge between them by what Allah has revealed, and do not follow their low desires (to turn away) from the truth that has come to you; for every one of you did We appoint a law

and a way, and if Allah had pleased He would have made you (all) a single people, but that He might try you in what He gave you, therefore strive with one another to hasten to virtuous deeds; to Allah is your return, of all (of you), so He will let you know that in which you differed;

49. And that you should judge between them by what Allah has revealed, and do not follow their low desires, and be cautious of them, lest they seduce you from part of what Allah has revealed to you; but if they turn back, then know that Allah desires to afflict them on account of some of their faults; and most surely many of the people are transgressors.

50. Is it then the judgment of (the times of) ignorance that they desire? And who is better than Allah to judge for a people who are sure?

51. O you who believe! do not take the Jews and the Christians for friends; they are friends of each other; and whoever amongst you takes them for a friend, then surely he is one of them; surely Allah does not guide the unjust people.

52. But you will see those in whose hearts is a disease, hastening towards them, saying: We fear lest a calamity should befall us; but it may be that Allah will bring the victory or a punishment from Himself, so that they shall be regretting on account of what they hid in their souls.

53. And those who believe will say: Are these they who swore by Allah with the most forcible of their oaths that they were most surely with you? Their deeds shall go for nothing, so they shall become losers.

54. O you who believe! whoever from among you turns back from his religion, then Allah will bring a people, He shall love them and they shall love Him, lowly before the believers, mighty against the unbelievers, they shall strive hard in Allah's way and shall not fear the censure of any censurer; this is Allah's grace, He gives it to whom He pleases, and Allah is Ample-giving, Knowing.

55. Only Allah is your Friend and His Apostle and those who believe, those who keep up prayers and pay the poor-rate while they bow.

56. And whoever takes Allah and His apostle and those who believe for a guardian, then surely the party of Allah are they that shall be triumphant.

57. O you who believe! do not take for guardians those who take your religion for a mockery and a joke, from among those

who were given the Book before you and the unbelievers; and be careful of (your duty to) Allah if you are believers.

58. And when you call to prayer they make it a mockery and a joke; this is because they are a people who do not understand.

59. Say: O followers of the Book! do you find fault with us (for aught) except that we believe in Allah and in what has been revealed to us and what was revealed before, and that most of you are transgressors?

60. Say: Shall I inform you of (him who is) worse than this in retribution from Allah? (Worse is he) whom Allah has cursed and brought His wrath upon, and of whom He made apes and swine, and he who served the Shaitan; these are worse in place and more erring from the straight path.

61. And when they come to you, they say: We believe; and indeed they come in with unbelief and indeed they go forth with it; and Allah knows best what they concealed.

62. And you will see many of them striving with one another to hasten in sin and exceeding the limits, and their eating of what is unlawfully acquired; certainly evil is that which they do.

63. Why do not the learned men and the doctors of law prohibit them from their speaking of what is sinful and their eating of what is unlawfully acquired? Certainly evil is that which they work.

64. And the Jews say: The hand of Allah is tied up! Their hands shall be shackled and they shall be cursed for what they say. Nay, both His hands are spread out, He expends as He pleases; and what has been revealed to you from your Lord will certainly make many of them increase in inordinacy and unbelief; and We have put enmity and hatred among them till the day of resurrection; whenever they kindle a fire for war Allah puts it out, and they strive to make mischief in the land; and Allah does not love the mischief-makers.

65. And if the followers of the Book had believed and guarded (against evil) We would certainly have covered their evil deeds and We would certainly have made them enter gardens of bliss,

66. And if they had kept up the Taurat and the Injeel and that which was revealed to them from their Lord, they would certainly have eaten from above them and from beneath their feet; there is a party of them keeping to the moderate course, and (as for) most of them, evil is that which they do.

67. O Apostle! deliver what has been revealed to you from your Lord; and if you do it not, then you have not delivered His

message, and Allah will protect you from the people; surely Allah will not guide the unbelieving people.

68. Say: O followers of the Book! you follow no good till you keep up the Taurat and the Injeel and that which is revealed to you from your Lord; and surely that which has been revealed to you from your Lord shall make many of them increase in inordinacy and unbelief; grieve not therefore for the unbelieving people.

69. Surely those who believe and those who are Jews and the Sebeans and the Christians whoever believes in Allah and the last day and does good—they shall have no fear nor shall they grieve.

70. Certainly We made a covenant with the children of Israel and We sent to them apostles; whenever there came to them an apostle with what that their souls did not desire, some (of them) did they call liars and some they slew.

71. And they thought that there would be no affliction, so they became blind and deaf; then Allah turned to them mercifully, but many of them became blind and deaf; and Allah is well seeing what they do.

72. Certainly they disbelieve who say: Surely Allah, He is the Messiah, son of Marium; and the Messiah said: O Children of Israel! serve Allah, my Lord and your Lord. Surely whoever associates (others) with Allah, then Allah has forbidden to him the garden, and his abode is the fire; and there shall be no helpers for the unjust.

73. Certainly they disbelieve who say: Surely Allah is the third (person) of the three; and there is no god but the one God, and if they desist not from what they say, a painful chastisement shall befall those among them who disbelieve.

74. Will they not then turn to Allah and ask His forgiveness? And Allah is Forgiving, Merciful.

75. The Messiah, son of Marium is but an apostle; apostles before him have indeed passed away; and his mother was a truthful woman; they both used to eat food. See how We make the communications clear to them, then behold, how they are turned away.

76. Say: Do you serve besides Allah that which does not control for you any harm, or any profit? And Allah—He is the Hearing, the Knowing.

77. Say: O followers of the Book! be not unduly immoderate in your religion, and do not follow the low desires of people who

went astray before and led many astray and went astray from the right path.

78. Those who disbelieved from among the children of Israel were cursed by the tongue of Dawood and Isa, son of Marium; this was because they disobeyed and used to exceed the limit.

79. They used not to forbid each other the hateful things (which) they did; certainly evil was that which they did.

80. You will see many of them befriending those who disbelieve; certainly evil is that which their souls have sent before for them, that Allah became displeased with them and in chastisement shall they abide.

81. And had they believed in Allah and the prophet and what was revealed to him, they would not have taken them for friends, but most of them are transgressors.

82. Certainly you will find the most violent of people in enmity for those who believe (to be) the Jews and those who are polytheists, and you will certainly find the nearest in friendship to those who believe (to be) those who say: We are Christians; this is because there are priests and monks among them and because they do not behave proudly.

83. And when they hear what has been revealed to the apostle, you will see their eyes overflowing with tears on account of the truth that they recognize; they say: Our Lord! we believe, so write us down with the witnesses (of truth).

84. And what (reason) have we that we should not believe in Allah and in the truth that has come to us, while we earnestly desire that our Lord should cause us to enter with the good people?

85. Therefore Allah rewarded them on account of what they said, with gardens in which rivers flow to abide in them; and this is the reward of those who do good (to others).

86. And (as for) those who disbelieve and reject Our communications, these are the companions of the flame.

87. O you who believe! do not forbid (yourselves) the good things which Allah has made lawful for you and do not exceed the limits; surely Allah does not love those who exceed the limits.

88. And eat of the lawful and good (things) that Allah has given you, and be careful of (your duty to) Allah, in Whom you believe.

89. Allah does not call you to account for what is vain in your oaths, but He calls you to account for the making of deliberate

oaths; so its expiation is the feeding of ten poor men out of the middling (food) you feed your families with, or their clothing, or the freeing of a neck; but whosoever cannot find (means) then fasting for three days; this is the expiation of your oaths when you swear; and guard your oaths. Thus does Allah make clear to you His communications, that you may be grateful.

90. O you who believe! intoxicants and games of chance and (sacrificing to) stones set up and (dividing by) arrows are only an uncleanness, the Shaitan's work; shun it therefore that you may be successful.

91. The Shaitan only desires to cause enmity and hatred to spring in your midst by means of intoxicants and games of chance, and to keep you off from the remembrance of Allah and from prayer. Will you then desist?

92. And obey Allah and obey the apostle and be cautious; but if you turn back, then know that only a clear deliverance of the message is (incumbent) on Our apostle.

93. On those who believe and do good there is no blame for what they eat, when they are careful (of their duty) and believe and do good deeds, then they are careful (of their duty) and believe, then they are careful (of their duty) and do good (to others), and Allah loves those who do good (to others).

94. O you who believe! Allah will certainly try you in respect of some game which your hands and your lances can reach, that Allah might know who fears Him in secret; but whoever exceeds the limit after this, he shall have a painful punishment.

95. O you who believe! do not kill game while you are on pilgrimage, and whoever among you shall kill it intentionally, the compensation (of it) is the like of what he killed, from the cattle, as two just persons among you shall judge, as an offering to be brought to the Kaaba or the expiation (of it) is the feeding of the poor or the equivalent of it in fasting, that he may taste the unwholesome result of his deed; Allah has pardoned what is gone by; and whoever returns (to it), Allah will inflict retribution on him; and Allah is Mighty, Lord of Retribution.

96. Lawful to you is the game of the sea and its food, a provision for you and for the travellers, and the game of the land is forbidden to you so long as you are on pilgrimage, and be careful of (your duty to) Allah, to Whom you shall be gathered.

97. Allah has made the Kaaba, the sacred house, a maintenance for the people, and the sacred month and the offerings and the sacrificial animals with garlands; this is that you may know

that Allah knows whatever is in the heavens and whatever is in the earth, and that Allah is the Knower of all things.

98. Know that Allah is severe in requiting (evil) and that Allah is Forgiving, Merciful.

99. Nothing is (incumbent) on the Apostle but to deliver (the message), and Allah knows what you do openly and what you hide.

100. Say: The bad and the good are not equal, though the abundance of the bad may please you; so be careful of (your duty to) Allah, O men of understanding, that you may be successful.

101. O you who believe! do not put questions about things which if declared to you may trouble you, and if you question about them when the Quran is being revealed, they shall be declared to you; Allah pardons this, and Allah is Forgiving, Forbearing.

102. A people before you indeed asked such questions, and then became disbelievers on account of them.

103. Allah has not ordained (the making of) a slit-ear she-camel, or a she-camel let loose for free pasture, or idol sacrifices for twin-births in animals, or stallion-camels freed from work, but those who disbelieve fabricate a lie against Allah, and most of them do not understand.

104. And when it is said to them, Come to what Allah has revealed and to the Apostle, they say: That on which we found our fathers is sufficient for us. What! even though their fathers knew nothing and did not follow the right way.

105. O you who believe! take care of your souls; he who errs cannot hurt you when you are on the right way; to Allah is your return, of all (of you), so He will inform you of what you did.

106. O you who believe! call to witness between you when death draws nigh to one of you, at the time of making the will, two just persons from among you, or two others from among others than you, if you are travelling in the land and the calamity of death befalls you; the two (witnesses) you should detain after the prayer; then if you doubt (them), they shall both swear by Allah, (saying): We will not take for it a price, though there be a relative, and we will not hide the testimony of Allah for then certainly we should be among the sinners.

107. Then if it becomes known that they both have been guilty of a sin, two others shall stand up in their place from among those who have a claim against them, the two nearest in kin; so they two should swear by Allah: Certainly our testimony is truer than the testimony of those two, and we have not

exceeded the limit, for then most surely we should be of the unjust.

108. This is more proper in order that they should give testimony truly or fear that other oaths be given after their oaths; and be careful of (your duty to) Allah, and hear; and Allah does not guide the transgressing people.

109. On the day when Allah will assemble the apostles, then say: What answer were you given? They shall say: We have no knowledge, surely Thou art the great Knower of the unseen things.

110. When Allah will say: O Isa son of Marium! Remember My favor on you and on your mother, when I strengthened you with the holy Spirit, you spoke to the people in the cradle and when of old age, and when I taught you the Book and the wisdom and the Taurat and the Injeel; and when you determined out of clay a thing like the form of a bird by My permission, then you breathed into it and it became a bird by My permission, and you healed the blind and the leprous by My permission; and when you brought forth the dead by My permission; and when I withheld the children of Israel from you when you came to them with clear arguments, but those who disbelieved among them said: This is nothing but clear enchantment.

111. And when I revealed to the disciples, saying, Believe in Me and My apostle, they said: We believe and bear witness that we submit (ourselves).

112. When the disciples said: O Isa son of Marium! will your Lord consent to send down to us food from heaven? He said: Be careful of (your duty to) Allah if you are believers.

113. They said: We desire that we should eat of it and that our hearts should be at rest, and that we may know that you have indeed spoken the truth to us and that we may be of the witnesses to it.

114. Isa the son of Marium said: O Allah, our Lord! send down to us food from heaven which should be to us an ever-recurring happiness, to the first of us and to the last of us, and a sign from Thee, and grant us means of subsistence, and Thou art the best of the Providers.

115. Allah said: Surely I will send it down to you, but whoever shall disbelieve afterwards from among you, surely I will chastise him with a chastisement with which I will not chastise anyone among the nations.

116. And when Allah will say: O Isa son of Marium! did you

say to men, Take me and my mother for two gods besides Allah, he will say: Glory be to Thee, it did not befit me that I should say what I had no right to (say); if I had said it, Thou wouldst indeed have known it; Thou knowest what is in my mind, and I do not know what is in Thy mind, surely Thou art the great Knower of the unseen things.

117. I did not say to them aught save what Thou didst enjoin me with: That serve Allah, my Lord and your Lord, and I was a witness of them so long as I was among them, but when Thou didst cause me to die, Thou wert the watcher over them, and Thou art witness of all things.

118. If Thou shouldst chastise them, then surely they are Thy servants; and if Thou shouldst forgive them, then surely Thou art the Mighty, the Wise.

119. Allah will say: This is the day when their truth shall benefit the truthful ones; they shall have gardens beneath which rivers flow to abide in them for ever: Allah is well pleased with them and they are well pleased with Allah; this is the mighty achievement.

120. Allah's is the kingdom of the heavens and the earth and what is in them; and He has power over all things.

THE CATTLE

In the name of Allah, the Beneficent, the Merciful.

1. All praise is due to Allah, Who created the heavens and the earth and made the darkness and the light; yet those who disbelieve set up equals with their Lord.

2. He it is Who created you from clay, then He decreed a term; and there is a term named with Him; still you doubt.

3. And He is Allah in the heavens and in the earth; He knows your secret (thoughts) and your open (words), and He knows what you earn.

4. And there does not come to them any communication of the communications of their Lord but they turn aside from it.

5. So they have indeed rejected the truth when it came to them; therefore the truth of what they mocked at will shine upon them.

6. Do they not consider how many a generation We have destroyed before them, whom We had established in the earth as We have not established you, and We sent the clouds pouring rain on them in abundance, and We made the rivers to flow beneath them, then We destroyed them on account of their faults and raised up after them another generation.

7. And if We had sent to you a writing on a paper, then they had touched it with their hands, certainly those who disbelieve would have said: This is nothing but clear enchantment.

8. And they say: Why has not an angel been sent down to him? And had We sent down an angel, the matter would have certainly been decided and then they would not have been respited.

9. And if We had made him angel, We would certainly have made him a man, and We would certainly have made confused to them what they make confused.

10. And certainly apostles before you were mocked at, but that which they mocked at encompassed the scoffers among them.

11. Say: Travel in the land, then see what was the end of the rejecters.

12. Say: To whom belongs what is in the heavens and the earth? Say: To Allah; He has ordained mercy on Himself; most certainly He will gather you on the resurrection day—there is no doubt about it. (As for) those who have lost their souls, they will not believe.

13. And to Him belongs whatever dwells in the night and the day; and He is the Hearing, the Knowing.

14. Say: Shall I take a guardian besides Allah, the Originator of the heavens and the earth, and He feeds (others) and is not (Himself) fed. Say: I am commanded to be the first who submits himself, and you should not be of the polytheists.

15. Say: Surely I fear, if I disobey my Lord, the chastisement of a grievous day.

16. He from whom it is averted on that day, Allah indeed has shown mercy to him; and this is a manifest achievement.

17. And if Allah touch you with affliction, there is none to take it off but He; and if He visit you with good, then He has power over all things.

18. And He is the Supreme, above His servants; and He is the Wise, the Aware.

19. Say: What thing is the weightiest in testimony? Say: Allah is witness between you and me; and this Quran has been revealed to me that with it I may warn you and whomsoever it reaches.

Do you really bear witness that there are other gods with Allah? Say: I do not bear witness. Say: He is only one God, and surely I am clear of that which you set up (with Him).

20. Those whom We have given the Book recognize him as they recognize their sons; (as for) those who have lost their souls, they will not believe.

21. And who is more unjust than he who forges a lie against Allah or (he who) gives the lie to His communications; surely the unjust will not be successful.

22. And on the day when We shall gather them all together, then shall We say to those who associated others (with Allah): Where are your associates whom you asserted?

23. Then their excuse would be nothing but that they would say: By Allah, our Lord, we were not polytheists.

24. See how they lie against their own souls, and that which they forged has passed away from them.

25. And of them is he who hearkens to you, and We have cast veils over their hearts lest they understand it and a heaviness into their ears; and even if they see every sign they will not believe in it; so much so that when they come to you they only dispute with you; those who disbelieve say: This is naught but the stories of the ancients.

26. And they prohibit (others) from it and go far away from it, and they only bring destruction upon their own souls while they do not perceive.

27. And could you see when they are made to stand before the fire, then they shall say: Would that we were sent back, and we would not reject the communications of our Lord and we would be of the believers.

28. Nay, what they concealed before shall become manifest to them; and if they were sent back, they would certainly go back to that which they are forbidden, and most surely they are liars.

29. And they say: There is nothing but our life of this world, and we shall not be raised.

30. And could you see when they are made to stand before their Lord. He will say: Is not this the truth? They will say: Yea! by our Lord. He will say: Taste then the chastisement because you disbelieved.

31. They are losers indeed who reject the meeting of Allah; until when the hour comes upon them all of a sudden they shall say: O our grief for our neglecting it! and they shall bear their burdens on their backs; now surely evil is that which they bear.

32. And this world's life is naught but a play and an idle sport; and certainly the abode of the hereafter is better for those who guard (against evil); do you not then understand?

33. We know indeed that what they say certainly grieves you, but surely they do not call you a liar; but the unjust deny the communications of Allah.

34. And certainly apostles before you were rejected, but they were patient on being rejected and persecuted until Our help came to them; and there is none to change the words of Allah, and certainly there has come to you some information about the messengers.

35. And if their turning away is hard on you, then if you can seek an opening (to go down) into the earth or a ladder (to ascend up) to heaven so that you should bring them a sign and if Allah had pleased He would certainly have gathered them all on guidance, therefore be not of the ignorant.

36. Only those accept who listen; and (as to) the dead, Allah will raise them, then to Him they shall be returned.

37. And they say: Why has not a sign been sent down to him from his Lord? Say: Surely Allah is able to send down a sign, but most of them do not know.

38. And there is no animal that walks upon the earth nor a bird that flies with its two wings but (they are) genera like yourselves; We have not neglected anything in the Book, then to their Lord shall they be gathered.

39. And they who reject Our communications are deaf and dumb, in utter darkness; whom Allah pleases He causes to err, and whom He pleases He puts on the right way.

40. Say: Tell me if the chastisement of Allah should overtake you or the hour should come upon you, will you call (on others) besides Allah, if you are truthful?

41. Nay, Him you call upon, so He clears away that for which you pray if He pleases and you forget what you set up (with Him).

42. And certainly We sent (apostles) to nations before you, then We seized them with distress and affliction in order that they might humble themselves.

43. Yet why did they not, when Our punishment came to them, humble themselves? But their hearts hardened and the Shaitan made what they did fair-seeming to them.

44. But when they neglected that with which they had been admonished, We opened for them the doors of all things, until

when they rejoiced in what they were given We seized them suddenly; then lo! they were in utter despair.

45. So the roots of the people who were unjust were cut off; and all praise is due to Allah, the Lord of the worlds.

46. Say: Have you considered that if Allah takes away your hearing and your sight and sets a seal on your hearts, who is the god besides Allah that can bring it to you? See how We repeat the communications, yet they turn away.

47. Say: Have you considered if the chastisement of Allah should overtake you suddenly or openly, will any be destroyed but the unjust people?

48. And We send not messengers but as announcers of good news and givers of warning; then whoever believes and acts aright, they shall have no fear, nor shall they grieve.

49. And (as for) those who reject Our communications, chastisement shall afflict them because they transgressed.

50. Say: I do not say to you, I have with me the treasures of Allah, nor do I know the unseen, nor do I say to you that I am an angel; I do not follow aught save that which is revealed to me. Say: Are the blind and the seeing one alike? Do you not then reflect?

51. And warn with it those who fear that they shall be gathered to their Lord—there is no guardian for them, nor any intercessor besides Him—that they may guard (against evil).

52. And do not drive away those who call upon their Lord in the morning and the evening, they desire only His favor; neither are you answerable for any reckoning of theirs, nor are they answerable for any reckoning of yours, so that you should drive them away and thus be of the unjust.

53. And thus do We try some of them by others so that they say: Are these they upon whom Allah has conferred benefit from among us? Does not Allah best know the grateful?

54. And when those who believe in Our communications come to you, say: Peace be on you, your Lord has ordained mercy on Himself, (so) that if any one of you does evil in ignorance, then turns after that and acts aright, then He is Forgiving, Merciful.

55. And thus do We make distinct the communications and so that the way of the guilty may become clear.

56. Say: I am forbidden to serve those whom you call upon besides Allah. Say: I do not follow your low desires, for then

indeed I should have gone astray and I should not be of those who go aright.

57. Say: Surely I have manifest proof from my Lord and you call it a lie; I have not with me that which you would hasten; the judgment is only Allah's; He relates the truth and He is the best of deciders.

58. Say: If that which you desire to hasten were with me, the matter would have certainly been decided between you and me; and Allah best knows the unjust.

59. And with Him are the keys of the unseen treasures—none knows them but He; and He knows what is in the land and the sea; and there falls not a leaf but He knows it, nor a grain in the darkness of the earth, nor anything green nor dry but (it is all) in a clear book.

60. And He it is Who takes your souls at night (in sleep), and He knows what you acquire in the day, then He raises you up therein that an appointed term may be fulfilled; then to Him is your return, then He will inform you of what you were doing.

61. And He is the Supreme, above His servants, and He sends keepers over you; until when death comes to one of you, Our messengers cause him to die, and they are not remiss.

62. Then are they sent back to Allah, their Master, the True one; now surely His is the judgment and He is swiftest in taking account.

63. Say: Who is it that delivers you from the dangers of the land and the sea (when) you call upon Him (openly) humiliating yourselves, and in secret: If He delivers us from this, we should certainly be of the grateful ones.

64. Say: Allah delivers you from them and from every distress, but again you set up others (with Him).

65. Say: He has the power that He should send on you a chastisement from above you or from beneath your feet, or that He should throw you into confusion, (making you) of different parties; and make some of you taste the fighting of others. See how We repeat the communications that they may understand.

66. And your people call it a lie and it is the very truth. Say: I am not placed in charge of you.

67. For every prophecy is a term, and you will come to know (it).

68. And when you see those who enter into false discourses about Our communications, withdraw from them until they

enter into some other discourse, and if the Shaitan causes you to forget, then do not sit after recollection with the unjust people.

69. And nought of the reckoning of their (deeds) shall be against those who guard (against evil), but (theirs) is only to remind, haply they may guard.

70. And leave those who have taken their religion for a play and an idle sport, and whom this world's life has deceived, and remind (them) thereby lest a soul should be given up to destruction for what it has earned; it shall not have besides Allah any guardian nor an intercessor, and if it should seek to give every compensation, it shall not be accepted from it; these are they who shall be given up to destruction for what they earned; they shall have a drink of boiling water and a painful chastisement because they disbelieved.

71. Say: Shall we call on that besides Allah, which does not benefit us nor harm us, and shall we be returned back on our heels after Allah has guided us, like him whom the Shaitans have made to fall down perplexed in the earth? He has companions who call him to the right way, (saying): Come to us. Say: Surely the guidance of Allah, that is the (true) guidance, and we are commanded that we should submit to the Lord of the worlds.

72. And that you should keep up prayer and be careful of (your duty to) Him; and He it is to Whom you shall be gathered.

73. And He it is Who has created the heavens and the earth with truth; and on the day He says: Be, it is. His word is the truth, and His is the kingdom on the day when the trumpet shall be blown; the Knower of the unseen and the seen; and He is the Wise, the Aware.

74. And when Ibrahim said to his sire, Azar: Do you take idols for gods? Surely I see you and your people in manifest error.

75. And thus did We show Ibrahim the kingdom of the heavens and the earth and that he might be of those who are sure.

76. So when the night over-shadowed him, he saw a star; said he: Is this my Lord? So when it set, he said: I do not love the setting ones.

77. Then when he saw the moon rising, he said: Is this my Lord? So when it set, he said: If my Lord had not guided me I should certainly be of the erring people.

78. Then when he saw the sun rising, he said: Is this my Lord? Is this the greatest? So when it set, he said: O my people! surely I am clear of what you set up (with Allah).

79. Surely I have turned myself, being upright, wholly to Him Who originated the heavens and the earth, and I am not of the polytheists.

80. And his people disputed with him. He said: Do you dispute with me respecting Allah? And He has guided me indeed; and I do not fear in any way those that you set up with Him, unless my Lord pleases; my Lord comprehends all things in His knowledge; will you not then mind?

81. And how should I fear what you have set up (with Him), while you do not fear that you have set up with Allah that for which He has not sent down to you any authority; which then of the two parties is surer of security, if you know?

82. Those who believe and do not mix up their faith with iniquity, those are they who shall have the security and they are those who go aright.

83. And this was Our argument which we gave to Ibrahim against his people; We exalt in dignity whom We please; surely your Lord is Wise, Knowing.

84. And We gave to him Ishaq and Yaqoob; each did We guide, and Nuh did We guide before, and of his descendants, Dawood and Sulaiman and Ayub and Yusuf and Haroon; and thus do We reward those who do good (to others).

85. And Zakariya and Yahya and Isa and Ilyas; every one was of the good;

86. And Ismail and Al-Yasha and Yunus and Lut; and every one We made to excel (in) the worlds:

87. And from among their fathers and their descendants and their brethren, and We chose them and guided them into the right way.

88. This is Allah's guidance, He guides thereby whom He pleases of His servants; and if they had set up others (with Him), certainly what they did would have become ineffectual for them.

89. These are they to whom We gave the book and the wisdom and the prophecy; therefore if these disbelieve in it We have already entrusted with it a people who are not disbelievers in it.

90. These are they whom Allah guided, therefore follow their guidance. Say: I do not ask you for any reward for it; it is nothing but a reminder to the nations.

91. And they do not assign to Allah the attributes due to Him when they say: Allah has not revealed anything to a mortal. Say: Who revealed the Book which Musa brought, a light and a guidance to men, which you make into scattered writings which

you show while you conceal much? And you were taught what you did not know, (neither) you nor your fathers. Say: Allah; then leave them sporting in their vain discourses.

92. And this is a Book We have revealed, blessed, verifying that which is before it, and that you may warn the metropolis and those around her; and those who believe in the hereafter believe in it, and they attend to their prayers constantly.

93. And who is more unjust than he who forges a lie against Allah, or says: It has been revealed to me; while nothing has been revealed to him, and he who says: I can reveal the like of what Allah has revealed? and if you had seen when the unjust shall be in the agonies of death and the angels shall spread forth their hands: Give up your souls; today shall you be recompensed with an ignominious chastisement because you spoke against Allah other than the truth and (because) you showed pride against His communications.

94. And certainly you have come to Us alone as We created you at first, and you have left behind your backs the things which We gave you, and We do not see with you your intercessors about whom you asserted that they were (Allah's) associates in respect to you; certainly the ties between you are now cut off and what you asserted is gone from you.

95. Surely Allah causes the grain and the stone to germinate; He brings forth the living from the dead and He is the bringer forth of the dead from the living; that is Allah! how are you then turned away.

96. He causes the dawn to break; and He has made the night for rest, and the sun and the moon for reckoning; this is an arrangement of the Mighty, the Knowing.

97. And He it is Who has made the stars for you that you might follow the right way thereby in the darkness of the land and the sea; truly We have made plain the communications for a people who know.

98. And He it is Who has brought you into being from a single soul, then there is (for you) a resting-place and a depository; indeed We have made plain the communications for a people who understand.

99. And He it is Who sends down water from the cloud, then We bring forth with it buds of all (plants), then We bring forth from it green (foliage) from which We produce grain piled up (in the ear); and of the palm-tree, of the sheaths of it, come forth

clusters (of dates) within reach, and gardens of grapes and olives and pomegranates, alike and unlike; behold the fruit of it when it yields the fruit and the ripening of it; most surely there are signs in this for a people who believe.

100. And they make the jinn associates with Allah, while He created them, and they falsely attribute to Him sons and daughters without knowledge; glory be to Him, and highly exalted is He above what they ascribe (to Him).

101. Wonderful Originator of the heavens and the earth! How could He have a son when He has no consort, and He (Himself) created everything, and He is the Knower of all things.

102. That is Allah, your Lord, there is no god but He; the Creator of all things, therefore serve Him, and He has charge of all things.

103. Vision comprehends Him not, and He comprehends (all) vision; and He is the Knower of subtleties, the Aware.

104. Indeed there have come to you clear proofs from your Lord; whoever will therefore see, it is for his own soul and whoever will be blind, it shall be against himself and I am not a keeper over you.

105. And thus do We repeat the communications and that they may say: You have read; and that We may make it clear to a people who know.

106. Follow what is revealed to you from your Lord; there is no god but He; and withdraw from the polytheists.

107. And if Allah had pleased, they would not have set up others (with Him) and We have not appointed you a keeper over them, and you are not placed in charge of them.

108. And do not abuse those whom they call upon besides Allah, lest exceeding the limits they should abuse Allah out of ignorance. Thus have We made fair seeming to every people their deeds; then to their Lord shall be their return, so He will inform them of what they did.

109. And they swear by Allah with the strongest of their oaths, that if a sign came to them they would most certainly believe in it. Say: Signs are only with Allah; and what should make you know that when it comes they will not believe?

110. And We will turn their hearts and their sights, even as they did not believe in it the first time, and We will leave them in their inordinacy, blindly wandering on.

111. And even if We had sent down to them the angels and

the dead had spoken to them and We had brought together all things before them, they would not believe unless Allah pleases, but most of them are ignorant.

112. And thus did We make for every prophet an enemy, the Shaitans from among men and jinn, some of them suggesting to others varnished falsehood to deceive (them), and had your Lord pleased they would not have done it, therefore leave them and that which they forge.

113. And that the hearts of those who do not believe in the hereafter may incline to it and that they may be well pleased with it and that they may earn what they are going to earn (of evil).

114. Shall I then seek a judge other than Allah? And He it is Who has revealed to you the Book (which is) made plain; and those whom We have given the Book know that it is revealed by your Lord with truth, therefore you should not be of the disputers.

115. And the word of your Lord has been accomplished truly and justly; there is none who can change His words, and He is the Hearing, the Knowing.

116. And if you obey most of those in the earth, they will lead you astray from Allah's way; they follow but conjecture and they only lie.

117. Surely your Lord—He best knows who goes astray from His way, and He best knows those who follow the right course.

118. Therefore eat of that on which Allah's name has been mentioned if you are believers in His communications.

119. And what reason have you that you should not eat of that on which Allah's name has been mentioned, and He has already made plain to you what He has forbidden to you—excepting what you are compelled to; and most surely many would lead (people) astray by their low desires out of ignorance; surely your Lord—He best knows those who exceed the limits.

120. And abandon open and secret sin; surely they who earn sin shall be recompensed with what they earned.

121. And do not eat of that on which Allah's name has not been mentioned, and that is most surely a transgression; and most surely the Shaitans suggest to their friends that they should contend with you; and if you obey them, you shall most surely be polytheists.

122. Is he who was dead then We raised him to life and made for him a light by which he walks among the people, like him

whose likeness is that of one in utter darkness whence he cannot come forth? Thus what they did was made fair seeming to the unbelievers.

123. And thus have We made in every town the great ones to be its guilty ones, that they may plan therein; and they do not plan but against their own souls, and they do not perceive.

124. And when a communication comes to them they say: We will not believe till we are given the like of what Allah's apostles are given. Allah best knows where He places His message. There shall befall those who are guilty humiliation from Allah and severe chastisement because of what they planned.

125. Therefore (for) whomsoever Allah intends that He would guide him aright, He expands his breast for Islam, and (for) whomsoever He intends that He should cause him to err, He makes his breast strait and narrow as though he were ascending upwards; thus does Allah lay uncleanness on those who do not believe.

126. And this is the path of your Lord, (a) right (path); indeed We have made the communications clear for a people who mind.

127. They shall have the abode of peace with their Lord, and He is their guardian because of what they did.

128. And on the day when He shall gather them all together: O assembly of jinn! you took away a great part of mankind. And their friends from among the men shall say: Our Lord! some of us profited by others and we have reached our appointed term which Thou didst appoint for us. He shall say: The fire is your abode, to abide in it, except as Allah is pleased; surely your Lord is Wise, Knowing.

129. And thus do We make some of the iniquitous to befriend others on account of what they earned.

130. O assembly of jinn and men! did there not come to you apostles from among you, relating to you My communications and warning you of the meeting of this day of yours? They shall say: We bear witness against ourselves; and this world's life deceived them, and they shall bear witness against their own souls that they were unbelievers.

131. This is because your Lord would not destroy towns unjustly while their people were negligent.

132. And all have degrees according to what they do; and your Lord is not heedless of what they do.

133. And your Lord is the Self-sufficient one, the Lord of

mercy; if He pleases, He may take you off, and make whom He pleases successors after you, even as He raised you up from the seed of another people.

134. Surely what you are threatened with must come to pass and you cannot escape (it).

135. Say: O my people! act according to your ability; I too am acting; so you will soon come to know, for whom (of us) will be the (good) end of the abode; surely the unjust shall not be successful.

136. And they set apart a portion for Allah out of what He has created of tilth and cattle, and say: This is for Allah—so they assert—and this for our associates; then what is for their associates, it reaches not to Allah, and whatever is (set apart) for Allah, it reaches to their associates; evil is that which they judge.

137. And thus their associates have made fair seeming to most of the polytheists the killing of their children, that they may cause them to perish and obscure for them their religion; and if Allah had pleased, they would not have done it, therefore leave them and that which they forge.

138. And they say: These are cattle and tilth prohibited; none shall eat them except such as We please—so they assert—and cattle whose backs are forbidden, and cattle on which they would not mention Allah's name—forging a lie against Him; He shall requite them for what they forged.

139. And they say: What is in the wombs of these cattle is specially for our males, and forbidden to our wives, and if it be stillborn, then they are all partners in it; He will reward them for their attributing (falsehood to Allah); surely He is Wise, Knowing.

140. They are lost indeed who kill their children foolishly without knowledge, and forbid what Allah has given to them, forging a lie against Allah; they have indeed gone astray, and they are not the followers of the right course.

141. And He it is Who produces gardens (of vine), trellised and untrellised, and palms and seed-produce of which the fruits are of various sorts, and olives and pomegranates, like and unlike; eat of its fruit when it bears fruit, and pay the due of it on the day of its reaping, and do not act extravagantly; surely He does not love the extravagant.

142. And of cattle (He created) beasts of burden and those which are fit for slaughter only; eat of what Allah has given you

and do not follow the footsteps of the Shaitan; surely he is your open enemy.

143. Eight in pairs—two of sheep and two of goats. Say: Has He forbidden the two males or the two females or that which the wombs of the two females contain? Inform me with knowledge if you are truthful.

144. And two of camels and two of cows. Say: Has He forbidden the two males or the two females or that which the wombs of the two females contain? Or were you witnesses when Allah enjoined you this? Who, then, is more unjust than he who forges a lie against Allah that he should lead astray men without knowledge? Surely Allah does not guide the unjust people.

145. Say: I do not find in that which has been revealed to me anything forbidden for an eater to eat of except that it be what has died of itself, or blood poured forth, or flesh of swine—for that surely is unclean—or that which is a transgression, other than (the name of) Allah having been invoked on it; but whoever is driven to necessity, not desiring nor exceeding the limit, then surely your Lord is Forgiving, Merciful.

146. And to those who were Jews We made unlawful every animal having claws, and of oxen and sheep We made unlawful to them the fat of both, except such as was on their backs or the entrails or what was mixed with bones: this was a punishment We gave them on account of their rebellion, and We are surely Truthful.

147. But if they give you the lie, then say: Your Lord is the Lord of All-encompassing mercy; and His punishment cannot be averted from the guilty people.

148. Those who are polytheists will say: If Allah had pleased we would not have associated (aught with Him) nor our fathers, nor would we have forbidden (to ourselves) anything; even so did those before them reject until they tasted Our punishment. Say: Have you any knowledge with you so you should bring it forth to us? You only follow a conjecture and you only tell lies.

149. Say: Then Allah's is the conclusive argument; so if He please, He would certainly guide you all.

150. Say: Bring your witnesses who should bear witness that Allah has forbidden this, then if they bear witness, do not bear witness with them; and follow not the low desires of those who reject Our communications and of those who do not believe in the hereafter, and they make (others) equal to their Lord.

151. Say: Come I will recite what your Lord has forbidden to you—(remember) that you do not associate anything with Him and show kindness to your parents, and do not slay your children for (fear of) poverty—We provide for you and for them—and do not draw nigh to indecencies, those of them which are apparent and those which are concealed, and do not kill the soul which Allah has forbidden except for the requirements of justice; this He has enjoined you with that you may understand.

152. And do not approach the property of the orphan except in the best manner until he attains his maturity; and give full measure and weight with justice—We do not impose on any soul a duty except to the extent of its ability; and when you speak, then be just though it be (against) a relative, and fulfill Allah's covenant; this He has enjoined you with that you may be mindful;

153. And (know) that this is My path, the right one, therefore follow it, and follow not (other) ways, for they will lead you away from His way; this He has enjoined you with that you may guard (against evil).

154. Again, We gave the Book to Musa to complete (Our blessings) on him who would do good (to others), and making plain all things and a guidance and a mercy, so that they should believe in the meeting of their Lord.

155. And this is a Book We have revealed, blessed; therefore follow it and guard (against evil) that mercy may be shown to you.

156. Lest you say that the Book was only revealed to two parties before us and We were truly unaware of what they read.

157. Or lest you should say: If the Book had been revealed to us, we would certainly have been better guided than they; so indeed there has come to you clear proof from your Lord, and guidance and mercy. Who then is more unjust than he who rejects Allah's communications and turns away from them? We will reward those who turn away from Our communications with an evil chastisement because they turned away.

158. They do not wait aught but that the angels should come to them, or that your Lord should come, or that some of the signs of your Lord should come. On the day when some of the signs of your Lord shall come, its faith shall not profit a soul which did not believe before, or earn good through its faith. Say: Wait; we too are waiting.

159. Surely they who divided their religion into parts and became sects, you have no concern with them; their affair is only with Allah, then He will inform them of what they did.

160. Whoever brings a good deed, he shall have ten like it, and whoever brings an evil deed, he shall be recompensed only with the like of it, and they shall not be dealt with unjustly.

161. Say: Surely, (as for) me, my Lord has guided me to the right path; (to) a most right religion, the faith of Ibrahim the upright one, and he was not of the polytheists.

162. Say: Surely my prayer and my sacrifice and my life and my death are (all) for Allah, the Lord of the worlds;

163. No associate has He; and this am I commanded, and I am the first of those who submit.

164. Say: What! shall I seek a Lord other than Allah? And He is the Lord of all things; and no soul earns (evil) but against itself, and no bearer of burden shall bear the burden of another; then to your Lord is your return, so He will inform you of that in which you differed.

165. And He it is Who has made you successors in the land and raised some of you above others by (various) grades, that He might try you by what He has given you; surely your Lord is quick to requite (evil), and He is most surely the Forgiving, the Merciful.

THE ELEVATED PLACES

In the name of Allah, the Beneficent, the Merciful.

1. Alif Lam Mim Suad.

2. A Book revealed to you—so let there be no straitness in your breast on account of it—that you may warn thereby, and a reminder close to the believers.

3. Follow what has been revealed to you from your Lord and do not follow guardians besides Him, how little do you mind.

4. And how many a town that We destroyed, so Our punishment came to it by night or while they slept at midday.

5. Yet their cry, when Our punishment came to them, was nothing but that they said: Surely we were unjust.

6. Most certainly then We will question those to whom (the apostles) were sent, and most certainly We will also question the apostles;

7. Then most certainly We will relate to them with knowledge, and We were not absent.

8. And the measuring out on that day will be just; then as for him whose measure (of good deeds) is heavy, those are they who shall be successful;

9. And as for him whose measure (of good deeds) is light, those are they who have made their souls suffer loss because they disbelieved in Our communications.

10. And certainly We have established you in the earth and made in it means of livelihood for you; little it is that you give thanks.

11. And certainly We created you, then We fashioned you, then We said to the angels: Make obeisance to Adam. So they did obeisance except Iblis; he was not of those who did obeisance.

12. He said: What hindered you so that you did not make obeisance when I commanded you? He said: I am better than he: Thou hast created me of fire, while him Thou didst create of dust.

13. He said: Then get forth from this (state), for it does not befit you to behave proudly therein. Go forth, therefore, surely you are of the abject ones.

14. He said: Respite me until the day when they are raised up.

15. He said: Surely you are of the respited ones.

16. He said: As Thou hast caused me to remain disappointed I will certainly lie in wait for them in Thy straight path.

17. Then I will certainly come to them from before them and from behind them, and from their right-hand side and from their left-hand side; and Thou shalt not find most of them thankful.

18. He said: Get out of this (state), despised, driven away; whoever of them will follow you, I will certainly fill hell with you all.

19. And (We said): O Adam! Dwell you and your wife in the garden; so eat from where you desire, but do not go near this tree, for then you will be of the unjust.

20. But the Shaitan made an evil suggestion to them that he might make manifest to them what had been hidden from them of their evil inclinations, and he said: Your Lord has not forbidden you this tree except that you may not both become two angels or that you may (not) become of the immortals.

21. And he swore to them both: Most surely I am a sincere adviser to you.

22. Then he caused them to fall by deceit; so when they tasted of the tree, their evil inclinations became manifest to them, and they both began to cover themselves with the leaves of the garden; and their Lord called out to them: Did I not forbid you both from that tree and say to you that the Shaitan is your open enemy?

23. They said: Our Lord! We have been unjust to ourselves, and if Thou forgive us not, and have (not) mercy on us, we shall certainly be of the losers.

24. He said: Get forth, some of you, the enemies of others, and there is for you in the earth an abode and a provision for a time.

25. He (also) said: Therein shall you live, and therein shall you die, and from it shall you be raised.

26. O children of Adam! We have indeed sent down to you clothing to cover your shame, and (clothing) for beauty and clothing that guards (against evil), that is the best. This is of the communications of Allah that they may be mindful.

27. O children of Adam! let not the Shaitan cause you to fall into affliction as he expelled your parents from the garden, pulling off from them both their clothing that he might show them their evil inclinations, he surely sees you, he as well as his host, from whence you cannot see them; surely We have made the Shaitans to be the guardians of those who do not believe.

28. And when they commit an indecency they say: We found our fathers doing this, and Allah has enjoined it on us. Say: Surely Allah does not enjoin indecency; do you say against Allah what you do not know?

29. Say: My Lord has enjoined justice, and set upright your faces at every time of prayer and call on Him, being sincere to Him in obedience; as He brought you forth in the beginning, so shall you also return.

30. A part has He guided aright and (as for another) part, error is justly their due, surely they took the Shaitans for guardians beside Allah, and they think that they are followers of the right way.

31. O children of Adam! attend to your embellishments at every time of prayer, and eat and drink and be not extravagant; surely He does not love the extravagant.

32. Say: Who has prohibited the embellishment of Allah which

He has brought forth for His servants and the good provisions?
Say: These are for the believers in the life of this world, purely
(theirs) on the resurrection day; thus do We make the communications clear for a people who know.

33. Say: My Lord has only prohibited indecencies, those of
them that are apparent as well as those that are concealed, and
sin and rebellion without justice, and that you associate with
Allah that for which He has not sent down any authority, and
that you say against Allah what you do not know.

34. And for every nation there is a doom, so when their doom
is come they shall not remain behind the least while, nor shall
they go before.

35. O children of Adam! if there come to you apostles from
among you relating to you My communications, then whoever
shall guard (against evil) and act aright—they shall have no fear,
nor shall they grieve.

36. And (as for) those who reject Our communications and
turn away from them haughtily—these are the inmates of the fire
they shall abide in it.

37. Who is then more unjust than he who forges a lie against
Allah or rejects His communications? (As for) those, their portion of the Book shall reach them, until when Our messengers
come to them causing them to die, they shall say: Where is that
which you used to call upon besides Allah? They would say:
They are gone away from us; and they shall bear witness against
themselves that they were unbelievers.

38. He will say: Enter into fire among the nations that have
passed away before you from among jinn and men; whenever a
nation shall enter, it shall curse its sister, until when they have all
come up with one another into it; the last of them shall say with
regard to the foremost of them: Our Lord! these led us astray,
therefore give them a double chastisement of the fire. He will
say: Every one shall have double but you do not know.

39. And the foremost of them will say to the last of them: So
you have no preference over us; therefore taste the chastisement
for what you earned.

40. Surely (as for) those who reject Our communications and
turn away from them haughtily, the doors of heaven shall not be
opened for them, nor shall they enter the garden until the camel
pass through the eye of the needle; and thus do We reward the
guilty.

41. They shall have a bed of hell-fire and from above them coverings (of it); and thus do We reward the unjust.

42. And (as for) those who believe and do good—We do not impose on any soul a duty except to the extent of its ability—they are the dwellers of the garden; in it they shall abide.

43. And We will remove whatever of ill-feeling is in their breasts; the rivers shall flow beneath them and they shall say: All praise is due to Allah Who guided us to this, and we would not have found the way had it not been that Allah had guided us; certainly the apostles of our Lord brought the truth; and it shall be cried out to them that this is the garden of which you are made heirs for what you did.

44. And the dwellers of the garden will call out to the inmates of the fire: Surely we have found what our Lord promised us to be true; have you too found what your Lord promised to be true? They will say: Yes. Then a crier will cry out among them that the curse of Allah is on the unjust.

45. Who hinder (people) from Allah's way and seek to make it crooked, and they are disbelievers in the hereafter.

46. And between the two there shall be a veil, and on the most elevated places there shall be men who know all by their marks, and they shall call out to the dwellers of the garden: Peace be on you; they shall not have yet entered it, though they hope.

47. And when their eyes shall be turned towards the inmates of the fire, they shall say: Our Lord! place us not with the unjust people.

48. And the dwellers of the most elevated places shall call out to men whom they will recognize by their marks saying: Of no avail were to you your amassings and your behaving haughtily:

49. Are these they about whom you swore that Allah will not bestow mercy on them? Enter the garden; you shall have no fear, nor shall you grieve.

50. And the inmates of the fire shall call out to the dwellers of the garden, saying: Pour on us some water or of that which Allah has given you. They shall say: Surely Allah has prohibited them both to the unbelievers.

51. Who take their religion for an idle sport and a play and this life's world deceives them; so today We forsake them, as they neglected the meeting of this day of theirs and as they denied Our communications.

52. And certainly We have brought them a Book which We

have made clear with knowledge, a guidance and a mercy for a people who believe.

53. Do they wait for aught but its final sequel? On the day when its final sequel comes about, those who neglected it before will say: Indeed the apostles of our Lord brought the truth; are there for us then any intercessors so that they should intercede on our behalf? Or could we be sent back so that we should do (deeds) other than those which we did? Indeed they have lost their souls, and that which they forged has gone away from them.

54. Surely your Lord is Allah, Who created the heavens and the earth in six periods of time, and He is firm in power; He throws the veil of night over the day, which it pursues incessantly; and (He created) the sun and the moon and the stars, made subservient by His command; surely His is the creation and the command; blessed is Allah, the Lord of the worlds.

55. Call on your Lord humbly and secretly; surely He does not love those who exceed the limits.

56. And do not make mischief in the earth after its reformation, and call on Him fearing and hoping; surely the mercy of Allah is nigh to those who do good (to others).

57. And He it is Who sends forth the winds bearing good news before His mercy, until, when they bring up a laden cloud, We drive it to a dead land, then We send down water on it, then bring forth with it of fruits of all kinds; thus shall We bring forth the dead that you may be mindful.

58. And as for the good land, its vegetation springs forth (abundantly) by the permission of its Lord, and (as for) that which is inferior (its herbage) comes forth but scantily; thus do We repeat the communications for a people who give thanks.

59. Certainly We sent Nuh to his people, so he said: O my people! serve Allah, you have no god other than Him; surely I fear for you the chastisement of a grievous day.

60. The chiefs of his people said: Most surely we see you in clear error.

61. He said: O my people! there is no error in me, but I am an apostle from the Lord of the worlds.

62. I deliver to you the messages of my Lord, and I offer you good advice and I know from Allah what you do not know.

63. What! do you wonder that a reminder has come to you from your Lord through a man from among you, that he might warn you and that you might guard (against evil) and so that mercy may be shown to you?

64. But they called him a liar, so We delivered him and those with him in the ark, and We drowned those who rejected Our communications; surely they were a blind people.

65. And to Ad (We sent) their brother Hud. He said: O my people! serve Allah, you have no god other than Him; will you not then guard (against evil)?

66. The chiefs of those who disbelieved from among his people said: Most surely we see you in folly, and most surely we think you to be of the liars.

67. He said: O my people! there is no folly in me, but I am an apostle of the Lord of the worlds.

68. I deliver to you the messages of my Lord and I am a faithful adviser to you.

69. What! do you wonder that a reminder has come to you from your Lord through a man from among you that he might warn you? And remember when He made you successors after Nuh's people and increased you in excellence in respect of make; therefore remember the benefits of Allah, that you may be successful.

70. They said: Have you come to us that we may serve Allah alone and give up what our fathers used to serve? Then bring to us what you threaten us with, if you are of the truthful ones.

71. He said: Indeed uncleanness and wrath from your Lord have lighted upon you; what! do you dispute with me about names which you and your fathers have given? Allah has not sent any authority for them; wait then, I too with you will be of those who wait.

72. So We delivered him and those with him by mercy from Us, and We cut off the last of those who rejected Our communications and were not believers.

73. And to Samood (We sent) their brother Salih. He said: O my people! serve Allah, you have no god other than Him; clear proof indeed has come to you from your Lord; this is (as) Allah's she-camel for you—a sign, therefore leave her alone to pasture on Allah's earth, and do not touch her with any harm, otherwise painful chastisement will overtake you.

74. And remember when He made you successors after Ad and settled you in the land—you make mansions on its plains and hew out houses in the mountains—remember therefore Allah's benefits and do not act corruptly in the land, making mischief.

75. The chief of those who behaved proudly among his people said to those who were considered weak, to those who believed

from among them: Do you know that Salih is sent by his Lord? They said: Surely we are believers in what he has been sent with.

76. Those who were haughty said: Surely we are deniers of what you believe in.

77. So they slew the she-camel and revolted against their Lord's commandment, and they said: O Salih! bring us what you threatened us with, if you are one of the apostles.

78. Then the earthquake overtook them, so they became motionless bodies in their abode.

79. Then he turned away from them and said: O my people I did certainly deliver to you the message of my Lord, and I gave you good advice, but you do not love those who give good advice.

80. And (We sent) Lut when he said to his people: What! do you commit an indecency which any one in the world has not done before you?

81. Most surely you come to males in lust besides females; nay, you are an extravagant people.

82. And the answer of his people was no other than that they said: Turn them out of your town, surely they are a people who seek to purify (themselves).

83. So We delivered him and his followers, except his wife; she was of those who remained behind.

84. And We rained upon them a rain; consider then what was the end of the guilty.

85. And to Madyan (We sent) their brother Shu'aib. He said: O my people! serve Allah, you have no god other than Him; clear proof indeed has come to you from your Lord, therefore give full measure and weight and do not diminish to men their things, and do not make mischief in the land after its reform; this is better for you if you are believers:

86. And do not lie in wait in every path, threatening and turning away from Allah's way him who believes in Him and seeking to make it crooked; and remember when you were few, then He multiplied you, and consider what was the end of the mischief-makers.

87. And if there is a party of you who believe in that with which I am sent, and another party who do not believe, then wait patiently until Allah judges between us; and He is the best of the Judges.

88. The chiefs, those who were proud from among his people, said: We will most certainly turn you out, O Shu'aib, and (also) those who believe with you, from our town, or you shall come back to our faith. He said: What! though we dislike (it)?

89. Indeed we shall have forged a lie against Allah if we go back to your religion after Allah has delivered us from it, and it befits us not that we should go back to it, except if Allah our Lord please: Our Lord comprehends all things in His knowledge; in Allah do we trust: Our Lord! decide between us and our people with truth; and Thou art the best of deciders.

90. And the chiefs of those who disbelieved from among his people said: If you follow Shu'aib, you shall then most surely be losers.

91. Then the earthquake overtook them, so they became motionless bodies in their abode.

92. Those who called Shu'aib a liar were as though they had never dwelt therein; those who called Shu'aib a liar, they were the losers.

93. So he turned away from them and said: O my people! certainly I delivered to you the messages of my Lord and I gave you good advice; how shall I then be sorry for an unbelieving people?

94. And We did not send a prophet in a town but We overtook its people with distress and affliction in order that they might humble themselves.

95. Then We gave them good in the place of evil until they became many and said: Distress and happiness did indeed befall our fathers. Then We took them by surprise while they did not perceive.

96. And if the people of the towns had believed and guarded (against evil) We would certainly have opened up for them blessings from the heaven and the earth, but they rejected, so We overtook them for what they had earned.

97. What! do the people of the towns then feel secure from Our punishment coming to them by night while they sleep?

98. What! do the people of the towns feel secure from Our punishment coming to them in the morning while they play?

99. What! do they then feel secure from Allah's plan? But none feels secure from Allah's plan except the people who shall perish.

100. Is it not clear to those who inherit the earth after its (former) residents that if We please We would afflict them on account of their faults and set a seal on their hearts so they would not hear.

101. These towns—We relate to you some of their stories, and certainly their apostles came to them with clear arguments, but

they would not believe in what they rejected at first; thus does Allah set a seal over the hearts of the unbelievers.

102. And We did not find in most of them any (faithfulness to) covenant, and We found most of them to be certainly transgressors.

103. Then we raised after them Musa with Our communications to Firon and his chiefs, but they disbelieved in them; consider then what was the end of the mischief makers.

104. And Musa said: O Firon! surely I am an apostle from the Lord of the worlds:

105. (I am) worthy of not saying anything about Allah except the truth: I have come to you indeed with clear proof from your Lord, therefore send with me the children of Israel.

106. He said: If you have come with a sign, then bring it, if you are of the truthful ones.

107. So he threw his rod, then lo! it was a clear serpent.

108. And he drew forth his hand, and lo! it was white to the beholders.

109. The chiefs of Firon's people said: most surely this is an enchanter possessed of knowledge:

110. He intends to turn you out of your land. What counsel do you then give?

111. They said: Put him off and his brother, and send collectors into the cities:

112. That they may bring to you every enchanter possessed of knowledge.

113. And the enchanters came to Firon (and) said: We must surely have a reward if we are the prevailing ones.

114. He said: Yes, and you shall certainly be of those who are near (to me).

115. They said: O Musa! will you cast, or shall we be the first to cast?

116. He said: Cast. So when they cast, they deceived the people's eyes and frightened them, and they produced a mighty enchantment.

117. And We revealed to Musa, saying: Cast your rod; then lo! it devoured the lies they told.

118. So the truth was established, and what they did became null.

119. Thus they were vanquished there, and they went back abased.

120. And the enchanters were thrown down, prostrating (themselves).

121. They said: We believe in the Lord of the worlds,

122. The Lord of Musa and Haroun.

123. Firon said: Do you believe in Him before I have given you permission? Surely this is a plot which you have secretly devised in this city, that you may turn out of it its people, but you shall know:

124. I will certainly cut off your hands and your feet on opposite sides, then will I crucify you all together.

125. They said: Surely to our Lord shall we go back:

126. And you do not take revenge on us except because we have believed in the communications of our Lord when they came to us! Our Lord: Pour out upon us patience and cause us to die in submission.

127. And the chiefs of Firon's people said: Do you leave Musa and his people to make mischief in the land and to forsake you and your gods? He said: We will slay their sons and spare their women, and surely we are masters over them.

128. Musa said to his people: Ask help from Allah and be patient; surely the land is Allah's; He causes such of His servants to inherit it as He pleases, and the end is for those who guard (against evil).

129. They said: We have been persecuted before you came to us and since you have come to us. He said: It may be that your Lord will destroy your enemy and make you rulers in the land, then He will see how you act.

130. And certainly We overtook Firon's people with droughts and diminution of fruits that they may be mindful.

131. But when good befell them they said: This is due to us; and when evil afflicted them, they attributed it to the ill-luck of Musa and those with him; surely their evil fortune is only from Allah, but most of them do not know.

132. And they said: Whatever sign you may bring to us to charm us with it—we will not believe in you.

133. Therefore We sent upon them widespread death, and the locusts and the lice and the frog and the blood, clear signs; but they behaved haughtily and they were a guilty people.

134. And when the plague fell upon them, they said: O Musa! pray for us to your Lord as He has promised with you, if you remove the plague from us, we will certainly believe in you and we will certainly send away with you the children of Israel.

135. But when We removed the plague from them till a term which they should attain, lo! they broke (the promise).

136. Therefore We inflicted retribution on them and drowned

them in the sea because they rejected Our signs and were heedless of them.

137. And We made the people who were deemed weak to inherit the eastern lands and the western ones which We had blessed; and the good word of your Lord was fulfilled in the children of Israel because they bore up (sufferings) patiently; and We utterly destroyed what Firon and his people had wrought and what they built.

138. And We made the children of Israel to pass the sea; then they came upon a people who kept to the worship of their idols. They said: O Musa! make for us a god as they have (their) gods. He said: Surely you are a people acting ignorantly:

139. (As to) these, surely that about which they are shall be brought to naught and that which they do is vain.

140. He said: What! shall I seek for you a god other than Allah while He has made you excel (all) created things?

141. And when We delivered you from Firon's people who subjected you to severe torment, killing your sons and sparing your women, and in this there was a great trial from your Lord.

142. And We appointed with Musa a time of thirty nights and completed them with ten (more), so the appointed time of his Lord was complete forty nights, and Musa said to his brother Haroun: Take my place among my people, and act well and do not follow the way of the mischief-makers.

143. And when Musa came at Our appointed time and his Lord spoke to him, he said: My Lord! show me (Thyself), so that I may look upon Thee. He said: You cannot (bear to) see Me, but look at the mountain, if it remains firm in its place, then will you see Me; but when his Lord manifested His glory to the mountain He made it crumble and Musa fell down in a swoon; then when he recovered, he said: Glory be to Thee, I turn to Thee, and I am the first of the believers.

144. He said: O Musa! surely I have chosen you above the people with My messages and with My words, therefore take hold of what I give to you and be of the grateful ones.

145. And We ordained for him in the tablets admonition of every kind and clear explanation of all things; so take hold of them with firmness and enjoin your people to take hold of what is best thereof; I will show you the abode of the transgressors.

146. I will turn away from My communications those who are unjustly proud in the earth; and if they see every sign they will not believe in it; and if they see the way of rectitude they do not take it for a way, and if they see the way of error, they take it for

a way; this is because they rejected Our communications and were heedless of them.

147. And (as to) those who reject Our communications and the meeting of the hereafter, their deeds are null. Shall they be rewarded except for what they have done?

148. And Musa's people made of their ornaments a calf after him, a (mere) body, which gave a mooing sound. What! could they not see that it did not speak to them nor guide them in the way? They took it (for worship) and they were unjust.

149. And when they repented and saw that they had gone astray, they said: If our Lord show not mercy to us and forgive us, we shall certainly be of the losers.

150. And when Musa returned to his people, wrathful (and) in violent grief, he said: Evil is it that you have done after me; did you turn away from the bidding of your Lord? And he threw down the tablets and seized his brother by the head, dragging him towards him. He said: Son of my mother! surely the people reckoned me weak and had well-nigh slain me, therefore make not the enemies to rejoice over me and count me not among the unjust people.

151. He said: My Lord! forgive me and my brother and cause us to enter into Thy mercy, and Thou art the most Merciful of the merciful ones.

152. (As for) those who took the calf (for a god), surely wrath from their Lord and disgrace in this world's life shall overtake them, and thus do We recompense the devisers of lies.

153. And (as to) those who do evil deeds, then repent after that and believe, your Lord after that is most surely Forgiving, Merciful.

154. And when Musa's anger calmed down he took up the tablets, and in the writing thereof was guidance and mercy for those who fear for the sake of their Lord.

155. And Musa chose out of his people seventy men for Our appointment; so when the earthquake overtook them, he said: My Lord! if Thou hadst pleased, Thou hadst destroyed them before and myself (too); wilt Thou destroy us for what the fools among us have done? It is naught but Thy trial, Thou makest err with it whom Thou pleasest and guidest whom Thou pleasest: Thou art our Guardian, therefore forgive us and have mercy on us, and Thou art the best of the forgivers.

156. And ordain for us good in this world's life and in the hereafter, for surely we turn to Thee. He said: (As for) My chastisement, I will afflict with it whom I please, and My mercy

encompasses all things; so I will ordain it (specially) for those who guard (against evil) and pay the poor-rate, and those who believe in Our communications.

157. Those who follow the Apostle-Prophet, the unlettered, whom they find written down with them in the Torah and the Gospel, (who) enjoins them good and forbids them evil, and makes lawful to them the good things and makes unlawful to them impure things, and removes from them their burden and the shackles which were upon them; so (as for) those who believe in him and honor him and help him, and follow the light which has been sent down with him, these it is that are the successful.

158. Say: O people! surely I am the Apostle of Allah to you all, of Him Whose is the kingdom of the heavens and the earth, there is no god but He; He brings to life and causes to die, therefore believe in Allah and His apostle, the Ummi Prophet who believes in Allah and His words, and follow him so that you may walk in the right way.

159. And of Musa's people was a party who guided (people) with the truth, and thereby did they do justice.

160. And We divided them into twelve tribes, as nations; and We revealed to Musa when his people asked him for water: Strike the rock with your staff, so outflowed from it twelve springs; each tribe knew its drinking place; and We made the clouds to give shade over them and We sent to them manna and quails: Eat of the good things We have given you. And they did not do Us any harm, but they did injustice to their own souls.

161. And when it was said to them: Reside in this town and eat from it wherever you wish, and say, Put down from us our heavy burdens: and enter the gate making obeisance, We will forgive you your wrongs: We will give more to those who do good (to others).

162. But those who were unjust among them changed it for a saying other than that which had been spoken to them; so We sent upon them a pestilence from heaven because they were unjust.

163. And ask them about the town which stood by the sea; when they exceeded the limits of the Sabbath, when their fish came to them on the day of their Sabbath, appearing on the surface of the water, and on the day on which they did not keep the Sabbath they did not come to them; thus did We try them because they transgressed.

164. And when a party of them said: Why do you admonish a people whom Allah would destroy or whom He would chastise

with a severe chastisement? They said: To be free from blame
before your Lord, and that haply they may guard (against evil).

165. So when they neglected what they had been reminded of,
We delivered those who forbade evil and We overtook those
who were unjust with an evil chastisement because they transgressed.

166. Therefore when they revoltingly persisted in what they
had been forbidden, We said to them: Be (as) apes, despised and
hated.

167. And when your Lord announced that He would certainly
send against them to the day of resurrection those who would
subject them to severe torment; most surely your Lord is quick
to requite (evil) and most surely He is Forgiving, Merciful.

168. And We cut them up on the earth into parties, (some) of
them being righteous and (others) of them falling short of that,
and We tried them with blessings and misfortunes that they
might turn.

169. Then there came after them an evil posterity who inherited the Book, taking only the frail good of this low life and
saying: It will be forgiven us. And if the like good came to them,
they would take it (too). Was not a promise taken from them in
the Book that they would not speak anything about Allah but
the truth, and they have read what is in it; and the abode of the
hereafter is better for those who guard (against evil). Do you not
then understand?

170. And (as for) those who hold fast by the Book and keep
up prayer, surely We do not waste the reward of the right doers.

171. And when We shook the mountain over them as if it
were a covering overhead, and they thought that it was going to
fall down upon them: Take hold of what We have given you with
firmness, and be mindful of what is in it, so that you may guard
(against evil).

172. And when your Lord brought forth from the children of
Adam, from their backs, their descendants, and made them bear
witness against their own souls: Am I not your Lord? They said:
Yes! we bear witness. Lest you should say on the day of resurrection: Surely we were heedless of this.

173. Or you should say: Only our fathers associated others
(with Allah) before, and we were an offspring after them: Wilt
Thou then destroy us for what the vain doers did?

174. And thus do We make clear the communications, and
that haply they might return.

175. And recite to them the narrative of him to whom We give

Our communications, but he withdraws himself from them, so the Shaitan overtakes him, so he is of those who go astray.

176. And if We had pleased, We would certainly have exalted him thereby; but he clung to the earth and followed his low desire, so his parable is as the parable of the dog; if you attack him he lolls out his tongue; and if you leave him alone he lolls out his tongue; this is the parable of the people who reject Our communications; therefore relate the narrative that they may reflect.

177. Evil is the likeness of the people who reject Our communications and are unjust to their own souls.

178. Whomsoever Allah guides, he is the one who follows the right way; and whomsoever He causes to err, these are the losers.

179. And certainly We have created for hell many of the jinn and the men; they have hearts with which they do not u ۱erstand, and they have eyes with which they do not see, and they have ears with which they do not hear; they are as cattle, nay, they are in worse errors; these are the heedless ones.

180. And Allah's are the best names, therefore call on Him thereby, and leave alone those who violate the sanctity of His names; they shall be recompensed for what they did.

181. And of those whom We have created are a people who guide with the truth and thereby they do justice.

182. And (as to) those who reject Our communications, We draw them near (to destruction) by degrees from whence they know not.

183. And I grant them respite; surely My scheme is effective.

184. Do they not reflect that their companion has not unsoundness in mind; he is only a plain warner.

185. Do they not consider the kingdom of the heavens and the earth and whatever things Allah has created, and that may be their doom shall have drawn nigh; what announcement would they then believe in after this?

186. Whomsoever Allah causes to err, there is no guide for him; and He leaves them alone in their inordinacy, blindly wandering on.

187. They ask you about the hour, when will be its taking place? Say: The knowledge of it is only with my Lord; none but He shall manifest it at its time; it will be momentous in the heavens and the earth; it will not come on you but of a sudden. They ask you as if you were solicitous about it. Say: Its knowledge is only with Allah, but most people do not know.

188. Say: I do not control any benefit or harm for my own soul except as Allah please; and had I known the unseen I would have had much of good and no evil would have touched me; I am nothing but a warner and the giver of good news to a people who believe.

189. He it is Who created you from a single being, and of the same (kind) did He make his mate, that he might incline to her; so when he covers her she bears a light burden, then moves about with it; but when it grows heavy, they both call upon Allah, their Lord: If Thou givest us a good one, we shall certainly be of the grateful ones.

190. But when He gives them a good one, they set up with Him associates in what He has given them; but high is Allah above what they associate (with Him).

191. What! they associate (with Him) that which does not create any thing, while they are themselves created!

192. And they have no power to give them help, nor can they help themselves.

193. And if you invite them to guidance, they will not follow you; it is the same to you whether you invite them or you are silent.

194. Surely those whom you call on besides Allah are in a state of subjugation like yourselves; therefore call on them, then let them answer you if you are truthful.

195. Have they feet with which they walk, or have they hands with which they hold, or have they eyes with which they see, or have they ears with which they hear? Say: Call your associates, then make a struggle (to prevail) against me and give me no respite.

196. Surely my guardian is Allah, Who revealed the Book, and He befriends the good.

197. And those whom you call upon besides Him are not able to help you, nor can they help themselves.

198. And if you invite them to guidance, they do not hear; and you see them looking towards you, yet they do not see.

199. Take to forgiveness and enjoin good and turn aside from the ignorant.

200. And if a false imputation from the Shaitan afflict you, seek refuge in Allah; surely He is Hearing, Knowing.

201. Surely those who guard (against evil), when a visitation from the Shaitan afflicts them they become mindful, then lo! they see.

202. And their brethren increase them in error, then they cease not.

203. And when you bring them not a revelation they say: Why do you not forge it? Say: I only follow what is revealed to me from my Lord; these are clear proofs from your Lord and a guidance and a mercy for a people who believe.

204. And when the Quran is recited, then listen to it and remain silent, that mercy may be shown to you.

205. And remember your Lord within yourself humbly and fearing and in a voice not loud in the morning and the evening, and be not of the heedless ones.

206. Surely those who are with your Lord are not too proud to serve Him, and they declare His glory and throw themselves down in humility before Him.

THE SPOILS OF WAR

In the name of Allah the Beneficent, the Merciful.

1. They ask you about the windfalls. Say: The windfalls are for Allah and the Apostle. So be careful of (your duty to) Allah and set aright matters of your difference, and obey Allah and His Apostle if you are believers.

2. Those only are believers whose hearts become full of fear when Allah is mentioned, and when His communications are recited to them they increase them in faith, and in their Lord do they trust.

3. Those who keep up prayer and spend (benevolently) out of what We have given them.

4. These are the believers in truth; they shall have from their Lord exalted grades and forgiveness and an honorable sustenance.

5. Even as your Lord caused you to go forth from your house with the truth, though a party of the believers were surely averse;

6. They disputed with you about the truth after it had become clear, (and they went forth) as if they were being driven to death while they saw (it).

7. And when Allah promised you one of the two parties that it shall be yours and you loved that the one not armed should be

yours, and Allah desired to manifest the truth of what was true by His words and to cut off the root of the unbelievers.

8. That He may manifest the truth of what was true and show the falsehood of what was false, though the guilty disliked.

9. When you sought aid from your Lord, so He answered you: I will assist you with a thousand of the angels following one another.

10. And Allah only gave it as a good news and that your hearts might be at ease thereby; and victory is only from Allah; surely Allah is Mighty, Wise.

11. When He caused calm to fall on you as a security from Him and sent down upon you water from the cloud that He might thereby purify you, and take away from you the uncleanness of the Shaitan, and that He might fortify your hearts and steady (your) footsteps thereby.

12. When your Lord revealed to the angels: I am with you, therefore make firm those who believe. I will cast terror into the hearts of those who disbelieve. Therefore strike off their heads and strike off every fingertip of them.

13. This is because they acted adversely to Allah and His Apostle; and whoever acts adversely to Allah and His Apostle — then surely Allah is severe in requiting (evil).

14. This—taste it, and (know) that for the unbelievers is the chastisement of fire.

15. O you who believe! when you meet those who disbelieve marching for war, then turn not your backs to them.

16. And whoever shall turn his back to them on that day—unless he turn aside for the sake of fighting or withdraws to a company—then he, indeed, becomes deserving of Allah's wrath, and his abode is hell; and an evil destination shall it be.

17. So you did not slay them, but it was Allah Who slew them, and you did not smite when you smote (the enemy), but it was Allah Who smote, and that He might confer upon the believers a good gift from Himself; surely Allah is Hearing, Knowing.

18. This, and that Allah is the weakener of the struggle of the unbelievers.

19. If you demanded a judgment, the judgment has then indeed come to you; and if you desist, it will be better for you; and if you turn back (to fight), We (too) shall turn back, and your forces shall avail you nothing, though they may be many, and (know) that Allah is with the believers.

20. O you who believe! obey Allah and His Apostle and do not turn back from Him while you hear.

21. And be not like those who said, We hear, and they did not obey.

22. Surely the vilest of animals, in Allah's sight, are the deaf, the dumb, who do not understand.

23. And if Allah had known any good in them He would have made them hear, and if He makes them hear they would turn back while they withdraw.

24. O you who believe! answer (the call of) Allah and His Apostle when he calls you to that which gives you life; and know that Allah intervenes between man and his heart, and that to Him you shall be gathered.

25. And fear an affliction which may not smite those of you in particular who are unjust; and know that Allah is severe in requiting (evil).

26. And remember when you were few, deemed weak in the land, fearing lest people might carry you off by force, but He sheltered you and strengthened you with His aid and gave you of the good things that you may give thanks.

27. O you who believe! be not unfaithful to Allah and the Apostle, nor be unfaithful to your trusts while you know.

28. And know that your property and your children are a temptation, and that Allah is He with Whom there is a mighty reward.

29. O you who believe! If you are careful of (your duty to) Allah, He will grant you a distinction and do away with your evils and forgive you; and Allah is the Lord of mighty grace.

30. And when those who disbelieved devised plans against you that they might confine you or slay you or drive you away; and they devised plans and Allah too had arranged a plan; and Allah is the best of planners.

31. And when Our communications are recited to them, they say: We have heard indeed; if we pleased we could say the like of it; this is nothing but the stories of the ancients.

32. And when they said: O Allah! if this is the truth from Thee, then rain upon us stones from heaven or inflict on us a painful punishment.

33. But Allah was not going to chastise them while you were among them, nor is Allah going to chastise them while yet they ask for forgiveness.

34. And what (excuse) have they that Allah should not chas-

tise them while they hinder (men) from the Sacred Mosque and they are not (fit to be) guardians of it; its guardians are only those who guard (against evil), but most of them do not know.

35. And their prayer before the House is nothing but whistling and clapping of hands; taste then the chastisement, for you disbelieved.

36. Surely those who disbelieve spend their wealth to hinder (people) from the way of Allah; so they shall spend it, then it shall be to them an intense regret, then they shall be overcome; and those who disbelieve shall be driven together to hell.

37. That Allah might separate the impure from the good, and put the impure, some of it upon the other, and pile it up together, then cast it into hell; these it is that are the losers.

38. Say to those who disbelieve, if they desist, that which is past shall be forgiven to them; and if they return, then what happened to the ancients has already passed.

39. And fight with them until there is no more persecution and religion should be only for Allah; but if they desist, then surely Allah sees what they do.

40. And if they turn back, then know that Allah is your Patron; most excellent is the Patron and most excellent the Helper.

41. And know that whatever thing you gain, a fifth of it is for Allah and for the Apostle and for the near of kin and the orphans and the needy and the wayfarer, if you believe in Allah and in that which We revealed to Our servant, on the day of distinction, the day on which the two parties met; and Allah has power over all things.

42. When you were on the nearer side (of the valley) and they were on the farthest side, while the caravan was in a lower place than you; and if you had mutually made an appointment, you would certainly have broken away from the appointment, but— in order that Allah might bring about a matter which was to be done, that he who would perish might perish by clear proof, and he who would live might live by clear proof; and most surely Allah is Hearing, Knowing;

43. When Allah showed them to you in your dream as few; and if He had shown them to you as many you would certainly have become weak-hearted and you would have disputed about the matter, but Allah saved (you); surely He is the Knower of what is in the breasts.

44. And when He showed them to you, when you met, as few

in your eyes and He made you to appear little in their eyes, in order that Allah might bring about a matter which was to be done, and to Allah are all affairs returned.

45. O you who believe! when you meet a party, then be firm, and remember Allah much, that you may be successful.

46. And obey Allah and His Apostle and do not quarrel for then you will be weak in hearts and your power will depart, and be patient; surely Allah is with the patient.

47. And be not like those who came forth from their homes in great exultation and to be seen of men, and (who) turn away from the way of Allah, and Allah comprehends what they do.

48. And when the Shaitan made their works fair seeming to them, and said: No one can overcome you this day, and surely I am your protector: but when the two parties came in sight of each other he turned upon his heels, and said: Surely I am clear of you, surely I see what you do not see, surely I fear Allah; and Allah is severe in requiting (evil).

49. When the hypocrites and those in whose hearts was disease said: Their religion has deceived them; and whoever trusts in Allah, then surely Allah is Mighty, Wise.

50. And had you seen when the angels will cause to die those who disbelieve, smiting their faces and their backs, and (saying): Taste the punishment of burning.

51. This is for what your own hands have sent on before, and because Allah is not in the least unjust to the servants;

52. In the manner of the people of Firon and those before them; they disbelieved in Allah's communications, therefore Allah destroyed them on account of their faults; surely Allah is strong, severe in requiting (evil).

53. This is because Allah has never changed a favor which He has conferred upon a people until they change their own condition; and because Allah is Hearing, Knowing;

54. In the manner of the people of Firon and those before them; they rejected the communications of their Lord, therefore We destroyed them on account of their faults and We drowned Firon's people, and they were all unjust.

55. Surely the vilest of animals in Allah's sight are those who disbelieve, then they would not believe.

56. Those with whom you make an agreement, then they break their agreement every time and they do not guard (against punishment).

57. Therefore if you overtake them in fighting, then scatter by (making an example of) them those who are in their rear, that they may be mindful.

58. And if you fear treachery on the part of a people, then throw back to them on terms of equality; surely Allah does not love the treacherous.

59. And let not those who disbelieve think that they shall come in first; surely they will not escape.

60. And prepare against them what force you can and horses tied at the frontier, to frighten thereby the enemy of Allah and your enemy and others besides them, whom you do not know (but) Allah knows them; and whatever thing you will spend in Allah's way, it will be paid back to you fully and you shall not be dealt with unjustly.

61. And if they incline to peace, then incline to it and trust in Allah; surely He is the Hearing, the Knowing.

62. And if they intend to deceive you—then surely Allah is sufficient for you; He it is Who strengthened you with His help and with the believers,

63. And united their hearts; had you spent all that is in the earth, you could not have united their hearts, but Allah united them; surely He is Mighty, Wise.

64. O Prophet! Allah is sufficient for you and (for) such of the believers as follow you.

65. O Prophet! urge the believers to war; if there are twenty patient ones of you they shall overcome two hundred, and if there are a hundred of you they shall overcome a thousand of those who disbelieve, because they are a people who do not understand.

66. For the present Allah has made light your burden, and He knows that there is weakness in you; so if there are a hundred patient ones of you they shall overcome two hundred, and if there are a thousand they shall overcome two thousand by Allah's permission; and Allah is with the patient.

67. It is not fit for a prophet that he should take captives unless he has fought and triumphed in the land; you desire the frail goods of this world, while Allah desires (for you) the hereafter; and Allah is Mighty, Wise.

68. Were it not for an ordinance from Allah that had already gone forth, surely there would have befallen you a great chastisement for what you had taken to.

69. Eat then of the lawful and good (things) which you have acquired in war, and be careful of (your duty to) Allah; surely Allah is Forgiving, Merciful.

70. O Prophet! say to those of the captives who are in your hands: If Allah knows anything good in your hearts, He will give to you better than that which has been taken away from you and will forgive you, and Allah is Forgiving, Merciful.

71. And if they intend to act unfaithfully towards you, so indeed they acted unfaithfully towards Allah before, but He gave (you) mastery over them; and Allah is Knowing, Wise.

72. Surely those who believed and fled (their homes) and struggled hard in Allah's way with their property and their souls, and those who gave shelter and helped—these are guardians of each other; and (as for) those who believed and did not fly, not yours is their guardianship until they fly; and if they seek aid from you in the matter of religion, aid is incumbent on you except against a people between whom and you there is a treaty, and Allah sees what you do.

73. And (as for) those who disbelieve, some of them are the guardians of others; if you will not do it, there will be in the land persecution and great mischief.

74. And (as for) those who believed and fled and struggled hard in Allah's way, and those who gave shelter and helped, these are the believers truly; they shall have forgiveness and honorable provision.

75. And (as for) those who believed afterwards and fled and struggled hard along with you, they are of you; and the possessors of relationships are nearer to each other in the ordinance of Allah; surely Allah knows all things.

REPENTANCE

1. (This is a declaration of) immunity by Allah and His Apostle towards those of the idolaters with whom you made an agreement.

2. So go about in the land for four months and know that you cannot weaken Allah and that Allah will bring disgrace to the unbelievers.

3. And an announcement from Allah and His Apostle to the

people on the day of the greater pilgrimage that Allah and His Apostle are free from liability to the idolaters; therefore if you repent, it will be better for you, and if you turn back, then know that you will not weaken Allah; and announce painful punishment to those who disbelieve.

4. Except those of the idolaters with whom you made an agreement, then they have not failed you in anything and have not backed up any one against you, so fulfill their agreement to the end of their term; surely Allah loves those who are careful (of their duty).

5. So when the sacred months have passed away, then slay the idolaters wherever you find them, and take them captives and besiege them and lie in wait for them in every ambush, then if they repent and keep up prayer and pay the poor-rate, leave their way free to them; surely Allah is Forgiving, Merciful.

6. And if one of the idolaters seek protection from you, grant him protection till he hears the word of Allah, then make him attain his place of safety; this is because they are a people who do not know.

7. How can there be an agreement for the idolaters with Allah and with His Apostle; except those with whom you made an agreement at the Sacred Mosque? So as long as they are true to you, be true to them; surely Allah loves those who are careful (of their duty).

8. How (can it be)! while if they prevail against you, they would not pay regard in your case to ties of relationship, nor those of covenant; they please you with their mouths while their hearts do not consent; and most of them are transgressors.

9. They have taken a small price for the communications of Allah, so they turn away from His way; surely evil is it that they do.

10. They do not pay regard to ties of relationship nor those of covenant in the case of a believer; and these are they who go beyond the limits.

11. But if they repent and keep up prayer and pay the poor-rate, they are your brethren in faith; and We make the communications clear for a people who know.

12. And if they break their oaths after their agreement and (openly) revile your religion, then fight the leaders of unbelief— surely their oaths are nothing—so that they may desist.

13. What! will you not fight a people who broke their oaths and aimed at the expulsion of the Apostle, and they attacked

you first; do you fear them? But Allah is most deserving that you should fear Him, if you are believers.

14. Fight them; Allah will punish them by your hands and bring them to disgrace, and assist you against them and heal the hearts of a believing people.

15. And remove the rage of their hearts; and Allah turns (mercifully) to whom He pleases, and Allah is Knowing, Wise.

16. What! do you think that you will be left alone while Allah has not yet known those of you who have struggled hard and have not taken any one as an adherent besides Allah and His Apostle and the believers; and Allah is aware of what you do.

17. The idolaters have no right to visit the mosques of Allah while bearing witness to unbelief against themselves; these it is whose doings are null, and in the fire shall they abide.

18. Only he shall visit the mosques of Allah who believes in Allah and the latter day, and keeps up prayer and pays the poor-rate and fears none but Allah; so (as for) these, it may be that they are of the followers of the right course.

19. What! do you make (one who undertakes) the giving of drink to the pilgrims and the guarding of the Sacred Mosque like him who believes in Allah and the latter day and strives hard in Allah's way? They are not equal with Allah; and Allah does not guide the unjust people.

20. Those who believed and fled (their homes), and strove hard in Allah's way with their property and their souls, are much higher in rank with Allah; and those are they who are the achievers (of their objects).

21. Their Lord gives them good news of mercy from Himself and (His) good pleasure and gardens, wherein lasting blessings shall be theirs;

22. Abiding therein for ever; surely Allah has a Mighty reward with Him.

23. O you who believe! do not take your fathers and your brothers for guardians if they love unbelief more than belief; and whoever of you takes them for a guardian, these it is that are the unjust.

24. Say: If your fathers and your sons and your brethren and your mates and your kinsfolk and property which you have acquired, and the slackness of trade which you fear and dwellings which you like, are dearer to you than Allah and His Apostle and striving in His way, then wait till Allah brings about His command; and Allah does not guide the transgressing people.

25. Certainly Allah helped you in many battlefields and on the day of battle of Hunain, when your great numbers made you vain, but they availed you nothing and the earth became strait to you notwithstanding its spaciousness, then you turned back retreating.

26. Then Allah sent down His tranquillity upon His Apostle and upon the believers, and sent down hosts which you did not see, and chastised those who disbelieved, and that is the reward of the unbelievers.

27. Then will Allah after this turn (mercifully) to whom He pleases, and Allah is Forgiving, Merciful.

28. O you who believe! the idolaters are nothing but unclean, so they shall not approach the Sacred Mosque after this year; and if you fear poverty then Allah will enrich you out of His grace if He please; surely Allah is Knowing, Wise.

29. Fight those who do not believe in Allah, nor in the latter day, nor do they prohibit what Allah and His Apostle have prohibited, nor follow the religion of truth, out of those who have been given the Book, until they pay the tax in acknowledgment of superiority and they are in a state of subjection.

30. And the Jews say: Uzair is the son of Allah; and the Christians say: The Messiah is the son of Allah; these are the words of their mouths; they imitate the saying of those who disbelieved before; may Allah destroy them; how they are turned away!

31. They have taken their doctors of law and their monks for lords besides Allah, and (also) the Messiah son of Marium and they were enjoined that they should serve one God only, there is no god but He; far from His glory be what they set up (with Him).

32. They desire to put out the light of Allah with their mouths, and Allah will not consent save to perfect His light, though the unbelievers are averse.

33. He it is Who sent His Apostle with guidance and the religion of truth, that He might cause it to prevail over all religions, though the polytheists may be averse.

34. O you who believe! most surely many of the doctors of law and the monks eat away the property of men falsely, and turn (them) from Allah's way; and (as for) those who hoard up gold and silver and do not spend it in Allah's way, announce to them a painful chastisement,

35. On the day when it shall be heated in the fire of hell, then

their foreheads and their sides and their backs shall be branded with it; this is what you hoarded up for yourselves, therefore taste what you hoarded.

36. Surely the number of months with Allah is twelve months in Allah's ordinance since the day when He created the heavens and the earth, of these four being sacred; that is the right reckoning; therefore be not unjust to yourselves regarding them, and fight the polytheists all together as they fight you all together; and know that Allah is with those who guard (against evil).

37. Postponing (of the sacred month) is only an addition in unbelief, wherewith those who disbelieve are led astray, violating it one year and keeping it sacred another, that they may agree in the number (of months) that Allah has made sacred, and thus violate what Allah has made sacred; the evil of their doings is made fairseeming to them; and Allah does not guide the unbelieving people.

38. O you who believe! What (excuse) have you that when it is said to you: Go forth in Allah's way, you should incline heavily to earth; are you contented with this world's life instead of the hereafter? But the provision of this world's life compared with the hereafter is but little.

39. If you do not go forth, He will chastise you with a painful chastisement and bring in your place a people other than you, and you will do Him no harm; and Allah has power over all things.

40. If you will not aid him, Allah certainly aided him when those who disbelieved expelled him, he being the second of the two, when they were both in the cave, when he said to his companion: Grieve not, surely Allah is with us. So Allah sent down His tranquillity upon him and strengthened him with hosts which you did not see, and made lowest the word of those who disbelieved; and the word of Allah, that is the highest; and Allah is Mighty, Wise.

41. Go forth light and heavy, and strive hard in Allah's way with your property and your persons; this is better for you, if you know.

42. Had it been a near advantage and a short journey, they would certainly have followed you, but the tedious journey was too long for them; and they swear by Allah: If we had been able, we would certainly have gone forth with you; they cause their own souls to perish, and Allah knows that they are most surely liars.

43. Allah pardon you! Why did you give them leave until those who spoke the truth had become manifest to you and you had known the liars?

44. They do not ask leave of you who believe in Allah and the latter day (to stay away) from striving hard with their property and their persons, and Allah knows those who guard (against evil).

45. They only ask leave of you who do not believe in Allah and the latter day and their hearts are in doubt, so in their doubt do they waver.

46. And if they had intended to go forth, they would certainly have provided equipment for it, but Allah did not like their going forth, so He withheld them, and it was said (to them): Hold back with those who hold back.

47. Had they gone forth with you, they would not have added to you aught save corruption, and they would certainly have hurried about among you seeking (to sow) dissension among you, and among you there are those who hearken for their sake; and Allah knows the unjust.

48. Certainly they sought (to sow) dissension before, and they meditated plots against you until the truth came, and Allah's commandment prevailed although they were averse (from it).

49. And among them there is he who says: Allow me and do not try me. Surely into trial have they already tumbled down, and most surely hell encompasses the unbelievers.

50. If good befalls you, it grieves them, and if hardship afflicts you, they say: Indeed we had taken care of our affair before; and they turn back and are glad.

51. Say: Nothing will afflict us save what Allah has ordained for us; He is our Patron; and on Allah let the believers rely.

52. Say: Do you await for us but one of two most excellent things? And we await for you that Allah will afflict you with punishment from Himself or by our hands. So wait; we too will wait with you.

53. Say: Spend willingly or unwillingly, it shall not be accepted from you; surely you are a transgressing people.

54. And nothing hinders their spendings being accepted from them, except that they disbelieve in Allah and in His Apostle and they do not come to prayer but while they are sluggish, and they do not spend but while they are unwilling.

55. Let not then their property and their children excite your admiration; Allah only wishes to chastise them with these in this

world's life and (that) their souls may depart while they are unbelievers.

56. And they swear by Allah that they are most surely of you, and they are not of you, but they are a people who are afraid (of you).

57. If they could find a refuge or cave or a place to enter into, they would certainly have turned thereto, running away in all haste.

58. And of them there are those who blame you with respect to the alms; so if they are given from it they are pleased, and if they are not given from it, lo! they are full of rage.

59. And if they were content with what Allah and His Apostle gave them, and had said: Allah is sufficient for us; Allah will soon give us (more) out of His grace and His Apostle too; surely to Allah do we make our petition.

60. Alms are only for the poor and the needy, and the officials (appointed) over them, and those whose hearts are made to incline (to truth) and the (ransoming of) captives and those in debts and in the way of Allah and the wayfarer; an ordinance from Allah; and Allah is knowing, Wise.

61. And there are some of them who molest the Prophet and say: He is one who believes every thing that he hears; say: A hearer of good for you (who) believes in Allah and believes the faithful and a mercy for those of you who believe; and (as for) those who molest the Apostle of Allah, they shall have a painful punishment.

62. They swear to you by Allah that they might please you and, Allah, as well as His Apostle, has a greater right that they should please Him, if they are believers.

63. Do they not know that whoever acts in opposition to Allah and His Apostle, he shall surely have the fire of hell to abide in it? That is the grievous abasement.

64. The hypocrites fear lest a chapter should be sent down to them telling them plainly of what is in their hearts. Say: Go on mocking, surely Allah will bring forth what you fear.

65. And if you should question them, they would certainly say: We were only idly discoursing and sporting. Say: Was it at Allah and His communications and His Apostle that you mocked?

66. Do not make excuses; you have denied indeed after you had believed; if We pardon a party of you, We will chastise (another) party because they are guilty.

67. The hypocritical men and the hypocritical women are all

alike; they enjoin evil and forbid good and withhold their hands; they have forsaken Allah, so He has forsaken them; surely the hypocrites are the transgressors.

68. Allah has promised the hypocritical men and the hypocritical women and the unbelievers the fire of hell to abide therein; it is enough for them; and Allah has cursed them and they shall have lasting punishment.

69. Like those before you; they were stronger than you in power and more abundant in wealth and children, so they enjoyed their portion; thus have you enjoyed your portion as those before you enjoyed their portion; and you entered into vain discourses like the vain discourses in which entered those before you. These are they whose works are null in this world and the hereafter; and these are they who are the losers.

70. Has not the news of those before them come to them; of the people of Nuh and Ad and Samood, and the people of Ibrahim and the dwellers of Madyan and the overthrown cities; their apostles came to them with clear arguments; so it was not Allah Who should do them injustice, but they were unjust to themselves.

71. And (as for) the believing men and the believing women, they are guardians of each other; they enjoin good and forbid evil and keep up prayer and pay the poor-rate, and obey Allah and His Apostle; (as for) these, Allah will show mercy to them; surely Allah is Mighty, Wise.

72. Allah has promised to the believing men and the believing women gardens, beneath which rivers flow, to abide in them, and goodly dwellings in gardens of perpetual abode; and best of all is Allah's goodly pleasure—that is the grand achievement.

73. O Prophet! strive hard against the unbelievers and the hypocrites and be unyielding to them; and their abode is hell, and evil is the destination.

74. They swear by Allah that they did not speak, and certainly they did speak, the word of unbelief, and disbelieved after their Islam, and they had determined upon what they have not been able to effect, and they did not find fault except because Allah and His Apostle enriched them out of His grace; therefore if they repent, it will be good for them; and if they turn back, Allah will chastise them with a painful chastisement in this world and the hereafter, and they shall not have in the land any guardian or a helper.

75. And there are those of them who made a covenant with

Allah: If He give us out of His grace, we will certainly give alms and we will certainly be of the good.

76. But when He gave them out of His grace, they became niggardly of it and they turned back and they withdrew.

77. So He made hypocrisy to follow as a consequence into their hearts till the day when they shall meet Him because they failed to perform towards Allah what they had promised with Him and because they told lies.

78. Do they not know that Allah knows their hidden thoughts and their secret counsels, and that Allah is the great Knower of the unseen things?

79. They who taunt those of the faithful who give their alms freely, and those who give to the extent of their earnings and scoff at them; Allah will pay them back their scoffing, and they shall have a painful chastisement.

80. Ask forgiveness for them or do not ask forgiveness for them; even if you ask forgiveness for them seventy times, Allah will not forgive them; this is because they disbelieve in Allah and His Apostle, and Allah does not guide the transgressing people.

81. Those who were left behind were glad on account of their sitting behind Allah's Apostle and they were averse from striving in Allah's way with their property and their persons, and said: Do not go forth in the heat. Say: The fire of hell is much severe in heat. Would that they understood (it).

82. Therefore they shall laugh little and weep much as a recompense for what they earned.

83. Therefore if Allah brings you back to a party of them, and then they ask your permission to go forth, say: By no means shall you ever go forth with me and by no means shall you fight an enemy with me; surely you chose to sit the first time, therefore sit (now) with those who remain behind.

84. And never offer prayer for any one of them who dies and do not stand by his grave; surely they disbelieve in Allah and His Apostle and they shall die in transgression.

85. And let not their property and their children excite your admiration; Allah only wishes to chastise them with these in this world and (that) their souls may depart while they are unbelievers

86. And whenever a chapter is revealed, saying: Believe in Allah and strive hard along with His Apostle, those having ampleness of means ask permission of you and say: Leave us (behind), that we may be with those who sit.

87. They preferred to be with those who remained behind, and a seal is set on their hearts so they do not understand.

88. But the Apostle and those who believe with him strive hard with their property and their persons; and these it is who shall have the good things and these it is who shall be successful.

89. Allah has prepared for them gardens beneath which rivers flow, to abide in them; that is the great achievement.

90. And the defaulters from among the dwellers of the desert came that permission may be given to them and they sat (at home) who lied to Allah and His Apostle; a painful chastisement shall afflict those of them who disbelieved.

91. It shall be no crime in the weak, nor in the sick, nor in those who do not find what they should spend (to stay behind), so long as they are sincere to Allah and His Apostle; there is no way (to blame) against the doers of good; and Allah is Forgiving, Merciful;

92. Nor in those who when they came to you that you might carry them, you said: I cannot find that on which to carry you; they went back while their eyes overflowed with tears on account of grief for not finding that which they should spend.

93. The way (to blame) is only against those who ask permission of you though they are rich; they have chosen to be with those who remained behind, and Allah has set a seal upon their hearts so they do not know.

94. They will excuse themselves to you when you go back to them. Say: Urge no excuse, by no means will we believe you; indeed Allah has informed us of matters relating to you; and now Allah and His Apostle will see your doings, then you shall be brought back to the Knower of the unseen and the seen, then He will inform you of what you did.

95. They will swear to you by Allah when you return to them so that you may turn aside from them; so do turn aside from them; surely they are unclean and their abode is hell; a recompense for what they earned.

96. They will swear to you that you may be pleased with them; but if you are pleased with them, yet surely Allah is not pleased with the transgressing people.

97. The dwellers of the desert are very hard in unbelief and hypocrisy, and more disposed not to know the limits of what Allah has revealed to His Apostle; and Allah is Knowing, Wise.

98. And of the dwellers of the desert are those who take what

they spend to be a fine, and they wait (the befalling of) calamities to you; on them (will be) the evil calamity; and Allah is Hearing, Knowing.

99. And of the dwellers of the desert are those who believe in Allah and the latter day and take what they spend to be (means of) the nearness of Allah and the Apostle's prayers; surely it shall be means of nearness for them; Allah will make them enter into His mercy; surely Allah is Forgiving, Merciful.

100. And (as for) the foremost, the first of the migrants from Makkah and the people of Medina, and those who followed them in goodness, Allah is well pleased with them and they are well pleased with Him, and He has prepared for them gardens beneath which rivers flow, to abide in them for ever; that is the mighty achievement.

101. And from among those who are round about you of the dwellers of the desert there are hypocrites, and from among the people of Medina (also); they are stubborn in hypocrisy; you do not know them; We know them; We will chastise them twice, then shall they be turned back to a grievous chastisement.

102. And others have confessed their faults, they have mingled a good deed and an evil one; may be Allah will turn to them (mercifully); surely Allah is Forgiving, Merciful.

103. Take alms out of their property, you would cleanse them and purify them thereby, and pray for them; surely your prayer is a relief to them; and Allah is Hearing, Knowing.

104. Do they not know that Allah accepts repentance from His servants and takes the alms, and that Allah is the Oft-returning (to mercy), the Merciful?

105. And say: Work; so Allah will see your work and (so will) His Apostle and the believers; and you shall be brought back to the Knower of the unseen and the seen, then He will inform you of what you did.

106. And others are made to await Allah's command, whether He chastise them or whether He turn to them (mercifully); and Allah is Knowing, Wise.

107. And those who built a masjid to cause harm and for unbelief and to cause disunion among the believers and an ambush to him who made war against Allah and His Apostle before; and they will certainly swear: We did not desire aught but good; and Allah bears witness that they are most surely liars.

108. Never stand in it; certainly a masjid founded on piety from the very first day is more deserving that you should stand

in it; in it are men who love that they should be purified; and Allah loves those who purify themselves.

109. Is he, therefore, better who lays his foundation on fear of Allah and (His) good pleasure, or he who lays his foundation on the edge of a cracking hollowed bank, so it broke down with him into the fire of hell; and Allah does not guide the unjust people.

110. The building which they have built will ever continue to be a source of disquiet in their hearts, except that their hearts get cut into pieces; and Allah is Knowing, Wise.

111. Surely Allah has bought of the believers their persons and their property for this, that they shall have the garden; they fight in Allah's way, so they slay and are slain; a promise which is binding on Him in the Taurat and the Injeel and the Quran; and who is more faithful to his covenant than Allah? Rejoice therefore in the pledge which you have made; and that is the mighty achievement.

112. They who turn (to Allah), who serve (Him), who praise (Him), who fast, who bow down, who prostrate themselves, who enjoin what is good and forbid what is evil, and who keep the limits of Allah; and give good news to the believers.

113. It is not (fit) for the Prophet and those who believe that they should ask forgiveness for the polytheists, even though they should be near relatives, after it has become clear to them that they are inmates of the flaming fire.

114. And Ibrahim asking forgiveness for his sire was only owing to a promise which he had made to him; but when it became clear to him that he was an enemy of Allah, he declared himself to be clear of him; most surely Ibrahim was very tender-hearted, forbearing.

115. It is not (attributable to) Allah that He should lead a people astray after He has guided them; He even makes clear to them what they should guard against; surely Allah knows all things.

116. Surely Allah's is the kingdom of the heavens and the earth; He brings to life and causes to die; and there is not for you besides Allah any Guardian or Helper.

117. Certainly Allah has turned (mercifully) to the Prophet and those who fled (their homes) and the helpers who followed him in the hour of straitness after the hearts of a part of them were about to deviate, then He turned to them (mercifully); surely to them He is Compassionate, Merciful.

118. And to the three who were left behind, until the earth became strait to them notwithstanding its spaciousness and their souls were also straitened to them; and they knew it for certain that there was no refuge from Allah but in Him; then He turned to them (mercifully) that they might turn (to Him); surely Allah is the Oft-returning (to mercy), the Merciful.

119. O you who believe! be careful of (your duty to) Allah and be with the true ones.

120. It did not beseem the people of Medina and those round about them of the dwellers of the desert to remain behind the Apostle of Allah, nor should they desire (anything) for themselves in preference to him; this is because there afflicts them not thirst or fatigue or hunger in Allah's way, nor do they tread a path which enrages the unbelievers, nor do they attain from the enemy what they attain, but a good work is written down to them on account of it; surely Allah does not waste the reward of the doers of good;

121. Nor do they spend anything that may be spent, small or great, nor do they traverse a valley, but it is written down to their credit, that Allah may reward them with the best of what they have done.

122. And it does not beseem the believers that they should go forth all together; why should not then a company from every party from among them go forth that they may apply themselves to obtain understanding in religion, and that they may warn their people when they come back to them that they may be cautious?

123. O you who believe! fight those of the unbelievers who are near to you and let them find in you hardness; and know that Allah is with those who guard (against evil).

124. And whenever a chapter is revealed, there are some of them who say: Which of you has it strengthened in faith? Then as for those who believe, it strengthens them in faith and they rejoice.

125. And as for those in whose hearts is a disease, it adds uncleanness to their uncleanness and they die while they are unbelievers.

126. Do they not see that they are tried once or twice in every year, yet they do not turn (to Allah) nor do they mind.

127. And whenever a chapter is revealed, they cast glances at one another: Does any one see you? Then they turn away: Allah

has turned away their hearts because they are a people who do not understand.

128. Certainly an Apostle has come to you from among yourselves; grievous to him is your falling into distress, excessively solicitous respecting you; to the believers (he is) compassionate, merciful.

129. But if they turn back, say: Allah is sufficient for me, there is no god but He; on Him do I rely, and He is the Lord of mighty power.

SURAH X   *Yunus*

YUNUS

In the name of Allah, the Beneficent, the Merciful.

1. Alif Lam Ra. These are the verses of the wise Book.

2. What! is it a wonder to the people that We revealed to a man from among themselves, saying: Warn the people and give good news to those who believe that theirs is a footing of firmness with their Lord. The unbelievers say: This is most surely a manifest enchanter.

3. Surely your Lord is Allah, Who created the heavens and the earth in six periods, and He is firm in power, regulating the affair; there is no intercessor except after His permission; this is Allah, your Lord, therefore serve Him; will you not then mind?

4. To Him is your return, of all (of you); the promise of Allah (made) in truth; surely He begins the creation in the first instance, then He reproduces it, that He may with justice recompense those who believe and do good; and (as for) those who disbelieve, they shall have a drink of hot water and painful punishment because they disbelieved.

5. He it is Who made the sun a shining brightness and the moon a light, and ordained for it mansions that you might know the computation of years and the reckoning. Allah did not create it but with truth; He makes the signs manifest for a people who know.

6. Most surely in the variation of the night and the day, and what Allah has created in the heavens and the earth, there are signs for a people who guard (against evil).

7. Surely those who do not hope in Our meeting and are pleased with this world's life and are content with it, and those who are heedless of Our communications:

8. (As for) those, their abode is the fire because of what they earned.

9. Surely (as for) those who believe and do good, their Lord will guide them by their faith; there shall flow from beneath them rivers in gardens of bliss.

10. Their cry in it shall be: Glory to Thee, O Allah! and their greeting in it shall be: Peace; and the last of their cry shall be: Praise be to Allah, the Lord of the worlds.

11. And if Allah should hasten the evil to men as they desire the hastening on of good, their doom should certainly have been decreed for them; but We leave those alone who hope not for Our meeting in their inordinacy, blindly wandering on.

12. And when affliction touches a man, he calls on Us, whether lying on his side or sitting or standing; but when We remove his affliction from him, he passes on as though he had never called on Us on account of an affliction that touched him; thus that which they do is made fair-seeming to the extravagant.

13. And certainly We did destroy generations before you when they were unjust, and their apostles had come to them with clear arguments, and they would not believe; thus do We recompense the guilty people.

14. Then We made you successors in the land after them so that We may see how you act.

15. And when Our clear communications are recited to them, those who hope not for Our meeting say: Bring a Quran other than this or change it. Say: It does not beseem me that I should change it of myself; I follow naught but what is revealed to me; surely I fear, if I disobey my Lord, the punishment of a mighty day.

16. Say: If Allah had desired (otherwise) I would not have recited it to you, nor would He have taught it to you; indeed I have lived a lifetime among you before it; do you not then understand?

17. Who is then more unjust than who forges a lie against Allah or (who) gives the lie to His communications? Surely the guilty shall not be successful.

18. And they serve beside Allah what can neither harm them nor profit them, and they say: These are our intercessors with Allah. Say: Do you (presume to) inform Allah of what He

knows not in the heavens and the earth? Glory be to Him, and supremely exalted is He above what they set up (with Him).

19. And people are naught but a single nation, so they disagree; and had not a word already gone forth from your Lord, the matter would have certainly been decided between them in respect of that concerning which they disagree.

20. And they say: Why is not a sign sent to him from his Lord? Say: The unseen is only for Allah; therefore wait—surely I too, with you am of those who wait.

21. And when We make people taste of mercy after an affliction touches them, lo! they devise plans against Our communication. Say: Allah is quicker to plan; surely Our messengers write down what you plan.

22. He it is Who makes you travel by land and sea; until when you are in the ships, and they sail on with them in a pleasant breeze, and they rejoice, a violent wind overtakes them and the billows surge in on them from all sides, and they become certain that they are encompassed about, they pray to Allah, being sincere to Him in obedience: If Thou dost deliver us from this, we will most certainly be of the grateful ones.

23. But when He delivers them, lo! they are unjustly rebellious in the earth. O men! your rebellion is against your own souls—provision (only) of this world's life—then to Us shall be your return, so We will inform you of what you did.

24. The likeness of this world's life is only as water which We send down from the cloud, then the herbage of the earth of which men and cattle eat grows luxuriantly thereby; until when the earth puts on its golden raiment and it becomes garnished, and its people think that they have power over it, Our command comes to it, by night or by day, so We render it as reaped seed-produce, as though it had not been in existence yesterday, thus do We make clear the communications for a people who reflect.

25. And Allah invites to the abode of peace and guides whom He pleases into the right path.

26. For those who do good is good (reward) and more (than this); and blackness or ignominy shall not cover their faces; these are the dwellers of the garden; in it they shall abide.

27. And (as for) those who have earned evil, the punishment of an evil is the like of it, and abasement shall come upon them—they shall have none to protect them from Allah—as if their faces had been covered with slices of the dense darkness of night; these are the inmates of the fire; in it they shall abide.

28. And on the day when We will gather them all together, then We will say to those who associated others (with Allah): Keep where you are, you and your associates; then We shall separate them widely one from another and their associates would say: It was not us that you served:

29. Therefore Allah is sufficient as a witness between us and you that we were quite unaware of your serving (us).

30. There shall every soul become acquainted with what it sent before, and they shall be brought back to Allah, their true Patron, and what they devised shall escape from them.

31. Say: Who gives you sustenance from the heaven and the earth? Or Who controls the hearing and the sight? And Who brings forth the living from the dead, and brings forth the dead from the living? And Who regulates the affairs? Then they will say: Allah. Say then: Will you not then guard (against evil)?

32. This then is Allah, your true Lord; and what is there after the truth but error; how are you then turned back?

33. Thus does the word of your Lord prove true against those who transgress that they do not believe.

34. Say: Is there any one among your associates who can bring into existence the creation in the first instance, then reproduce it? Say: Allah brings the creation into existence, then He reproduces it; how are you then turned away?

35. Say: Is there any of your associates who guides to the truth? Say: Allah guides to the truth. Is He then Who guides to the truth more worthy to be followed, or he who himself does not go aright unless he is guided? What then is the matter with you; how do you judge?

36. And most of them do not follow (anything) but conjecture; surely conjecture will not avail aught against the truth; surely Allah is cognizant of what they do.

37. And this Quran is not such as could be forged by those besides Allah, but it is a verification of that which is before it and a clear explanation of the book, there is no doubt in it, from the Lord of the worlds.

38. Or do they say: He has forged it? Say: Then bring a chapter like this and invite whom you can besides Allah, if you are truthful.

39. Nay, they reject that of which they have no comprehensive knowledge, and the final sequel of it has not yet come to them; even thus did those before them reject (the truth); see then what was the end of the unjust.

40. And of them is he who believes in it, and of them is he who does not believe in it, and your Lord best knows the mischief-makers.

41. And if they call you a liar, say: My work is for me and your work for you; you are clear of what I do and I am clear of what you do.

42. And there are those of them who hear you, but can you make the deaf to hear though they will not understand?

43. And there are those of them who look at you, but can you show the way to the blind though they will not see?

44. Surely Allah does not do any injustice to men, but men are unjust to themselves.

45. And on the day when He will gather them as though they had not stayed but an hour of the day, they will know each other. They will perish indeed who called the meeting with Allah to be a lie, and they are not followers of the right direction.

46. And if We show you something of what We threaten them with, or cause you to die, yet to Us is their return, and Allah is the bearer of witness to what they do.

47. And every nation had an apostle; so when their apostle came, the matter was decided between them with justice and they shall not be dealt with unjustly.

48. And they say: When will this threat come about, if you are truthful?

49. Say: I do not control for myself any harm, or any benefit except what Allah pleases; every nation has a term; when their term comes, they shall not then remain behind for an hour, nor can they go before (their time).

50. Say: Tell me if His punishment overtakes you by night or by day! what then is there of it that the guilty would hasten on?

51. And when it comes to pass, will you believe in it? What! now (you believe), and already you wished to have it hastened on.

52. Then it shall be said to those who were unjust: Taste abiding chastisement; you are not requited except for what you earned.

53. And they ask you: Is that true? Say: Aye! by my Lord! it is most surely the truth, and you will not escape.

54. And if every soul that has done injustice had all that is in the earth, it would offer it for ransom, and they will manifest regret when they see the chastisement and the matter shall be decided between them with justice and they shall not be dealt with unjustly.

55. Now surely Allah's is what is in the heavens and the earth; now surely Allah's promise is true, but most of them do not know.

56. He gives life and causes death, and to Him you shall be brought back.

57. O men! there has come to you indeed an admonition from your Lord and a healing for what is in the breasts and a guidance and a mercy for the believers.

58. Say: In the grace of Allah and in His mercy—in that they should rejoice; it is better than that which they gather.

59. Say: Tell me what Allah has sent down for you of sustenance, then you make (a part) of it unlawful and (a part) lawful. Say: Has Allah commanded you, or do you forge a lie against Allah?

60. And what will be the thought of those who forge lies against Allah on the day of resurrection? Most surely Allah is the Lord of grace towards men, but most of them do not give thanks.

61. And you are not (engaged) in any affair, nor do you recite concerning it any portion of the Quran, nor do you do any work but We are witnesses over you when you enter into it, and there does not lie concealed from your Lord the weight of an atom in the earth or in the heaven, nor any thing less than that nor greater, but it is in a clear book.

62. Now surely the friends of Allah—they shall have no fear nor shall they grieve.

63. Those who believe and guarded (against evil):

64. They shall have good news in this world's life and in the hereafter; there is no changing the words of Allah; that is the mighty achievement.

65. And let not their speech grieve you; surely might is wholly Allah's; He is the Hearing, the Knowing.

66. Now, surely, whatever is in the heavens and whatever is in the earth is Allah's; and they do not (really) follow any associates, who call on others besides Allah; they do not follow (anything) but conjectures, and they, only lie.

67. He it is Who made for you the night that you might rest in it, and the day giving light; most surely there are signs in it for a people who would hear.

68. They say: Allah has taken a son (to Himself)! Glory be to Him; He is the Self-sufficient; His is what is in the heavens and

what is in the earth; you have no authority for this; do you say against Allah what you do not know?

69. Say: Those who forge a lie against Allah shall not be successful.

70. (It is only) a provision in this world, then to Us shall be their return; then We shall make them taste severe punishment because they disbelieved.

71. And recite to them the story of Nuh when he said to his people: O my people! if my stay and my reminding (you) by the communications of Allah is hard on you—yet on Allah do I rely—then resolve upon your affair and (gather) your associates, then let not your affair remain dubious to you, then have it executed against me and give me no respite:

72. But if you turn back, I did not ask for any reward from you; my reward is only with Allah, and I am commanded that I should be of those who submit.

73. But they rejected him, so We delivered him and those with him in the ark, and We made them rulers and drowned those who rejected Our communications; see then what was the end of the (people) warned.

74. Then did We raise up after him apostles to their people, so they came to them with clear arguments, but they would not believe in what they had rejected before; thus it is that We set seals upon the hearts of those who exceed the limits.

75. Then did We send up after them Musa and Haroun to Firon and his chiefs with Our signs, but they showed pride and they were a guilty people.

76. So when the truth came to them from Us they said: This is most surely clear enchantment!

77. Musa said: Do you say (this) of the truth when it has come to you? Is it magic? And the magicians are not successful.

78. They said: Have you come to us to turn us away from what we found our fathers upon, and (that) greatness in the land should be for you two? And we are not going to believe in you.

79. And Firon said: Bring to me every skilful magician.

80. And when the magicians came, Musa said to them: Cast down what you have to cast.

81. So when they cast down, Musa said to them: What you have brought is deception; surely Allah will make it naught; surely Allah does not make the work of mischief-makers to thrive.

82. And Allah will show the truth to be the truth by His words, though the guilty may be averse (to it).

83. But none believed in Musa except the offspring of his people, on account of the fear of Firon and their chiefs, lest he should persecute them; and most surely Firon was lofty in the land; and most surely he was of the extravagant.

84. And Musa said: O my people! if you believe in Allah, then rely on Him (alone) if you submit (to Allah).

85. So they said: On Allah we rely: O our Lord! make us not subject to the persecution of the unjust people:

86. And do Thou deliver us by Thy mercy from the unbelieving people.

87. And We revealed to Musa and his brother, saying: Take for your people houses to abide in Egypt and make your houses places of worship and keep up prayer and give good news t the believers.

88. And Musa said: Our Lord! surely Thou hast given to Firon and his chiefs finery and riches in this world's life, to this end, our Lord, that they lead (people) astray from Thy way: Our Lord! destroy their riches and harden their hearts so that they believe not until they see the painful punishment.

89. He said: The prayer of you both has indeed been accepted, therefore continue in the right way and do not follow the path of those who do not know.

90. And We made the children of Israel to pass through the sea, then Firon and his hosts followed them for oppression and tyranny; until when drowning overtook him, he said: I believe that there is no god but He in Whom the children of Israel believe and I am of those who submit.

91. What! now! and indeed you disobeyed before and you were of the mischief-makers.

92. But We will this day deliver you with your body that you may be a sign to those after you, and most surely the majority of the people are heedless to Our communications.

93. And certainly.We lodged the children of Israel in a goodly abode and We provided them with good things; but they did not disagree until the knowledge had come to them; surely your Lord will judge between them on the resurrection day concerning that in which they disagreed.

94. But if you are in doubt as to what We have revealed to you, ask those who read the Book before you; certainly the truth

has come to you from your Lord, therefore you should not be of the disputers.

95. And you should not be of those who reject the communications of Allah, (for) then you should be one of the losers.

96. Surely those against whom the word of your Lord has proved true will not believe,

97. Though every sign should come to them, until they witness the painful chastisement.

98. And wherefore was there not a town which should believe so that their belief should have profited them but the people of Yunus? When they believed, We removed from them the chastisement of disgrace in this world's life and We gave them provision till a time.

99. And if your Lord had pleased, surely all those who are in the earth would have believed, all of them; will you then force men till they become believers?

100. And it is not for a soul to believe except by Allah's permission; and He casts uncleanness on those who will not understand.

101. Say: Consider what is it that is in the heavens and the earth; and signs and warners do not avail a people who would not believe.

102. What do they wait for then but the like of the days of those who passed away before them? Say: Wait then; surely I too am with you of those who wait.

103. Then We deliver Our apostles and those who believe— even so (now), it is binding on Us (that) We deliver the believers.

104. Say: O people! if you are in doubt as to my religion, then (know that) I do not serve those whom you serve besides Allah, but I do serve Allah, Who will cause you to die, and I am commanded that I should be of the believers.

105. And that you should keep your course towards the religion uprightly; and you should not be of the polytheists.

106. And do not call besides Allah on that which can neither benefit you nor harm you, for if you do then surely you will in that case be of the unjust.

107. And if Allah should afflict you with harm, then there is none to remove it but He; and if He intends good to you there is none to repel His grace; He brings it to whom He pleases of His servants; and He is the Forgiving, the Merciful.

108. Say: O people! indeed there has come to you the truth

from your Lord, therefore whoever goes aright, he goes aright only for the good of his own soul, and whoever goes astray, he goes astray only to the detriment of it, and I am not a custodian over you.

109. And follow what is revealed to you and be patient till Allah should give judgment, and He is the best of the judges.

HUD

In the name of Allah, the Beneficent, the Merciful.

1. Alif Lam Ra (This is) a Book, whose verses are made decisive, then are they made plain, from the Wise, All-aware:

2. That you shall not serve (any) but Allah; surely I am a warner for you from Him and a giver of good news;

3. And you that ask forgiveness of your Lord, then turn to Him; He will provide you with a goodly provision to an appointed term and bestow His grace on every one endowed with grace, and if you turn back, then surely I fear for you the chastisement of a great day.

4. To Allah is your return, and He has power over all things.

5. Now surely they fold up their breasts that they may conceal (their enmity) from Him; now surely, when they use their garments as a covering, He knows what they conceal and what they make public; surely He knows what is in the breasts.

6. And there is no animal in the earth but on Allah is the sustenance of it, and He knows its resting place and its depository; all (things) are in a manifest book.

7. And He it is Who created the heavens and the earth in six periods—and His dominion (extends) on the water—that He might manifest to you, which of you is best in action, and if you say, surely you shall be raised up after death, those who disbelieve would certainly say: This is nothing but clear magic.

8. And if We hold back from them the punishment until a stated period of time, they will certainly say: What prevents it? Now surely on the day when it will come to them, it shall not be averted from them and that which they scoffed at shall beset them.

9. And if We make man taste mercy from Us, then take it off from him, most surely he is despairing, ungrateful.

10. And if We make him taste a favor after distress has afflicted him, he will certainly say: The evils are gone away from me. Most surely he is exulting, boasting;

11. Except those who are patient and do good, they shall have forgiveness and a great reward.

12. Then, it may be that you will give up part of what is revealed to you and your breast will become straitened by it because they say: Why has not a treasure been sent down upon him or an angel come with him? You are only a warner; and Allah is custodian over all things.

13. Or, do they say: He has forged it. Say: Then bring ten forged chapters like it and call upon whom you can besides Allah, if you are truthful.

14. But if they do not answer you, then know that it is revealed by Allah's knowledge and that there is no god but He; will you then submit?

15. Whoever desires this world's life and its finery, We will pay them in full their deeds therein, and they shall not be made to suffer loss in respect of them.

16. These are they for whom there is nothing but fire in the hereafter, and what they wrought in it shall go for nothing, and vain is what they do.

17. Is he then who has with him clear proof from his Lord, and a witness from Him recites it and before it (is) the Book of Musa, a guide and a mercy? These believe in it; and whoever of the (different) parties disbelieves in it, surely it is the truth from your Lord, but most men do not believe.

18. And who is more unjust than he who forges a lie against Allah? These shall be brought before their Lord, and the witnesses shall say: These are they who lied against their Lord. Now surely the curse of Allah is on the unjust.

19. Who turn away from the path of Allah and desire to make it crooked; and they are disbelievers in the hereafter.

20. These shall not escape in the earth, nor shall they have any guardians besides Allah; the punishment shall be doubled for them; they could not bear to hear and they did not see.

21. These are they who have lost their souls, and what they forged is gone from them.

22. Truly in the hereafter they are the greatest losers.

23. Surely (as to) those who believe and do good and humble themselves to their Lord, these are the dwellers of the garden, in it they will abide.

24. The likeness of the two parties is as the blind and the deaf, and the seeing and the hearing: are they equal in condition? Will you not then mind?

25. And certainly We sent Nuh to his people: Surely I am a plain warner for you:

26. That you shall not serve any but Allah, surely I fear for you the punishment of a painful day.

27. But the chiefs of those who disbelieved from among his people said: We do not consider you but a mortal like ourselves, and we do not see any have followed you but those who are the meanest of us at first thought and we do not see in you any excellence over us; nay, we deem you liars.

28. He said: O my people! tell me if I have with me clear proof from my Lord, and He has granted me mercy from Himself and it has been made obscure to you; shall we constrain you to (accept) it while you are averse from it?

29. And, O my people! I ask you not for wealth in return for it; my reward is only with Allah and I am not going to drive away those who believe; surely they shall meet their Lord, but I consider you a people who are ignorant:

30. And, O my people! who will help me against Allah if I drive them away? Will you not then mind?

31. And I do not say to you that I have the treasures of Allah; and I do not know the unseen, nor do I say that I am an angel; nor do I say about those whom your eyes hold in mean estimation (that) Allah will never grant them (any) good—Allah knows best what is in their souls—for then most surely I should be of the unjust.

32. They said: O Nuh! indeed you have disputed with us and lengthened dispute with us, therefore bring to us what you threaten us with, if you are of the truthful ones.

33. He said: Allah only will bring it to you if He please, and you will not escape:

34. And if I intend to give you good advice, my advice will not profit you if Allah intended that He should leave you to go astray; He is your Lord, and to Him shall you be returned.

35. Or do they say: He has forged it? Say: If I have forged it, on me is my guilt, and I am clear of that of which you are guilty.

36. And it was revealed to Nuh: That none of your people will believe except those who have already believed, therefore do not grieve at what they do:

37. And make the ark before Our eyes and (according to) Our

revelation, and do not speak to Me in respect of those who are unjust; surely they shall be drowned.

38. And he began to make the ark; and whenever the chiefs from among his people passed by him they laughed at him. He said: If you laugh at us, surely we too laugh at you as you laugh (at us).

39. So shall you know who it is on whom will come a chastisement which will disgrace him, and on whom will lasting chastisement come down.

40. Until when Our command came and water came forth from the valley, We said: Carry in it two of all things, a pair, and your own family—except those against whom the word has already gone forth, and those who believe. And there believed not with him but a few.

41. And he said: Embark in it, in the name of Allah be its sailing and its anchoring; most surely my Lord is Forgiving, Merciful.

42. And it moved on with them amid waves like mountains; and Nuh called out to his son, and he was aloof: O my son! embark with us and be not with the unbelievers.

43. He said: I will betake myself for refuge to a mountain that shall protect me from the water. Nuh said: There is no protector today from Allah's punishment but He Who has mercy; and a wave intervened between them, so he was of the drowned.

44. And it was said: O earth, swallow down your water, and O cloud, clear away; and the water was made to abate and the affair was decided, and the ark rested on the Judi, and it was said: Away with the unjust people.

45. And Nuh cried out to his Lord and said: My Lord! surely my son is of my family, and Thy promise is surely true, and Thou art the most just of the judges.

46. He said: O Nuh! surely he is not of your family; surely he is (the doer of) other than good deeds, therefore ask not of Me that of which you have no knowledge; surely I admonish you lest you may be of the ignorant.

47. He said: My Lord! I seek refuge in Thee from asking Thee that of which I have no knowledge; and if Thou shouldst not forgive me and have mercy on me, I should be of the losers.

48. It was said: O Nuh! descend with peace from Us and blessings on you and on the people from among those who are with you, and there shall be nations whom We will afford provisions, then a painful punishment from Us shall afflict them.

49. These are announcements relating to the unseen which We reveal to you, you did not know them—(neither) you nor your people—before this; therefore be patient; surely the end is for those who guard (against evil).

50. And to Ad (We sent) their brother Hud. He said: O my people! serve Allah, you have no god other than He; you are nothing but forgers (of lies).

51. O my people! I do not ask of you any reward for it; my reward is only with Him Who created me; do you not then understand?

52. And, O my people! ask forgiveness of your Lord, then turn to Him, He will send on you clouds pouring down abundance of rain and add strength to your strength, and do not turn back guilty.

53. They said: O Hud! you have not brought to us any clear argument and we are not going to desert our gods for your word, and we are not believers in you:

54. We cannot say aught but that some of our gods have smitten you with evil. He said: Surely I call Allah to witness, and do you bear witness too, that I am clear of what you associate (with Allah).

55. Besides Him, therefore scheme against me all together; then give me no respite:

56. Surely I rely on Allah, my Lord and your Lord; there is no living creature but He holds it by its forelock; surely my Lord is on the right path.

57. But if you turn back, then indeed I have delivered to you the message with which I have been sent to you, and my Lord will bring another people in your place, and you cannot do Him any harm; surely my Lord is the Preserver of all things.

58. And when Our decree came to pass, We delivered Hud and those who believed with him with mercy from Us, and We delivered them from a hard chastisement.

59. And this was Ad; they denied the communications of their Lord, and disobeyed His apostles and followed the bidding of every insolent opposer (of truth).

60. And they were overtaken by curse in this world and on the resurrection day; now surely Ad disbelieved in their Lord; now surely, away with Ad, the people of Hud.

61. And to Samood (We sent) their brother Salih. He said: O my people! serve Allah, you have no god other than He; He brought you into being from the earth, and made you dwell in it,

therefore ask forgiveness of Him, then turn to Him; surely my Lord is Nigh, Answering.

62. They said: O Salih! surely you were one amongst us in whom great expectations were placed before this; do you (now) forbid us from worshipping what our fathers worshipped? And as to that which you call us to, most surely we are in disquieting doubt.

63. He said: O my people! tell me if I have clear proof from my Lord and He has granted to me mercy from Himself—who will then help me against Allah if I disobey Him? Therefore you do not add to me other than loss:

64. And, O my people! this will be (as) Allah's she-camel for you, a sign; therefore leave her to pasture on Allah's earth and do not touch her with evil, for then a near chastisement will overtake you.

65. But they slew her, so he said: Enjoy yourselves in your abode for three days, that is a promise not to be belied.

66. So when Our decree came to pass, We delivered Salih and those who believed with him by mercy from Us, and (We saved them) from the disgrace of that day; surely your Lord is the Strong, the Mighty.

67. And the rumbling overtook those who were unjust, so they became motionless bodies in their abodes,

68. As though they had never dwelt in them; now surely did Samood disbelieve in their Lord; now surely, away with Samood.

69. And certainly Our messengers came to Ibrahim with good news. They said: Peace. Peace, said he, and he made no delay in bringing a roasted calf.

70. But when he saw that their hands were not extended towards it, he deemed them strange and conceived fear of them. They said: Fear not, surely we are sent to Lut's people.

71. And his wife was standing (by), so she laughed, then We gave her the good news of Ishaq and after Ishaq of (a son's son) Yaqoub.

72. She said: O wonder! shall I bear a son when I am an extremely old woman and this my husband an extremely old man? Most surely this is a wonderful thing.

73. They said: Do you wonder at Allah's bidding? The mercy of Allah and His blessings are on you, O people of the house, surely He is Praised, Glorious.

74. So when fear had gone away from Ibrahim and good news came to him, he began to plead with Us for Lut's people.

75. Most surely Ibrahim was forbearing, tender-hearted, oft-returning (to Allah):

76. O Ibrahim! leave off this, surely the decree of your Lord has come to pass, and surely there must come to them a chastisement that cannot be averted.

77. And when Our messengers came to Lut, he was grieved for them, and he lacked strength to protect them, and said: This is a hard day.

78. And his people came to him, (as if) rushed on towards him, and already they did evil deeds. He said: O my people! these are my daughters—they are purer for you, so guard against (the punishment of) Allah and do not disgrace me with regard to my guests; is there not among you one right-minded man?

79. They said: Certainly you know that we have no claim on your daughters, and most surely you know what we desire.

80. He said: Ah! that I had power to suppress you, rather I shall have recourse to a strong support.

81. They said: O Lut! we are the messengers of your Lord; they shall by no means reach you; so remove your followers in a part of the night—and let none of you turn back—except your wife, for surely whatsoever befalls them shall befall her; surely their appointed time is the morning; is not the morning nigh?

82. So when Our decree came to pass, We turned them upside down and rained down upon them stones, of what had been decreed, one after another.

83. Marked (for punishment) with your Lord and it is not far off from the unjust.

84. And to Madyan (We sent) their brother Shu'aib. He said: O my people! serve Allah, you have no god other than He, and do not give short measure and weight: surely I see you in prosperity and surely I fear for you the punishment of an all-encompassing day.

85. And, O my people! give full measure and weight fairly, and defraud not men their things, and do not act corruptly in the land, making mischief:

86. What remains with Allah is better for you if you are believers, and I am not a keeper over you.

87. They said: O Shu'aib! does your prayer enjoin you that we should forsake what our fathers worshipped or that we should not do what we please with regard to our property? Forsooth you are the forbearing, the right-directing one.

88. He said: O my people! have you considered if I have a

clear proof from my Lord and He has given me a goodly
sustenance from Himself; and I do not desire that in opposition
to you I should betake myself to that which I forbid you: I desire
nothing but reform so far as I am able, and with none but Allah
is the direction of my affair to a right issue; on Him do I rely and
to Him do I turn:

89. And, O my people! let not opposition to me make you
guilty so that there may befall you the like of what befell the
people of Nuh, or the people of Hud, or the people of Salih, nor
are the people of Lut far off from you;

90. And ask forgiveness of your Lord, then turn to Him;
surely my Lord is Merciful, Loving-kind.

91. They said: O Shu'aib! we do not understand much of what
you say and most surely we see you to be weak among us, and
were it not for your family we would surely stone you, and you
are not mighty against us.

92. He said: O my people! is my family more esteemed by you
than Allah? And you neglect Him as a thing cast behind your
back; surely my Lord encompasses what you do:

93. And, O my people! act according to your ability, I too am
acting; you will come to know soon who it is on whom will light
the punishment that will disgrace him and who it is that is a liar,
and watch, surely I too am watching with you.

94. And when Our decree came to pass We delivered Shu'aib,
and those who believed with him by mercy from Us, and the
rumbling overtook those who were unjust so they became motionless bodies in their abodes,

95. As though they had never dwelt in them; now surely
perdition overtook Madyan as had perished Samood.

96. And certainly We sent Musa with Our communications
and a clear authority,

97. To Firon and his chiefs, but they followed the bidding of
Firon, and Firon's bidding was not right-directing.

98. He shall lead his people on the resurrection day, and bring
them down to the fire; and evil the place to which they are
brought.

99. And they are overtaken by curse in this (world), and on
the resurrection day; evil the gift which shall be given.

100. This is an account of (the fate of) the towns which We
relate to you; of them are some that stand and (others) mown
down.

101. And We did not do them injustice, but they were unjust

to themselves, so their gods whom they called upon besides Allah did not avail them aught when the decree of your Lord came to pass; and they added but to their ruin.

102. And such is the punishment of your Lord when He punishes the towns while they are unjust; surely His punishment is painful, severe.

103. Most surely there is a sign in this for him who fears the chastisement of the hereafter; this is a day on which the people shall be gathered together and this is a day that shall be witnessed.

104. And We do not delay it but to an appointed term.

105. On the day when it shall come, no soul shall speak except with His permission, then (some) of them shall be unhappy and (others) happy.

106. So as to those who are unhappy, they shall be in th fire; for them shall be sighing and groaning in it:

107. Abiding therein so long as the heavens and the earth endure, except as your Lord please; surely your Lord is the mighty doer of what He intends.

108. And as to those who are made happy, they shall be in the garden, abiding in it as long as the heavens and the earth endure, except as your Lord please; a gift which shall never be cut off.

109. Therefore be not in doubt as to what these worship; they do not worship but as their fathers worshipped before; and most surely We will pay them back in full their portion undiminished.

110. And certainly We gave the book to Musa, but it was gone against; and had not a word gone forth from your Lord, the matter would surely have been decided between them; and surely they are in a disquieting doubt about it.

111. And your Lord will most surely pay back to all their deeds in full; surely He is aware of what they do.

112. Continue then in the right way as you are commanded, as also he who has turned (to Allah) with you, and be not inordinate (O men!), surely He sees what you do.

113. And do not incline to those who are unjust, lest the fire touch you, and you have no guardians besides Allah, then you shall not be helped.

114. And keep up prayer in the two parts of the day and in the first hours of the night; surely good deeds take away evil deeds; this is a reminder to the mindful.

115. And be patient, for surely Allah does not waste the reward of the good-doers.

116. But why were there not among the generations before you those possessing understanding, who should have forbidden the making of mischief in the earth, except a few of those whom We delivered from among them? And those who were unjust went after what they are made to enjoy of plenty, and they were guilty.

117. And it did not beseem your Lord to have destroyed the towns tyrannously, while their people acted well.

118. And if your Lord had pleased He would certainly have made people a single nation, and they shall continue to differ.

119. Except those on whom your Lord has mercy; and for this did He create them; and the word of your Lord is fulfilled: Certainly I will fill hell with the jinn and the men, all together.

120. And all we relate to you of the accounts of the apostles is to strengthen your heart therewith; and in this has come to you the truth and an admonition, and a reminder to the believers.

121. And say to those who do not believe: Act according to your state; surely we too are acting.

122. And wait; surely we are waiting also.

123. And Allah's is the unseen in the heavens and the earth, and to Him is returned the whole of the affair; therefore serve Him and rely on Him, and your Lord is not heedless of what you do.

YUSUF

In the name of Allah, the Beneficent, the Merciful.

1. Alif Lam Ra. These are the verses of the Book that makes (things) manifest.

2. Surely We have revealed it—an Arabic Quran—that you may understand.

3. We narrate to you the best of narratives, by Our revealing to you this Quran, though before this you were certainly one of those who did not know.

4. When Yusuf said to his father: O my father! surely I saw eleven stars and the sun and the moon—I saw them making obeisance to me.

5. He said: O my son! do not relate your vision to your brothers, lest they devise a plan against you; surely the Shaitan is an open enemy to man.

6. And thus will your Lord choose you and teach you the interpretation of sayings and make His favor complete to you and to the children of Yaqoub, as He made it complete before to your fathers, Ibrahim and Ishaq; surely your Lord is Knowing, Wise.

7. Certainly in Yusuf and his brothers there are signs for the inquirers.

8. When they said: Certainly Yusuf and his brother are dearer to our father than we, though we are a (stronger) company; most surely our father is in manifest error:

9. Slay Yusuf or cast him (forth) into some land, so that your father's regard may be exclusively for you, and after that you may be a righteous people.

10. A speaker from among them said: Do not slay Yusuf, and cast him down into the bottom of the pit if you must do (it), (so that) some of the travellers may pick him up.

11. They said: O our father! what reason have you that you do not trust in us with respect to Yusuf? And most surely we are his sincere well-wishers:

12. Send him with us tomorrow that he may enjoy himself and sport, and surely we will guard him well.

13. He said: Surely it grieves me that you should take him off, and I fear lest the wolf devour him while you are heedless of him.

14. They said: Surely if the wolf should devour him notwithstanding that we are a (strong) company, we should then certainly be losers.

15. So when they had gone off with him and agreed that they should put him down at the bottom of the pit, and We revealed to him: You will most certainly inform them of this their affair while they do not perceive.

16. And they came to their father at nightfall, weeping.

17. They said: O our father! surely we went off racing and left Yusuf by our goods, so the wolf devoured him, and you will not believe us though we are truthful.

18. And they brought his shirt with false blood upon it. He said: Nay, your souls have made the matter light for you, but patience is good and Allah is He Whose help is sought for against what you describe.

19. And there came travellers and they sent their water-drawer and he let down his bucket. He said: O good news! this is a

youth; and they concealed him as an article of merchandise, and Allah knew what they did.

20. And they sold him for a small price, a few pieces of silver, and they showed no desire for him.

21. And the Egyptian who bought him said to his wife: Give him an honorable abode, maybe he will be useful to us, or we may adopt him as a son. And thus did We establish Yusuf in the land and that We might teach him the interpretation of sayings; and Allah is the master of His affair, but most people do not know.

22. And when he had attained his maturity, We gave him wisdom and knowledge: and thus do We reward those who do good.

23. And she in whose house he was sought to make himself yield (to her), and she made fast the doors and said: Come forward. He said: I seek Allah's refuge, surely my Lord made good my abode: Surely the unjust do not prosper.

24. And certainly she made for him, and he would have made for her, were it not that he had seen the manifest evidence of his Lord; thus (it was) that We might turn away from him evil and indecency, surely he was one of Our sincere servants.

25. And they both hastened to the door, and she rent his shirt from behind and they met her husband at the door. She said: What is the punishment of him who intends evil to your wife except imprisonment or a painful chastisement?

26. He said: She sought to make me yield (to her); and a witness of her own family bore witness: If his shirt is rent from front, she speaks the truth and he is one of the liars:

27. And if his shirt is rent from behind, she tells a lie and he is one of the truthful.

28. So when he saw his shirt rent from behind, he said: Surely it is a guile of you women; surely your guile is great:

29. O Yusuf! turn aside from this; and (O my wife)! ask forgiveness for your fault, surely you are one of the wrong-doers.

30. And women in the city said: The chief's wife seeks her slave to yield himself (to her), surely he has affected her deeply with (his) love; most surely we see her in manifest error.

31. So when she heard of their sly talk she sent for them and prepared for them a repast, and gave each of them a knife, and said (to Yusuf): Come forth to them. So when they saw him, they deemed him great, and cut their hands (in amazement), and said: Remote is Allah (from imperfection); this is not a mortal; this is but a noble angel.

32. She said: This is he with respect to whom you blamed me, and certainly I sought his yielding himself (to me), but he abstained, and if he does not do what I bid him, he shall certainly be imprisoned, and he shall certainly be of those who are in a state of ignominy.

33. He said: My Lord! the prison house is dearer to me than that to which they invite me; and if Thou turn not away their device from me, I will yearn towards them and become (one) of the ignorant.

34. Thereupon his Lord accepted his prayer and turned away their guile from him; surely He is the Hearing, the Knowing.

35. Then it occurred to them after they had seen the signs that they should imprison him till a time.

36. And two youths entered the prison with him. One of them said: I saw myself pressing wine. And the other said: I saw myself carrying bread on my head, of which birds ate. Inform us of its interpretation; surely we see you to be of the doers of good.

37. He said: There shall not come to you the food with which you are fed, but I will inform you both of its interpretation before it comes to you; this is of what my Lord has taught me; surely I have forsaken the religion of a people who do not believe in Allah, and they are deniers of the hereafter:

38. And I follow the religion of my fathers, Ibrahim and Ishaq and Yaqoub; it beseems us not that we should associate aught with Allah; this is by Allah's grace upon us and on mankind, but most people do not give thanks:

39. O my two mates of the prison! are sundry lords better or Allah the One, the Supreme?

40. You do not serve besides Him but names which you have named, you and your fathers; Allah has not sent down any authority for them; judgment is only Allah's; He has commanded that you shall not serve aught but Him; this is the right religion but most people do not know:

41. O my two mates of the prison! as for one of you, he shall give his lord to drink wine; and as for the other, he shall be crucified, so that the birds shall eat from his head; the matter is decreed concerning which you inquired.

42. And he said to him whom he knew would be delivered of the two: Remember me with your lord; but the Shaitan caused him to forget mentioning (it) to his lord, so he remained in the prison a few years.

43. And the king said: Surely I see seven fat kine which seven lean ones devoured; and seven green ears and (seven) others dry;

O chiefs! explain to me my dream, if you can interpret the dream.

44. They said: Confused dreams, and we do not know the interpretation of dreams.

45. And of the two (prisoners) he who had found deliverance and remembered after a long time said: I will inform you of its interpretation, so let me go:

46. Yusuf! O truthful one! explain to us seven fat kine which seven lean ones devoured, and seven green ears and (seven) others dry, that I may go back to the people so that they may know.

47. He said: You shall sow for seven years continuously, then what you reap leave it in its ear except a little of which you eat.

48. Then there shall come after that seven years of hardship which shall eat away all that you have beforehand laid up in store for them, except a little of what you shall have preserved:

49. Then there will come after that a year in which people shall have rain and in which they shall press (grapes).

50. And the king said: Bring him to me. So when the messenger came to him, he said: Go back to your lord and ask him, what is the case of the women who cut their hands; surely my Lord knows their guile.

51. He said: How was your affair when you sought Yusuf to yield himself (to you)? They said: Remote is Allah (from imperfection), we knew of no evil on his part. The chief's wife said: Now has the truth become established: I sought him to yield himself (to me), and he is most surely of the truthful ones.

52. This is that he might know that I have not been unfaithful to him in secret and that Allah does not guide the device of the unfaithful.

53. And I do not declare myself free, most surely (man's) self is wont to command (him to do) evil, except such as my Lord has had mercy on, surely my Lord is Forgiving, Merciful.

54. And the king said: Bring him to me, I will choose him for myself. So when he had spoken with him, he said: Surely you are in our presence today an honorable, a faithful one.

55. He said: Place me (in authority) over the treasures of the land, surely I am a good keeper, knowing well.

56. And thus did We give to Yusuf power in the land—he had mastery in it wherever he liked; We send down Our mercy on whom We please, and We do not waste the reward of those who do good.

57. And certainly the reward of the hereafter is much better for those who believe and guard (against evil).

58. And Yusuf's brothers came and went in to him, and he knew them, while they did not recognize him.

59. And when he furnished them with their provision, he said: Bring to me a brother of yours from your father; do you not see that I give full measure and that I am the best of hosts?

60. But if you do not bring him to me, you shall have no measure (of corn) from me, nor shall you come near me.

61. They said: We will strive to make his father yield in respect of him, and we are sure to do (it).

62. And he said to his servants: Put their money into their bags that they may recognize it when they go back to their family, so that they may come back.

63. So when they returned to their father, they said: O our father, the measure is withheld from us, therefore send with us our brother, (so that) we may get the measure, and we will most surely guard him.

64. He said: I cannot trust in you with respect to him, except as I trusted in you with respect to his brother before; but Allah is the best Keeper, and He is the most Merciful of the merciful ones.

65. And when they opened their goods, they found their money returned to them. They said: O our father! what (more) can we desire? This is our property returned to us, and we will bring corn for our family and guard our brother, and will have in addition the measure of a camel-(load); this is an easy measure.

66. He said: I will by no means send him with you until you give me a firm covenant in Allah's name that you will most certainly bring him back to me, unless you are completely surrounded. And when they gave him their covenant, he said: Allah is the One in Whom trust is placed as regards what we say.

67. And he said: O my sons! do not (all) enter by one gate and enter by different gates and I cannot avail you aught against Allah; judgment is only Allah's; on Him do I rely, and on Him let those who are reliant rely.

68. And when they had entered as their father had bidden them, it did not avail them aught against Allah, but (it was only) a desire in the soul of Yaqoub which he satisfied; and surely he was possessed of knowledge because We had given him knowledge, but most people do not know.

69. And when they went in to Yusuf, he lodged his brother

with himself, saying: I am your brother, therefore grieve not at what they do.

70. So when he furnished them with their provisions, (someone) placed the drinking cup in his brother's bag. Then a crier cried out: O caravan! you are most surely thieves.

71. They said while they were facing them: What is it that you miss?

72. They said: We miss the king's drinking cup, and he who shall bring it shall have a camel-load and I am responsible for it.

73. They said: By Allah! you know for certain that we have not come to make mischief in the land, and we are not thieves.

74. They said: But what shall be the requital of this, if you are liars?

75. They said: The requital of this is that the person in whose bag it is found shall himself be (held for) the satisfaction thereof; thus do we punish the wrongdoers.

76. So he began with their sacks before the sack of his brother, then he brought it out from his brother's sack. Thus did We plan for the sake of Yusuf; it was not (lawful) that he should take his brother under the king's law unless Allah pleased; We raise the degrees of whomsoever We please, and above every one possessed of knowledge is the All-knowing one.

77. They said: If he steal, a brother of his did indeed steal before; but Yusuf kept it secret in his heart and did not disclose it to them. He said: You are in an evil condition and Allah knows best what you state.

78. They said: O chief! he has a father, a very old man, therefore retain one of us in his stead; surely we see you to be of the doers of good.

79. He said: Allah protect us that we should seize other than him with whom we found our property, for then most surely we would be unjust.

80. Then when they despaired of him, they retired, conferring privately together. The eldest of them said: Do you not know that your father took from you a covenant in Allah's name, and how you fell short of your duty with respect to Yusuf before? Therefore I will by no means depart from this land until my father permits me or Allah decides for me, and He is the best of the judges:

81. Go back to your father and say: O our father! surely your son committed theft, and we do not bear witness except to what we have known, and we could not keep watch over the unseen:

82. And inquire in the town in which we were and the caravan with which we proceeded, and most surely we are truthful.

83. He (Yaquob) said: Nay, your souls have made a matter light for you, so patience is good; maybe Allah will bring them all together to me; surely He is the Knowing, the Wise.

84. And he turned away from them, and said: O my sorrow for Yusuf! and his eyes became white on account of the grief, and he was a repressor (of grief).

85. They said: By Allah! you will not cease to remember Yusuf until you are a prey to constant disease or (until) you are of those who perish.

86. He said: I only complain of my grief and sorrow to Allah, and I know from Allah what you do not know.

87. O my sons! Go and inquire respecting Yusuf and his brother, and despair not of Allah's mercy; surely none despairs of Allah's mercy except the unbelieving people.

88. So when they came in to him, they said: O chief! distress has afflicted us and our family and we have brought scanty money, so give us full measure and be charitable to us; surely Allah rewards the charitable.

89. He said: Do you know how you treated Yusuf and his brother when you were ignorant?

90. They said: Are you indeed Yusuf? He said: I am Yusuf and this is my brother; Allah has indeed been gracious to us; surely he who guards (against evil) and is patient (is rewarded) for surely Allah does not waste the reward of those who do good.

91. They said: By Allah! now has Allah certainly chosen you over us, and we were certainly sinners.

92. He said: (There shall be) no reproof against you this day; Allah may forgive you, and He is the most Merciful of the merciful.

93. Take this my shirt and cast it on my father's face; he will (again) be able to see, and come to me with all your families.

94. And when the caravan had departed, their father said: Most surely I perceive the greatness of Yusuf, unless you pronounce me to be weak in judgment.

95. They said: By Allah, you are most surely in your old error.

96. So when the bearer of good news came he cast it on his face, so forthwith he regained his sight. He said: Did I not say to you that I know from Allah what you do not know?

97. They said: O our father! ask forgiveness of our faults for us, surely we were sinners.

98. He said: I will ask for you forgiveness from my Lord; surely He is the Forgiving, the Merciful.

99. Then when they came in to Yusuf, he took his parents to lodge with him and said: Enter safe into Egypt, if Allah please.

100. And he raised his parents upon the throne and they fell down in prostration before him, and he said: O my father! this is the significance of my vision of old; my Lord has indeed made it to be true; and He was indeed kind to me when He brought me forth from the prison and brought you from the desert after the Shaitan had sown dissensions between me and my brothers, surely my Lord is benignant to whom He pleases; surely He is the Knowing, the Wise.

101. My Lord! Thou hast given me of the kingdom and taught me of the interpretation of sayings: Originator of the heavens and the earth! Thou art my guardian in this world and the hereafter; make me die a muslim and join me with the good.

102. This is of the announcements relating to the unseen (which) We reveal to you, and you were not with them when they resolved upon their affair, and they were devising plans.

103. And most men will not believe though you desire it eagerly.

104. And you do not ask them for a reward for this; it is nothing but a reminder for all mankind.

105. And how many a sign in the heavens and the earth which they pass by, yet they turn aside from it.

106. And most of them do not believe in Allah without associating others (with Him).

107. Do they then feel secure that there may come to them an extensive chastisement from Allah or (that) the hour may come to them suddenly while they do not perceive?

108. Say: This is my way: I call to Allah, I and those who follow me being certain, and glory be to Allah, and I am not one of the polytheists.

109. And We have not sent before you but men from (among) the people of the towns, to whom We sent revelations. Have they not then travelled in the land and seen what was the end of those before them? And certainly the abode of the hereafter is best for those who guard (against evil); do you not then understand?

110. Until when the apostles despaired and the people became

sure that they were indeed told a lie, Our help came to them and whom We pleased was delivered; and Our punishment is not averted from the guilty people.

111. In their histories there is certainly a lesson for men of understanding. It is not a narrative which could be forged, but a verification of what is before it and a distinct explanation of all things and a guide and a mercy to a people who believe.

SURAH XIII   *The Thunder*

THE THUNDER

In the name of Allah, the Beneficent, the Merciful.

1. Alif Lam Mim Ra. These are the verses of the Book; and that which is revealed to you from your Lord is the truth, but most people do not believe.

2. Allah is He Who raised the heavens without any pillars that you see, and He is firm in power and He made the sun and the moon subservient (to you); each one pursues its course to an appointed time; He regulates the affair, making clear the signs that you may be certain of meeting your Lord.

3. And He it is Who spread the earth and made in it firm mountains and rivers, and of all fruits He has made in it two kinds; He makes the night cover the day; most surely there are signs in this for a people who reflect.

4. And in the earth there are tracts side by side and gardens of grapes and corn and palm trees having one root and (others) having distinct roots—they are watered with one water, and We make some of them excel others in fruit; most surely there are signs in this for a people who understand.

5. And if you would wonder, then wondrous is their saying: What! when we are dust, shall we then certainly be in a new creation? These are they who disbelieve in their Lord, and these have chains on their necks, and they are the inmates of the fire; in it they shall abide.

6. And they ask you to hasten on the evil before the good, and indeed there have been exemplary punishments before them; and most surely your Lord is the Lord of forgiveness to people, notwithstanding their injustice; and most surely your Lord is severe in requiting (evil).

7. And those who disbelieve say: Why has not a sign been sent down upon him from his Lord? You are only a warner and (there is) a guide for every people.

8. Allah knows what every female bears, and that of which the wombs fall short of completion and that in which they increase; and there is a measure with Him of everything.

9. The knower of the unseen and the seen, the Great, the Most High.

10. Alike (to Him) among you is he who conceals (his) words and he who speaks them openly, and he who hides himself by night and (who) goes forth by day.

11. For his sake there are angels following one another, before him and behind him, who guard him by Allah's commandment; surely Allah does not change the condition of a people until they change their own condition; and when Allah intends evil to a people, there is no averting it, and besides Him they have no protector.

12. He it is Who shows you the lightning causing fear and hope and (Who) brings up the heavy cloud.

13. And the thunder declares His glory with His praise, and the angels too for awe of Him; and He sends the thunderbolts and smites with them whom He pleases, yet they dispute concerning Allah, and He is mighty in prowess.

14. To Him is due the true prayer; and those whom they pray to besides Allah give them no answer; but (they are) like one who stretches forth his two hands towards water that it may reach his mouth, but it will not reach it; and the prayer of the unbelievers is only in error.

15. And whoever is in the heavens and the earth makes obeisance to Allah only, willingly and unwillingly, and their shadows too at morn and eve.

16. Say: Who is the Lord of the heavens and the earth?—Say: Allah. Say: Do you take then besides Him guardians who do not control any profit or harm for themselves? Say: Are the blind and the seeing alike? Or can the darkness and the light be equal? Or have they set up with Allah associates who have created creation like His, so that what is created became confused to them? Say: Allah is the Creator of all things, and He is the One, the Supreme.

17. He sends down water from the cloud, then watercourses flow (with water) according to their measure, and the torrent

bears along the swelling foam, and from what they melt in the fire for the sake of making ornaments or apparatus arises a scum like it; thus does Allah compare truth and falsehood; then as for the scum, it passes away as a worthless thing; and as for that which profits the people, it tarries in the earth; thus does Allah set forth parables.

18. For those who respond to their Lord is good; and (as for) those who do not respond to Him, had they all that is in the earth and the like thereof with it they would certainly offer it for a ransom. (As for) those, an evil reckoning shall be theirs and their abode is hell, and evil is the resting-place.

19. Is he then who knows that what has been revealed to you from your Lord is the truth like him who is blind? Only those possessed of understanding will mind,

20. Those who fulfil the promise of Allah and do not break the covenant,

21. And those who join that which Allah has bidden to be joined and have awe of their Lord and fear the evil reckoning.

22. And those who are constant, seeking the pleasure of their Lord, and keep up prayer and spend (benevolently) out of what We have given them secretly and openly and repel evil with good; as for those, they shall have the (happy) issue of the abode,

23. The gardens of perpetual abode which they will enter along with those who do good from among their parents and their spouses and their offspring; and the angels will enter in upon them from every gate:

24. Peace be on you because you were constant, how excellent, is then, the issue of the abode.

25. And those who break the covenant of Allah after its confirmation and cut asunder that which Allah has ordered to be joined and make mischief in the land; (as for) those, upon them shall be curse and they shall have the evil (issue) of the abode.

26. Allah amplifies and straitens the means of subsistence for whom He pleases; and they rejoice in this world's life, and this world's life is nothing compared with the hereafter but a temporary enjoyment.

27. And those who disbelieve say: Why is not a sign sent down upon him by his Lord? Say: Surely Allah makes him who will go astray, and guides to Himself those who turn (to Him).

28. Those who believe and whose hearts are set at rest by the remembrance of Allah; now surely by Allah's remembrance are the hearts set at rest.

29. (As for) those who believe and do good, a good final state shall be theirs and a goodly return.

30. And thus We have sent you among a nation before which other nations have passed away, that you might recite to them what We have revealed to you and (still) they deny the Beneficent God. Say: He is my Lord, there is no god but He; on Him do I rely and to Him is my return.

31. And even if there were a Quran with which the mountains were made to pass away, or the earth were travelled over with it, or the dead were made to speak thereby; nay! the commandment is wholly Allah's. Have not yet those who believe known that if Allah please He would certainly guide all the people? And (as for) those who disbelieve, there will not cease to afflict them because of what they do a repelling calamity, or it will alight close by their abodes, until the promise of Allah comes about; surely Allah will not fail in (His) promise.

32. And apostles before you were certainly mocked at, but I gave respite to those who disbelieved, then I destroyed them; how then was My requital (of evil)?

33. Is He then Who watches every soul as to what it earns? And yet they give associates to Allah! Say: Give them a name; nay, do you mean to inform Him of what He does not know in the earth, or (do you affirm this) by an outward saying? Rather, their plans are made to appear fair-seeming to those who disbelieve, and they are kept back from the path; and whom Allah makes err, he shall have no guide.

34. They shall have chastisement in this world's life, and the chastisement of the hereafter is certainly more grievous, and they shall have no protector against Allah.

35. A likeness of the garden which the righteous are promised; there flow beneath it rivers, its food and shades are perpetual; this is the requital of those who guarded (against evil), and the requital of the unbelievers is the fire.

36. And those to whom We have given the Book rejoice in that which has been revealed to you, and of the confederates are some who deny a part of it. Say: I am only commanded that I should serve Allah and not associate anything with Him, to Him do I invite (you) and to Him is my return.

37. And thus have We revealed it, a true judgment in Arabic, and if you follow their low desires after what has come to you of knowledge, you shall not have against Allah any guardian or a protector.

38. And certainly We sent apostles before you and gave them wives and children, and it is not in (the power of) an apostle to bring a sign except by Allah's permission; for every term there is an appointment.

39. Allah makes to pass away and establishes what He pleases, and with Him is the basis of the Book.

40. And We will either let you see part of what We threaten them with or cause you to die, for only the delivery of the message is (incumbent) on you, while calling (them) to account is Our (business).

41. Do they not see that We are bringing destruction upon the land by curtailing it of its sides? And Allah pronounces a doom—there is no repeller of His decree, and He is swift to take account.

42. And those before them did indeed make plans, but all planning is Allah's; He knows what every soul earns, and the unbelievers shall come to know for whom is the (better) issue of the abode.

43. And those who disbelieve say: You are not a messenger. Say: Allah is sufficient as a witness between me and you and whoever has knowledge of the Book.

SURAH XIV *Ibrahim*

IBRAHIM

In the name of Allah, the Beneficent, the Merciful.

1. Alif Lam Ra. (This is) a Book which We have revealed to you that you may bring forth men, by their Lord's permission from utter darkness into light—to the way of the Mighty, the Praised One,

2. (Of) Allah, Whose is whatever is in the heavens and whatever is in the earth; and woe to the unbelievers on account of the severe chastisement,

3. (To) those who love this world's life more than the hereafter, and turn away from Allah's path and desire to make it crooked; these are in a great error.

4. And We did not send any apostle but with the language of his people, so that he might explain to them clearly; then Allah makes whom He pleases err and He guides whom He pleases, and He is the Mighty, the Wise.

5. And certainly We sent Musa with Our communications, saying: Bring forth your people from utter darkness into light and remind them of the days of Allah; most surely there are signs in this for every patient, grateful one.

6. And when Musa said to his people: Call to mind Allah's favor to you when He delivered you from Firon's people, who subjected you to severe torment, and slew your sons and spared your women; and in this there was a great trial from your Lord.

7. And when your Lord made it known: If you are grateful, I would certainly give to you more, and if you are ungrateful, My chastisement is truly severe.

8. And Musa said: If you are ungrateful, you and those on earth all together, most surely Allah is Self-sufficient, Praised;

9. Has not the account reached you of those before you, of the people of Nuh and Ad and Samood, and those after them? None knows them but Allah. Their apostles come to them with clear arguments, but they thrust their hands into their mouths and said: Surely we deny that with which you are sent, and most surely we are in serious doubt as to that to which you invite us.

10. Their apostles said: Is there doubt about Allah, the Maker of the heavens and the earth? He invites you to forgive you your faults and to respite you till an appointed term. They said: You are nothing but mortals like us; you wish to turn us away from what our fathers used to worship; bring us therefore some clear authority.

11. Their apostles said to them: We are nothing but mortals like yourselves, but Allah bestows (His) favors on whom He pleases of His servants, and it is not for us that we should bring you an authority except by Allah's permission; and on Allah should the believers rely.

12. And what reason have we that we should not rely on Allah? And He has indeed guided us in our ways; and certainly we would bear with patience your persecution of us; and on Allah should the reliant rely.

13. And those who disbelieved said to their apostles: We will most certainly drive you forth from our land, or else you shall come back into our religion. So their Lord revealed to them: Most certainly We will destroy the unjust.

14. And most certainly We will settle you in the land after them; this is for him who fears standing in My presence and who fears My threat.

15. And they asked for judgment and every insolent opposer was disappointed:

16. Hell is before him and he shall be given to drink of festering water:

17. He will drink it little by little and will not be able to swallow it agreeably, and death will come to him from every quarter, but he shall not die; and there shall be vehement chastisement before him.

18. The parable of those who disbelieve in their Lord: their actions are like ashes on which the wind blows hard on a stormy day; they shall not have power over any thing out of what they have earned; this is the great error.

19. Do you not see that Allah created the heavens and the earth with truth? If He please He will take you off and bring a new creation,

20. And this is not difficult for Allah.

21. And they shall all come forth before Allah, then the weak shall say to those who were proud: Surely we were your followers, can you therefore avert from us any part of the chastisement of Allah? They would say: If Allah had guided us, we too would have guided you; it is the same to us whether we are impatient (now) or patient, there is no place for us to fly to.

22. And the Shaitan shall say after the affair is decided: Surely Allah promised you the promise of truth, and I gave you promises, then failed to keep them to you, and I had no authority over you, except that I called you and you obeyed me, therefore do not blame me but blame yourselves: I cannot be your aider (now) nor can you be my aiders; surely I disbelieved in your associating me with Allah before; surely it is the unjust that shall have the painful punishment.

23. And those who believe and do good are made to enter gardens, beneath which rivers flow, to abide in them by their Lord's permission; their greeting therein is, Peace.

24. Have you not considered how Allah sets forth a parable of a good word (being) like a good tree, whose root is firm and whose branches are in heaven,

25. Yielding its fruit in every season by the permission of its Lord? And Allah sets forth parables for men that they may be mindful.

26. And the parable of an evil word is as an evil tree pulled up from the earth's surface; it has no stability.

27. Allah confirms those who believe with the sure word in this world's life and in the hereafter, and Allah causes the unjust to go astray, and Allah does what He pleases.

28. Have you not seen those who have changed Allah's favor for ungratefulness and made their people to alight into the abode of perdition;

29. (Into) hell? They shall enter into it and an evil place it is to settle in.

30. And they set up equals with Allah that they may lead (people) astray from His path. Say: Enjoy yourselves, for surely your return is to the fire.

31. Say to My servants who believe that they should keep up prayer and spend out of what We have given them secretly and openly before the coming of the day in which there shall be no bartering nor mutual befriending.

32. Allah is He Who created the heavens and the earth and sent down water from the clouds, then brought forth with it fruits as a sustenance for you, and He has made the ships subservient to you, that they might run their course in the sea by His command, and He has made the rivers subservient to you.

33. And He has made subservient to you the sun and the moon pursuing their courses, and He has made subservient to you the night and the day.

34. And He gives you of all that you ask Him; and if you count Allah's favors, you will not be able to number them; most surely man is very unjust, very ungrateful.

35. And when Ibrahim said: My Lord! make this city secure, and save me and my sons from worshipping idols:

36. My Lord! surely they have led many men astray; then whoever follows me, he is surely of me, and whoever disobeys me, Thou surely art Forgiving, Merciful:

37. O our Lord! surely I have settled a part of my offspring in a valley unproductive of fruit near Thy Sacred House, our Lord! that they may keep up prayer; therefore make the hearts of some people yearn towards them and provide them with fruits; haply they may be grateful:

38. O our Lord! Surely Thou knowest what we hide and what we make public, and nothing in the earth nor any thing in heaven is hidden from Allah:

39. Praise be to Allah, Who has given me in old age Ismail and Ishaq; most surely my Lord is the Hearer of prayer:

40. My Lord! make me keep up prayer and from my offspring (too), O our Lord, and accept my prayer:

41. O our Lord! grant me protection and my parents and the believers on the day when the reckoning shall come to pass!

42. And do not think Allah to be heedless of what the unjust do; He only respites them to a day on which the eyes shall be fixedly open,

43. Hastening forward, their heads upraised, their eyes not reverting to them and their hearts vacant.

44. And warn people of the day when the chastisement shall come to them, then those who were unjust will say: O our Lord! respite us to a near term, (so) we shall respond to Thy call and follow the apostles. What! did you not swear before (that) there will be no passing away for you!

45. And you dwell in the abodes of those who were unjust to themselves, and it is clear to you how We dealt with them and We have made (them) examples to you.

46. And they have indeed planned their plan, but their plan is with Allah, though their plan was such that the mountains should pass away thereby.

47. Therefore do not think Allah (to be one) failing in His promise to His apostles; surely Allah is Mighty, the Lord of Retribution.

48. On the day when the earth shall be changed into a different earth, and the heavens (as well), and they shall come forth before Allah, the One, the Supreme.

49. And you will see the guilty on that day linked together in chains.

50. Their shirts made of pitch and the fire covering their faces,

51. That Allah may requite each soul (according to) what it has earned; surely Allah is swift in reckoning.

52. This is a sufficient exposition for the people and that they may be warned thereby, and that they may know that He is One God and that those possessed of understanding may mind.

THE ROCK

In the name of Allah, the Beneficent, the Merciful.

1. Alif Lam Ra. These are the verses of the Book and (of) a Quran that makes (things) clear.

2. Often will those who disbelieve wish that they had been Muslims.

3. Leave them that they may eat and enjoy themselves and (that) hope may beguile them, for they will soon know.

4. And never did We destroy a town but it had a term made known.

5. No people can hasten on their doom nor can they postpone (it).

6. And they say: O you to whom the Reminder has been revealed! you are most surely insane:

7. Why do you not bring to us the angels if you are of the truthful ones?

8. We do not send the angels but with truth, and then they would not be respited.

9. Surely We have revealed the Reminder and We will most surely be its guardian.

10. And certainly We sent (apostles) before you among the nations of yore.

11. And there never came an apostle to them but they mocked him.

12. Thus do We make it to enter into the hearts of the guilty;

13. They do not believe in it, and indeed the example of the former people has already passed.

14. And even if We open to them a gateway of heaven, so that they ascend into it all the while,

15. They would certainly say: Only our eyes have been covered over, rather we are an enchanted people.

16. And certainly We have made strongholds in the heaven and We have made it fair seeming to the beholders.

17. And We guard it against every accursed Shaitan,

18. But he who steals a hearing, so there follows him a visible flame.

19. And the earth— We have spread it forth and made in it firm mountains and caused to grow in it of every suitable thing.

20. And We have made in it means of subsistence for you and for him for whom you are not the suppliers.

21. And there is not a thing but with Us are the treasures of it, and We do not send it down but in a known measure.

22. And We send the winds fertilizing, then send down water from the cloud so We give it to you to drink of, nor is it you who store it up.

23. And most surely We bring to life and cause to die and We are the heirs.

24. And certainly We know those of you who have gone before and We certainly know those who shall come later.

25. And surely your Lord will gather them together; surely He is Wise, Knowing.

26. And certainly We created man of clay that gives forth sound, of mud fashioned in shape.

27. And the jinn We created before, of intensely hot fire.

28. And when your Lord said to the angels: Surely I am going to create a mortal of the essence of black mud fashioned in shape.

29. So when I have made him complete and breathed into him of My spirit, fall down making obeisance to him.

30. So the angels made obeisance, all of them together,

31. But Iblis (did it not); he refused to be with those who made obeisance.

32. He said: O Iblis! what excuse have you that you are not with those who make obeisance?

33. He said: I am not such that I should make obeisance to a mortal whom Thou hast created of the essence of mud fashioned in shape.

34. He said: Then get out of it, for surely you are driven away:

35. And surely on you is curse until the day of judgment.

36. He said: My Lord! then respite me till the time when they are raised.

37. He said: So surely you are of the respited ones,

38. Till the period of the time made known.

39. He said: My Lord! because Thou hast made life evil to me, I will certainly make (evil) fair-seeming to them on earth, and I will certainly cause them all to deviate,

40. Except Thy servants from among them, the devoted ones.

41. He said: This is a right way with Me:

42. Surely, as regards My servants, you have no authority over them except those who follow you of the deviators.

43. And surely Hell is the promised place of them all:

44. It has seven gates; for every gate there shall be a separate party of them.

45. Surely those who guard (against evil) shall be in the midst of gardens and fountains:

46. Enter them in peace, secure.

47. And We will root out whatever of rancor is in their

breasts—(they shall be) as brethren, on raised couches, face to face.

48. Toil shall not afflict them in it, nor shall they be ever ejected from it.

49. Inform My servants that I am the Forgiving, the Merciful,

50. And that My punishment—that is the painful punishment.

51. And inform them of the guests of Ibrahim:

52. When they entered upon him, they said, Peace. He said: Surely we are afraid of you.

53. They said: Be not afraid, surely we give you the good news of a boy, possessing knowledge.

54. He said: Do you give me good news (of a son) when old age has come upon me?—Of what then do you give me good news!

55. They said: We give you good news with truth, therefore be not of the despairing.

56. He said: And who despairs of the mercy of his Lord but the erring ones?

57. He said: What is your business then, O messengers?

58. They said: Surely we are sent towards a guilty people,

59. Except Lut's followers: We will most surely deliver them all,

60. Except his wife; We ordained that she shall surely be of those who remain behind.

61. So when the messengers came to Lut's followers,

62. He said: Surely you are an unknown people.

63. They said: Nay, we have come to you with that about which they disputed.

64. And we have come to you with the truth, and we are most surely truthful.

65. Therefore go forth with your followers in a part of the night and yourself follow their rear, and let not any one of you turn round, and go forth whither you are commanded.

66. And We revealed to him this decree, that the roots of these shall be cut off in the morning.

67. And the people of the town came rejoicing.

68. He said: Surely these are my guests, therefore do not disgrace me,

69. And guard against (the punishment of) Allah and do not put me to shame.

70. They said: Have we not forbidden you from (other) people?

71. He said: These are my daughters, if you will do (aught).

72. By your life! they were blindly wandering on in their intoxication.

73. So the rumbling overtook them (while) entering upon the time of sunrise;

74. Thus did We turn it upside down, and rained down upon them stones of what had been decreed.

75. Surely in this are signs for those who examine.

76. And surely it is on a road that still abides.

77. Most surely there is a sign in this for the believers.

78. And the dwellers of the thicket also were most surely unjust.

79. So We inflicted retribution on them, and they are both, indeed, on an open road (still) pursued.

80. And the dwellers of the Rock certainly rejected the messengers;

81. And We gave them Our communications, but they turned aside from them;

82. And they hewed houses in the mountains in security.

83. So the rumbling overtook them in the morning;

84. And what they earned did not avail them.

85. And We did not create the heavens and the earth and what is between them two but in truth; and the hour is most surely coming, so turn away with kindly forgiveness.

86. Surely your Lord is the Creator of all things, the Knowing.

87. And certainly We have given you seven of the oft-repeated (verses) and the grand Quran.

88. Do not strain your eyes after what We have given certain classes of them to enjoy, and do not grieve for them, and make yourself gentle to the believers.

89. And say: Surely I am the plain warner.

90. Like as We sent down on the dividers,

91. Those who made the Quran into shreds.

92. So, by your Lord, We would most certainly question them all,

93. As to what they did.

94. Therefore declare openly what you are bidden and turn aside from the polytheists.

95. Surely We will suffice you against the scoffers,

96. Those who set up another god with Allah; so they shall soon know.

97. And surely We know that your breast straitens at what they say;

98. Therefore celebrate the praise of your Lord, and be of those who make obeisance.

99. And serve your Lord until there comes to you that which is certain.

THE BEE

In the Name of Allah, the Beneficent, the Merciful.

1. Allah's commandment has come, therefore do not desire to hasten it; glory be to Him, and highly exalted be He above what they associate (with Him).

2. He sends down the angels with the inspiration by His commandment on whom He pleases of His servants, saying: Give the warning that there is no god but Me, therefore be careful (of your duty) to Me.

3. He created the heavens and the earth with the truth, highly exalted be He above what they associate (with Him).

4. He created man from a small seed and lo! he is an open contender.

5. And He created the cattle for you; you have in them warm clothing and (many) advantages, and of them do you eat.

6. And there is beauty in them for you when you drive them back (to home), and when you send them forth (to pasture).

7. And they carry your heavy loads to regions which you could not reach but with distress of the souls; most surely your Lord is Compassionate, Merciful.

8. And (He made) horses and mules and asses that you might ride upon them and as an ornament; and He creates what you do not know.

9. And upon Allah it rests to show the right way, and there are some deviating (ways); and if He please He would certainly guide you all aright.

10. He it is Who sends down water from the cloud for you; it gives drink, and by it (grow) the trees upon which you pasture.

11. He causes to grow for you thereby herbage, and the olives, and the palm trees, and the grapes, and of all the fruits; most surely there is a sign in this for a people who reflect.

12. And He has made subservient for you the night and the day and the sun and the moon, and the stars are made subservient by His commandment; most surely there are signs in this for a people who ponder;

13. And what He has created in the earth of varied hues; most surely there is a sign in this for a people who are mindful.

14. And He it is Who has made the sea subservient that you may eat fresh flesh from it and bring forth from it ornaments which you wear, and you see the ships cleaving through it, and that you might seek of His bounty and that you may give thanks.

15. And He has cast great mountains in the earth lest it might be convulsed with you, and rivers and roads that you may go aright,

16. And landmarks; and by the stars they find the right way.

17. Is He then Who creates like him who does not create? Do you not then mind?

18. And if you would count Allah's favors, you will not be able to number them; most surely Allah is Forgiving, Merciful.

19. And Allah knows what you conceal and what you do openly.

20. And those whom they call on besides Allah have not created anything while they are themselves created;

21. Dead (are they), not living, and they know not when they shall be raised.

22. Your God is one God; so (as for) those who do not believe in the hereafter, their hearts are ignorant and they are proud.

23. Truly Allah knows what they hide and what they manifest; surely He does not love the proud.

24. And when it is said to them, what is it that your Lord has revealed? They say: Stories of the ancients;

25. That they may bear their burdens entirely on the day of resurrection and also of the burdens of those whom they lead astray without knowledge; now surely evil is what they bear.

26. Those before them did indeed devise plans, but Allah demolished their building from the foundations, so the roof fell down on them from above them, and the punishment came to them from whence they did not perceive.

27. Then on the resurrection day He will bring them to disgrace and say: Where are the associates you gave Me, for whose sake you became hostile? Those who are given the knowledge will say: Surely the disgrace and the evil are this day upon the unbelievers:

28. Those whom the angels cause to die while they are unjust to themselves. Then would they offer submission: We used not to do any evil. Aye! surely Allah knows what you did.

29. Therefore enter the gates of hell, to abide therein; so certainly evil is the dwelling place of the proud.

30. And it is said to those who guard (against evil): What is it that your Lord has revealed? They say, Good. For those who do good in this world is good, and certainly the abode of the hereafter is better; and certainly most excellent is the abode of those who guard (against evil);

31. The gardens of perpetuity, they shall enter them, rivers flowing beneath them; they shall have in them what they please. Thus does Allah reward those who guard (against evil),

32. Those whom the angels cause to die in a good state, saying: Peace be on you: enter the garden for what you did.

33. They do not wait aught but that the angels should come to them or that the commandment of your Lord should come to pass. Thus did those before them; and Allah was not unjust to them, but they were unjust to themselves.

34. So the evil (consequences) of what they did shall afflict them and that which they mocked shall encompass them.

35. And they who give associates (to Allah) say: If Allah had pleased, we would not have served anything besides Allah, (neither) we nor our fathers, nor would we have prohibited anything without (order from) Him. Thus did those before them; is then aught incumbent upon the apostles except a plain delivery (of the message)?

36. And certainly We raised in every nation an apostle saying: Serve Allah and shun the Shaitan. So there were some of them whom Allah guided and there were others against whom error was due; therefore travel in the land, then see what was the end of the rejecters.

37. If you desire for their guidance, yet surely Allah does not guide him who leads astray, nor shall they have any helpers.

38. And they swear by Allah with the most energetic of their oaths: Allah will not raise up him who dies. Yea! it is a promise binding on Him, quite true, but most people do not know;

39. So that He might make manifest to them that about which they differ, and that those who disbelieve might know that they were liars.

40. Our word for a thing when We intend it, is only that We say to it, Be, and it is.

41. And those who fly for Allah's sake after they are oppressed, We will most certainly give them a good abode in the world, and the reward of the hereafter is certainly much greater, did they but know;

42. Those who are patient and on their Lord do they rely.

43. And We did not send before you any but men to whom We sent revelation—so ask the followers of the Reminder if you do not know—

44. With clear arguments and scriptures; and We have revealed to you the Reminder that you may make clear to men what has been revealed to them, and that haply they may reflect.

45. Do they then who plan evil (deeds) feel secure (of this) that Allah will not cause the earth to swallow them or that punishment may not overtake them from whence they do not perceive?

46. Or that He may not seize them in the course of their journeys, then shall they not escape;

47. Or that He may not seize them by causing them to suffer gradual loss, for your Lord is most surely Compassionate, Merciful.

48. Do they not consider every thing that Allah has created? Its (very) shadows return from right and left, making obeisance to Allah while they are in utter abasement.

49. And whatever creature that is in the heavens and that is in the earth makes obeisance to Allah (only), and the angels (too) and they do not show pride.

50. They fear their Lord above them and do what they are commanded.

51. And Allah has said: Take not two gods, He is only one God; so of Me alone should you be afraid.

52. And whatever is in the heavens and the earth is His, and to Him should obedience be (rendered) constantly; will you then guard against other than (the punishment of) Allah?

53. And whatever favor is (bestowed) on you it is from Allah; then when evil afflicts you, to Him do you cry for aid.

54. Yet when He removes the evil from you, lo! a party of you associate others with their Lord;

55. So that they be ungrateful for what We have given them; then enjoy yourselves; for soon will you know.

56. And they set apart for what they do not know a portion of what We have given them. By Allah, you shall most certainly be questioned about that which you forged.

57. And they ascribe daughters to Allah, glory be to Him; and for themselves (they would have) what they desire.

58. And when a daughter is announced to one of them his face becomes black and he is full of wrath.

59. He hides himself from the people because of the evil of that which is announced to him. Shall he keep it with disgrace or bury it (alive) in the dust? Now surely evil is what they judge.

60. For those who do not believe in the hereafter is an evil attribute, and Allah's is the loftiest attribute; and He is the Mighty, the Wise.

61. And if Allah had destroyed men for their iniquity, He would not leave on the earth a single creature, but He respites them till an appointed time; so when their doom will come they shall not be able to delay (it) an hour nor can they bring (it) on (before its time).

62. And they ascribe to Allah what they (themselves) hate and their tongues relate the lie that they shall have the good; there is no avoiding it that for them is the fire and that they shall be sent before.

63. By Allah, most certainly We sent (apostles) to nations before you, but the Shaitan made their deeds fair-seeming to them, so he is their guardian today, and they shall have a painful punishment.

64. And We have not revealed to you the Book except that you may make clear to them that about which they differ, and (as) a guidance and a mercy for a people who believe.

65. And Allah has sent down water from the cloud and therewith given life to the earth after its death; most surely there is a sign in this for a people who would listen.

66. And most surely there is a lesson for you in the cattle; We give you to drink of what is in their bellies—from betwixt the feces and the blood—pure milk, easy and agreeable to swallow for those who drink.

67. And of the fruits of the palms and the grapes—you obtain from them intoxication and goodly provision; most surely there is a sign in this for a people who ponder.

68. And your Lord revealed to the bee saying: Make hives in the mountains and in the trees and in what they build:

69. Then eat of all the fruits and walk in the ways of your Lord submissively. There comes forth from within it a beverage of many colours, in which there is healing for men; most surely there is a sign in this for a people who reflect.

70. And Allah has created you, then He causes you to die, and of you is he who is brought back to the worst part of life, so that after having knowledge he does not know anything; surely Allah is Knowing, Powerful.

71. And Allah has made some of you excel others in the means of subsistence, so those who are made to excel do not give away their sustenance to those whom their right hands possess, so that they should be equal therein; is it then the favor of Allah which they deny?

72. And Allah has made wives for you from among yourselves, and has given you sons and grandchildren from your wives, and has given you of the good things; is it then in the falsehood that they believe while it is in the favor of Allah that they disbelieve?

73. And they serve besides Allah that which does not control for them any sustenance at all from the heavens and the earth, nor have they any power.

74. Therefore do not give likenesses to Allah; surely Allah knows and you do not know.

75. Allah sets forth a parable: (consider) a slave, the property of another, (who) has no power over anything, and one whom We have granted from Ourselves a goodly sustenance so he spends from it secretly and openly; are the two alike? (All) praise is due to Allah! Nay, most of them do not know.

76. And Allah sets forth a parable of two men; one of them is dumb, not able to do anything, and he is a burden to his master; wherever he sends him, he brings no good; can he be held equal with him who enjoins what is just, and he (himself) is on the right path?

77. And Allah's is the unseen of the heavens and the earth; and the matter of the hour is but as the twinkling of an eye or it is higher still; surely Allah has power over all things.

78. And Allah has brought you forth from the wombs of your mothers—you did not know anything—and He gave you hearing and sight and hearts that you may give thanks.

79. Do they not see the birds, constrained in the middle of the sky? None withholds them but Allah; most surely there are signs in this for a people who believe.

80. And Allah has given you a place to abide in your houses, and He has given you tents of the skins of cattle which you find light to carry on the day of your march and on the day of your

halting, and of their wool and their fur and their hair (He has given you) household stuff and a provision for a time.

81. And Allah has made for you of what He has created shelters, and He has given you in the mountains places of retreat, and He has given you garments to preserve you from the heat and coats of mail to preserve you in your fighting; even thus does He complete His favor upon you, that haply you may submit.

82. But if they turn back, then on you devolves only the clear deliverance (of the message).

83. They recognize the favor of Allah, yet they deny it, and most of them are ungrateful.

84. And on the day when We will raise up a witness out of every nation, then shall no permission be given to those who disbelieve, nor shall they be made to solicit favor.

85. And when those who are unjust shall see the chastisement, it shall not be lightened for them, nor shall they be respited.

86. And when those who associate (others with Allah) shall see their associate-gods, they shall say: Our Lord, these are our associate-gods on whom we called besides Thee. But they will give them back the reply: Most surely you are liars.

87. And they shall tender submission to Allah on that day; and what they used to forge shall depart from them.

88. (As for) those who disbelieve and turn away from Allah's way, We will add chastisement to their chastisement because they made mischief.

89. And on the day when We will raise up in every people a witness against them from among themselves, and bring you as a witness against these—and We have revealed the Book to you explaining clearly everything, and a guidance and mercy and good news for those who submit.

90. Surely Allah enjoins the doing of justice and the doing of good (to others) and the giving to the kindred, and He forbids indecency and evil and rebellion; He admonishes you that you may be mindful.

91. And fulfill the covenant of Allah when you have made a covenant, and do not break the oaths after making them fast, and you have indeed made Allah a surety for you; surely Allah knows what you do.

92. And be not like her who unravels her yarn, disintegrating it into pieces after she has spun it strongly. You make your oaths to be means of deceit between you because (one) nation is more

numerous than (another) nation. Allah only tries you by this; and He will most certainly make clear to you on the resurrection day that about which you differed.

93. And if Allah please He would certainly make you a single nation, but He causes to err whom He pleases and guides whom He pleases; and most certainly you will be questioned as to what you did.

94. And do not make your oaths a means of deceit between you, lest a foot should slip after its stability and you should taste evil because you turned away from Allah's way and grievous punishment be your (lot).

95. And do not take a small price in exchange for Allah's covenant; surely what is with Allah is better for you, did you but know.

96. What is with you passes away and what is with Allah is enduring; and We will most certainly give to those who are patient their reward for the best of what they did.

97. Whoever does good whether male or female and he is a believer, We will most certainly make him live a happy life, and We will most certainly give them their reward for the best of what they did.

98. So when you recite the Quran, seek refuge with Allah from the accursed Shaitan,

99. Surely he has no authority over those who believe and rely on their Lord.

100. His authority is only over those who befriend him and those who associate others with Him.

101. And when We change (one) communication for (another) communication, and Allah knows best what He reveals, they say: You are only a forger. Nay, most of them do not know.

102. Say: The Holy spirit has revealed it from your Lord with the truth, that it may establish those who believe and as a guidance and good news for those who submit.

103. And certainly We know that they say: Only a mortal teaches him. The tongue of him whom they reproach is barbarous, and this is clear Arabic tongue.

104. (As for) those who do not believe in Allah's communications, surely Allah will not guide them, and they shall have a painful punishment.

105. Only they forge the lie who do not believe in Allah's communications, and these are the liars.

106. He who disbelieves in Allah after his having believed, not he who is compelled while his heart is at rest on account of faith, but he who opens (his) breast to disbelief—on these is the wrath of Allah, and they shall have a grievous chastisement.

107. This is because they love this world's life more than the hereafter, and because Allah does not guide the unbelieving people.

108. These are they on whose hearts and their hearing and their eyes Allah has set a seal, and these are the heedless ones.

109. No doubt that in the hereafter they will be the losers.

110. Yet surely your Lord, with respect to those who fly after they are persecuted, then they struggle hard and are patient, most surely your Lord after that is Forgiving, Merciful.

111. (Remember) the day when every soul shall come, pleading for itself and every soul shall be paid in full what it has done, and they shall not be dealt with unjustly.

112. And Allah sets forth a parable: (Consider) a town safe and secure to which its means of subsistence come in abundance from every quarter; but it became ungrateful to Allah's favors, therefore Allah made it to taste the utmost degree of hunger and fear because of what they wrought.

113. And certainly there came to them an Apostle from among them, but they rejected him, so the punishment overtook them while they were unjust.

114. Therefore eat of what Allah has given you, lawful and good (things), and give thanks for Allah's favor if Him do you serve.

115. He has only forbidden you what dies of itself and blood and flesh of swine and that over which any other name than that of Allah has been invoked, but whoever is driven to necessity, not desiring nor exceeding the limit, then surely Allah is Forgiving, Merciful.

116. And, for what your tongues describe, do not utter the lie, (saying) This is lawful and this is unlawful, in order to forge a lie against Allah; surely those who forge the lie against Allah shall not prosper.

117. A little enjoyment and they shall have a painful punishment.

118. And for those who were Jews We prohibited what We have related to you already, and We did them no injustice, but they were unjust to themselves.

119. Yet surely your Lord, with respect to those who do an evil in ignorance, then turn after that and make amends, most surely your Lord after that is Forgiving, Merciful.

120. Surely Ibrahim was an exemplar, obedient to Allah, upright, and he was not of the polytheists.

121. Grateful for His favors; He chose him and guided him on the right path.

122. And We gave him good in this world, and in the next he will most surely be among the good.

123. Then We revealed to you: Follow the faith of Ibrahim, the upright one, and he was not of the polytheists.

124. The Sabbath was ordained only for those who differed about it, and most surely your Lord will judge between them on the resurrection day concerning that about which they differed.

125. Call to the way of your Lord with wisdom and goodly exhortation, and have disputations with them in the best manner; surely your Lord best knows those who go astray from His path, and He knows best those who follow the right way.

126. And if you take your turn, then retaliate with the like of that with which you were afflicted; but if you are patient, it will certainly be best for those who are patient.

127. And be patient and your patience is not but by (the assistance of) Allah, and grieve not for them, and do not distress yourself at what they plan.

128. Surely Allah is with those who guard (against evil) and those who do good (to others).

THE ISRAELITES

In the name of Allah, the Beneficent, the Merciful.

1. Glory be to Him Who made His servant to go on a night from the Sacred Mosque to the remote mosque of which We have blessed the precincts, so that We may show to him some of Our signs; surely He is the Hearing, the Seeing.

2. And We gave Musa the Book and made it a guidance to the children of Israel, saying: Do not take a protector besides Me;

3. The offspring of those whom We bore with Nuh; surely he was a grateful servant.

4. And We had made known to the children of Israel in the Book: Most certainly you will make mischief in the land twice, and most certainly you will behave insolently with great insolence.

5. So when the promise for the first of the two came, We sent over you Our servants, of mighty prowess, so they went to and fro among the houses, and it was a promise to be accomplished.

6. Then We gave you back the turn to prevail against them, and aided you with wealth and children and made you a numerous band.

7. If you do good, you will do good for your own souls, and if you do evil, it shall be for them. So when the second promise came (We raised another people) that they may bring you to grief and that they may enter the mosque as they entered it the first time, and that they might destroy whatever they gained ascendancy over with utter destruction.

8. It may be that your Lord will have mercy on you, and if you again return (to disobedience) We too will return (to punishment), and We have made hell a prison for the unbelievers.

9. Surely this Quran guides to that which is most upright and gives good news to the believers who do good that they shall have a great reward.

10. And that (as for) those who do not believe in the hereafter, We have prepared for them a painful chastisement.

11. And man prays for evil as he ought to pray for good, and man is ever hasty.

12. And We have made the night and the day two signs, then We have made the sign of the night to pass away and We have made the sign of the day manifest, so that you may seek grace from your Lord, and that you might know the numbering of years and the reckoning; and We have explained everything with distinctness.

13. And We have made every man's actions to cling to his neck, and We will bring forth to him on the resurrection day a book which he will find wide open:

14. Read your book; your own self is sufficient as a reckoner against you this day.

15. Whoever goes aright, for his own soul does he go aright; and whoever goes astray, to its detriment only does he go astray;

nor can the bearer of a burden bear the burden of another, nor do We chastise until We raise an apostle.

16. And when We wish to destroy a town, We send Our commandment to the people of it who lead easy lives, but they transgress therein; thus the word proves true against it, so We destroy it with utter destruction.

17. And how many of the generations did We destroy after Nuh! and your Lord is sufficient as Knowing and Seeing with regard to His servants' faults.

18. Whoever desires this present life, We hasten to him therein what We please for whomsoever We desire, then We assign to him the hell; he shall enter it despised, driven away.

19. And whoever desires the hereafter and strives for it as he ought to strive and he is a believer; (as for) these, their striving shall surely be accepted.

20. All do We aid—these as well as those—out of the bounty of your Lord, and the bounty of your Lord is not confined.

21. See how We have made some of them to excel others, and certainly the hereafter is much superior in respect of excellence.

22. Do not associate with Allah any other god, lest you sit down despised, neglected.

23. And your Lord has commanded that you shall not serve (any) but Him, and goodness to your parents. If either or both of them reach old age with you, say not to them (so much as) "Ugh" nor chide them, and speak to them a generous word.

24. And make yourself submissively gentle to them with compassion, and say: O my Lord! have compassion on them, as they brought me up (when I was) little.

25. Your Lord knows best what is in your minds; if you are good, then He is surely Forgiving to those who turn (to Him) frequently.

26. And give to the near of kin his due and (to) the needy and the wayfarer, and do not squander wastefully.

27. Surely the squanderers are the fellows of the Shaitans and the Shaitan is ever ungrateful to his Lord.

28. And if you turn away from them to seek mercy from your Lord, which you hope for, speak to them a gentle word.

29. And do not make your hand to be shackled to your neck nor stretch it forth to the utmost (limit) of its stretching forth, lest you should (afterwards) sit down blamed, stripped off.

30. Surely your Lord makes plentiful the means of subsist-

ence for whom He pleases and He straitens (them); surely He is ever Aware of, Seeing, His servants.

31. And do not kill your children for fear of poverty; We give them sustenance and yourselves (too); surely to kill them is a great wrong.

32. And go not nigh to fornication; surely it is an indecency and an evil way.

33. And do not kill any one whom Allah has forbidden, except for a just cause, and whoever is slain unjustly, We have indeed given to his heir authority, so let him not exceed the just limits in slaying; surely he is aided.

34. And draw not near to the property of the orphan except in a goodly way till he attains his maturity and fulfill the promise; surely (every) promise shall be questioned about.

35. And give full measure when you measure out, and weigh with a true balance; this is fair and better in the end.

36. And follow not that of which you have not the knowledge; surely the hearing and the sight and the heart, all of these, shall be questioned about that.

37. And do not go about in the land exultingly, for you cannot cut through the earth nor reach the mountains in height.

38. All this—the evil of it—is hateful in the sight of your Lord.

39. This is of what your Lord has revealed to you of wisdom, and do not associate any other god with Allah lest you should be thrown into hell, blamed, cast away.

40. What! has then your Lord preferred to give you sons, and (for Himself) taken daughters from among the angels? Most surely you utter a grievous saying.

41. And certainly We have repeated (warnings) in this Quran that they may be mindful, but it does not add save to their aversion.

42. Say: If there were with Him gods as they say, then certainly they would have been able to seek a way to the Lord of power.

43. Glory be to Him and exalted be He in high exaltation above what they say.

44. The seven heavens declare His glory and the earth (too), and those who are in them; and there is not a single thing but glorifies Him with His praise, but you do not understand their glorification; surely He is Forbearing, Forgiving.

45. And when you recite the Quran, We place between you and those who do not believe in the hereafter a hidden barrier;

46. And We have placed coverings on their hearts and a heaviness in their ears lest they understand it, and when you mention your Lord alone in the Quran they turn their backs in aversion.

47. We know best what they listen to when they listen to you, and when they take counsel secretly, when the unjust say: You follow only a man deprived of reason.

48. See what they liken you to! So they have gone astray and cannot find the way.

49. And they say: What! when we shall have become bones and decayed particles, shall we then certainly be raised up, being a new creation?

50. Say: Become stones or iron,

51. Or some other creature of those which are too hard (to receive life) in your minds! But they will say: Who will return us? Say: Who created you at first. Still they will shake their heads at you and say: When will it be? Say: Maybe it has drawn nigh.

52. On the day when He will call you forth, then shall you obey Him, giving Him praise, and you will think that you tarried but a little (while).

53. And say to My servants (that) they speak that which is best; surely the Shaitan sows dissensions among them; surely the Shaitan is an open enemy to man.

54. Your Lord knows you best; He will have mercy on you if He pleases, or He will chastise you if He pleases; and We have not sent you as being in charge of them.

55. And your Lord best knows those who are in the heavens and the earth; and certainly We have made some of the prophets to excel others, and to Dawood We gave a scripture.

56. Say: Call on those whom you assert besides Him, so they shall not control the removal of distress from you nor (its) transference.

57. Those whom they call upon, themselves seek the means of access to their Lord—whoever of them is nearest—and they hope for His mercy and fear His chastisement; surely the chastisement of your Lord is a thing to be cautious of.

58. And there is not a town but We will destroy it before the day of resurrection or chastise it with a severe chastisement; this is written in the Divine ordinance.

59. And nothing could have hindered Us that We should send

signs except that the ancients rejected them; and We gave to Samood the she-camel—a manifest sign—but on her account they did injustice, and We do not send signs but to make (men) fear.

60. And when We said to you: Surely your Lord encompasses men; and We did not make the vision which We showed you but a trial for men and the cursed tree in the Quran as well; and We cause them to fear, but it only adds to their great inordinacy.

61. And when We said to the angels: Make obeisance to Adam; they made obeisance, but Iblis (did it not). He said: Shall I make obeisance to him whom Thou hast created of dust?

62. He said: Tell me, is this he whom Thou hast honored above me? If Thou shouldst respite me to the day of resurrection, I will most certainly cause his progeny to perish except a few.

63. He said: Be gone! for whoever of them will follow you, then surely hell is your recompense, a full recompense:

64. And beguile whomsoever of them you can with your voice, and collect against them your forces riding and on foot, and share with them in wealth and children, and hold out promises to them; and the Shaitan makes not promises to them but to deceive:

65. Surely (as for) My servants, you have no authority over them; and your Lord is sufficient as a Protector.

66. Your Lord is He Who speeds the ships for you in the sea that you may seek of His grace; surely He is ever Merciful to you.

67. And when distress afflicts you in the sea, away go those whom you call on except He; but when He brings you safe to the land, you turn aside; and man is ever ungrateful.

68. What! Do you then feel secure that He will not cause a tract of land to engulf you or send on you a tornado? Then you shall not find a protector for yourselves.

69. Or, do you feel secure that He will (not) take you back into it another time, then send on you a fierce gale and thus drown you on account of your ungratefulness? Then you shall not find any aider against Us in the matter.

70. And surely We have honored the children of Adam, and We carry them in the land and the sea, and We have given them of the good things, and We have made them to excel by an appropriate excellence over most of those whom We have created.

71. (Remember) the day when We will call every people with

their Imam; then whoever is given his book in his right hand, these shall read their book; and they shall not be dealt with a whit unjustly.

72. And whoever is blind in this, he shall (also) be blind in the hereafter; and more erring from the way.

73. And surely they had purposed to turn you away from that which We have revealed to you, that you should forge against Us other than that, and then they would certainly have taken you for a friend.

74. And had it not been that We had already established you, you would certainly have been near to incline to them a little;

75. In that case We would certainly have made you to taste a double (punishment) in this life and a double (punishment) after death, then you would not have found any helper against Us.

76. And surely they purposed to unsettle you from the land that they might expel you from it, and in that case they will not tarry behind you but a little.

77. (This is Our) course with regard to those of Our apostles whom We sent before you, and you shall not find a change in Our course.

78. Keep up prayer from the declining of the sun till the darkness of the night and the morning recitation; surely the morning recitation is witnessed.

79. And during a part of the night, pray an additional prayer beyond what is incumbent on you; maybe your Lord will raise you to a position of great glory.

80. And say: My Lord! make me to enter a goodly entering, and cause me to go forth a goodly going forth, and grant me from near Thee power to assist (me).

81. And say: The truth has come and the falsehood has vanished; surely falsehood is a vanishing (thing).

82. And We reveal of the Quran that which is a healing and a mercy to the believers, and it adds only to the perdition of the unjust.

83. And when We bestow favor on man, he turns aside and behaves proudly, and when evil afflicts him, he is despairing.

84. Say: Every one acts according to his manner; but your Lord best knows who is best guided in the path.

85. And they ask you about the soul. Say: The soul is one of the commands of my Lord, and you are not given aught of knowledge but a little.

86. And if We please, We should certainly take away that which We have revealed to you, then you would not find for it any protector against Us.

87. But on account of mercy from your Lord—surely His grace to you is abundant.

88. Say: If men and jinn should combine together to bring the like of this Quran, they could not bring the like of it, though some of them were aiders of others.

89. And certainly We have explained for men in this Quran every kind of similitude, but most men do not consent to aught but denying.

90. And they say: We will by no means believe in you until you cause a fountain to gush forth from the earth for us.

91. Or you should have a garden of palms and grapes in the midst of which you should cause rivers to flow forth, gushing out.

92. Or you should cause the heaven to come down upon us in pieces as you think, or bring Allah and the angels face to face (with us).

93. Or you should have a house of gold, or you should ascend into heaven, and we will not believe in your ascending until you bring down to us a book which we may read. Say: Glory be to my Lord; am I aught but a mortal apostle?

94. And nothing prevented people from believing when the guidance came to them except that they said: What! has Allah raised up a mortal to be an apostle?

95. Say: Had there been in the earth angels walking about as settlers, We would certainly have sent down to them from the heaven an angel as an apostle.

96. Say: Allah suffices as a witness between me and you; surely He is Aware of His servants, Seeing.

97. And whomsoever Allah guides, he is the follower of the right way, and whomsoever He causes to err, you shall not find for him guardians besides Him; and We will gather them together on the day of resurrection on their faces, blind and dumb and deaf; their abode is hell; whenever it becomes allayed We will add to their burning.

98. This is their retribution because they disbelieved in Our communications and said: What! when we shall have become bones and decayed particles, shall we then indeed be raised up into a new creation?

99. Do they not consider that Allah, Who created the heavens and the earth, is able to create their like, and He has appointed for them a doom about which there is no doubt? But the unjust do not consent to aught but denying.

100. Say: If you control the treasures of the mercy of my Lord, then you would withhold (them) from fear of spending, and man is miserly.

101. And certainly We gave Musa nine clear signs; so ask the children of Israel. When he came to them, Firon said to him: Most surely I deem you, O Musa, to be a man deprived of reason.

102. He said: Truly you know that none but the Lord of the heavens and the earth has sent down these as clear proof, and most surely I believe you, O Firon, to be given over to perdition.

103. So he desired to destroy them out of the earth, but We drowned him and those with him all together;

104. And We said to the Israelites after him: Dwell in the land: and when the promise of the next life shall come to pass, we will bring you both together in judgment.

105. And with truth have We revealed it, and with truth did it come; and We have not sent you but as the giver of good news and as a warner.

106. And it is a Quran which We have revealed in portions so that you may read it to the people by slow degrees, and We have revealed it, revealing in portions.

107. Say: Believe in it or believe not; surely those who are given the knowledge before it fall down on their faces, making obeisance when it is recited to them.

108. And they say: Glory be to our Lord! most surely the promise of our Lord was to be fulfilled.

109. And they fall down on their faces weeping, and it adds to their humility.

110. Say: Call upon Allah or call upon, the Beneficent God; whichever you call upon, He has the best names; and do not utter your prayer with a very raised voice nor be silent with regard to it, and seek a way between these.

111. And say: (All) praise is due to Allah, Who has not taken a son and Who has not a partner in the kingdom, and Who has not a helper to save Him from disgrace; and proclaim His greatness magnifying (Him).

THE CAVE

In the name of Allah, the Beneficent, the Merciful.

1. (All) praise is due to Allah, Who revealed the Book to His servant and did not make in it any crookedness.

2. Rightly directing, that he might give warning of severe punishment from Him and give good news to the believers who do good that they shall have a goodly reward,

3. Staying in it for ever;

4. And warn those who say: Allah has taken a son.

5. They have no knowledge of it, nor had their fathers; a grievous word it is that comes out of their mouths; they speak nothing but a lie.

6. Then maybe you will kill yourself with grief, sorrowing after them, if they do not believe in this announcement.

7. Surely We have made whatever is on the earth an embellishment for it, so that We may try them (as to) which of them is best in works.

8. And most surely We will make what is on it bare ground without herbage.

9. Or, do you think that the Fellows of the Cave and the Inscription were of Our wonderful signs?

10. When the youths sought refuge in the cave, they said: Our Lord! grant us mercy from Thee, and provide for us a right course in our affair.

11. So We prevented them from hearing in the cave for a number of years.

12. Then We raised them up that We might know which of the two parties was best able to compute the time for which they remained.

13. We relate to you their story with the truth; surely they were youths who believed in their Lord and We increased them in guidance.

14. And We strengthened their hearts with patience, when they stood up and said: Our Lord is the Lord of the heavens and the earth; we will by no means call upon any god besides Him, for then indeed we should have said an extravagant thing.

15. These our people have taken gods besides Him; why do they not produce any clear authority in their support? Who is then more unjust than he who forges a lie against Allah?

16. And when you forsake them and what they worship save Allah, betake yourselves for refuge to the cave; your Lord will extend to you largely of His mercy and provide for you a profitable course in your affair.

17. And you might see the sun when it rose, decline from their cave towards the right hand, and when it set, leave them behind on the left while they were in a wide space thereof. This is of the signs of Allah; whomsoever Allah guides, he is the rightly guided one, and whomsoever He causes to err, you shall not find for him any friend to lead (him) aright.

18. And you might think them awake while they were asleep, and We turned them about to the right and to the left, while their dog (lay) outstretching its paws at the entrance; if you looked at them you would certainly turn back from them in flight, and you would certainly be filled with awe because of them.

19. And thus did We rouse them that they might question each other. A speaker among them said: How long have you tarried? They said: We have tarried for a day or a part of a day. (Others) said: Your Lord knows best how long you have tarried. Now send one of you with this silver (coin) of yours to the city, then let him see which of them has purest food, so let him bring you provision from it, and let him behave with gentleness, and by no means make your case known to any one:

20. For surely if they prevail against you they would stone you to death or force you back to their religion, and then you will never succeed.

21. And thus did We make (men) to get knowledge of them, that they might know that Allah's promise is true and that as for the hour there is no doubt about it. When they disputed among themselves about their affair and said: Erect an edifice over them—their Lord best knows them. Those who prevailed in their affair said: We will certainly raise a masjid over them.

22. (Some) say: (They are) three, the fourth of them being their dog; and (others) say: Five, the sixth of them being their dog, making conjectures at what is unknown; and (others yet) say: Seven, and the eighth of them is their dog. Say: My Lord best knows their number, none knows them but a few; therefore contend not in the matter of them but with an outward contention, and do not question concerning them any of them.

23. And do not say of anything: Surely I will do it tomorrow,

24. Unless Allah pleases; and remember your Lord when you

forget and say: Maybe my Lord will guide me to a nearer course to the right than this.

25. And they remained in their cave three hundred years and (some) add (another) nine.

26. Say: Allah knows best how long they remained; to Him are (known) the unseen things of the heavens and the earth; how clear His sight and how clear His hearing! There is none to be a guardian for them besides Him, and He does not make any one His associate in His Judgment.

27. And recite what has been revealed to you of the Book of your Lord; there is none who can alter His words; and you shall not find any refuge besides Him.

28. And withhold yourself with those who call on their Lord morning and evening desiring His goodwill, and let not your eyes pass from them, desiring the beauties of this world's life; and do not follow him whose heart We have made unmindful to Our remembrance, and he follows his low desires and his case is one in which due bounds are exceeded.

29. And say: The truth is from your Lord, so let him who please believe, and let him who please disbelieve; surely We have prepared for the iniquitous a fire, the curtains of which shall encompass them about; and if they cry for water, they shall be given water like molten brass which will scald their faces; evil the drink and ill the resting-place.

30. Surely (as for) those who believe and do good, We do not waste the reward of him who does a good work.

31. These it is for whom are gardens of perpetuity beneath which rivers flow; ornaments shall be given to them therein of bracelets of gold, and they shall wear green robes of fine silk and thick silk brocade interwoven with gold, reclining therein on raised couches; excellent the recompense and goodly the resting place.

32. And set forth to them a parable of two men; for one of them We made two gardens of grape vines, and We surrounded them both with palms, and in the midst of them We made cornfields.

33. Both these gardens yielded their fruits, and failed not aught thereof, and We caused a river to gush forth in their midst,

34. And he possessed much wealth; so he said to his companion, while he disputed with him: I have greater wealth than you, and am mightier in followers.

35. And he entered his garden while he was unjust to himself. He said: I do not think that this will ever perish,

36. And I do not think the hour will come, and even if I am returned to my Lord I will most certainly find a returning place better than this:

37. His companion said to him while disputing with him: Do you disbelieve in Him Who created you from dust, then from a small seed, then He made you a perfect man?

38. But as for me, He, Allah, is my Lord, and I do not associate anyone with my Lord.

39. And wherefore did you not say when you entered your garden: It is as Allah has pleased, there is no power save in Allah? If you consider me to be inferior to you in wealth and children,

40. Then maybe my Lord will give me what is better than your garden, and send on it a thunderbolt from heaven so that it shall become even ground without plant,

41. Or its waters should sink down into the ground so that you are unable to find it.

42. And his wealth was destroyed; so he began to wring his hands for what he had spent on it, while it lay, having fallen down upon its roofs, and he said: Ah me! would that I had not associated anyone with my Lord.

43. And he had no host to help him besides Allah nor could he defend himself.

44. Here is protection only Allah's, the True One; He is best in (the giving of) reward and best in requiting.

45. And set forth to them parable of the life of this world: like water which We send down from the cloud so the herbage of the earth becomes tangled on account of it, then it becomes dry, broken into pieces which the winds scatter; and Allah is the holder of power over all things.

46. Wealth and children are an adornment of the life of this world; and the ever-abiding, the good works, are better with your Lord in reward and better in expectation.

47. And the day on which We will cause the mountains to pass away and you will see the earth a levelled plain and We will gather them and leave not any one of them behind.

48. And they shall be brought before your Lord, standing in ranks: Now certainly you have come to Us as We created you at first. Nay, you thought that We had not appointed to you a time of the fulfillment of the promise.

49. And the Book shall be placed, then you will see the guilty fearing from what is in it, and they will say: Ah! woe to us! what a book is this! it does not omit a small one nor a great one, but numbers them (all); and what they had done they shall find present (there); and your Lord does not deal unjustly with anyone.

50. And when We said to the angels: Make obeisance to Adam; they made obeisance but Iblis (did it not). He was of the jinn, so he transgressed the commandment of his Lord. What! would you then take him and his offspring for friends rather than Me, and they are your enemies? Evil is (this) change for the unjust.

51. I did not make them witnesses of the creation of the heavens and the earth, nor of the creation of their own souls; nor could I take those who lead (others) astray for aiders.

52. And on the day when He shall say: Call on those whom you considered to be My associates. So they shall call on them, but they shall not answer them, and We will cause a separation between them.

53. And the guilty shall see the fire, then they shall know that they are going to fall into it, and they shall not find a place to which to turn away from it.

54. And certainly We have explained in this Quran every kind of example; and man is most of all given to contention.

55. And nothing prevents men from believing when the guidance comes to them, and from asking forgiveness of their Lord, except that what happened to the ancients should overtake them, or that the chastisement should come face to face with them.

56. And We do not send apostles but as givers of good news and warning, and those who disbelieve make a false contention that they may render null thereby the truth, and they take My communications and that with which they are warned for a mockery.

57. And who is more unjust than he who is reminded of the communications of his Lord, then he turns away from them and forgets what his two hands have sent before? Surely We have placed veils over their hearts lest they should understand it and a heaviness in their ears; and if you call them to the guidance, they will not ever follow the right course in that case.

58. And your Lord is Forgiving, the Lord of Mercy; were He to punish them for what they earn, He would certainly have

hastened the chastisement for them; but for them there is an appointed time from which they shall not find a refuge.

59. And (as for) these towns, We destroyed them when they acted unjustly, and We have appointed a time for their destruction.

60. And when Musa said to his servant: I will not cease until I reach the junction of the two rivers or I will go on for years.

61. So when they had reached the junction of the two (rivers), they forgot their fish, and it took its way into the sea, going away.

62. But when they had gone farther, he said to his servant: Bring to us our morning meal, certainly we have met with fatigue from this our journey.

63. He said: Did you see when we took refuge on the rock, then I forgot the fish, and nothing made me forget to speak of it but the Shaitan, and it took its way into the river; what a wonder!

64. He said: This is what we sought for; so they returned retracing their footsteps.

65. Then they found one from among Our servants whom We had granted mercy from Us and whom We had taught knowledge from Ourselves.

66. Musa said to him: Shall I follow you on condition that you should teach me right knowledge of what you have been taught?

67. He said: Surely you cannot have patience with me:

68. And how can you have patience in that of which you have not got a comprehensive knowledge?

69. He said: If Allah pleases, you will find me patient and I shall not disobey you in any matter.

70. He said: If you would follow me, then do not question me about any thing until I myself speak to you about it.

71. So they went (their way) until when they embarked in the boat he made a hole in it. (Musa) said: Have you made a hole in it to drown its inmates? Certainly you have done a grievous thing.

72. He said: Did I not say that you will not be able to have patience with me?

73. He said: Blame me not for what I forgot, and do not constrain me to a difficult thing in my affair.

74. So they went on until, when they met a boy, he slew him.

(Musa) said: Have you slain an innocent person otherwise than for manslaughter? Certainly you have done an evil thing.

75. He said: Did I not say to you that you will not be able to have patience with me?

76. He said: If I ask you about anything after this, keep me not in your company; indeed you shall have (then) found an excuse in my case.

77. So they went on until when they came to the people of a town, they asked them for food, but they refused to entertain them as guests. Then they found in it a wall which was on the point of falling, so he put it into a right state. (Musa) said: If you had pleased, you might certainly have taken a recompense for it.

78. He said: This shall be separation between me and you; now I will inform you of the significance of that with which you could not have patience.

79. As for the boat, it belonged to (some) poor men who worked on the river and I wished that I should damage it, and there was behind them a king who seized every boat by force.

80. And as for the boy, his parents were believers and we feared lest he should make disobedience and ingratitude to come upon them:

81. So we desired that their Lord might give them in his place one better than him in purity and nearer to having compassion.

82. And as for the wall, it belonged to two orphan boys in the city, and there was beneath it a treasure belonging to them, and their father was a righteous man; so your Lord desired that they should attain their maturity and take out their treasure, a mercy from your Lord, and I did not do it of my own accord. This is the significance of that with which you could not have patience.

83. And they ask you about Zulqarnain. Say: I will recite to you an account of him.

84. Surely We established him in the land and granted him means of access to every thing.

85. So he followed a course.

86. Until when he reached the place where the sun set, he found it going down into a black sea, and found by it a people. We said: O Zulqarnain! either give them a chastisement or do them a benefit.

87. He said: As to him who is unjust, we will chastise him, then shall he be returned to his Lord, and He will chastise him with an exemplary chastisement:

88. And as for him who believes and does good, he shall have goodly reward, and We will speak to him an easy word of Our command.

89. Then he followed (another) course.

90. Until when he reached the land of the rising of the sun, he found it rising on a people to whom We had given no shelter from it;

91. Even so! and We had a full knowledge of what he had.

92. Then he followed (another) course.

93. Until when he reached (a place) between the two mountains, he found on that side of them a people who could hardly understand a word.

94. They said: O Zulqarnain! surely Gog and Magog make mischief in the land. Shall we then pay you a tribute on condition that you should raise a barrier between us and them.

95. He said: That in which my Lord has established me is better, therefore you only help me with workers, I will make a fortified barrier between you and them;

96. Bring me blocks of iron; until when he had filled up the space between the two mountain sides, he said: Blow; until when he had made it (as) fire, he said: Bring me molten brass which I may pour over it.

97. So they were not able to scale it nor could they make a hole in it.

98. He said: This is a mercy from my Lord, but when the promise of my Lord comes to pass He will make it level with the ground, and the promise of my Lord is ever true.

99. And on that day We will leave a part of them in conflict with another part, and the trumpet will be blown, so We will gather them all together;

100. And We will bring forth hell, exposed to view, on that day before the unbelievers.

101. They whose eyes were under a cover from My reminder, and they could not even hear.

102. What! do then those who disbelieve think that they can take My servants to be guardians besides Me? Surely We have prepared hell for the entertainment of the unbelievers.

103. Say: Shall We inform you of the greatest losers in (their) deeds?

104. (These are) they whose labor is lost in this world's life and they think that they are well versed in skill of the work of hands.

105. These are they who disbelieve in the communications of their Lord and His meeting, so their deeds become null, and therefore We will not set up a balance for them on the day of resurrection.

106. Thus it is that their recompense is hell, because they disbelieved and held My communications and My apostles in mockery.

107. Surely (as for) those who believe and do good deeds, their place of entertainment shall be the gardens of paradise,

108. Abiding therein; they shall not desire removal from them.

109. Say: If the sea were ink for the words of my Lord, the sea would surely be consumed before the words of my Lord are exhausted, though We were to bring the like of that (sea) to add thereto.

110. Say: I am only a mortal like you; it is revealed to me that your god is one God, therefore whoever hopes to meet his Lord, he should do good deeds, and not join any one in the service of his Lord.

MARIUM

In the name of Allah, The Beneficent, The Merciful.

1. Kaf Ha Ya Ain Suad.

2. A mention of the mercy of your Lord to His servant Zakariya.

3. When he called upon his Lord in a low voice,

4. He said: My Lord! surely my bones are weakened and my head flares with hoariness, and, my Lord! I have never been unsuccessful in my prayer to Thee:

5. And surely I fear my cousins after me, and my wife is barren, therefore grant me from Thyself an heir,

6. Who should inherit me and inherit from the children of Yaqoub, and make him, my Lord, one in whom Thou art well pleased.

7. O Zakariya! surely We give you good news of a boy whose name shall be Yahya: We have not made before anyone his equal.

8. He said: O my Lord! when shall I have a son, and my wife is barren, and I myself have reached indeed the extreme degree of old age?

9. He said: So shall it be; your Lord says: It is easy to Me, and indeed I created you before, when you were nothing.

10. He said: My Lord! give me a sign. He said: Your sign is that you will not be able to speak to the people three nights while in sound health.

11. So he went forth to his people from his place of worship, then he made known to them that they should glorify (Allah) morning and evening.

12. O Yahya! take hold of the Book with strength, and We granted him wisdom while yet a child,

13. And tenderness from Us and purity, and he was one who guarded (against evil),

14. And dutiful to his parents, and he was not insolent, disobedient.

15. And peace on him on the day he was born, and on the day he dies, and on the day he is raised to life.

16. And mention Marium in the Book when she drew aside from her family to an eastern place;

17. So she took a veil (to screen herself) from them; then We sent to her Our spirit, and there appeared to her a well-made man.

18. She said: Surely I fly for refuge from you to the Beneficent God, if you are one guarding (against evil).

19. He said: I am only a messenger of your Lord: That I will give you a pure boy.

20. She said: When shall I have a boy and no mortal has yet touched me, nor have I been unchaste?

21. He said: Even so; your Lord says: It is easy to Me: and that We may make him a sign to men and a mercy from Us; and it is a matter which has been decreed.

22. So she conceived him; then withdrew herself with him to a remote place.

23. And the throes (of childbirth) compelled her to betake herself to the trunk of a palm tree. She said: Oh, would that I had died before this, and had been a thing quite forgotten!

24. Then (the child) called out to her from beneath her: Grieve not, surely your Lord has made a stream to flow beneath you;

25. And shake towards you the trunk of the palmtree, it will drop on you fresh ripe dates:

26. So eat and drink and refresh the eye. Then if you see any mortal, say: Surely I have vowed a fast to the Beneficent God, so I shall not speak to any man today.

27. And she came to her people with him, carrying him (with her). They said: O Marium! surely you have done a strange thing.

28. O sister of Haroun! your father was not a bad man, nor was your mother an unchaste woman.

29. But she pointed to him. They said: How should we speak to one who was a child in the cradle?

30. He said: Surely I am a servant of Allah; He has given me the Book and made me a prophet;

31. And He has made me blessed wherever I may be, and He has enjoined on me prayer and poor-rate so long as I live;

32. And dutiful to my mother, and He has not made me insolent, unblessed;

33. And peace on me on the day I was born, and on the day I die, and on the day I am raised to life.

34. Such is Isa, son of Marium; (this is) the saying of truth about which they dispute.

35. It beseems not Allah that He should take to Himself a son, glory to be Him; when He has decreed a matter He only says to it "Be," and it is.

36. And surely Allah is my Lord and your Lord, therefore serve Him; this is the right path.

37. But parties from among them disagreed with each other, so woe to those who disbelieve, because of presence on a great day.

38. How clearly shall they hear and how clearly shall they see on the day when they come to Us; but the unjust this day are in manifest error.

39. And warn them of the day of intense regret, when the matter shall have been decided; and they are (now) in negligence and they do not believe.

40. Surely We inherit the earth and all those who are on it, and to Us they shall be returned.

41. And mention Ibrahim in the Book; surely he was a truthful man, a prophet.

42. When he said to his father; O my father! why do you

worship what neither hears nor sees, nor does it avail you in the least:

43. O my father! truly the knowledge has come to me which has not come to you, therefore follow me, I will guide you on a right path:

44. O my father! serve not the Shaitan, surely the Shaitan is disobedient to the Beneficent God:

45. O my father! surely I fear that a punishment from the Beneficent God should afflict you so that you should be a friend of the Shaitan.

46. He said: Do you dislike my gods, O Ibrahim? If you do not desist I will certainly revile you, and leave me for a time.

47. He said: Peace be on you, I will pray to my Lord to forgive you; surely He is ever Affectionate to me:

48. And I will withdraw from you and what you call on besides Allah, and I will call upon my Lord; may be I shall not remain unblessed in calling upon my Lord.

49. So when he withdrew from them and what they worshipped besides Allah, We gave to him Ishaq and Yaqoub, and each one of them We made a prophet.

50. And We granted to them of Our mercy, and We left (behind them) a truthful mention of eminence for them.

51. And mention Musa in the Book; surely he was one purified, and he was an apostle, a prophet.

52. And We called to him from the blessed side of the mountain, and We made him draw nigh, holding communion (with Us).

53. And We gave to him out of Our mercy his brother Haroun a prophet.

54. And mention Ismail in the Book; surely he was truthful in (his) promise, and he was an apostle, a prophet.

55. And he enjoined on his family prayer and almsgiving, and was one in whom his Lord was well pleased.

56. And mention Idris in the Book; surely he was a truthful man, a prophet,

57. And We raised him high in Heaven.

58. These are they on whom Allah bestowed favors, from among the prophets of the seed of Adam, and of those whom We carried with Nuh, and of the seed of Ibrahim and Israel, and of those whom We guided and chose; when the communications of the Beneficent God were recited to them, they fell down making obeisance and weeping.

59. But there came after them an evil generation, who neg-

lected prayers and followed and sensual desires, so they will meet perdition,

60. Except such as repent and believe and do good, these shall enter the garden, and they shall not be dealt with unjustly in any way:

61. The gardens of perpetuity which the Beneficent God has promised to His servants while unseen; surely His promise shall come to pass.

62. They shall not hear therein any vain discourse, but only: Peace, and they shall have their sustenance therein morning and evening.

63. This is the garden which We cause those of Our servants to inherit who guard (against evil).

64. And we do not descend but by the command of your Lord; to Him belongs whatever is before us and whatever is behind us and whatever is between these, and your Lord is not forgetful.

65. The Lord of the heavens and the earth and what is between them, so serve Him and be patient in His service. Do you know any one equal to Him?

66. And says man: What! when I am dead shall I truly be brought forth alive?

67. Does not man remember that We created him before, when he was nothing?

68. So by your Lord! We will most certainly gather them together and the Shaitans, then shall We certainly cause them to be present round hell on their knees.

69. Then We will most certainly draw forth from every sect of them him who is most exorbitantly rebellious against the Beneficent God.

70. Again We do certainly know best those who deserve most to be burned therein.

71. And there is not one of you but shall come to it; this is an unavoidable decree of your Lord.

72. And We will deliver those who guarded (against evil), and We will leave the unjust therein on their knees.

73. And when Our clear communications are recited to them, those who disbelieve say to those who believe: Which of the two parties is best in abiding and best in assembly?

74. And how many of the generations have We destroyed before them who were better in respect of goods and outward appearance!

75. Say: As for him who remains in error, the Beneficent God will surely prolong his length of days, until they see what they were threatened with, either the punishment or the hour; then they shall know who is in more evil plight and weaker in forces.

76. And Allah increases in guidance those who go aright; and ever-abiding good works are with your Lord best in recompense and best in yielding fruit.

77. Have you, then, seen him who disbelieves in Our communications and says: I shall certainly be given wealth and children?

78. Has he gained knowledge of the unseen, or made a covenant with the Beneficent God?

79. By no means! We write down what he says, and We will lengthen to him the length of the chastisement,

80. And We will inherit of him what he says, and he shall come to Us alone.

81. And they have taken gods besides Allah, that they should be to them a source of strength;

82. By no means! They shall soon deny their worshipping them, and they shall be adversaries to them.

83. Do you not see that We have sent the Shaitans against the unbelievers, inciting them by incitement?

84. Therefore be not in haste against them, We only number out to them a number (of days).

85. The day on which We will gather those who guard (against evil) to the Beneficent God to receive honors,

86. And We will drive the guilty to hell thirsty.

87. They shall not control intercession, save he who has made a covenant with the Beneficent God.

88. And they say: The Beneficent God has taken (to Himself) a son.

89. Certainly you have made an abominable assertion:

90. The heavens may almost be rent thereat, and the earth cleave asunder, and the mountains fall down in pieces,

91. That they ascribe a son to the Beneficent God.

92. And it is not worthy of the Beneficent God that He should take (to Himself) a son.

93. There is no one in the heavens and the earth but will come to the Beneficent God as a servant.

94. Certainly He has a comprehensive knowledge of them, and He has numbered them a (comprehensive) numbering.

95. And every one of them will come to Him on the day of resurrection alone.

96. Surely (as for) those who believe and do good deeds for them will Allah bring about love.

97. So We have only made it easy in your tongue that you may give good news thereby to those who guard (against evil) and warn thereby a vehemently contentious people.

98. And how many a generation have We destroyed before them! Do you see any one of them or hear a sound of them?

TA HA

In the name of Allah, the Beneficent, the Merciful.

1. Ta Ha.

2. We have not revealed the Quran to you that you may be unsuccessful.

3. Nay, it is a reminder to him who fears:

4. A revelation from Him Who created the earth and the high heavens.

5. The Beneficent God is firm in power.

6. His is what is in the heavens and what is in the earth and what is between them two and what is beneath the ground.

7. And if you utter the saying aloud, then surely He knows the secret, and what is yet more hidden.

8. Allah—there is no god but He; His are the very best names.

9. And has the story of Musa come to you?

10. When he saw fire, he said to his family: Stop, for surely I see a fire, haply I may bring to you therefrom a live coal or find a guidance at the fire.

11. So when he came to it, a voice was uttered: O Musa:

12. Surely I am your Lord, therefore put off your shoes; surely you are in the sacred valley, Tuwa,

13. And I have chosen you, so listen to what is revealed:

14. Surely I am Allah, there is no god but I, therefore serve Me and keep up prayer for My remembrance:

15. Surely the hour is coming—I am about to make it manifest—so that every soul may be rewarded as it strives:

16. Therefore let not him who believes not in it and follows his low desires turn you away from it so that you should perish;

17. And what is this in your right hand, O Musa!

18. He said: This is my staff: I recline on it and I beat the leaves with it to make them fall upon my sheep, and I have other uses for it.

19. He said: Cast it down, O Musa!

20. So he cast it down; and lo! it was a serpent running.

21. He said: Take hold of it and fear not; We will restore it to its former state:

22. And press your hand to your side, it shall come out white without evil: another sign:

23. That We may show you of Our greater signs:

24. Go to Firon, surely he has exceeded all limits.

25. He said: O my Lord! Expand my breast for me,

26. And make my affair easy to me,

27. And loose the knot from my tongue,

28. (That) they may understand my word;

29. And give to me an aider from my family:

30. Haroun, my brother,

31. Strengthen my back by him,

32. And associate him (with me) in my affair,

33. So that we should glorify Thee much,

34. And remember Thee oft.

35. Surely, Thou art seeing us.

36. He said: You are indeed granted your petition, O Musa;

37. And certainly We bestowed on you a favor at another time;

38. When We revealed to your mother what was revealed;

39. Saying: Put him into a chest, then cast it down into the river, then the river shall throw him on the shore; there shall take him up one who is an enemy to Me and enemy to him; and I cast down upon you love from Me, and that you might be brought up before My eyes;

40. When your sister went and said: Shall I direct you to one who will take charge of him? So We brought you back to your mother, that her eye might be cooled and she should not grieve; and you killed a man, then We delivered you from the grief, and We tried you with (a severe) trying. Then you stayed for years among the people of Madyan; then you came hither as ordained, O Musa.

41. And I have chosen you for Myself:

42. Go you and your brother with My communications and be not remiss in remembering Me;

43. Go both to Firon, surely he has become inordinate;

44. Then speak to him a gentle word haply he may mind or fear.

45. Both said: O our Lord! Surely we fear that he may hasten to do evil to us or that he may become inordinate.

46. He said: Fear not, surely I am with you both: I do hear and see.

47. So go you both to him and say: Surely we are two apostles of your Lord; therefore send the children of Israel with us and do not torment them! Indeed we have brought to you a communication from your Lord, and peace is on him who follows the guidance;

48. Surely it has been revealed to us that the chastisement will surely come upon him who rejects and turns back.

49. (Firon) said: And who is your Lord, O Musa?

50. He said: Our Lord is He Who gave to everything its creation, then guided it (to its goal).

51. He said: Then what is the state of the former generations?

52. He said: The knowledge thereof is with my Lord in a book; my Lord errs not, nor does He forget;

53. Who made the earth for you an expanse and made for you therein paths and sent down water from the cloud; then thereby We have brought forth many species of various herbs.

54. Eat and pasture your cattle; most surely there are signs in this for those endowed with understanding.

55. From it We created you and into it We shall send you back and from it will We raise you a second time.

56. And truly We showed him Our signs, all of them, but he rejected and refused.

57. Said he: Have you come to us that you should turn us out of our land by your magic, O Musa?

58. So we too will produce before you magic like it, therefore make between us and you an appointment, which we should not break, (neither) we nor you, (in) a central place.

59. (Musa) said: Your appointment is the day of the Festival and let the people be gathered together in the early forenoon.

60. So Firon turned his back and settled his plan, then came.

61. Musa said to them: Woe to you! do not forge a lie against Allah, lest He destroy you by a punishment, and he who forges (a lie) indeed fails to attain (his desire).

62. So they disputed with one another about their affair and kept the discourse secret.

63. They said: These are most surely two magicians who wish to turn you out from your land by their magic and to take away your best traditions.

64. Therefore settle your plan, then come standing in ranks, and he will prosper indeed this day who overcomes.

65. They said: O Musa! will you cast, or shall we be the first who cast down?

66. He said: Nay! cast down. then lo! their cords and their rods—it was imaged to him on account of their magic as if they were running.

67. So Musa conceived in his mind a fear.

68. We said: Fear not, surely you shall be the uppermost,

69. And cast down what is in your right hand; it shall devour what they have wrought; they have wrought only the plan of a magician, and the magician shall not be successful wheresoever he may come from.

70. And the magicians were cast down making obeisance; they said: We believe in the Lord of Haroun and Musa.

71. (Firon) said: You believe in him before I give you leave; most surely he is the chief of you who taught you enchantment, therefore I will certainly cut off your hands and your feet on opposite sides, and I will certainly crucify you on the trunks of the palm trees, and certainly you will come to know which of us is the more severe and the more abiding in chastising.

72. They said: We do not prefer you to what has come to us of clear arguments and to He Who made us, therefore decide what you are going to decide; you can only decide about this world's life.

73. Surely we believe in our Lord that He may forgive us our sins and the magic to which you compelled us; and Allah is better and more abiding.

74. Whoever comes to his Lord (being) guilty, for him is surely hell; he shall not die therein, nor shall he live.

75. And whoever comes to Him a believer (and) he has done good deeds indeed, these it is who shall have the high ranks,

76. The gardens of perpetuity, beneath which rivers flow, to abide therein; and this is the reward of him who has purified himself.

77. And certainly We revealed to Musa, saying: Travel by

night with My servants, then make for them a dry path in the sea, not fearing to be overtaken, nor being afraid.

78. And Firon followed them with his armies, so there came upon them of the sea that which came upon them.

79. And Firon led astray his people and he did not guide (them) aright.

80. O children of Israel! indeed We delivered you from your enemy, and We made a covenant with you on the blessed side of the mountain, and We sent to you the manna and the quails.

81. Eat of the good things We have given you for sustenance, and be not inordinate with respect to them, lest My wrath should be due to you, and to whomsoever My wrath is due he shall perish indeed.

82. And most surely I am most Forgiving to him who repents and believes and does good, then continues to follow the right direction.

83. And what caused you to hasten from your people, O Musa?

84. He said: They are here on my track and I hastened on to Thee, my Lord, that Thou mightest be pleased.

85. He said: So surely We have tried your people after you, and the Samiri has led them astray.

86. So Musa returned to his people wrathful, sorrowing. Said he: O my people! did not your Lord promise you a goodly promise: did then the time seem long to you, or did you wish that displeasure from your Lord should be due to you, so that you broke (your) promise to me?

87. They said: We did not break (our) promise to you of our own accord, but we were made to bear the burdens of the ornaments of the people, then we made a casting of them, and thus did the Samiri suggest.

88. So he brought forth for them a calf, a (mere) body, which had a mooing sound, so they said: This is your god and the god of Musa, but he forgot.

89. What! could they not see that it did not return to them a reply, and (that) it did not control any harm or benefit for them?

90. And certainly Haroun had said to them before: O my people! you are only tried by it, and surely your Lord is the Beneficent God, therefore follow me and obey my order.

91. They said: We will by no means cease to keep to its worship until Musa returns to us.

92. (Musa) said: O Haroun! what prevented you, when you saw them going astray,

93. So that you did not follow me? Did you then disobey my order?

94. He said: O son of my mother! seize me not by my beard nor by my head; surely I was afraid lest you should say: You have caused a division among the children of Israel and not waited for my word.

95. He said: What was then your object, O Samiri?

96. He said: I saw (Jibreel) what they did not see, so I took a handful (of the dust) from the footsteps of the messenger, then I threw it in the casting; thus did my soul commend to me.

97. He said: Begone then, surely for you it will be in this life to say, Touch (me) not; and surely there is a threat for you, which shall not be made to fail to you, and look at your god to whose worship you kept (so long); we will certainly burn it, then we will certainly scatter it a (wide) scattering in the sea.

98. Your God is only Allah, there is no god but He; He comprehends all things in (His) knowledge.

99. Thus do We relate to you (some) of the news of what has gone before; and indeed We have given to you a Reminder from Ourselves.

100. Whoever turns aside from it, he shall surely bear a burden on the day of resurrection,

101. Abiding in this (state), and evil will it be for them to bear on the day of resurrection;

102. On the day when the trumpet shall be blown, and We will gather the guilty, blue-eyed, on that day;

103. They shall consult together secretly: You did tarry but ten (centuries).

104. We know best what they say, when the fairest of them in course would say: You tarried but a day.

105. And they ask you about the mountains. Say: My Lord will carry them away from the roots.

106. Then leave it a plain, smooth level;

107. You shall not see therein any crookedness or unevenness.

108. On that day they shall follow the inviter, there is no crookedness in him, and the voices shall be low before the Beneficent God so that you shall not hear aught but a soft sound.

109. On that day shall no intercession avail except of him

whom the Beneficent God allows and whose word He is pleased with.

110. He knows what is before them and what is behind them, while they do not comprehend it in knowledge.

111. And the faces shall be humbled before the Living, the Self-subsistent God, and he who bears iniquity is indeed a failure.

112. And whoever does good works and he is a believer, he shall have no fear of injustice nor of the withholding of his due.

113. And thus have We sent it down an Arabic Quran, and have distinctly set forth therein of threats that they may guard (against evil) or that it may produce a reminder for them.

114. Supremely exalted is therefore Allah, the King, the Truth; and do not make haste with the Quran before its revelation is made complete to you and say: O my Lord! increase me in knowledge.

115. And certainly We gave a commandment to Adam before, but he forgot; and We did not find in him any determination.

116. And when We said to the angels: Make obeisance to Adam, they made obeisance, but Iblis (did it not); he refused.

117. So We said: O Adam! This is an enemy to you and to your wife; therefore let him not drive you both forth from the garden so that you should be unhappy;

118. Surely it is (ordained) for you that you shall not be hungry therein nor bare of clothing;

119. And that you shall not be thirsty therein nor shall you feel the heat of the sun.

120. But the Shaitan made an evil suggestion to him; he said: O Adam! Shall I guide you to the tree of immortality and a kingdom which decays not?

121. Then they both ate of it, so their evil inclinations became manifest to them, and they both began to cover themselves with leaves of the garden, and Adam disobeyed his Lord, so his life became evil (to him).

122. Then his Lord chose him, so He turned to him and guided (him).

123. He said: Get forth you two therefrom, all (of you), one of you (is) enemy to another. So there will surely come to you guidance from Me, then whoever follows My guidance, he shall not go astray nor be unhappy;

124. And whoever turns away from My reminder, his shall

surely be a straitened life, and We will raise him on the day of resurrection, blind.

125. He shall say: My Lord! why hast Thou raised me blind, and I was a seeing one indeed?

126. He will say: Even so, Our communications came to you, but you neglected them; even thus shall you be forsaken this day.

127. And thus do We recompense him who is extravagant and does not believe in the communications of his Lord; and certainly the chastisement of the hereafter is severer and more lasting.

128. Does it not then direct them aright how many of the generations in whose dwelling-places they go about We destroyed before them? Most surely there are signs in this for those endowed with understanding.

129. And had there not been a word (that had) already gone forth from your Lord and an appointed term, it would surely have been made to cleave (to them).

130. Bear then patiently what they say, and glorify your Lord by the praising of Him before the rising of the sun and before its setting, and during hours of the night do also glorify (Him) and during parts of the day, that you may be well pleased.

131. And do not stretch your eyes after that with which We have provided different classes of them, (of) the splendor of this world's life, that We may thereby try them; and the sustenance (given) by your Lord is better and more abiding.

132. And enjoin prayer on your followers, and steadily adhere to it; We do not ask you for subsistence; We do give you subsistence, and the (good) end is for guarding (against evil).

133. And they say: Why does he not bring to us a sign from his Lord? Has not there come to them a clear evidence of what is in the previous books?

134. And had We destroyed them with chastisement before this, they would certainly have said: O our Lord! why didst Thou not send to us an apostle, for then we should have followed Thy communications before that we met disgrace and shame.

135. Say: Every one (of us) is awaiting, therefore do await: So you will come to know who is the follower of the even path and who goes aright.

THE PROPHETS

In the name of Allah, the Beneficent, the Merciful.

1. Their reckoning has drawn near to men, and in heedlessness are they turning aside.

2. There comes not to them a new reminder from their Lord but they hear it while they sport,

3. Their hearts trifling; and those who are unjust counsel together in secret: He is nothing but a mortal like yourselves; what! will you then yield to enchantment while you see?

4. He said: My Lord knows what is spoken in the heaven and the earth, and He is the Hearing, the Knowing.

5. Nay! say they: Medleys of dreams; nay! he has forged it; nay! he is a poet; so let him bring to us a sign as the former (prophets) were sent (with).

6. There did not believe before them any town which We destroyed; will they then believe?

7. And We did not send before you any but men to whom We sent revelation, so ask the followers of the reminder if you do not know.

8. And We did not make them bodies not eating the food, and they were not to abide (forever).

9. Then We made Our promise good to them, so We delivered them and those whom We pleased, and We destroyed the extravagant.

10. Certainly We have revealed to you a Book in which is your good remembrance; what! do you not then understand?

11. And how many a town which was iniquitous did We demolish, and We raised up after it another people!

12. So when they felt Our punishment, lo! they began to fly from it.

13. Do not fly (now) and come back to what you were made to lead easy lives in and to your dwellings, haply you will be questioned.

14. They said: O woe to us! surely we were unjust.

15. And this ceased not to be their cry till We made them cut off, extinct.

16. And We did not create the heaven and the earth and what is between them for sport.

17. Had We wished to make a diversion, We would have made it from before Ourselves: by no means would We do (it).

18. Nay! We cast the truth against the falsehood, so that it breaks its head, and lo! it vanishes; and woe to you for what you describe;

19. And whoever is in the heavens and the earth is His; and those who are with Him are not proud to serve Him, nor do they grow weary.

20. They glorify (Him) by night and day; they are never languid.

21. Or have they taken gods from the earth who raise (the dead).

22. If there had been in them any gods except Allah, they would both have certainly been in a state of disorder; therefore glory be to Allah, the Lord of the dominion, above what they attribute (to Him).

23. He cannot be questioned concerning what He does and they shall be questioned.

24. Or, have they taken gods besides Him? Say: Bring your proof; this is the reminder of those with me and the reminder of those before me. Nay! most of them do not know the truth, so they turn aside.

25. And We did not send before you any apostle but We revealed to him that there is no god but Me, therefore serve Me.

26. And they say: The Beneficent God has taken to Himself a son. Glory be to Him. Nay! they are honored servants;

27. They do not precede Him in speech and (only) according to His commandment do they act.

28. He knows what is before them and what is behind them, and they do not intercede except for him whom He approves, and for fear of Him they tremble.

29. And whoever of them should say: Surely I am a god besides Him, such a one do We recompense with hell; thus do We recompense the unjust.

30. Do not those who disbelieve see that the heavens and the earth were closed up, but We have opened them; and We have made of water everything living, will they not then believe?

31. And We have made great mountains in the earth lest it might be convulsed with them, and We have made in it wide ways that they may follow a right direction.

32. And We have made the heaven a guarded canopy and (yet) they turn aside from its signs.

33. And He it is Who created the night and the day and the sun and the moon; all (orbs) travel along swiftly in their celestial spheres.

34. And We did not ordain abiding for any mortal before you. What! Then if you die, will they abide?

35. Every soul must taste of death and We try you by evil and good by way of probation; and to Us you shall be brought back.

36. And when those who disbelieve see you, they do not take you but for one to be scoffed at: Is this he who speaks of your gods? And they are deniers at the mention of the Beneficent God.

37. Man is created of haste; now will I show to you My signs, therefore do not ask Me to hasten (them) on.

38. And they say: When will this threat come to pass if you are truthful?

39. Had those who disbelieve but known (of the time) when they shall not be able to ward off the fire from their faces nor from their backs, nor shall they be helped.

40. Nay, it shall come on them all of a sudden and cause them to become confounded, so they shall not have the power to avert it, nor shall they be respited.

41. And certainly apostles before you were scoffed at, then there befell those of them who scoffed that at which they had scoffed.

42. Say: Who guards you by night and by day from the Beneficent God? Nay, they turn aside at the mention of their Lord.

43. Or, have they gods who can defend them against Us? They shall not be able to assist themselves, nor shall they be defended from Us.

44. Nay, We gave provision to these and their fathers until life was prolonged to them. Do they not then see that We are visiting the land, curtailing it of its sides? Shall they then prevail?

45. Say: I warn you only by revelation; and the deaf do not hear the call whenever they are warned.

46. And if a blast of the chastisement of your Lord were to touch them, they will certainly say: O woe to us! surely we were unjust.

47. And We will set up a just balance on the day of resurrection, so no soul shall be dealt with unjustly in the least; and though there be the weight of a grain of mustard seed, (yet) will We bring it, and sufficient are We to take account.

48. And certainly We gave to Musa and Haroun the Furqan and a light and a reminder for those who would guard (against evil).

49. (For) those who fear their Lord in secret and they are fearful of the hour.

50. And this is a blessed Reminder which We have revealed; will you then deny it?

51. And certainly We gave to Ibrahim his rectitude before, and We knew him fully well.

52. When he said to his father and his people: What are these images to whose worship you cleave?

53. They said: We found our fathers worshipping them.

54. He said: Certainly you have been, (both) you and your fathers, in manifest error.

55. They said: Have you brought to us the truth, or are you one of the triflers?

56. He said: Nay! your Lord is the Lord of the heavens and the earth, Who brought them into existence, and I am of those who bear witness to this:

57. And, by Allah! I will certainly do something against your idols after you go away, turning back.

58. So he broke them into pieces, except the chief of them, that haply they may return to it.

59. They said: Who has done this to our gods? Most surely he is one of the unjust.

60. They said: We heard a youth called Ibrahim speak of them.

61. Said they: Then bring him before the eyes of the people, perhaps they may bear witness.

62. They said: Have you done this to our gods, O Ibrahim?

63. He said: Surely (some doer) has done it; the chief of them is this, therefore ask them, if they can speak.

64. Then they turned to themselves and said: Surely you yourselves are the unjust;

65. Then they were made to hang down their heads: Certainly you know that they do not speak.

66. He said: What! do you then serve besides Allah what brings you not any benefit at all, nor does it harm you?

67. Fie on you and on what you serve besides Allah; what! do you not then understand?

68. They said: Burn him and help your gods, if you are going to do (anything).

69. We said: O fire! be a comfort and peace to Ibrahim;

70. And they desired a war on him, but We made them the greatest losers.

71. And We delivered him as well as Lut (removing them) to the land which We had blessed for all people.

72. And We gave him Ishaq and Yaqoub, a son's son, and We made (them) all good.

73. And We made them Imams who guided (people) by Our command, and We revealed to them the doing of good and the keeping up of prayer and the giving of the alms, and Us (alone) did they serve;

74. And (as for) Lut, We gave him wisdom and knowledge, and We delivered him from the town which wrought abominations; surely they were an evil people, transgressors;

75. And We took him into Our mercy; surely he was of the good.

76. And Nuh, when he cried aforetime, so We answered him, and delivered him and his followers from the great calamity.

77. And We helped him against the people who rejected Our communications; surely they were an evil people, so We drowned them all.

78. And Dawood and Sulaiman when they gave judgment concerning the field when the people's sheep pastured therein by night, and We were bearers of witness to their judgment.

79. So We made Sulaiman to understand it; and to each one We gave wisdom and knowledge; and We made the mountains, and the birds to celebrate Our praise with Dawood; and We were the doers.

80. And We taught him the making of coats of mail for you, that they might protect you in your wars; will you then be grateful?

81. And (We made subservient) to Sulaiman the wind blowing violent, pursuing its course by his command to the land which We had blessed, and We are knower of all things.

82. And of the rebellious people there were those who dived for him and did other work besides that, and We kept guard over them;

83. And Ayub, when he cried to his Lord, (saying): Harm has afflicted me, and Thou art the most Merciful of the merciful.

84. Therefore We responded to him and took off what harm he had, and We gave him his family and the like of them with them: a mercy from Us and a reminder to the worshippers.

85. And Ismail and Idris and Zulkifl; all were of the patient ones;

86. And We caused them to enter into Our mercy; surely they were of the good ones.

87. And Yunus, when he went away in wrath, so he thought that We would not straiten him, so he called out among afflictions: There is no god but Thou, glory be to Thee; surely I am of those who make themselves to suffer loss.

88. So We responded to him and delivered him from the grief, and thus do We deliver the believers.

89. And Zakariya, when he cried to his Lord: O my Lord! leave me not alone; and Thou art the best of inheritors.

90. So We responded to him and gave him Yahya and made his wife fit for him; surely they used to hasten, one with another, in deeds of goodness and to call upon Us, hoping and fearing; and they were humble before Us.

91. And she who guarded her chastity, so We breathed into her of Our inspiration and made her and her son a sign for the nations.

92. Surely this Islam is your religion, one religion (only), and I am your Lord, therefore serve Me.

93. And they broke their religion (into sects) between them: to Us shall all come back.

94. Therefore whoever shall do of good deeds and he is a believer, there shall be no denying of his exertion, and surely We will write (it) down for him.

95. And it is binding on a town which We destroy that they shall not return.

96. Even when Gog and Magog are let loose and they shall break forth from every elevated place.

97. And the true promise shall draw nigh, then lo! the eyes of those who disbelieved shall be fixedly open: O woe to us! surely we were in a state of heedlessness as to this; nay, we were unjust.

98. Surely you and what you worship besides Allah are the firewood of hell; to it you shall come.

99. Had these been gods, they would not have come to it and all shall abide therein.

100. For them therein shall be groaning and therein they shall not hear.

101. Surely (as for) those for whom the good has already gone forth from Us, they shall be kept far off from it;

102. They will not hear its faintest sound, and they shall abide in that which their souls long for.

103. The great fearful event shall not grieve them, and the angels shall meet them: This is your day which you were promised.

104. On the day when We will roll up heaven like the rolling up of the scroll for writings; as We originated the first creation, (so) We shall reproduce it; a promise (binding on Us); surely We will bring it about.

105. And certainly We wrote in the Book after the reminder that (as for) the land, My righteous servants shall inherit it.

106. Most surely in this is a message to a people who serve (Us).

107. And We have not sent you but as a mercy to the worlds.

108. Say: It is only revealed to me that your God is one God; will you then submit?

109. But if they turn back, say: I have given you warning in fairness and I do not know whether what you are threatened with is near or far:

110. Surely He knows what is spoken openly and He knows what you hide:

111. And I do not know if this may be a trial for you and a provision till a time.

112. He said: O my Lord! judge Thou with truth; and our Lord is the Beneficent God, Whose help is sought against what you ascribe (to Him).

THE PILGRIMAGE

In the name of Allah, the Beneficent, the Merciful.

1. O people! guard against (the punishment from) your Lord; surely the violence of the hour is a grievous thing.

2. On the day when you shall see it, every woman giving suck shall quit in confusion what she suckled, and every pregnant woman shall lay down her burden, and you shall see men intoxicated, and they shall not be intoxicated but the chastisement of Allah will be severe.

3. And among men there is he who disputes about Allah without knowledge and follows every rebellious Shaitan;

4. Against him it is written down that whoever takes him for a friend, he shall lead him astray and conduct him to the chastisement of the burning fire.

5. O people! if you are in doubt about the raising, then surely We created you from dust, then from a small seed, then from a clot, then from a lump of flesh, complete in make and incomplete, that We may make clear to you; and We cause what We please to stay in the wombs till an appointed time, then We bring you forth as babies, then that you may attain your maturity; and of you is he who is caused to die, and of you is he who is brought back to the worst part of life, so that after having knowledge he does not know anything; and you see the earth sterile land, but when We send down on it the water, it stirs and swells and brings forth of every kind a beautiful herbage.

6. This is because Allah is the Truth and because He gives life to the dead and because He has power over all things,

7. And because the hour is coming, there is no doubt about it; and because Allah shall raise up those who are in the graves.

8. And among men there is he who disputes about Allah without knowledge and without guidance and without an illuminating book,

9. Turning away haughtily that he may lead (others) astray from the way of Allah; for him is disgrace in this world, and on the day of resurrection We will make him taste the punishment of burning:

10. This is due to what your two hands have sent before, and because Allah is not in the least unjust to the servants.

11. And among men is he who serves Allah (standing) on the verge, so that if good befalls him he is satisfied therewith, but if a trial afflict him he turns back headlong; he loses this world as well as the hereafter; that is a manifest loss.

12. He calls besides Allah upon that which does not harm him and that which does not profit him; that is the great straying.

13. He calls upon him whose harm is nearer than his profit; evil certainly is the guardian and evil certainly is the associate.

14. Surely Allah will cause those who believe and do good deeds to enter gardens beneath which rivers flow; surely Allah does what He pleases.

15. Whoever thinks that Allah will not assist him in this life

and the hereafter, let him stretch a rope to the ceiling, then let him cut (it) off, then let him see if his struggle will take away that at which he is enraged.

16. And thus have We revealed it, being clear arguments, and because Allah guides whom He intends.

17. Surely those who believe and those who are Jews and the Sabeans and the Christians and the Magians and those who associate (others with Allah)—surely Allah will decide between them on the day of resurrection; surely Allah is a witness over all things.

18. Do you not see that Allah is He, Whom obeys whoever is in the heavens and whoever is in the earth, and the sun and the moon and the stars, and the mountains and the trees, and the animals and many of the people; and many there are against whom chastisement has become necessary; and whomsoever Allah abases, there is none who can make him honorable; surely Allah does what He pleases.

19. These are two adversaries who dispute about their Lord; then (as to) those who disbelieve, for them are cut out garments of fire; boiling water shall be poured over their heads.

20. With it shall be melted what is in their bellies and (their) skins as well.

21. And for them are whips of iron.

22. Whenever they will desire to go forth from it, from grief, they shall be turned back into it, and taste the chastisement of burning.

23. Surely Allah will make those who believe and do good deeds enter gardens beneath which rivers flow; they shall be adorned therein with bracelets of gold and (with) pearls, and their garments therein shall be of silk.

24. And they are guided to goodly words and they are guided into the path of the Praised One.

25. Surely (as for) those who disbelieve, and hinder (men) from Allah's way and from the Sacred Mosque which We have made equally for all men, (for) the dweller therein and (for) the visitor, and whoever shall incline therein to wrong unjustly, We will make him taste of a painful chastisement.

26. And when We assigned to Ibrahim the place of the House, saying: Do not associate with Me aught, and purify My House for those who make the circuit and stand to pray and bow and prostrate themselves.

27. And proclaim among men the Pilgrimage: they will come to you on foot and on every lean camel, coming from every remote path,

28. That they may witness advantages for them and mention the name of Allah during stated days over what He has given them of the cattle quadrupeds, then eat of them and feed the distressed one, the needy.

29. Then let them accomplish their needful acts of shaving and cleansing, and let them fulfil their vows and let them go round the Ancient House.

30. That (shall be so); and whoever respects the sacred ordinances of Allah, it is better for him with his Lord; and the cattle are made lawful for you, except that which is recited to you, therefore avoid the uncleanness of the idols and avoid false words,

31. Being upright for Allah, not associating aught with Him and whoever associates (others) with Allah, it is as though he had fallen from on high, then the birds snatch him away or the wind carries him off to a far-distant place.

32. That (shall be so); and whoever respects the signs of Allah, this surely is (the outcome) of the piety of hearts.

33. You have advantages in them till a fixed time, then their place of sacrifice is the Ancient House.

34. And to every nation We appointed acts of devotion that they may mention the name of Allah on what He has given them of the cattle quadrupeds; so your God is One God, therefore to Him should you submit, and give good news to the humble,

35. (To) those whose hearts tremble when Allah is mentioned, and those who are patient under that which afflicts them, and those who keep up prayer, and spend (benevolently) out of what We have given them.

36. And (as for) the camels, We have made them of the signs of the religion of Allah for you; for you therein is much good; therefore mention the name of Allah on them as they stand in a row, then when they fall down eat of them and feed the poor man who is contented and the beggar; thus have We made them subservient to you, that you may be grateful.

37. There does not reach Allah their flesh nor their blood, but to Him is acceptable the guarding (against evil) on your part; thus has He made them subservient to you, that you may magnify Allah because He has guided you aright; and give good news to those who do good (to others).

38. Surely Allah will defend those who believe; surely Allah does not love any one who is unfaithful, ungrateful.

39. Permission (to fight) is given to those upon whom war is made because they are oppressed, and most surely Allah is well able to assist them;

40. Those who have been expelled from their homes without a just cause except that they say: Our Lord is Allah. And had there not been Allah's repelling some people by others, certainly there would have been pulled down cloisters and churches and synagogues and mosques in which Allah's name is much remembered; and surely Allah will help him who helps His cause; most surely Allah is Strong, Mighty.

41. Those who, should We establish them in the land, will keep up prayer and pay the poor-rate and enjoin good and forbid evil; and Allah's is the end of affairs.

42. And if they reject you, then already before you did the people of Nuh and Ad and Samood reject (prophets).

43. And the people of Ibrahim and the people of Lut,

44. As well as those of Madyan and Musa (too) was rejected, but I gave respite to the unbelievers, then did I overtake them, so how (severe) was My disapproval.

45. So how many a town did We destroy while it was unjust, so it was fallen down upon its roofs, and (how many a) deserted well and palace raised high.

46. Have they not travelled in the land so that they should have hearts with which to understand, or ears with which to hear? For surely it is not the eyes that are blind, but blind are the hearts which are in the breasts.

47. And they ask you to hasten on the punishment, and Allah will by no means fail in His promise, and surely a day with your Lord is as a thousand years of what you number.

48. And how many a town to which I gave respite while it was unjust, then I overtook it, and to Me is the return.

49. Say: O people! I am only a plain warner to you.

50. Then (as for) those who believe and do good, they shall have forgiveness and an honorable sustenance.

51. And (as for) those who strive to oppose Our communications, they shall be the inmates of the flaming fire.

52. And We did not send before you any apostle or prophet, but when he desired, the Shaitan made a suggestion respecting his desire; but Allah annuls that which the Shaitan casts, then does Allah establish His communications, and Allah is Knowing, Wise,

53. So that He may make what the Shaitan casts a trial for those in whose hearts is disease and those whose hearts are hard; and most surely the unjust are in a great opposition,

54. And that those who have been given the knowledge may know that it is the truth from your Lord, so they may believe in it and their hearts may be lowly before it; and most surely Allah is the Guide of those who believe into a right path.

55. And those who disbelieve shall not cease to be in doubt concerning it until the hour overtakes them suddenly, or there comes on them the chastisement of a destructive day.

56. The kingdom on that day shall be Allah's; He will judge between them; so those who believe and do good will be in gardens of bliss.

57. And (as for) those who disbelieve in and reject Our communications, these it is who shall have a disgraceful chastisement.

58. And (as for) those who fly in Allah's way and are then slain or die, Allah will most certainly grant them a goodly sustenance, and most surely Allah is the best Giver of sustenance.

59. He will certainly cause them to enter a place of entrance which they shall be well pleased with; and most surely Allah is Knowing, Forbearing.

60. That (shall be so); and he who retaliates with the like of that with which he has been afflicted and he has been oppressed, Allah will most certainly aid him; most surely Allah is Pardoning, Forgiving.

61. That is because Allah causes the night to enter into the day and causes the day to enter into the night, and because Allah is Hearing, Seeing.

62. That is because Allah is the Truth, and that what they call upon besides Him—that is the falsehood, and because Allah is the High, the Great.

63. Do you not see that Allah sends down water from the cloud so the earth becomes green? Surely Allah is Benignant, Aware.

64. His is whatsoever is in the heavens and whatsoever is in the earth; and most surely Allah is the Self-sufficient, the Praised.

65. Do you not see that Allah has made subservient to you whatsoever is in the earth and the ships running in the sea by His command? And He withholds the heaven from falling on the

earth except with His permission; most surely Allah is Compassionate, Merciful to men.

66. And He it is Who has brought you to life, then He will cause you to die, then bring you to life (again); most surely man is ungrateful.

67. To every nation We appointed acts of devotion which they observe, therefore they should not dispute with you about the matter and call to your Lord; most surely you are on a right way.

68. And if they contend with you, say: Allah best knows what you do.

69. Allah will judge between you on the day of resurrection respecting that in which you differ.

70. Do you not know that Allah knows what is in the heaven and the earth? Surely this is in a book; surely this is easy to Allah.

71. And they serve besides Allah that for which He has not sent any authority, and that of which they have no knowledge; and for the unjust there shall be no helper.

72. And when Our clear communications are recited to them, you will find denial on the faces of those who disbelieve; they almost spring upon those who recite to them Our communications. Say: Shall I inform you of what is worse than this? The fire; Allah has promised it to those who disbelieve; and how evil the resort!

73. O people! a parable is set forth, therefore listen to it; surely those whom you call upon besides Allah cannot create a fly, though they should all gather for it, and should the fly snatch away anything from them, they could not take it back from it; weak are the invoker and the invoked.

74. They have not estimated Allah with the estimation that is due to Him; most surely Allah is Strong, Mighty.

75. Allah chooses messengers from among the angels and from among the men; surely Allah is Hearing, Seeing.

76. He knows what is before them and what is behind them, and to Allah are all affairs turned back.

77. O you who believe! bow down and prostrate yourselves and serve your Lord, and do good that you may succeed.

78. And strive hard in (the way of) Allah, (such) a striving as is due to Him; He has chosen you and has not laid upon you any hardship in religion; the faith of your father Ibrahim; He named

you Muslims before and in this, that the Apostle may be a bearer of witness to you, and you may be bearers of witness to the people; therefore keep up prayer and pay the poor-rate and hold fast by Allah; He is your Guardian; how excellent the Guardian and how excellent the Helper!

THE BELIEVERS

In the name of Allah, the Beneficent, the Merciful.

1. Successful indeed are the believers,
2. Who are humble in their prayers,
3. And who keep aloof from what is vain,
4. And who are givers of poor-rate,
5. And who guard their private parts,
6. Except before their mates or those whom their right hands possess, for they surely are not blameable,
7. But whoever seeks to go beyond that, these are they that exceed the limits;
8. And those who are keepers of their trusts and their covenant,
9. And those who keep a guard on their prayers;
10. These are they who are the heirs,
11. Who shall inherit the Paradise; they shall abide therein.
12. And certainly We created man of an extract of clay,
13. Then We made him a small seed in a firm resting-place,
14. Then We made the seed a clot, then We made the clot a lump of flesh, then We made (in) the lump of flesh bones, then We clothed the bones with flesh, then We caused it to grow into another creation, so blessed be Allah, the best of the creators.
15. Then after that you will most surely die.
16. Then surely on the day of resurrection you shall be raised.
17. And certainly We made above you seven heavens; and never are We heedless of creation.
18. And We send down water from the cloud according to a measure, then We cause it to settle in the earth, and most surely We are able to carry it away.

19. Then We cause to grow thereby gardens of palm trees and grapes for you; you have in them many fruits and from them do you eat;

20. And a tree that grows out of Mount Sinai which produces oil and a condiment for those who eat.

21. And most surely there is a lesson for you in the cattle: We make you to drink of what is in their bellies, and you have in them many advantages and of them you eat,

22. And on them and on the ships you are borne.

23. And certainly We sent Nuh to his people, and he said: O my people! serve Allah, you have no god other than Him; will you not then guard (against evil)?

24. And the chiefs of those who disbelieved from among his people said: He is nothing but a mortal like yourselves who desires that he may have superiority over you, and if Allah had pleased, He could certainly have sent down angels. We have not heard of this among our fathers of yore:

25. He is only a madman, so bear with him for a time.

26. He said: O my Lord! help me against their calling me a liar.

27. So We revealed to him, saying: Make the ark before Our eyes and (according to) Our revelation; and when Our command is given and the valley overflows, take into it of every kind a pair, two, and your followers, except those among them against whom the word has gone forth, and do not speak to Me in respect of those who are unjust; surely they shall be drowned.

28. And when you are firmly seated, you and those with you, in the ark, say: All praise is due to Allah who delivered us from the unjust people:

29. And say: O my Lord! cause me to disembark a blessed alighting, and Thou art the best to cause to alight.

30. Most surely there are signs in this, and most surely We are ever trying (men).

31. Then We raised up after them another generation.

32. So We sent among them an apostle from among them, saying: Serve Allah, you have no god other than Him; will you not then guard (against evil)?

33. And the chiefs of his people who disbelieved and called the meeting of the hereafter a lie, and whom We had given plenty to enjoy in this world's life, said: This is nothing but a mortal like yourselves, eating of what you eat from and drinking of what you drink.

34. And if you obey a mortal like yourselves, then most surely you will be losers:

35. What! does he threaten you that when you are dead and become dust and bones that you shall then be brought forth?

36. Far, far is that which you are threatened with.

37. There is naught but our life in this world; we die and we live and we shall not be raised again.

38. He is naught but a man who has forged a lie against Allah, and we are not going to believe in him.

39. He said: O my Lord! help me against their calling me a liar.

40. He said: In a little while they will most certainly be repenting.

41. So the punishment overtook them in justice, and We made them as rubbish; so away with the unjust people.

42. Then We raised after them other generations.

43. No people can hasten on their doom nor can they postpone (it).

44. Then We sent Our apostles one after another; whenever there came to a people their apostle, they called him a liar, so We made some of them follow others and We made them stories; so away with a people who do not believe!

45. Then We sent Musa and his brother Haroun, with Our communications and a clear authority,

46. To Firon and his chiefs, but they behaved haughtily and they were an insolent people.

47. And they said: What! shall we believe in two mortals like ourselves while their people serve us?

48. So they rejected them and became of those who were destroyed.

49. And certainly We gave Musa the Book that they may follow a right direction.

50. And We made the son of Marium and his mother a sign, and We gave them a shelter on a lofty ground having meadows and springs.

51. O apostles! eat of the good things and do good; surely I know what you do.

52. And surely this your religion is one religion and I am your Lord, therefore be careful (of your duty) to Me.

53. But they cut off their religion among themselves into sects, each part rejoicing in that which is with them.

54. Therefore leave them in their overwhelming ignorance till a time.

55. Do they think that by what We aid them with of wealth and children,

56. We are hastening to them of good things? Nay, they do not perceive.

57. Surely they who from fear of their Lord are cautious,

58. And those who believe in the communications of their Lord,

59. And those who do not associate (aught) with their Lord,

60. And those who give what they give (in alms) while their hearts are full of fear that to their Lord they must return,

61. These hasten to good things and they are foremost in (attaining) them.

62. And We do not lay on any soul a burden except to the extent of its ability, and with Us is a book which speaks the truth, and they shall not be dealt with unjustly.

63. Nay, their hearts are in overwhelming ignorance with respect to it and they have besides this other deeds which they do.

64. Until when We overtake those who lead easy lives among them with punishment, lo! they cry for succor.

65. Cry not for succor this day; surely you shall not be given help from Us.

66. My communications were indeed recited to you, but you used to turn back on your heels,

67. In arrogance; talking nonsense about the Quran, and left him like one telling fables by night.

68. Is it then that they do not ponder over what is said, or is it that there has come to them that which did not come to their fathers of old?

69. Or is it that they have not recognized their Apostle, so that they deny him?

70. Or do they say. There is madness in him? Nay! he has brought them the truth, and most of them are averse from the truth.

71. And should the truth follow their low desires, surely the heavens and the earth and all those who are therein would have perished. Nay! We have brought to them their reminder, but from their reminder they turn aside.

72. Or is it that you ask them a recompense? But the recompense of your Lord is best, and He is the best of those who provide sustenance.

73. And most surely you invite them to a right way.

74. And most surely those who do not believe in the hereafter are deviating from the way.

75. And if We show mercy to them and remove the distress they have, they would persist in their inordinacy, blindly wandering on.

76. And already We overtook them with chastisement, but they were not submissive to their Lord, nor do they humble themselves.

77. Until when We open upon them a door of severe chastisement, lo! they are in despair at it.

78. And He it is Who made for you the ears and the eyes and the hearts; little is it that you give thanks.

79. And He it is Who multiplied you in the earth, and to Him you shall be gathered.

80. And He it is Who gives life and causes death, and (in) His (control) is the alternation of the night and the day; do you not then understand?

81. Nay, they say the like of what the ancients said:

82. They say: What! When we are dead and become dust and bones, shall we then be raised?

83. Certainly we are promised this, and (so were) our fathers aforetime; this is naught but stories of those of old.

84. Say: Whose is the earth, and whoever is therein, if you know?

85. They will say: Allah's. Say: Will you not then mind?

86. Say: Who is the Lord of the seven heavens and the Lord of the mighty dominion?

87. They will say: (This is) Allah's. Say: Will you not then guard (against evil)?

88. Say: Who is it in Whose hand is the kingdom of all things and Who gives succor, but against Him Succor is not given, if you do but know?

89. They will say: (This is) Allah's. Say: From whence are you then deceived?

90. Nay! We have brought to them the truth, and most surely they are liars.

91. Never did Allah take to Himself a son, and never was there with him any (other) god—in that case would each god have certainly taken away what he created, and some of them would certainly have overpowered others; glory be to Allah above what they describe!

92. The Knower of the unseen and the seen, so may He be exalted above what they associate (with Him).

93. Say: O my Lord! if Thou shouldst make me see what they are threatened with:

94. My Lord! then place me not with the unjust.

95. And most surely We are well able to make you see what We threaten them with.

96. Repel evil by what is best; We know best what they describe.

97. And say: O my Lord! I seek refuge in Thee from the evil suggestions of the Shaitans;

98. And I seek refuge in Thee! O my Lord! from their presence.

99. Until when death overtakes one of them, he says: Send me back, my Lord, send me back;

100. Haply I may do good in that which I have left. By no means! it is a (mere) word that he speaks; and before them is a barrier until the day they are raised.

101. So when the trumpet is blown, there shall be no ties of relationship between them on that day, nor shall they ask of each other.

102. Then as for him whose good deeds are preponderant, these are the successful.

103. And as for him whose good deeds are light, these are they who shall have lost their souls, abiding in hell.

104. The fire shall scorch their faces, and they therein shall be in severe affliction.

105. Were not My communications recited to you? But you used to reject them.

106. They shall say: O our Lord! our adversity overcame us and we were an erring people:

107. O our Lord! Take us out of it; then if we return (to evil) surely we shall be unjust.

108. He shall say: Go away into it and speak not to Me;

109. Surely there was a party of My servants who said: O our Lord! we believe, so do Thou forgive us and have mercy on us, and Thou art the best of the Merciful ones.

110. But you took them for a mockery until they made you forget My remembrance and you used to laugh at them.

111. Surely I have rewarded them this day because they were patient, that they are the achievers.

112. He will say: How many years did you tarry in the earth?

113. They will say: We tarried a day or part of a day, but ask those who keep account.

114. He will say: You did tarry but a little—had you but known (it):

115. What! did you then think that We had created you in vain and that you shall not be returned to Us?

116. So exalted be Allah, the True King; no god is there but He, the Lord of the honorable dominion.

117. And whoever invokes with Allah another god—he has no proof of this—his reckoning is only with his Lord; surely the unbelievers shall not be successful.

118. And say: O my Lord! forgive and have mercy, and Thou art the best of the Merciful ones.

THE LIGHT

In the name of Allah, the Beneficent, the Merciful.

1. (This is) a chapter which We have revealed and made obligatory and in which We have revealed clear communications that you may be mindful.

2. (As for) the fornicatress and the fornicator, flog each of them, (giving) a hundred stripes, and let not pity for them detain you in the matter of obedience to Allah, if you believe in Allah and the last day, and let a party of believers witness their chastisement.

3. The fornicator shall not marry any but a fornicatress or idolatress, and (as for) the fornicatress, none shall marry her but a fornicator or an idolater; and it is forbidden to the believers.

4. And those who accuse free women then do not bring four witnesses, flog them, (giving) eighty stripes, and do not admit any evidence from them ever; and these it is that are the transgressors,

5. Except those who repent after this and act aright, for surely Allah is Forgiving, Merciful.

6. And (as for) those who accuse their wives and have no witnesses except themselves, the evidence of one of these (should be taken) four times, bearing Allah to witness that he is most surely of the truthful ones.

7. And the fifth (time) that the curse of Allah be on him if he is one of the liars.

8. And it shall avert the chastisement from her if she testify

four times, bearing Allah to witness that he is most surely one of the liars;

9. And the fifth (time) that the wrath of Allah be on her if he is one of the truthful.

10. And were it not for Allah's grace upon you and His mercy—and that Allah is Oft-returning (to mercy), Wise!

11. Surely they who concocted the lie are a party from among you. Do not regard it an evil to you; nay, it is good for you. Every man of them shall have what he has earned of sin; and (as for) him who took upon himself the main part thereof, he shall have a grievous chastisement.

12. Why did not the believing men and the believing women, when you heard it, think well of their own people, and say: This is an evident falsehood?

13. Why did they not bring four witnesses of it? But as they have not brought witnesses they are liars before Allah.

14. And were it not for Allah's grace upon you and His mercy in this world and the hereafter, a grievous chastisement would certainly have touched you on account of the discourse which you entered into.

15. When you received it with your tongues and spoke with your mouths what you had no knowledge of, and you deemed it an easy matter while with Allah it was grievous.

16. And why did you not, when you heard it, say: It does not beseem us that we should talk of it; glory be to Thee! this is a great calumny?

17. Allah admonishes you that you should not return to the like of it ever again if you are believers.

18. And Allah makes clear to you the communications; and Allah is Knowing, Wise.

19. Surely (as for) those who love that scandal should circulate respecting those who believe, they shall have a grievous chastisement in this world and the hereafter; and Allah knows, while you do not know.

20. And were it not for Allah's grace on you and His mercy, and that Allah is Compassionate, Merciful.

21. O you who believe! do not follow the footsteps of the Shaitan; and whoever follows the footsteps of the Shaitan, then surely he bids the doing of indecency and evil; and were it not for Allah's grace upon you and His mercy, not one of you would have ever been pure, but Allah purifies whom He pleases; and Allah is Hearing, Knowing.

22. And let not those of you who possess grace and abun-

dance swear against giving to the near of kin and the poor and those who have fled in Allah's way, and they should pardon and turn away. Do you not love that Allah should forgive you? And Allah is Forgiving, Merciful.

23. Surely those who accuse chaste believing women, unaware (of the evil), are cursed in this world and the hereafter, and they shall have a grievous chastisement.

24. On the day when their tongues and their hands and their feet shall bear witness against them as to what they did.

25. On that day Allah will pay back to them in full their just reward, and they shall know that Allah is the evident Truth.

26. Unclean things are for unclean ones and unclean ones are for unclean things, and the good things are for good ones and the good ones are for good things; these are free from what they say; they shall have forgiveness and an honorable sustenance.

27. O you who believe! Do not enter houses other than your own houses until you have asked permission and saluted their inmates; this is better for you, that you may be mindful.

28. But if you do not find any one therein, then do not enter them until permission is given to you; and if it is said to you: Go back, then go back; this is purer for you; and Allah is Cognizant of what you do.

29. It is no sin in you that you enter uninhabited houses wherein you have your necessaries; and Allah knows what you do openly and what you hide.

30. Say to the believing men that they cast down their looks and guard their private parts; that is purer for them; surely Allah is Aware of what they do.

31. And say to the believing women that they cast down their looks and guard their private parts and do not display their ornaments except what appears thereof, and let them wear their head-coverings over their bosoms, and not display their ornaments except to their husbands or their fathers, or the fathers of their husbands, or their sons, or the sons of their husbands, or their brothers, or their brothers' sons, or their sisters' sons, or their women, or those whom their right hands possess, or the male servants not having need (of women), or the children who have not attained knowledge of what is hidden of women; and let them not strike their feet so that what they hide of their ornaments may be known; and turn to Allah all of you, O believers! so that you may be successful.

32. And marry those among you who are single and those

who are fit among your male slaves and your female slaves; if they are needy, Allah will make them free from want out of His grace; and Allah is Ample-giving, Knowing.

33. And let those who do not find the means to marry keep chaste until Allah makes them free from want out of His grace. And (as for) those who ask for a writing from among those whom your right hands possess, give them the writing if you know any good in them, and give them of the wealth of Allah which He has given you; and do not compel your slave girls to prostitution, when they desire to keep chaste, in order to seek the frail good of this world's life; and whoever compels them, then surely after their compulsion Allah is Forgiving, Merciful.

34. And certainly We have sent to you clear communications and a description of those who have passed away before you, and an admonition to those who guard (against evil).

35. Allah is the light of the heavens and the earth; a likeness of His light is as a niche in which is a lamp, the lamp is in a glass, (and) the glass is as it were a brightly shining star, lit from a blessed olive-tree, neither eastern nor western, the oil whereof almost gives light though fire touch it not—light upon light— Allah guides to His light whom He pleases, and Allah sets forth parables for men, and Allah is Cognizant of all things.

36. In houses which Allah has permitted to be exalted and that His name may be remembered in them; there glorify Him therein in the mornings and the evenings,

37. Men whom neither merchandise nor selling diverts from the remembrance of Allah and the keeping up of prayer and the giving of poor-rate; they fear a day in which the hearts and eyes shall turn about;

38. That Allah may give them the best reward of what they have done, and give them more out of His grace; and Allah gives sustenance to whom He pleases without measure.

39. And (as for) those who disbelieve, their deeds are like the mirage in a desert, which the thirsty man deems to be water; until when he comes to it he finds it to be naught, and there he finds Allah, so He pays back to him his reckoning in full; and Allah is quick in reckoning;

40. Or like utter darkness in the deep sea: there covers it a wave above which is another wave, above which is a cloud, (layers of) utter darkness one above another; when he holds out his hand, he is almost unable to see it; and to whomsoever Allah does not give light, he has no light.

41. Do you not see that Allah is He Whom do glorify all those who are in the heavens and the earth, and the (very) birds with expanded wings? He knows the prayer of each one and its glorification, and Allah is Cognizant of what they do.

42. And Allah's is the kingdom of the heavens and the earth, and to Allah is the eventual coming.

43. Do you not see that Allah drives along the clouds, then gathers them together, then piles them up, so that you see the rain coming forth from their midst? And He sends down of the clouds that are (like) mountains wherein is hail, afflicting therewith whom He pleases and turning it away from whom He pleases; the flash of His lightning almost takes away the sight.

44. Allah turns over the night and the day; most surely there is a lesson in this for those who have sight.

45. And Allah has created from water every living creature: so of them is that which walks upon its belly, and of them is that which walks upon two feet, and of them is that which walks upon four; Allah creates what He pleases; surely Allah has power over all things.

46. Certainly We have revealed clear communications, and Allah guides whom He pleases to the right way.

47. And they say: We believe in Allah and in the apostle and we obey; then a party of them turn back after this, and these are not believers.

48. And when they are called to Allah and His Apostle that he may judge between them, lo! a party of them turn aside.

49. And if the truth be on their side, they come to him quickly, obedient.

50. Is there in their hearts a disease, or are they in doubt, or do they fear that Allah and His Apostle will act wrongfully towards them? Nay! they themselves are the unjust.

51. The response of the believers, when they are invited to Allah and His Apostle that he may judge between them, is only to say: We hear and we obey; and these it is that are the successful.

52. And he who obeys Allah and His Apostle, and fears Allah, and is careful of (his duty to) Him, these it is that are the achievers.

53. And they swear by Allah with the most energetic of their oaths that if you command them they would certainly go forth. Say: Swear not; reasonable obedience (is desired); surely Allah is aware of what you do.

54. Say: Obey Allah and obey the Apostle; but if you turn back, then on him rests that which is imposed on him and on you rests that which is imposed on you; and if you obey him, you are on the right way; and nothing rests on the Apostle but clear delivering (of the message).

55. Allah has promised to those of you who believe and do good that He will most certainly make them rulers in the earth as He made rulers those before them, and that He will most certainly establish for them their religion which He has chosen for them, and that He will most certainly, after their fear, give them security in exchange; they shall serve Me, not associating aught with Me; and whoever is ungrateful after this, these it is who are the transgressors.

56. And keep up prayer and pay the poor-rate and obey the Apostle, so that mercy may be shown to you.

57. Think not that those who disbelieve shall escape in the earth, and their abode is the fire; and certainly evil is the resort!

58. O you who believe! let those whom your right hands possess and those of you who have not attained to puberty ask permission of you three times; before the morning prayer, and when you put off your clothes at midday in summer, and after the prayer of the nightfall; these are three times of privacy for you; neither is it a sin for you nor for them besides these, some of you must go round about (waiting) upon others; thus does Allah make clear to you the communications, and Allah is Knowing, Wise.

59. And when the children among you have attained to puberty, let them seek permission as those before them sought permission; thus does Allah make clear to you His communications, and Allah is knowing, Wise.

60. And (as for) women advanced in years who do not hope for a marriage, it is no sin for them if they put off their clothes without displaying their ornaments; and if they restrain themselves it is better for them; and Allah is Hearing, Knowing.

61. There is no blame on the blind man, nor is there blame on the lame, nor is there blame on the sick, nor on yourselves that you eat from your houses, or your fathers' houses or your mothers' houses, or your brothers' houses, or your sisters' houses, or your paternal uncles' houses, or your paternal aunts' houses, or your maternal uncles' houses, or your maternal aunts' houses, or what you possess the keys of, or your friends' (houses). It is no sin in you that you eat together or separately. So when you enter

houses, greet your people with a salutation from Allah, blessed (and) goodly; thus does Allah make clear to you the communications that you may understand.

62. Only those are believers who believe in Allah and His Apostle, and when they are with him on a momentous affair they go not away until they have asked his permission; surely they who ask your permission are they who believe in Allah and His Apostle; so when they ask your permission for some affair of theirs, give permission to whom you please of them and ask forgiveness for them from Allah; surely Allah is Forgiving, Merciful.

63. Do not hold the Apostle's calling (you) among you to be like your calling one to the other; Allah indeed knows those who steal away from among you, concealing themselves; therefore let those beware who go against his order lest a trial afflict them or there befall them a painful chastisement.

64. Now surely Allah's is whatever is in the heavens and the earth; He knows indeed that to which you are conforming yourselves; and on the day on which they are returned to Him, He will inform them of what they did; and Allah is Cognizant of all things.

THE CRITERION

In the name of Allah, the Beneficent, the Merciful.

1. Blessed is He Who sent down the Furqan upon His servant that he may be a warner to the nations;

2. He, Whose is the kingdom of the heavens and the earth, and Who did not take to Himself a son, and Who has no associate in the kingdom, and Who created everything, then ordained for it a measure.

3. And they have taken besides Him gods, who do not create anything while they are themselves created, and they control not for themselves any harm or profit, and they control not death, nor life, nor raising (the dead) to life.

4. And those who disbelieve say: This is nothing but a lie

which he has forged, and other people have helped him at it; so indeed they have done injustice and (uttered) a falsehood.

5. And they say: The stories of the ancients—he has got them written—so these are read out to him morning and evening.

6. Say: He has revealed it Who knows the secret in the heavens and the earth; surely He is ever Forgiving, Merciful.

7. And they say: What is the matter with this Apostle that he eats food and goes about in the markets; why has not an angel been sent down to him, so that he should have been a warner with him?

8. Or (why is not) a treasure sent down to him, or he is made to have a garden from which he should eat? And the unjust say: You do not follow any but a man deprived of reason.

9. See what likenesses do they apply to you, so they have gone astray, therefore they shall not be able to find a way.

10. Blessed is He Who, if He please, will give you what is better than this, gardens beneath which rivers flow, and He will give you palaces.

11. But they reject the hour, and We have prepared a burning fire for him who rejects the hour.

12. When it shall come into their sight from a distant place, they shall hear its vehement raging and roaring.

13. And when they are cast into a narrow place in it, bound, they shall there call out for destruction.

14. Call not this day for one destruction, but call for destructions many.

15. Say: Is this better or the abiding garden which those who guard (against evil) are promised? That shall be a reward and a resort for them.

16. They shall have therein what they desire abiding (in it); it is a promise which it is proper to be prayed for from your Lord.

17. And on the day when He shall gather them, and whatever they served besides Allah, He shall say: Was it you who led astray these My servants, or did they themselves go astray from the path?

18. They shall say: Glory be to Thee; it was not beseeming for us that we should take any guardians besides Thee, but Thou didst make them and their fathers to enjoy until they forsook the reminder, and they were a people in perdition,

19. So they shall indeed give you the lie in what you say, then you shall not be able to ward off or help, and whoever among you is unjust, We will make him taste a great chastisement.

20. And We have not sent before you any messengers but they most surely ate food and went about in the markets; and We have made some of you a trial for others; will you bear patiently? And your Lord is ever Seeing.

21. And those who do not hope for Our meeting, say: Why have not angels been sent down upon us, or (why) do we not see our Lord? Now certainly they are too proud of themselves and have revolted in great revolt.

22. On the day when they shall see the angels, there shall be no joy on that day for the guilty, and they shall say: It is a forbidden thing totally prohibited.

23. And We will proceed to what they have done of deeds, so We shall render them as scattered floating dust.

24. The dwellers of the garden shall on that day be in a better abiding-place and a better resting-place.

25. And on the day when the heaven shall burst asunder with the clouds, and the angels shall be sent down descending (in ranks).

26. The kingdom on that day shall rightly belong to the Beneficent God, and a hard day shall it be for the unbelievers.

27. And the day when the unjust one shall bite his hands, saying: O! would that I had taken a way with the Apostle;

28. O woe is me! would that I had not taken such a one for a friend!

29. Certainly he led me astray from the reminder after it had come to me; and the Shaitan fails to aid man.

30. And the Apostle cried out: O my Lord! surely my people have treated this Quran as a forsaken thing.

31. And thus have We made for every prophet an enemy from among the sinners and sufficient is your Lord as a Guide and a Helper.

32. And those who disbelieve say: Why has not the Quran been revealed to him all at once? Thus, that We may strengthen your heart by it and We have arranged it well in arranging.

33. And they shall not bring to you any argument, but We have brought to you (one) with truth and best in signficance.

34. (As for) those who shall be gathered upon their faces to hell, they are in a worse plight and straying farther away from the path.

35. And certainly We gave Musa the Book and We appointed with him his brother Haroun an aider.

36. Then We said: Go you both to the people who rejected

Our communications; so We destroyed them with utter destruction.

37. And the people of Nuh, when they rejected the apostles, We drowned them, and made them a sign for men, and We have prepared a painful punishment for the unjust;

38. And Ad and Samood and the dwellers of the Rass and many generations between them.

39. And to every one We gave examples and every one did We destroy with utter destruction.

40. And certainly they have (often) passed by the town on which was rained an evil rain; did they not then see it? Nay! they did not hope to be raised again.

41. And when they see you, they do not take you for aught but a mockery: Is this he whom Allah has raised to be an apostle?

42. He had well-nigh led us astray from our gods had we not adhered to them patiently! And they will know, when they see the punishment, who is straying farther off from the path.

43. Have you seen him who takes his low desires for his god? Will you then be a protector over him?

44. Or do you think that most of them do hear or understand? They are nothing but as cattle; nay, they are straying farther off from the path.

45. Have you not considered (the work of) your Lord, how He extends the shade? And if He had pleased He would certainly have made it stationary; then We have made the sun an indication of it;

46. Then We take it to Ourselves, taking little by little.

47. And He it is Who made the night a covering for you, and the sleep a rest, and He made the day to rise up again.

48. And He it is Who sends the winds as good news before His mercy; and We send down pure water from the cloud,

49. That We may give life thereby to a dead land and give it for drink, out of what We have created, to cattle and many people.

50. And certainly We have repeated this to them that they may be mindful, but the greater number of men do not consent to aught except denying.

51. And if We had pleased We would certainly have raised a warner in every town.

52. So do not follow the unbelievers, and strive against them a mighty striving with it.

53. And He it is Who has made two seas to flow freely, the one sweet that subdues thirst by its sweetness, and the other salt that burns by its saltness; and between the two He has made a barrier and inviolable obstruction.

54. And He it is Who has created man from the water, then He has made for him blood relationship and marriage relationship, and your Lord is powerful.

55. And they serve besides Allah that which neither profits them nor causes them harm; and the unbeliever is a partisan against his Lord.

56. And We have not sent you but as a giver of good news and as a warner.

57. Say: I do not ask you aught in return except that he who will, may take the way to his Lord.

58. And rely on the Ever-living Who dies not, and celebrate His praise; and Sufficient is He as being aware of the faults of His servants,

59. Who created the heavens and the earth and what is between them in six periods, and He is firmly established on the throne of authority; the Beneficent God, so ask respecting it one aware.

60. And when it is said to them: Make obeisance to the Beneficent God, they say: And what is the God of beneficence? Shall we make obeisance to what you bid us? And it adds to their aversion.

61. Blessed is He Who made the constellations in the heavens and made therein a lamp and a shining moon.

62. And He it is Who made the night and the day to follow each other for him who desires to be mindful or desires to be thankful.

63. And the servants of the Beneficent God are they who walk on the earth in humbleness, and when the ignorant address them, they say: Peace.

64. And they who pass the night prostrating themselves before their Lord and standing.

65. And they who say: O our Lord! turn away from us the punishment of hell, surely the punishment thereof is a lasting evil.

66. Surely it is an evil abode and (evil) place to stay.

67. And they who when they spend, are neither extravagant nor parsimonious, and (keep) between these the just mean.

68. And they who do not call upon another god with Allah and do not slay the soul, which Allah has forbidden except in the

requirements of justice, and (who) do not commit fornication and he who does this shall find a requital of sin;

69. The punishment shall be doubled to him on the day of resurrection, and he shall abide therein in abasement;

70. Except him who repents and believes and does a good deed; so these are they of whom Allah changes the evil deeds to good ones; and Allah is Forgiving, Merciful.

71. And whoever repents and does good, he surely turns to Allah a (goodly) turning.

72. And they who do not bear witness to what is false, and when they pass by what is vain, they pass by nobly.

73. And they who, when reminded of the communications of their Lord, do not fall down thereat deaf and blind.

74. And they who say: O our Lord! grant us in our wives and our offspring the joy of our eyes, and make us guides to those who guard (against evil).

75. These shall be rewarded with high places because they were patient, and shall be met therein with greetings and salutations.

76. Abiding therein; goodly the abode and the resting-place.

77. Say: My Lord would not care for you were it not for your prayer; but you have indeed rejected (the truth), so that which shall cleave shall come.

THE POETS

In the name of Allah, the Beneficent, the Merciful.

1. Ta Sin Mim.

2. These are the verses of the Book that makes (things) clear.

3. Perhaps you will kill yourself with grief because they do not believe.

4. If We please, We should send down upon them a sign from the heaven so that their necks should stoop to it.

5. And there does not come to them a new reminder from the Beneficent God but they turn aside from it.

6. So they have indeed rejected (the truth), therefore the news of that which they mock shall soon come to them.

7. Do they not see the earth, how many of every noble kind We have caused to grow in it? '

8. Most surely there is a sign in that, but most of them will not believe.

9. And most surely your Lord is the Mighty, the Merciful.

10. And when your Lord called out to Musa, saying: Go to the unjust people,

11. The people of Firon: Will they not guard (against evil)?

12. He said: O my Lord! surely I fear that they will reject me;

13. And my breast straitens, and my tongue is not eloquent, therefore send Thou to Haroun (to help me);

14. And they have a crime against me, therefore I fear that they may slay me.

15. He said: By no means, so go you both with Our signs; surely We are with you, hearing;

16. Then come to Firon and say: Surely we are the messengers of the Lord of the worlds:

17. Then send with us the children of Israel.

18. (Firon) said: Did we not bring you up as a child among us, and you tarried among us for (many) years of your life?

19. And you did (that) deed of yours which you did, and you are one of the ungrateful.

20. He said: I did it then while I was of those unable to see the right course;

21. So I fled from you when I feared you, then my Lord granted me wisdom and made me of the apostles;

22. And is it a favor of which you remind me that you have enslaved the children of Israel?

23. Firon said: And what is the Lord of the worlds?

24. He said: The Lord of the heavens and the earth and what is between them, if you would be sure.

25. (Firon) said to those around him: Do you not hear?

26. He said: Your Lord and the Lord of your fathers of old.

27. Said he: Most surely your Apostle who is sent to you is mad.

28. He said: The Lord of the east and the west and what is between them, if you understand.

29. Said he: If you will take a god besides me, I will most certainly make you one of the imprisoned.

30. He said: What! even if I bring to you something manifest?

31. Said he: Bring it then, if you are of the truthful ones.

32. So he cast down his rod, and lo! it was an obvious serpent,

33. And he drew forth his hand, and lo! it appeared white to the onlookers.

34. (Firon) said to the chiefs around him: Most surely this is a skillful magician,

35. Who desires to turn you out of your land with his magic; what is it then that you advise?

36. They said: Give him and his brother respite and send heralds into the cities;

37. That they should bring to you every skillful magician.

38. So the magicians were gathered together at the appointed time on the fixed day,

39. And it was said to the people: Will you gather together?

40. Haply we may follow the magicians, if they are the vanquishers.

41. And when the magicians came, they said to Firon: Shall we get a reward if we are the vanquishers?

42. He said: Yes, and surely you will then be of those who are made near.

43. Musa said to them: Cast what you are going to cast.

44. So they cast down their cords and their rods and said: By Firon's power, we shall most surely be victorious.

45. Then Musa cast down his staff and lo! it swallowed up the lies they told.

46. And the magicians were thrown down prostrate;

47. They said: We believe in the Lord of the worlds:

48. The Lord of Musa and Haroun.

49. Said he: You believe in him before I give you permission; most surely he is the chief of you who taught you the magic, so you shall know: certainly I will cut off your hands and your feet on opposite sides, and certainly I will crucify you all.

50. They said: No harm; surely to our Lord we go back;

51. Surely we hope that our Lord will forgive us our wrongs because we are the first of the believers.

52. And We revealed to Musa, saying: Go away with My servants travelling by night, surely you will be pursued.

53. So Firon sent heralds into the cities;

54. Most surely these are a small company;

55. And most surely they have enraged us;

56. And most surely we are a vigilant multitude.

57. So We turned them out of gardens and springs,

58. And treasures and goodly dwellings,

59. Even so. And We gave them as a heritage to the children of Israel.

60. Then they pursued them at sunrise.

61. So when the two hosts saw each other, the companions of Musa cried out: Most surely we are being overtaken.

62. He said: By no means; surely my Lord is with me: He will show me a way out.

63. Then We revealed to Musa: Strike the sea with your staff. So it had cloven asunder, and each part was like a huge mound.

64. And We brought near, there, the others.

65. And We saved Musa and those with him, all of them.

66. Then We drowned the others.

67. Most surely there is a sign in this, but most of them do not believe.

68. And most surely your Lord is the Mighty, the Merciful.

69. And recite to them the story of Ibrahim.

70. When he said to his father and his people: What do you worship?

71. They said: We worship idols, so we shall be their votaries.

72. He said: Do they hear you when you call?

73. Or do they profit you or cause you harm?

74. They said: Nay, we found our fathers doing so.

75. He said: Have you then considered what you have been worshipping:

76. You and your ancient sires.

77. Surely they are enemies to me, but not (so) the Lord of the worlds;

78. Who created me, then He has shown me the way:

79. And He Who gives me to eat and gives me to drink:

80. And when I am sick, then He restores me to health;

81. And He Who will cause me to die, then give me life;

82. And Who, I hope, will forgive me my mistakes on the day of judgment.

83. My Lord: Grant me wisdom, and join me with the good;

84. And ordain for me a goodly mention among posterity;

85. And make me of the heirs of the garden of bliss;

86. And forgive my father, for surely he is of those who have gone astray;

87. And disgrace me not on the day when they are raised,

88. The day on which property will not avail, nor sons,

89. Except him who comes to Allah with a heart free (from evil).

90. And the garden shall be brought near for those who guard (against evil),

91. And the hell shall be made manifest to the erring ones,

92. And it shall be said to them: Where are those that you used to worship;

93. Besides Allah? Can they help you or yet help themselves?

94. So they shall be thrown down into it, they and the erring ones,

95. And the hosts of the Shaitan, all.

96. They shall say while they contend therein:

97. By Allah! we were certainly in manifest error,

98. When we made you equal to the Lord of the worlds;

99. And none but the guilty led us astray;

100. So we have no intercessors,

101. Nor a true friend;

102. But if we could but once return, we would be of the believers.

103. Most surely there is a sign in this, but most of them do not believe.

104. And most surely your Lord is the Mighty, the Merciful.

105. The people of Nuh rejected the apostles.

106. When their brother Nuh said to them: Will you not guard (against evil)?

107. Surely I am a faithful apostle to you;

108. Therefore guard against (the punishment of) Allah and obey me;

109. And I do not ask you any reward for it; my reward is only with the Lord of the worlds:

110. So guard against (the punishment of) Allah and obey me.

111. They said: Shall we believe in you while the meanest follow you?

112. He said: And what knowledge have I of what they do?

113. Their account is only with my Lord, if you could perceive;

114. And I am not going to drive away the believers;

115. I am naught but a plain warner.

116. They said: If you desist not, O Nuh, you shall most certainly be of those stoned to death.

117. He said: My Lord! Surely my people give me the lie!

118. Therefore judge Thou between me and them with a (just) judgment, and deliver me and those who are with me of the believers.

119. So We delivered him and those with him in the laden ark.

120. Then We drowned the rest afterwards.

121. Most surely there is a sign in this, but most of them do not believe.

122. And most surely your Lord is the Mighty, the Merciful.

123. Ad gave the lie to the apostles.

124. When their brother Hud said to them: Will you not guard (against evil)?

125. Surely I am a faithful apostle to you;

126. Therefore guard against (the punishment of) Allah and obey me:

127. And I do not ask you any reward for it; surely my reward is only with the Lord of the worlds;

128. Do you build on every height a monument? Vain is it that you do:

129. And you make strong fortresses that perhaps you may abide;

130. And when you lay hands (on men) you lay hands (like) tyrants;

131. So guard against (the punishment of) Allah and obey me;

132. And be careful of (your duty to) Him Who has given you abundance of what you know.

133. He has given you abundance of cattle and children,

134. And gardens and fountains;

135. Surely I fear for you the chastisement of a grievous day.

136. They said: It is the same to us whether you admonish or are not one of the admonishers;

137. This is naught but a custom of the ancients;

138. And we are not going to be punished.

139. So they gave him the lie, then We destroyed them. Most surely there is a sign in this, but most of them do not believe.

140. And most surely your Lord is the Mighty, the Merciful.

141. Samood gave the lie to the apostles.

142. When their brother Salih said to them: Will you not guard (against evil)?

143. Surely I am a faithful apostle to you;

144. Therefore guard against (the punishment of) Allah and obey me:

145. And I do not ask you any reward for it; my reward is only with the Lord of the worlds:

146. Will you be left secure in what is here;

147. In gardens and fountains,

148. And cornfields and palm-trees having fine spadices?

149. And you hew houses out of the mountains exultingly;

150. Therefore guard against (the punishment of) Allah and obey me;

151. And do not obey the bidding of the extravagant,

152. Who make mischief in the land and do not act aright.

153. They said: You are only of the deluded ones;

154. You are naught but a mortal like ourselves; so bring a sign if you are one of the truthful.

155. He said: This is a she-camel; she shall have her portion of water, and you have your portion of water on an appointed time;

156. And do not touch her with evil, lest the punishment of a grievous day should overtake you.

157. But they hamstrung her, then regretted;

158. So the punishment overtook them. Most surely there is a sign in this, but most of them do not believe.

159. And most surely your Lord is the Mighty, the Merciful.

160. The people of Lut gave the lie to the apostles.

161. When their brother Lut said to them: Will you not guard (against evil)?

162. Surely I am a faithful apostle to you;

163. Therefore guard against (the punishment of) Allah and obey me:

164. And I do not ask you any reward for it; my reward is only with the Lord of the worlds;

165. What! do you come to the males from among the creatures,

166. And leave what your Lord has created for you of your wives? Nay, you are a people exceeding limits.

167. They said: If you desist not, O Lut! you shall surely be of those who are expelled.

168. He said: Surely I am of those who utterly abhor your doing;

169. My Lord! deliver me and my followers from what they do.

170. So We delivered him and his followers all,

171. Except an old woman, among those who remained behind.

172. Then We utterly destroyed the others.

173. And We rained down upon them a rain, and evil was the rain on those warned.

174. Most surely there is a sign in this, but most of them do not believe.

175. And most surely your Lord is the Mighty, the Merciful.

176. The dwellers of the thicket gave the lie to the apostles.

177. When Shu'aib said to them: Will you not guard (against evil)?

178. Surely I am a faithful apostle to you;

179. Therefore guard against (the punishment of) Allah and obey me:

180. And I do not ask you any reward for it; my reward is only with the Lord of the worlds;

181. Give a full measure and be not of those who diminish;

182. And weigh (things) with a right balance,

183. And do not wrong men of their things, and do not act corruptly in the earth, making mischief.

184. And guard against (the punishment of) Him who created you and the former nations.

185. They said: You are only of those deluded;

186. And you are naught but a mortal like ourselves, and we know you to be certainly of the liars.

187. Therefore cause a portion of the heaven to come down upon us, if you are one of the truthful.

188. He said: My Lord knows best what you do.

189. But they called him a liar, so the punishment of the day of covering overtook them; surely it was the punishment of a grievous day.

190. Most surely there is a sign in this, but most of them do not believe.

191. And most surely your Lord is Mighty, the Merciful.

192. And most surely this is a revelation from the Lord of the worlds.

193. The Faithful Spirit has descended with it,

194. Upon your heart that you may be of the warners,

195. In plain Arabic language.

196. And most surely the same is in the scriptures of the ancients.

197. Is it not a sign to them that the learned men of the Israelites know it?

198. And if we had revealed it to any of the foreigners,

199. So that he should have recited it to them, they would not have believed therein.

200. Thus have We caused it to enter into the hearts of the guilty.

201. They will not believe in it until they see the painful punishment.

202. And it shall come to them all of a sudden, while they shall not perceive;

203. Then they will say: Shall we be respited?

204. What! do they still seek to hasten on Our punishment?

205. Have you then considered if We let them enjoy themselves for years,

206. Then there comes to them that with which they are threatened,

207. That which they were made to enjoy shall not avail them?

208. And We did not destroy any town but it had (its) warners,

209. To remind, and We are never unjust.

210. And the Shaitans have not come down with it.

211. And it behoves them not, and they have not the power to do (it).

212. Most surely they are far removed from the hearing of it.

213. So call not upon another god with Allah, lest you be of those who are punished.

214. And warn your nearest relations,

215. And be kind to him who follows you of the believers.

216. But if they disobey you, then say: Surely I am clear of what you do.

217. And rely on the Mighty, the Merciful,

218. Who sees you when you stand up.

219. And your turning over and over among those who prostrate themselves before Allah.

220. Surely He is the Hearing, the Knowing.

221. Shall I inform you (of him) upon whom the Shaitans descend?

222. They descend upon every lying, sinful one,

223. They incline their ears, and most of them are liars.

224. And as to the poets, those who go astray follow them.

225. Do you not see that they wander about bewildered in every valley?

226. And that they say that which they do not do;

227. Except those who believe and do good and remember Allah much, and defend themselves after they are oppressed; and they who act unjustly shall know to what final place of turning they shall turn back.

THE ANT

In the name of Allah, the Beneficent, the Merciful.

1. Ta Sin! These are the verses of the Quran and the Book that makes (things) clear,

2. A guidance and good news for the believers,

3. Who keep up prayer and pay the poor-rate, and of the hereafter, they are sure.

4. As to those who do not believe in the hereafter, We have surely made their deeds fair-seeming to them, but they blindly wander on.

5. These are they who shall have an evil punishment, and in the hereafter they shall be the greatest losers.

6. And most surely you are made to receive the Quran from the Wise, the Knowing God.

7. When Musa said to his family: Surely I see fire; I will bring to you from it some news, or I will bring to you therefrom a burning firebrand so that you may warm yourselves.

8. So when he came to it a voice was uttered saying: Blessed is Whoever is in the fire and whatever is about it; and glory be to Allah, the Lord of the worlds;

9. O Musa! surely I am Allah, the Mighty, the Wise;

10. And cast down your staff. So when he saw it in motion as if it were a serpent, he turned back retreating and did not return: O Musa! fear not; surely the apostles shall not fear in My presence;

11. Neither he who has been unjust, then he does good instead after evil, for surely I am the Forgiving, the Merciful:

12. And enter your hand into the opening of your bosom, it shall come forth white without evil; among nine signs to Firon and his people, surely they are a transgressing people.

13. So when Our clear signs came to them, they said: This is clear enchantment.

14. And they denied them unjustly and proudly while their soul had been convinced of them; consider, then how was the end of the mischief-makers.

15. And certainly We gave knowledge to Dawood and Sulaiman, and they both said: Praise be to Allah, Who has made us to excel many of His believing servants.

16. And Sulaiman was Dawood's heir, and he said: O men! we have been taught the language of birds, and we have been given all things; most surely this is manifest grace.

17. And his hosts of the jinn and the men and the birds were gathered to him, and they were formed into groups.

18. Until when they came to the valley of the Naml, a Namlite said: O Naml! enter your houses, (that) Sulaiman and his hosts may not crush you while they do not know.

19. So he smiled, wondering at her word, and said: My Lord! grant me that I should be grateful for Thy favor which Thou hast bestowed on me and on my parents, and that I should do good such as Thou art pleased with, and make me enter, by Thy mercy, into Thy servants, the good ones.

20. And he reviewed the birds, then said: How is it I see not the hoopoe or is it that he is of the absentees?

21. I will most certainly punish him with a severe punishment, or kill him, or he shall bring to me a clear plea.

22. And he tarried not long, then said: I comprehend that which you do not comprehend and I have brought to you a sure information from Sheba.

23. Surely I found a woman ruling over them, and she has been given abundance and she has a mighty throne:

24. I found her and her people adoring the sun instead of Allah, and the Shaitan has made their deeds fair-seeming to them and thus turned them from the way, so they do not go aright;

25. That they do not make obeisance to Allah, Who brings forth what is hidden in the heavens and the earth and knows what you hide and what you make manifest:

26. Allah, there is no god but He: He is the Lord of mighty power.

27. He said: We will see whether you have told the truth or whether you are of the liars:

28. Take this my letter and hand it over to them, then turn away from them and see what (answer) they return.

29. She said: O chief! surely an honorable letter has been delivered to me;

30. Surely it is from Sulaiman, and surely it is in the name of Allah, the Beneficent, the Merciful;

31. Saying: exalt not yourselves against me and come to me in submission.

32. She said: O chiefs! give me advice respecting my affair: I never decide an affair until you are in my presence.

33. They said: We are possessors of strength and possessors of mighty prowess, and the command is yours, therefore see what you will command.

34. She said: Surely the kings, when they enter a town, ruin it and make the noblest of its people to be low, and thus they (always) do;

35. And surely I am going to send a present to them, and shall wait to see what (answer) do the messengers bring back.

36. So when he came to Sulaiman, he said: What! will you help me with wealth? But what Allah has given me is better than what He has given you. Nay, you are exultant because of your present;

37. Go back to them, so we will most certainly come to them with hosts which they shall have no power to oppose, and we will most certainly expel them therefrom in abasement, and they shall be in a state of ignominy.

38. He said: O chiefs! which of you can bring to me her throne before they come to me in submission?

39. One audacious among the jinn said: I will bring it to you before you rise up from your place; and most surely I am strong (and) trusty for it.

40. One who had the knowledge of the Book said: I will bring it to you in the twinkling of an eye. Then when he saw it settled beside him, he said: This is of the grace of my Lord that He may try me whether I am grateful or ungrateful; and whoever is grateful, he is grateful only for his own soul, and whoever is ungrateful, then surely my Lord is Self-sufficient, Honored.

41. He said: Alter her throne for her; we will see whether she follows the right way or is of those who do not go aright.

42. So when she came, it was said: Is your throne like this? She said: It is as it were the same, and we were given the knowledge before it, and we were submissive.

43. And what she worshipped besides Allah prevented her, surely she was of an unbelieving people.

44. It·was said to her: Enter the palace; but when she saw it she deemed it to be a great expanse of water, and bared her legs. He said: Surely it is a palace made smooth with glass. She said: My Lord! surely I have been unjust to myself, and I submit with Sulaiman to Allah, the Lord of the worlds.

45. And certainly We sent to Samood their brother Salih,

saying: Serve Allah; and lo! they became two sects quarrelling with each other.

46. He said: O my people! why do you seek to hasten on the evil before the good? Why do you not ask forgiveness of Allah so that you may be dealt with mercifully?

47. They said: We have met with ill luck on account of you and on account of those with you. He said: The cause of your evil fortune is with Allah; nay, you are a people who are tried.

48. And there were in the city nine persons who made mischief in the land and did not act aright.

49. They said: Swear to each other by Allah that we will certainly make a sudden attack on him and his family by night, then we will say to his heir: We did not witness the destruction of his family, and we are most surely truthful.

50. And they planned a plan, and We planned a plan while they perceived not.

51. See, then, how was the end of their plan that We destroyed them and their people, all (of them).

52. So those are their houses fallen down because they were unjust; most surely there is a sign in this for a people who know.

53. And We delivered those who believed and who guarded (against evil).

54. And (We sent) Lut, when he said to his people: What! do you commit indecency while you see?

55. What! do you indeed approach men lustfully rather than women? Nay, you are a people who act ignorantly.

56. But the answer of his people was no other except that they said: Turn out Lut's followers from your town; surely they are a people who would keep pure!

57. But We delivered him and his followers except his wife; We ordained her to be of those who remained behind.

58. And We rained on them a rain, and evil was the rain of those who had been warned.

59. Say: Praise be to Allah and peace on His servants whom He has chosen: is Allah better, or what they associate (with Him)?

60. Nay, He Who created the heavens and the earth, and sent down for you water from the cloud; then We cause to grow thereby beautiful gardens; it is not possible for you that you should make the trees thereof to grow. Is there a god with Allah? Nay! they are people who deviate.

61. Or, Who made the earth a restingplace, and made in it

rivers, and raised on it mountains, and placed between the two seas a barrier. Is there a god with Allah? Nay! most of them do not know!

62. Or, Who answers the distressed one when he calls upon Him and removes the evil, and He will make you successors in the earth. Is there a god with Allah? Little is it that you mind!

63. Or, Who guides you in utter darkness of the land and the sea, and Who sends the winds as good news before His mercy. Is there a god with Allah? Exalted by Allah above what they associate (with Him).

64. Or, Who originates the creation, then reproduces it, and Who gives you sustenance from the heaven and the earth. Is there a god With Allah? Say: Bring your proof if you are truthful.

65. Say: No one in the heavens and the earth knows the unseen but Allah; and they do not know when they shall be raised.

66. Nay, their knowledge respecting the hereafter is slight and hasty; nay, they are in doubt about it; nay, they are quite blind to it.

67. And those who disbelieve say: What! when we have become dust and our fathers (too), shall we certainly be brought forth?

68. We have certainly been promised this, we and our fathers before; these are naught but stories of the ancients.

69. Say: Travel in the earth, then see how was the end of the guilty.

70. And grieve not for them and be not distressed because of what they plan.

71. And they say: When will this threat come to pass, if you are truthful?

72. Say: Maybe there may have drawn near to you somewhat of that which you seek to hasten on.

73. And surely your Lord is the Lord of grace to men, but most of them are not grateful.

74. And most surely your Lord knows what their breasts conceal and what they manifest.

75. And there is nothing concealed in the heaven and the earth but it is in a clear book.

76. Surely this Quran declares to the children of Israel most of what they differ in.

77. And most surely it is a guidance and a mercy for the believers.

78. Surely your Lord will judge between them by his judgment, and He is the Mighty, the knowing.

79. Therefore rely on Allah; surely you are on the clear truth.

80. Surely you do not make the dead to hear, and you do not make the deaf to hear the call when they go back retreating.

81. Nor can you be a guide to the blind out of their error; you cannot make to bear (any one) except those who believe in Our communications, so they submit.

82. And when the word shall come to pass against them, We shall bring forth for them a creature from the earth that shall wound them, because people did not believe in Our communications.

83. And on the day when We will gather from every nation a party from among those who rejected Our communications, then they shall be formed into groups.

84. Until when they come, He will say: Did you reject My communications while you had no comprehensive knowledge of them? Or what was it that you did?

85. And the word shall come to pass against them because they were unjust, so they shall not speak.

86. Do they not consider that We have made the night that they may rest therein, and the day to give light? Most surely there are signs in this for a people who believe.

87. And on the day when the trumpet shall be blown, then those who are in the heavens and those who are in the earth shall be terrified except such as Allah please, and all shall come to him abased.

88. And you see the mountains, you think them to be solid, and they shall pass away as the passing away of the cloud—the handiwork of Allah Who has made every thing thoroughly; surely He is Aware of what you do.

89. Whoever brings good, he shall have better than it; and they shall be secure from terror on the day.

90. And whoever brings evil, these shall be thrown down on their faces into the fire; shall you be rewarded (for) aught except what you did?

91. I am commanded only that I should serve the Lord of this city, Who has made it sacred, and His are all things; and I am commanded that I should be of these who submit;

92. And that I should recite the Quran. Therefore whoever goes aright, he goes aright for his own soul, and whoever goes astray, then say: I am only one of the warners.

93. And say: Praise be to Allah, He will show you His signs so that you shall recognize them; nor is your Lord heedless of what you do.

THE NARRATIVE

In the name of Allah, the Beneficient, the Merciful.

1. Ta sin Mim.

2. These are the verses of the Book that makes (things) clear.

3. We recite to you from the account of Musa and Firon with truth for people who believe.

4. Surely Firon exalted himself in the land and made its people into parties, weakening one party from among them; he slaughtered their sons and let their women live; surely he was one of the mischiefmakers.

5. And We desired to bestow a favor upon those who were deemed weak in the land, and to make them the Imams, and to make them the heirs,

6. And to grant them power in the land, and to make Firon and Haman and their hosts see from them what they feared.

7. And We revealed to Musa's mothers, saying: Give him suck, then when you fear for him, cast him into the river and do not fear nor grieve; surely We will bring him back to you and make him one of the apostles.

8. And Firon's family took him up that he might be an enemy and a grief for them; surely Firon and Haman and their hosts were wrongdoers.

9. And Firon's wife said: A refreshment of the eye to me and to you; do not slay him; maybe he will be useful to us, or we may take him for a son; and they did not perceive.

10. And the heart of Musa's mother was free (from anxiety); she would have almost disclosed it had We not strengthened her heart so that she might be of the believers.

11. And she said to his sister: Follow him up. So she watched him from a distance while they did not perceive,

12. And We ordained that he refused to suck any foster mother before, so she said: Shall I point out to you the people of a house who will take care of him for you, and they will be benevolent to him?

13. So We gave him back to his mother that her eye might be refreshed, and that she might not grieve, and that she might know that the promise of Allah is true, but most of them do not know.

14. And when he attained his maturity and became full grown, We granted him wisdom and knowledge; and thus do We reward those who do good (to others).

15. And he went into the city at a time of unvigilance on the part of its people, so he found therein two men fighting, one being of his party and the other of his foes, and he who was of his party cried out to him for help against him who was of his enemies, so Musa struck him with his fist and killed him. He said: This is on account of the Shaitan's doing; surely he is an enemy, openly leading astray.

16. He said: My Lord! surely I have done harm to myself, so do Thou protect me. So He protected him; surely He is the Forgiving, the Merciful.

17. He said: My Lord! because Thou hast bestowed a favor on me, I shall never be a backer of the guilty.

18. And he was in the city, fearing, awaiting, when lo! he who had asked his assistance the day before was crying out to him for aid. Musa said to him: You are most surely one erring manifestly.

19. So when he desired to seize him who was an enemy to them both, he said: O Musa! do you intend to kill me as you killed a person yesterday? You desire nothing but that you should be a tyrant in the land, and you do not desire to be of those who act aright.

20. And a man came running from the remotest part of the city. He said: O Musa! surely the chiefs are consulting together to slay you, therefore depart (at once); surely I am of those who wish well to you.

21. So he went forth therefrom, fearing, awaiting, (and) he said: My Lord! deliver me from the unjust people.

22. And when he turned his face towards Madyan, he said: Maybe my Lord will guide me in the right path.

23. And when he came to the water of Madyan, he found on it

a group of men watering, and he found besides them two women keeping back (their flocks). He said: What is the matter with you? They said: We cannot water until the shepherds take away (their sheep) from the water, and our father is a very old man.

24. So he watered (their sheep) for them, then went back to the shade and said: My Lord! surely I stand in need of whatever good Thou mayest send down to me.

25. Then one of the two women came to him walking bashfully. She said: My father invites you that he may give you the reward of your having watered for us. So when he came to him and gave to him the account, he said: Fear not, you are secure from the unjust people.

26. Said one of them: O my father! employ him, surely the best of those that you can employ is the strong man, the faithful one.

27. He said: I desire to marry one of these two daughters of mine to you on condition that you should serve me for eight years; but if you complete ten, it will be of your own free will, and I do not wish to be hard to you; if Allah please, you will find me one of the good.

28. He said: This shall be (an agreement) between me and you; whichever of the two terms I fulfill, there shall be no wrongdoing to me; and Allah is a witness of what we say.

29. So when Musa had fulfilled the term, and he journeyed with his family, he perceived on this side of the mountain a fire. He said to his family: Wait, I have seen a fire, maybe I will bring to you from it some news or a brand of fire, so that you may warm yourselves.

30. And when he came to it, a voice was uttered from the right side of the valley in the blessed spot of the bush, saying: O Musa! surely I am Allah, the Lord of the worlds.

31. And saying: Cast down you staff. So when he saw it in motion as if it were a serpent, he turned back retreating, and did not return. O Musa! come forward and fear not; surely you are of those who are secure;

32. Enter your hand into the opening of your bosom, it will come forth white without evil, and draw your hand to yourself to ward off fear: so these two shall be two arguments from your Lord to Firon and his chiefs, surely they are a transgressing people.

33. He said: My Lord! surely I killed one of them, so I fear lest they should slay me;

34. And my brother, Haroun, he is more eloquent of tongue than I, therefore send him with me as an aider, verifying me: surely I fear that they would reject me.

35. He said: We will strengthen your arm with your brother, and We will give you both an authority, so that they shall not reach you; (go) with Our signs; you two and those who follow you shall be uppermost.

36. So when Musa came to them with Our clear signs, they said: This is nothing but forged enchantment, and we never heard of it amongst our fathers of old.

37. And Musa said: My Lord knows best who comes with guidance from Him, and whose shall be the good end of the abode; surely the unjust shall not be successful.

38. And Firon said: O chiefs! I do not know of any god for you besides myself; therefore kindle a fire for me, O Haman, from brick, then prepare for me a lofty building so that I may obtain knowledge of Musa's God, and most surely I think him to be one of the liars.

39. And he was unjustly proud in the land, he and his hosts, and they deemed that they would not be brought back to Us.

40. So We caught hold of him and his hosts, then We cast them into the sea, and see how was the end of the unjust.

41. And We made them Imams who call to the fire, and on the day of resurrection they shall not be assisted.

42. And We caused a curse to follow them in this world, and on the day of resurrection they shall be of those made to appear hideous.

43. And certainly We gave Musa the Book after We had destroyed the former generations, clear arguments for men and a guidance and a mercy, that they may be mindful.

44. And you were not on the western side when We revealed to Musa the commandment, and you were not among the witnesses;

45. But We raised up generations, then life became prolonged to them; and you were not dwelling among the people of Madyan, reciting to them Our communications, but We were the senders.

46. And you were not on this side of the mountain when We called, but a mercy from your Lord that you may warn a people to whom no warner came before you, that they may be mindful.

47. And were it not that there should befall them a disaster for what their hands have sent before, then they should say: Our

Lord! why didst Thou not send to us an apostle so that we should have followed Thy communications and been of the believers!

48. But (now) when the truth has come to them from Us, they say: Why is he not given the like of what was given to Musa? What! did they not disbelieve in what Musa was given before? They say: Two magicians backing up each other; and they say: Surely we are unbelievers in all.

49. Say: Then bring some (other) book from Allah which is a better guide than both of them, (that) I may follow it, if you are truthful.

50. But if they do not answer you, then know that they only follow their low desires; and who is more erring than he who follows his low desires without any guidance from Allah? Surely Allah does not guide the unjust people.

51. And certainly We have made the word to reach them so that they may be mindful.

52. (As to) those whom We gave the Book before it, they are believers in it.

53. And when it is recited to them they say: We believe in it; surely it is the truth from our Lord; surely we were submitters before this.

54. These shall be granted their reward twice, because they are steadfast and they repel evil with good and spend out of what We have given them.

55. And when they hear idle talk they turn aside from it and say: We shall have our deeds and you shall have your deeds; peace be on you, we do not desire the ignorant.

56. Surely you cannot guide whom you love, but Allah guides whom He pleases, and He knows best the followers of the right way.

57. And they say: If we follow the guidance with you, we shall be carried off from our country. What! have We not settled them in a safe, sacred territory to which fruits of every kind shall be drawn?—a sustenance from Us; but most of them do not know.

58. And how many a town have We destroyed which exulted in its means of subsistence; so these are their abodes; they have not been dwelt in after them except a little, and We are the inheritors,

59. And your Lord never destroyed the towns until He raised in their metropolis an apostle, reciting to them Our communi-

cations, and We never destroyed the towns except when their people were unjust.

60. And whatever things you have been given are only a provision of this world's life and its adornment, and whatever is with Allah is better and more lasting; do you not then understand?

61. Is he to whom We have promised a goodly promise which he shall meet with like him whom We have provided with the provisions of this world's life, then on the day of resurrection he shall be of those who are brought up?

62. And on the day when He will call them and say: Where are those whom you deemed to be My associates?

63. Those against whom the sentence has become confirmed will say: Our Lord! these are they whom we caused to err; we caused them to err as we ourselves did err; to Thee we declare ourselves to be clear (of them); they never served Us.

64. And it will be said: Call your associate-gods. So they will call upon them, but they will not answer them, and they shall see the punishment; would that they had followed the right way!

65. And on the day when He shall call them and say: What was the answer you gave to the apostles?

66. Then the pleas shall become obscure to them on that day, so they shall not ask each other.

67. But as to him who repents and believes and does good, maybe he will be among the successful:

68. And your Lord creates and chooses whom He pleases; to choose is not theirs; glory be to Allah, and exalted be He above what they associate (with Him).

69. And your Lord knows what their breasts conceal and what they manifest.

70. And He is Allah, there is no god but He! All praise is due to Him in this (life) and the hereafter, and His is the judgment, and to Him you shall be brought back.

71. Say: Tell me, if Allah were to make the night to continue incessantly on you till the day of resurrection, who is the god besides Allah that could bring you light? Do you not then hear?

72. Say: Tell me, if Allah were to make the day to continue incessantly on you till the day of resurrection, who is the god besides Allah that could bring you the night in which you take rest? Do you not then see?

73. And out of His mercy He has made for you the night and

the day, that you may rest therein, and that you may seek of His grace, and that you may give thanks.

74. And on the day when He shall call them and say: Where are those whom you deemed to be My associates?

75. And We will draw forth from among every nation a witness and say: Bring your proof; then shall they know that the truth is Allah's, and that which they forged shall depart from them.

76. Surely Qaroun was of the people of Musa, but he rebelled against them, and We had given him of the treasures, so much so that his hoards of wealth would certainly weigh down a company of men possessed of great strength. When his people said to him: Do not exult, surely Allah does not love the exultant;

77. And seek by means of what Allah has given you the future abode, and do not neglect your portion of this world, and do good (to others) as Allah has done good to you, and do not seek to make mischief in the land, surely Allah does not love the mischief-makers.

78. He said: I have been given this only on account of the knowledge I have. Did he not know that Allah had destroyed before him of the generations those who were mightier in strength than he and greater in assemblage? And the guilty shall not be asked about their faults.

79. So he went forth to his people in his finery. Those who desire this world's life said: O would that we had the like of what Qaroun is given; most surely he is possessed of mighty good fortune.

80. And those who were given the knowledge said: Woe to you! Allah's reward is better for him who believes and does good, and none is made to receive this except the patient.

81. Thus We made the earth to swallow up him and his abode; so he had no body of helpers to assist him against Allah, nor was he of those who can defend themselves.

82. And those who yearned for his place only the day before began to say: Ah! (know) that Allah amplifies and straitens the means of subsistence for whom He pleases of His servants; had not Allah been gracious to us, He would most surely have abased us; ah! (know) that the ungrateful are never successful.

83. (As for) that future abode, We assign it to those who have no desire to exalt themselves in the earth nor to make mischief and the good end is for those who guard (against evil).

84. Whoever brings good, he shall have better than it, and

whoever brings evil, those who do evil shall not be rewarded (for) aught except what they did.

85. Most surely He Who has made the Quran binding on you will bring you back to the destination. Say: My Lord knows best him who has brought the guidance and him who is in manifest error.

86. And you did not expect that the Book would be inspired to you, but it is a mercy from your Lord, therefore be not a backer-up of the unbelievers.

87. And let them not turn you aside from the communications of Allah after they have been revealed to you, and call (men) to your Lord and be not of the polytheists.

88. And call not with Allah any other god; there is no god but He; every thing is perishable but He; His is the judgment, and to Him you shall be brought back.

THE SPIDER

In the name of Allah, the Beneficent, the Merciful.

1. Alif Lam Mim.

2. Do men think that they will be left alone on saying, We believe, and not be tried?

3. And certainly We tried those before them, so Allah will certainly know those who are true and He will certainly know the liars.

4. Or do they who work evil think that they will escape Us? Evil is it that they judge!

5. Whoever hopes to meet Allah, the term appointed by Allah will then most surely come; and He is the Hearing, the Knowing.

6. And whoever strives hard, he strives only for his own soul; most surely Allah is Self-sufficient, above (need of) the worlds.

7. And (as for) those who believe and do good, We will most certainly do away with their evil deeds and We will most certainly reward them the best of what they did.

8. And We have enjoined on man goodness to his parents, and if they contend with you that you should associate (others) with

Me, of which you have no knowledge, do not obey them; to Me is your return, so I will inform you of what you did.

9. And (as for) those who believe and do good, We will most surely cause them to enter among the good.

10. And among men is he who says: We believe in Allah; but when he is persecuted in (the way of) Allah he thinks the persecution of men to be as the chastisement of Allah; and if there come assistance from your Lord, they would most certainly say: Surely we were with you. What! is not Allah the best knower of what is in the breasts of mankind.

11. And most certainly Allah will know those who believe, and most certainly He will know the hypocrites.

12. And those who disbelieve say to those who believe: Follow our path and we will bear your wrongs. And never shall they be the bearers of any of their wrongs; most surely they are liars.

13. And most certainly they shall carry their own burdens, and other burdens with their own burdens, and most certainly they shall be questioned on the resurrection day as to what they forged.

14. And certainly We sent Nuh to his people, so he remained among them a thousand years save fifty years. And the deluge overtook them, while they were unjust.

15. So We delivered him and the inmates of the ark, and made it a sign to the nations.

16. And (We sent) Ibrahim, when he said to his people: Serve Allah and be careful of (your duty to) Him; this is best for you, if you did but know:

17. You only worship idols besides Allah and you create a lie; surely they whom you serve besides Allah do not control for you any sustenance, therefore seek the sustenance from Allah and serve Him and be grateful to Him; to Him you shall be brought back.

18. And if you reject (the truth), nations before you did indeed reject (the truth); and nothing is incumbent on the apostle but a plain delivering (of the message).

19. What! do they not consider how Allah originates the creation, then reproduces it? Surely that is easy to Allah.

20. Say: Travel in the earth and see how He makes the first creation, then Allah creates the latter creation; surely Allah has power over all things.

21. He punishes whom He pleases and has mercy on whom He pleases, and to Him you shall be turned back.

22. And you shall not escape in the earth nor in the heaven, and you have neither a protector nor a helper besides Allah.

23. And (as to) those who disbelieve in the communications of Allah and His meeting, they have despaired of My mercy, and these it is that shall have a painful punishment.

24. So naught was the answer of his people except that they said: Slay him or burn him; then Allah delivered him from the fire; most surely there are signs in this for a people who believe.

25. And he said: You have only taken for yourselves idols besides Allah by way of friendship between you in this world's life, then on the resurrection day some of you shall deny others, and some of you shall curse others, and your abode is the fire, and you shall not have any helpers.

26. And Lut believed in Him, and he said: I am fleeing to my Lord, surely He is the Mighty, the Wise.

27. And We granted him Ishaq and Yaqoub, and caused the prophethood and the book to remain in his seed, and We gave him his reward in this world, and in the hereafter he will most surely be among the good.

28. And (We sent) Lut when he said to his people: Most surely you are guilty of an indecency which none of the nations has ever done before you;

29. What! do you come to the males and commit robbery on the highway, and you commit evil deeds in your assemblies? But nothing was the answer of his people except that they said: Bring on us Allah's punishment, if you are one of the truthful.

30. He said: My Lord! help me against the mischievous people.

31. And when Our messengers came to Ibrahim with the good news, they said: Surely we are going to destroy the people of this town, for its people are unjust.

32. He said: Surely in it is Lut. They said: We know well who is in it; we shall certainly deliver him and his followers, except his wife; she shall be of those who remain behind.

33. And when Our messengers came to Lut he was grieved on account of them, and he felt powerless (to protect) them; and they said: Fear not, nor grieve; surely we will deliver you and your followers, except your wife; she shall be of those who remain behind.

34. Surely We will cause to come down upon the people of this town a punishment from heaven, because they transgressed.

35. And certainly We have left a clear sign of it for a people who understand.

36. And to Madyan (We sent) their brother Shuaib, so he said: O my people! serve Allah and fear the latter day and do not act corruptly in the land, making mischief.

37. But they rejected him, so a severe earthquake overtook them, and they became motionless bodies in their abode.

38. And (We destroyed) Ad and Samood, and from their dwellings (this) is apparent to you indeed; and the Shaitan made their deeds fair-seeming to them, so he kept them back from the path, though they were endowed with intelligence and skill,

39. And (We destroyed) Qaroun and Firon and Haman; and certainly Musa came to them with clear arguments, but they behaved haughtily in the land; yet they could not outstrip (Us).

40. So each We punished for his sin; of them was he on whom We sent down a violent storm, and of them was he whom the rumbling overtook, and of them was he whom We made to be swallowed up by the earth, and of them was he whom We drowned; and it did not beseem Allah that He should be unjust to them, but they were unjust to their own souls.

41. The parable of those who take guardians besides Allah is as the parable of the spider that makes for itself a house; and most surely the frailest of the houses is the spider's house—did they but know.

42. Surely Allah knows whatever thing they call upon besides Him; and He is the Mighty, the Wise.

43. And (as for) these examples, We set them forth for men, and none understand them but the learned.

44. Allah created the heavens and the earth with truth; most surely there is a sign in this for the believers.

45. Recite that which has been revealed to you of the Book and keep up prayer; surely prayer keeps (one) away from indecency and evil, and certainly the remembrance of Allah is the greatest, and Allah knows what you do.

46. And do not dispute with the followers of the Book except by what is best, except those of them who act unjustly, and say: We believe in that which has been revealed to us and revealed to you, and our God and your God is One, and to Him do we submit.

47. And thus have We revealed the Book to you. So those whom We have given the Book believe in it, and of these there are those who believe in it, and none deny Our communications except the unbelievers.

48. And you did not recite before it any book, nor did you

transcribe one with your right hand, for then could those who say untrue things have doubted.

49. Nay! these are clear communications in the breasts of those who are granted knowledge; and none deny Our communications except the unjust.

50. And they say: Why are not signs sent down upon him from his Lord? Say: The signs are only with Allah, and I am only a plain warner.

51. Is it not enough for them that We have revealed to you the Book which is recited to them? Most surely there is mercy in this and a reminder for a people who believe.

52. Say: Allah is sufficient as a witness between me and you; He knows what is in the heavens and the earth. And (as for) those who believe in the falsehood and disbelieve in Allah, these it is that are the losers.

53. And they ask you to hasten on the chastisement; and had not a term been appointed, the chastisement would certainly have come to them; and most certainly it will come to them all of a sudden while they will not perceive.

54. They ask you to hasten on the chastisement, and most surely hell encompasses the unbelievers;

55. On the day when the chastisement shall cover them from above them, and from beneath their feet; and He shall say: Taste what you did.

56. O My servants who believe! surely My earth is vast, therefore Me alone should you serve.

57. Every soul must taste of death, then to Us you shall be brought back.

58. And (as for) those who believe and do good, We will certainly give them abode in the nigh places in gardens beneath which rivers flow, abiding therein; how good the reward of the workers:

59. Those who are patient, and on their Lord do they rely.

60. And how many a living creature that does not carry its sustenance: Allah sustains it and yourselves; and He is the Hearing, the Knowing.

61. And if you ask them, Who created the heavens and the earth and made the sun and the moon subservient, they will certainly say, Allah. Whence are they then turned away?

62. Allah makes abundant the means of subsistence for whom He pleases of His servants, and straitens them for whom (He pleases) surely Allah is Cognizant of all things.

63. And if you ask them Who is it that sends down water from the clouds, then gives life to the earth with it after its death, they will certainly say, Allah. Say: All praise is due to Allah. Nay, most of them do not understand.

64. And this life of the world is nothing but a sport and a play; and as for the next abode, that most surely is the life—did they but know!

65. So when they ride in the ships they call upon Allah, being sincerely obedient to Him, but when He brings them safe to the land, lo! they associate others (with Him);

66. Thus they become ungrateful for what We have given them, so that they may enjoy; but they shall soon know.

67. Do they not see that We have made a sacred territory secure, while men are carried off by force from around them? Will they still believe in the falsehood and disbelieve in the favour of Allah?

68. And who is more unjust than one who forges a lie against Allah, or gives the lie to the truth when it has come to him? Will not in hell be the abode of the unbelievers?

69. And (as for) those who strive hard for Us, We will most certainly guide them in Our ways; and Allah is most surely with the doers of good.

THE ROMANS

In the name of Allah, the Beneficent, the Merciful.

1. Alif Lam Mim.

2. The Romans are vanquished,

3. In a near land, and they, after being vanquished, shall overcome,

4. Within a few years. Allah's is the command before and after; and on that day the believers shall rejoice,

5. With the help of Allah; He helps whom He pleases; and He is the Mighty, the Merciful;

6. (This is) Allah's promise! Allah will not fail His promise, but most people do not know.

7. They know the outward of this world's life, but of the hereafter they are absolutely heedless.

8. Do they not reflect within themselves: Allah did not create the heavens and the earth and what is between them two but with truth, and (for) an appointed term? And most surely most of the people are deniers of the meeting of their Lord.

9. Have they not travelled in the earth and seen how was the end of those before them? They were stronger than these in prowess, and dug up the earth, and built on it in greater abundance than these have built on it, and there came to them their apostles with clear arguments; so it was not beseeming for Allah that He should deal with them unjustly, but they dealt unjustly with their own souls.

10. Then evil was the end of those who did evil, because they rejected the communications of Allah and used to mock them.

11. Allah originates the creation, then reproduces it, then to Him you shall be brought back.

12. And at the time when the hour shall come the guilty shall be in despair.

13. And they shall not have any intercessors from among their gods they have joined with God, and they shall be deniers of their associate-gods.

14. And at the time when the hour shall come, at that time they shall become separated one from the other.

15. Then as to those who believed and did good, they shall be made happy in a garden.

16. And as to those who disbelieved and rejected Our communications and the meeting of the hereafter, these shall be brought over to the chastisement.

17. Therefore glory be to Allah when you enter upon the time of the evening and when you enter upon the time of the morning.

18. And to Him belongs praise in the heavens and the earth, and at nightfall and when you are at midday.

19. He brings forth the living from the dead and brings forth the dead from the living, and gives life to the earth after its death, and thus shall you be brought forth.

20. And one of His signs is that He created you from dust, then lo! you are mortals (who) scatter.

21. And one of His signs is that He created mates for you from yourselves that you may find rest in them, and He put between you love and compassion; most surely there are signs in this for a people who reflect.

22. And one of His signs is the creation of the heavens and the earth and the diversity of your tongues and colors; most surely there are signs in this for the learned.

23. And one of His signs is your sleeping and your seeking of His grace by night and (by) day; most surely there are signs in this for a people who would hear.

24. And one of His signs is that He shows you the lightning for fear and for hope, and sends down water from the clouds, then gives life therewith to the earth after its death; most surely there are signs in this for a people who understand.

25. And one of His signs is that the heaven and the earth subsist by His command, then when He calls you with a (single) call from out of the earth, lo! you come forth.

26. And His is whosoever is in the heavens and the earth; all are obedient to Him.

27. And He it is Who originates the creation, then reproduces it, and it is easy to Him; and His are the most exalted attributes in the heavens and the earth, and He is the Mighty, the Wise.

28. He sets forth to you a parable relating to yourselves: Have you among those whom your right hands possess partners in what We have given you for sustenance, so that with respect to it you are alike; you fear them as you fear each other? Thus do We make the communications distinct for a people who understand.

29. Nay! those who are unjust follow their low desires without any knowledge; so who can guide him whom Allah makes err? And they shall have no helpers.

30. Then set your face upright for religion in the right state—the nature made by Allah in which He has made men; there is no altering of Allah's creation; that is the right religion, but most people do not know—

31. Turn to Him, and be careful of (your duty to) Him, and keep up prayer and be not of the polytheists,

32. Of those who divided their religion and became sects, every sect rejoicing in what they had with them.

33. And when harm afflicts men, they call upon their Lord, turning to Him, then when He makes them taste of mercy from Him, lo! some of them begin to associate (others) with their Lord,

34. So as to be ungrateful for what We have given them; but enjoy yourselves (for a while), for you shall soon come to know.

35. Or, have We sent down upon them an authority so that it speaks of that which they associate with Him?

36. And when We make people taste of mercy they rejoice in it, and if an evil befall them for what their hands have already wrought, lo! they are in despair.

37. Do they not see that Allah makes ample provision for

whom He pleases, or straitens? Most surely there are signs in this for a people who believe.

38. Then give to the near of kin his due, and to the needy and the wayfarer; this is best for those who desire Allah's pleasure, and these it is who are successful.

39. And whatever you lay out as usury, so that it may increase in the property of men, it shall not increase with Allah; and whatever you give in charity, desiring Allah's pleasure—it is these (persons) that shall get manifold.

40. Allah is He Who created you, then gave you sustenance, then He causes you to die, then brings you to life. Is there any of your associate-gods who does aught of it? Glory be to Him, and exalted be He above what they associate (with Him).

41. Corruption has appeared in the land and the sea on account of what the hands of men have wrought, that He may make them taste a part of that which they have done, so that they may return.

42. Say: Travel in the land, then see how was the end of those before; most of them were polytheists.

43. Then turn thy face straight to the right religion before there come from Allah the day which cannot be averted; on that day they shall become separated.

44. Whoever disbelieves, he shall be responsible for his disbelief, and whoever does good, they prepare (good) for their own souls,

45. That He may reward those who believe and do good out of His grace; surely He does not love the unbelievers.

46. And one of His signs is that He sends forth the winds bearing good news, and that He may make you taste of His mercy, and that the ships may run by His command, and that you may seek of His grace, and that you may be grateful.

47. And certainly We sent before you apostles to their people, so they came to them with clear arguments, then We gave the punishment to those who were guilty; and helping the believers is ever incumbent on Us.

48. Allah is he Who sends forth the winds so they raise a cloud, then He spreads it forth in the sky as He pleases, and He breaks it up so that you see the rain coming forth from inside it; then when He causes it to fall upon whom He pleases of His servants, lo! they are joyful,

49. Though they were before this, before it was sent down upon them, confounded in sure despair.

50. Look then at the signs of Allah's mercy, how He gives life

to the earth after its death, most surely He will raise the dead to life; and He has power over all things.

51. And if We send a wind and they see it to be yellow, they would after that certainly continue to disbelieve.

52. For surely you cannot make the dead to hear and you cannot make the deaf to hear the call, when they turn back and flee.

53. Nor can you lead away the blind out of their error. You cannot make to hear any but those who believe in Our communications so they shall submit.

54. Allah is He Who created you from a state of weakness, then He gave strength after weakness, then ordained weakness and hoary hair after strength; He creates what He pleases, and He is the Knowing, the Powerful.

55. And at the time when the hour shall come, the guilty shall swear (that) they did not tarry but an hour; thus are they ever turned away.

56. And those who are given knowledge and faith will say: Certainly you tarried according to the ordinance of Allah till the day of resurrection, so this is the day of resurrection, but you did not know.

57. But on that day their excuse shall not profit those who were unjust, nor shall they be regarded with goodwill.

58. And certainly We have set forth for men every kind of example in this Quran; and if you should bring them a communication, those who disbelieve would certainly say: You are naught but false claimants.

59. Thus does Allah set a seal on the hearts of those who do not know.

60. Therefore be patient; surely the promise of Allah is true, and let not those who have no certainty hold you in light estimation.

LUQMAN

In the name of Allah, the Beneficent, the Merciful.

1. Alif Lam Mim.
2. These are verses of the Book of Wisdom,
3. A guidance and a mercy for the doers of goodness,

4. Those who keep up prayer and pay the poor-rate and they are certain of the hereafter.

5. These are on a guidance from their Lord, and these are they who are successful.

6. And of men is he who takes instead frivolous discourse to lead astray from Allah's path without knowledge, and to take it for a mockery; these shall have an abasing chastisement.

7. And when Our communications are recited to him, he turns back proudly, as if he had not heard them, as though in his ears were a heaviness, therefore announce to him a painful chastisement.

8. (As for) those who believe and do good, they shall surely have gardens of bliss,

9. Abiding in them; the promise of Allah; (a) true (promise), and He is the Mighty, the Wise.

10. He created the heavens without pillars as you see them, and put mountains upon the earth lest it might convulse with you, and He spread in it animals of every kind; and We sent down water from the cloud, then caused to grow therein (vegetation) of every noble kind.

11. This is Allah's creation, but show Me what those besides Him have created. Nay, the unjust are in manifest error.

12. And certainly We gave wisdom to Luqman, saying: Be grateful to Allah. And whoever is grateful, he is only grateful for his own soul; and whoever is ungrateful, then surely Allah is Self-sufficient, Praised.

13. And when Luqman said to his son while he admonished him: O my son! do not associate aught with Allah; most surely polytheism is a grievous iniquity—

14. And We have enjoined man in respect of his parents—his mother bears him with faintings upon faintings and his weaning takes two years—saying: Be grateful to Me and to both your parents; to Me is the eventual coming.

15. And if they contend with you that you should associate with Me what you have no knowledge of, do not obey them, and keep company with them in this world kindly, and follow the way of him who turns to Me, then to Me is your return, then will I inform you of what you did—

16. O my son! surely if it is the very weight of the grain of a mustard-seed, even though it is in (the heart of) rock, or (high above) in the heaven or (deep down) in the earth, Allah will bring it (to light); surely Allah is Knower of subtleties, Aware;

17. O my son! keep up prayer and enjoin the good and forbid

the evil, and bear patiently that which befalls you; surely these acts require courage;

18. And do not turn your face away from people in contempt, nor go about in the land exulting overmuch; surely Allah does not love any self-conceited boaster;

19. And pursue the right course in your going about and lower your voice; surely the most hateful of voices is braying of the asses.

20. Do you not see that Allah has made what is in the heavens and what is in the earth subservient to you, and made complete to you His favors outwardly and inwardly? And among men is he who disputes in respect of Allah though having no knowledge, nor guidance, nor a book giving light.

21. And when it is said to them: Follow what Allah has revealed, they say: Nay, we follow that on which we found our fathers. What! though the Shaitan calls them to the chastisement of the burning fire!

22. And whoever submits himself wholly to Allah and he is the doer of good (to others), he indeed has taken hold of the firmest thing upon which one can lay hold; and Allah's is the end of affairs.

23. And whoever disbelieves, let not his disbelief grieve you; to Us is their return, then will We inform them of what they did; surely Allah is the Knower of what is in the breasts.

24. We give them to enjoy a little, then will We drive them to a severe chastisement.

25. And if you ask them who created the heavens and the earth, they will certainly say: Allah. Say: (All) praise is due to Allah; nay! most of them do not know.

26. What is in the heavens and the earth is Allah's; surely Allah is the Self-sufficient, the Praised.

27. And were every tree that is in the earth (made into) pens and the sea (to supply it with ink), with seven more seas to increase it, the words of Allah would not come to an end; surely Allah is Mighty, Wise.

28. Neither your creation nor your raising is anything but as a single soul; surely Allah is Hearing, Seeing.

29. Do you not see that Allah makes the night to enter into the day, and He makes the day to enter into the night, and He has made the sun and the moon subservient (to you); each pursues its course till an appointed time; and that Allah is Aware of what you do?

30. This is because Allah is the Truth, and that which they call upon besides Him is the falsehood, and that Allah is the High, the Great.

31. Do you not see that the ships run on in the sea by Allah's favor, that He may show you of His signs? Most surely there are signs in this for every patient endurer, grateful one.

32. And when a wave like mountains covers them they call upon Allah, being sincere to Him in obedience, but when He brings them safe to the land, some of them follow the middle course; and none denies Our signs but every perfidious, ungrateful one.

33. O people! guard against (the punishment of) your Lord and dread the day when a father shall not make any satisfaction for his son, nor shall the child be the maker of any satisfaction for his father; surely the promise of Allah is true, therefore let not this world's life deceive you, nor let the arch-deceiver deceive you in respect of Allah.

34. Surely Allah is He with Whom is the knowledge of the hour, and He sends down the rain and He knows what is in the wombs; and no one knows what he shall earn on the morrow; and no one knows in what land he shall die; surely Allah is Knowing, Aware.

THE ADORATION

In the name of Allah, the Beneficent, the Merciful.

1. Alif Lam Mim.

2. The revelation of the Book, there is no doubt in it, is from the Lord of the worlds.

3. Or do they say: He has forged it? Nay! it is the truth from your Lord that you may warn a people to whom no warner has come before you, that they may follow the right direction.

4. Allah is He Who created the heavens and the earth and what is between them in six periods, and He mounted the throne (of authority); you have not besides Him any guardian or any intercessor; will you not then mind?

5. He regulates the affair from the heaven to the earth; then

shall it ascend to Him in a day the measure of which is a thousand years of what you count.

6. This is the Knower of the unseen and the seen, the Mighty, the Merciful,

7. Who made good everything that He has created, and He began the creation of man from dust.

8. Then He made his progeny of an extract, of water held in light estimation.

9. Then He made him complete and breathed into him of His spirit, and made for you the ears and the eyes and the hearts; little is it that you give thanks.

10. And they say: What! when we have become lost in the earth, shall we then certainly be in a new creation? Nay! they are disbelievers in the meeting of their Lord.

11. Say: The angel of death who is given charge of you shall cause you to die, then to your Lord you shall be brought back.

12. And could you but see when the guilty shall hang down their heads before their Lord: Our Lord! we have seen and we have heard, therefore send us back, we will do good; surely (now) we are certain.

13. And if We had pleased We would certainly have given to every soul its guidance, but the word (which had gone forth) from Me was just: I will certainly fill hell with the jinn and men together.

14. So taste, because you neglected the meeting of this day of yours; surely We forsake you; and taste the abiding chastisement for what you did.

15. Only they believe in Our communications who, when they are reminded of them, fall down making obeisance and celebrate the praise of their Lord, and they are not proud.

16. Their sides draw away from (their) beds, they call upon their Lord in fear and in hope, and they spend (benevolently) out of what We have given them.

17. So no soul knows what is hidden for them of that which will refresh the eyes; a reward for what they did.

18. Is he then who is a believer like him who is a transgressor? They are not equal.

19. As for those who believe and do good, the gardens are their abiding-place; an entertainment for what they did.

20. And as for those who transgress, their abode is the fire; whenever they desire to go forth from it they shall be brought back into it, and it will be said to them: Taste the chastisement of the fire which you called a lie.

21. And most certainly We will make them taste of the nearer chastisement before the greater chastisement that haply they may turn.

22. And who is more unjust than he who is reminded of the communications of his Lord, then he turns away from them? Surely We will give punishment to the guilty.

23. And certainly We gave the Book to Musa, so be not in doubt concerning the receiving of it, and We made it a guide for the children of Israel.

24. And We made of them Imams to guide by Our command when they were patient, and they were certain of Our communications.

25. Surely your Lord will judge between them on the day of resurrection concerning that wherein they differ.

26. Does it not point out to them the right way, how many of the generations, in whose abodes they go about, did We destroy before them? Most surely there are signs in this; will they not then hear?

27. Do they not see that We drive the water to a land having no herbage, then We bring forth thereby seed-produce of which their cattle and they themselves eat; will they not then see?

28. And they say: When will this judgment take place, if you are truthful?

29. Say: On the day of judgment the faith of those who (now) disbelieve will not profit them, nor will they be respited.

30. Therefore turn away from them and wait, surely they too are waiting.

THE ALLIES

In the name of Allah, the Beneficent, the Merciful.

1. O Prophet! be careful of (your duty to) Allah and do not comply with (the wishes of) the unbelievers and the hypocrites; surely Allah is Knowing, Wise;

2. And follow what is revealed to you from your Lord; surely Allah is Aware of what you do;

3. And rely on Allah; and Allah is sufficient for a Protector.

4. Allah has not made for any man two hearts within him; nor has He made your wives whose backs you liken to the backs of

your mothers as your mothers, nor has He made those whom you assert to be your sons your real sons; these are the words of your mouths; and Allah speaks the truth and He guides to the way.

5. Assert their relationship to their fathers; this is more equitable with Allah; but if you do not know their fathers, then they are your brethren in faith and your friends; and there is no blame on you concerning that in which you made a mistake, but (concerning) that which your hearts do purposely (blame may rest on you), and Allah is Forgiving, Merciful.

6. The Prophet has a greater claim on the faithful than they have on themselves, and his wives are (as) their mothers; and the possessors of relationship have the better claim in the ordinance of Allah to inheritance, one with respect to another, than (other) believers, and (than) those who have fled (their homes), except that you do some good to your friends; this is written in the Book.

7. And when We made a covenant with the prophets and with you, and with Nuh and Ibrahim and Musa and Isa, son of Marium, and We made with them a strong covenant,

8. That He may question the truthful of their truth, and He has prepared for the unbelievers a painful punishment.

9. O you who believe! call to mind the favor of Allah to you when there came down upon you hosts, so We sent against them a strong wind and hosts, that you saw not, and Allah is Seeing what you do.

10. When they came upon you from above you and from below you, and when the eyes turned dull, and the hearts rose up to the throats, and you began to think diverse thoughts of Allah.

11. There the believers were tried and they were shaken with severe shaking.

12. And when the hypocrites and those in whose hearts was a disease began to say: Allah and His Apostle did not promise us (victory) but only to deceive.

13. And when a party of them said: O people of Yathrib! (old name of Medina) there is no place to stand for you (here), therefore go back; and a party of them asked permission of the prophet, saying: Surely our houses are exposed; and they were not exposed; they only desired to fly away.

14. And if an entry were made upon them from the outlying parts of it, then they were asked to wage war, they would certainly have done it, and they would not have stayed in it but a little while.

15. And certainly they had made a covenant with Allah before,

(that) they would not turn (their) backs; and Allah's covenant shall be inquired of.

16. Say: Flight shall not do you any good if you fly from death or slaughter, and in that case you will not be allowed to enjoy yourselves but a little.

17. Say: Who is it that can withhold you from Allah if He intends to do you evil, rather He intends to show you mercy? And they will not find for themselves besides Allah any guardian or a helper.

18. Allah knows indeed those among you who hinder others and those who say to their brethren: Come to us; and they come not to the fight but a little,

19. Being niggardly with respect to you; but when fear comes, you will see them looking to you, their eyes rolling like one swooning because of death; but when the fear is gone they smite you with sharp tongues, being niggardly of the good things. These have not believed, therefore Allah has made their doing naught; and this is easy to Allah.

20. They think the allies are not gone, and if the allies should come (again) they would fain be in the deserts with the desert Arabs asking for news about you, and if they were among you they would not fight save a little.

21. Certainly you have in the Apostle of Allah an excellent exemplar for him who hopes in Allah and the latter day and remembers Allah much.

22. And when the believers saw the allies, they said: This is what Allah and His Apostle promised us, and Allah and His Apostle spoke the truth; and it only increased them in faith and submission.

23. Of the believers are men who are true to the covenant which they made with Allah; so of them is he who accomplished his vow, and of them is he who yet waits, and they have not changed in the least;

24. That Allah may reward the truthful for their truth, and punish the hypocrites if He please or turn to them (mercifully); surely Allah is Forgiving, Merciful.

25. And Allah turned back the unbelievers in their rage; they did not obtain any advantage, and Allah sufficed the believers in fighting; and Allah is Strong, Mighty.

26. And He drove down those of the followers of the Book who backed them from their fortresses and He cast awe into their hearts; some you killed and you took captive another part.

27. And He made you heirs to their land and their dwellings

and their property, and (to) a land which you have not yet trodden, and Allah has power over all things.

28. O Prophet! say to your wives: If you desire this world's life and its adornment, then come, I will give you a provision and allow you to depart a goodly departing;

29. And if you desire Allah and His Apostle and the latter abode, then surely Allah has prepared for the doers of good among you a mighty reward.

30. O wives of the prophet! whoever of you commits an open indecency, the punishment shall be increased to her doubly; and this is easy to Allah.

31. And whoever of you is obedient to Allah and His Apostle and does good, We will give to her her reward doubly, and We have prepared for her an honorable sustenance.

32. O wives of the Prophet! you are not like any other of the women; if you will be on your guard, then be not soft in (your) speech, lest he in whose heart is a disease yearn; and speak a good word.

33. And stay in your houses and do not display your finery like the displaying of the ignorance of yore; and keep up prayer, and pay the poor-rate, and obey Allah and His Apostle. Allah only desires to keep away the uncleanness from you, O people of the House! and to purify you a (thorough) purifying.

34. And keep to mind what is recited in your houses of the communications of Allah and the wisdom; surely Allah is Knower of subtleties, Aware.

35. Surely the men who submit and the women who submit, and the believing men and the believing women, and the obeying men and the obeying women, and the truthful men and the truthful women, and the patient men and the patient women, and the humble men and the humble women, and the almsgiving men and the almsgiving women, and the fasting men and the fasting women, and the men who guard their private parts and the women who guard, and the men who remember Allah much and the women who remember—Allah has prepared for them forgiveness and a mighty reward.

36. And it behoves not a believing man and a believing woman that they should have any choice in their matter when Allah and His Apostle have decided a matter; and whoever disobeys Allah and His Apostle, he surely strays off a manifest straying.

37. And when you said to him to whom Allah had shown favor and to whom you had shown a favor: Keep your wife to

yourself and be careful of (your duty to) Allah; and you concealed in your soul what Allah would bring to light, and you feared men, and Allah had a greater right that you should fear Him. But when Zaid had accomplished his want of her, We gave her to you as a wife, so that there should be no difficulty for the believers in respect of the wives of their adopted sons, when they have accomplished their want of them; and Allah's command shall be performed.

38. There is no harm in the Prophet doing that which Allah has ordained for him; such has been the course of Allah with respect to those who have gone before; and the command of Allah is a decree that is made absolute:

39. Those who deliver the messages of Allah and fear Him, and do not fear any one but Allah; and Allah is sufficient to take account.

40. Muhammad is not the father of any of your men, but he is the Apostle of Allah and the Last of the prophets; and Allah is Cognizant of all things.

41. O you who believe! remember Allah, remembering frequently,

42. And glorify Him morning and evening.

43. He it is Who sends His blessings on you, and (so do) His angels, that He may bring you forth out of utter darkness into the light; and He is Merciful to the believers.

44. Their salutation on the day that they meet Him shall be, Peace, and He has prepared for them an honourable reward.

45. O Prophet! surely We have sent you as a witness, and as a bearer of good news and as a warner,

46. And as one inviting to Allah by His permission, and as a light-giving torch.

47. And give to the believers the good news that they shall have a great grace from Allah.

48. And be not compliant to the unbelievers and the hypocrites, and leave unregarded their annoying talk, and rely on Allah; and Allah is sufficient as a Protector.

49. O you who believe! when you marry the believing women, then divorce them before you touch them, you have in their case no term which you should reckon; so make some provision for them and send them forth a goodly sending forth.

50. O Prophet! surely We have made lawful to you your wives whom you have given their dowries, and those whom your right hand possesses out of those whom Allah has given to you as

prisoners of war, and the daughters of your paternal uncles and the daughters of your paternal aunts, and the daughters of your maternal uncles and the daughters of your maternal aunts who fled with you; and a believing woman if she gave herself to the Prophet, if the Prophet desired to marry her—specially for you, not for the (rest of) believers; We know what We have ordained for them concerning their wives and those whom their right hands possess in order that no blame may attach to you; and Allah is Forgiving, Merciful.

51. You may put off whom you please of them, and you may take to you whom you please, and whom you desire of those whom you had separated provisionally; no blame attaches to you; this is most proper, so that their eyes may be cool and they may not grieve, and that they should be pleased, all of them, with what you give them, and Allah knows what is in your hearts; and Allah is Knowing, Forbearing.

52. It is not allowed to you to take women afterwards, nor that you should change them for other wives, though their beauty be pleasing to you, except what your right hand possesses; and Allah is Watchful over all things.

53. O you who believe! do not enter the houses of the Prophet unless permission is given to you for a meal, not waiting for its cooking being finished—but when you are invited, enter, and when you have taken the food, then disperse—not seeking to listen to talk; surely this gives the Prophet trouble, but he forbears from you, and Allah does not forbear from the truth. And when you ask of them any goods, ask of them from behind a curtain; this is purer for your hearts and (for) their hearts; and it does not behove you that you should give trouble to the Apostle of Allah, nor that you should marry his wives after him ever; surely this is grievous in the sight of Allah.

54. If you do a thing openly or do it in secret, then surely Allah is Cognizant of all things.

55. There is no blame on them in respect of their fathers, nor their brothers, nor their brothers' sons, nor their sisters' sons, nor their own women, nor of what their right hands possess; and be careful of (your duty to) Allah; surely Allah is a witness of all things.

56. Surely Allah and His angels bless the Prophet; O you who believe! call for (Divine) blessings on him and salute him with a (becoming) salutation.

57. Surely (as for) those who speak evil things of Allah and

His Apostle, Allah has cursed them in this world and the hereafter, and He has prepared for them a chastisement bringing disgrace.

58. And those who speak evil things of the believing men and the believing women without their having earned (it), they are guilty indeed of a false accusation and a manifest sin.

59. O Prophet! say to your wives and your daughters and the women of the believers that they let down upon them their overgarments; this will be more proper, that they may be known, and thus they will not be given trouble; and Allah is Forgiving, Merciful.

60. If the hypocrites and those in whose hearts is a disease and the agitators in the city do not desist, We shall most certainly set you over them, then they shall not be your neighbors in it but for a little while;

61. Cursed: wherever they are found they shall be seized and murdered, a (horrible) murdering.

62. (Such has been) the course of Allah with respect to those who have gone before; and you shall not find any change in the course of Allah.

63. Men ask you about the hour; say: The knowledge of it is only with Allah, and what will make you comprehend that the hour may be nigh.

64. Surely Allah has cursed the unbelievers and has prepared for them a burning fire,

65. To abide therein for a long time; they shall not find a protector or a helper.

66. On the day when their faces shall be turned back into the fire, they shall say: O would that we had obeyed Allah and obeyed the Apostle!

67. And they shall say: O our Lord! surely we obeyed our leaders and our great men, so they led us astray from the path;

68. O our Lord! give them a double punishment and curse them with a great curse.

69. O you who believe! be not like those who spoke evil things of Musa, but Allah cleared him of what they said, and he was worthy of regard with Allah.

70. O you who believe! be careful of (your duty to) Allah and speak the right word,

71. He will put your deeds into a right state for you, and forgive you your faults; and whoever obeys Allah and His Apostle, he indeed achieves a mighty success.

72. Surely We offered the trust to the heavens and the earth and the mountains, but they refused to be unfaithful to it and feared from it, and man has turned unfaithful to it; surely he is unjust, ignorant;

73. So Allah will chastise the hypocritical men and the hypocritical women and the polytheistic men and the polytheistic women, and Allah will turn (mercifully) to the believing women, and Allah is Forgiving, Merciful.

SABA

In the name of Allah, the Beneficent, the Merciful.

1. (All) praise is due to Allah, Whose is what is in the heavens and what is in the earth, and to Him is due (all) praise in the hereafter; and He is the Wise, the Aware.

2. He knows that which goes down into the earth and that which comes out of it, and that which comes down from the heaven and that which goes up to it; and He is the Merciful, the Forgiving.

3. And those who disbelieve say: The hour shall not come upon us. Say: Yea! by my Lord, the Knower of the unseen, it shall certainly come upon you; not the weight of an atom becomes absent from Him, in the heavens or in the earth, and neither less than that nor greater, but (all) is in a clear book,

4. That He may reward those who believe and do good; these it is for whom is forgiveness and an honorable sustenance.

5. And (as for) those who strive hard in opposing Our communications, these it is for whom is a painful chastisement of an evil kind.

6. And those to whom the knowledge has been given see that which has been revealed to you from your Lord, that is the truth, and it guides into the path of the Mighty, the Praised.

7. And those who disbelieve say: Shall we point out to you a man who informs you that when you are scattered the utmost scattering you shall then be most surely (raised) in (to) a new creation?

8. He has forged a lie against Allah or there is madness in

him. Nay! those who do not believe in the hereafter are in torment and in great error.

9. Do they not then consider what is before them and what is behind them of the heaven and the earth? If We please We will make them disappear in the land or bring down upon them a portion from the heaven; most surely there is a sign in this for every servant turning (to Allah).

10. And certainly We gave to Dawood excellence from Us: O mountains! sing praises with him, and the birds; and We made the iron pliant to him,

11. Saying: Make ample (coats of mail), and assign a time to the making of coats of mail and do good; surely I am Seeing what you do.

12. And (We made) the wind (subservient) to Sulaiman, which made a month's journey in the morning and a month's journey in the evening, and We made a fountain of molten copper to flow out for him; and of the jinn there were those who worked before him by the command of his Lord; and whoever turned aside from Our command from among them, We made him taste of the punishment of burning.

13. They made for him what he pleased of fortresses and images, and bowls (large) as watering-troughs and cooking-pots that will not move from their place; give thanks, O family of Dawood! and very few of My servants are grateful.

14. But when We decreed death for him, naught showed them his death but a creature of the earth that ate away his staff; and when it fell down, the jinn came to know plainly that if they had known the unseen, they would not have tarried in abasing torment.

15. Certainly there was a sign for Saba in their abode; two gardens on the right and the left; eat of the sustenance of your Lord and give thanks to Him: a good land and a Forgiving Lord!

16. But they turned aside, so We sent upon them a torrent of which the rush could not be withstood, and in place of their two gardens We gave to them two gardens yielding bitter fruit and (growing) tamarisk and a few lote-trees.

17. This We requited them with because they disbelieved; and We do not punish any but the ungrateful.

18. And We made between them and the towns which We had blessed (other) towns to be easily seen, and We apportioned the journey therein: Travel through them nights and days, secure.

19. And they said: O our Lord! make spaces to be longer

between our journeys; and they were unjust to themselves; so We made them stories and scattered them with an utter scattering; most surely there are signs in this for every patient, grateful one.

20. And certainly the Shaitan found true his conjecture concerning them, so they follow him, except a party of the believers.

21. And he has no authority over them, but that We may distinguish him who believes in the hereafter from him who is in doubt concerning it; and your Lord is the Preserver of all things.

22. Say: Call upon those whom you assert besides Allah; they do not control the weight of an atom in the heavens or in the earth, nor have they any partnership in either, nor has He among them any one to back (Him) up.

23. And intercession will not avail aught with Him save of him whom He permits. Until when fear shall be removed from their hearts, They shall say: What is it that your Lord said? They shall say: The truth. And He is the Most High, the Great.

24. Say: Who gives you the sustenance from the heavens and the earth? Say: Allah. And most surely we or you are on a right way or in manifest error.

25. Say: You will not be questioned as to what we are guilty of, nor shall we be questioned as to what you do.

26. Say: Our Lord will gather us together, then will He judge between us with the truth; and He is the greatest Judge, the All-knowing.

27. Say: Show me those whom you have joined with Him as associates; by no means (can you do it). Nay! He is Allah, the Mighty, the Wise.

28. And We have not sent you but to all the men as a bearer of good news and as a warner, but most men do not know.

29. And they say: When will this promise be (fulfilled) if you are truthful?

30. Say: You have the appointment of a day from which you cannot hold back any while, nor can you bring it on.

31. And those who disbelieve say: By no means will we believe in this Quran, nor in that which is before it; and could you see when the unjust shall be made to stand before their Lord, bandying words one with another! Those who were reckoned weak shall say to those who were proud: Had it not been for you, we would certainly have been believers.

32. Those who were proud shall say to those who were deemed weak: Did we turn you away from the guidance after it had come to you? Nay, you (yourselves) were guilty.

33. And those who were deemed weak shall say to those who

were proud: Nay, (it was) planning by night and day when you told us to disbelieve in Allah and to set up likes with Him. And they shall conceal regret when they shall see the punishment; and We will put shackles on the necks of those who disbelieved; they shall not be requited but what they did.

34. And We never sent a warner to a town but those who led lives in ease in it said: We are surely disbelievers in what you are sent with.

35. And they say: We have more wealth and children, and we shall not be punished.

36. Say: Surely my Lord amplifies the means of subsistence for whom He pleases and straitens (for whom He pleases), but most men do not know.

37. And not your wealth nor your children, are the things which bring you near Us in station, but whoever believes and does good, these it is for whom is a double reward for what they do, and they shall be secure in the highest places.

38. And (as for) those who strive in opposing Our communications, they shall be caused to be brought to the chastisement.

39. Say: Surely my Lord amplifies the means of subsistence for whom He pleases of His servants and straitens (them) for whom (He pleases), and whatever thing you spend, He exceeds it in reward, and He is the best of Sustainers.

40. And on the day when He will gather them all together, then will He say to the angels: Did these worship you?

41. They shall say: Glory be to Thee! Thou art our Guardian, not they; nay! they worshipped the jinn; most of them were believers in them.

42. So on that day one of you shall not control profit or harm for another, and We will say to those who were unjust: Taste the chastisement of the fire which you called a lie.

43. And when Our clear communications are recited to them, they say: This is naught but a man who desires to turn you away from that which your fathers worshipped. And they say: This is naught but a lie that is forged. And those who disbelieve say of the truth when it comes to them: This is only clear enchantment.

44. And We have not given them any books which they read, nor did We send to them before you a warner.

45. And those before them rejected (the truth), and these have not yet attained a tenth of what We gave them, but they gave the lie to My apostles, then how was the manifestation of My disapproval?

46. Say: I exhort you only to one thing, that rise up for Allah's

sake in twos and singly, then ponder: there is no madness in your fellow-citizen; he is only a warner to you before a severe chastisement.

47. Say: Whatever reward I have asked of you, that is only for yourselves; my reward is only with Allah, and He is a witness of all things.

48. Say: Surely my Lord utters the truth, the great Knower of the unseen.

49. Say: The truth has come, and the falsehood shall vanish and shall not come back.

50. Say: If I err, I err only against my own soul, and if I follow a right direction, it is because of what my Lord reveals to me; surely He is Hearing, Nigh.

51. And could you see when they shall become terrified, but (then) there shall be no escape and they shall be seized upon from a near place,

52. And they shall say: We believe in it. And how shall the attaining (of faith) be possible to them from a distant place?

53. And they disbelieved in it before, and they utter conjectures with regard to the unseen from a distant place.

54. And a barrier shall be placed between them and that which they desire, as was done with the likes of them before; surely they are in a disquieting doubt.

SURAH XXXV *The Originator*

THE ORIGINATOR

In the name of Allah, the Beneficent, the Merciful.

1. All praise is due to Allah, the Originator of the heavens and the earth, the Maker of the angels, messengers flying on wings, two, and three, and four; He increases in creation what He pleases; surely Allah has power over all things.

2. Whatever Allah grants to men of (His) mercy, there is none to withhold it, and what He withholds there is none to send it forth after that, and He is the Mighty, the Wise.

3. O men! call to mind the favor of Allah on you; is there any creator besides Allah who gives you sustenance from the heaven and the earth? There is no god but He; whence are you then turned away?

4. And if they call you a liar, truly apostles before you were called liars, and to Allah are all affairs returned.

5. O men! surely the promise of Allah is true, therefore let not the life of this world deceive you, and let not the arch-deceiver deceive you respecting Allah.

6. Surely the Shaitan is your enemy, so take him for an enemy; he only invites his party that they may be inmates of the burning fire.

7. (As for) those who disbelieve, they shall have a severe punishment, and (as for) those who believe and do good, they shall have forgiveness and a great reward.

8. What! is he whose evil deed is made fairseeming to him so much so that he considers it good? Now surely Allah makes err whom He pleases and guides aright whom He pleases, so let not your soul waste away in grief for them; surely Allah is Cognizant of what they do.

9. And Allah is He Who sends the winds so they raise a cloud, then We drive it on to a dead country, and therewith We give life to the earth after its death; even so is the quickening.

10. Whoever desires honor, then to Allah belongs the honor wholly. To Him do ascend the good words; and the good deeds, lift them up; and (as for) those who plan evil deeds, they shall have a severe chastisement; and (as for) their plan, it shall perish.

11. And Allah created you of dust, then of the life-germ, then He made you pairs; and no female bears, nor does she bring forth, except with His knowledge; and no one whose life is lengthened has his life lengthened, nor is aught diminished of one's life, but it is all in a book; surely this is easy to Allah.

12. And the two seas are not alike: the one sweet, that subdues thirst by its excessive sweetness, pleasant to drink; and the other salt, that burns by its saltness; yet from each of them you eat fresh flesh and bring forth ornaments which you wear; and you see the ships cleave through it that you may seek of His bounty and that you may be grateful.

13. He causes the night to enter in upon the day, and He causes the day to enter in upon the night, and He has made subservient (to you) the sun and the moon; each one follows its course to an appointed time; this is Allah, your Lord, His is the kingdom; and those whom you call upon besides Him do not control a straw.

14. If you call on them they shall not hear your call, and even if they could hear they shall not answer you; and on the resurrection day they will deny your associating them (with Allah); and none can inform you like the One Who is Aware.

15. O men! you are they who stand in need of Allah, and Allah is He Who is the Self-sufficient, the Praised One.

16. If He please, He will take you off and bring a new generation.

17. And this is not hard to Allah.

18. And a burdened soul cannot bear the burden of another; and if one weighed down by burden should cry for (another to carry) its burden, not aught of it shall be carried, even though he be near of kin. You warn only those who fear their Lord in secret and keep up prayer; and whoever purifies himself, he purifies himself only for (the good of) his own soul; and to Allah is the eventual coming.

19. And the blind and the seeing are not alike,

20. Nor the darkness and the light,

21. Nor the shade and the heat,

22. Neither are the living and the dead alike. Surely Allah makes whom He pleases hear, and you cannot make those hear who are in the graves.

23. You are naught but a warner.

24. Surely We have sent you with the truth as a bearer of good news and a warner; and there is not a people but a warner has gone among them.

25. And if they call you a liar, so did those before them indeed call (their apostles) liars; their apostles had come to them with clear arguments, and with scriptures, and with the illuminating book.

26. Then did I punish those who disbelieved, so how was the manifestation of My disapproval?

27. Do you not see that Allah sends down water from the cloud, then We bring forth therewith fruits of various colors; and in the mountains are streaks, white and red, of various hues and (others) intensely black?

28. And of men and beasts and cattle are various species of it likewise; those of His servants only who are possessed of knowledge fear Allah; surely Allah is Mighty, Forgiving.

29. Surely they who recite the Book of Allah and keep up prayer and spend out of what We have given them secretly and openly, hope for a gain which will not perish.

30. That He may pay them back fully their rewards and give them more out of His grace: surely He is Forgiving, Multiplier of rewards.

31. And that which We have revealed to you of the Book, that

is the truth verifying that which is before it; most surely with respect to His servants Allah is Aware, Seeing.

32. Then We gave the Book for an inheritance to those whom We chose from among Our servants; but of them is he who makes his soul to suffer a loss, and of them is he who takes a middle course, and of them is he who is foremost in deeds of goodness by Allah's permission; this is the great excellence.

33. Gardens of perpetuity, they shall enter therein; they shall be made to wear therein bracelets of gold and pearls, and their dress therein shall be silk.

34. And they shall say: (All) praise is due to Allah, Who has made grief to depart from us; most surely our Lord is Forgiving, Multiplier of rewards,

35. Who has made us alight in a house abiding for ever out of His grace; toil shall not touch us therein, nor shall fatigue therein afflict us.

36. And (as for) those who disbelieve, for them is the fire of hell; it shall not be finished with them entirely so that they should die, nor shall the chastisement thereof be lightened to them: even thus do We retribute every ungrateful one.

37. And they shall cry therein for succour: O our Lord! take us out, we will do good deeds other than those which we used to do. Did We not preserve you alive long enough, so that he who would be mindful in it should mind? And there came to you the warner; therefore taste; because for the unjust, there is no helper.

38. Surely Allah is the Knower of what is unseen in the heavens and the earth; surely He is Cognizant of what is in the hearts.

39. He it is Who made you rulers in the land; therefore whoever disbelieves, his unbelief is against himself; and their unbelief does not increase the disbelievers with their Lord in anything except hatred, and their unbelief does not increase the disbelievers in anything except loss.

40. Say: Have you considered your associates which you call upon besides Allah? Show me what part of the earth they have created, or have they any share in the heavens; or, have We given them a book so that they follow a clear argument thereof? Nay, the unjust do not hold out promises one to another but only to deceive.

41. Surely Allah upholds the heavens and the earth lest they come to naught; and if they should come to naught, there is none who can uphold them after Him; surely He is the Forbearing, the Forgiving.

42. And they swore by Allah with the strongest of their oaths that if there came to them a warner they would be better guided than any of the nations; but when there came to them a warner it increased them in naught but aversion,

43. (In) behaving proudly in the land and in planning evil; and the evil plans shall not beset any save the authors of it. Then should they wait for aught except the way of the former people? For you shall not find any alteration in the course of Allah; and you shall not find any change in the course of Allah.

44. Have they not travelled in the land and seen how was the end of those before them while they were stronger than these in power? And Allah is not such that any thing in the heavens or in the earth should escape Him; surely He is Knowing, Powerful.

45. And were Allah to punish men for what they earn, He would not leave on the back of it any creature, but He respites them till an appointed term; so when their doom shall come, then surely Allah is Seeing with respect to His servants.

YA SEEN

In the name of Allah, the Beneficent, the Merciful.

1. Ya Seen.
2. I swear by the Quran full of wisdom;
3. Most surely you are one of the apostles,
4. On a right way.
5. A revelation of the Mighty, the Merciful.
6. That you may warn a people whose fathers were not warned, so they are heedless.
7. Certainly the word has proved true of most of them, so they do not believe.
8. Surely We have placed chains on their necks, and these reach up to their chins, so they have their heads raised aloft.
9. And We have made before them a barrier and a barrier behind them, then We have covered them over so that they do not see.
10. And it is alike to them whether you warn them or warn them not: they do not believe.

11. You can only warn him who follows the reminder and fears the Beneficent God in secret; so announce to him forgiveness and an honorable reward.

12. Surely We give life to the dead, and We write down what they have sent before and their footprints, and We have recorded everything in a clear writing.

13. And set out to them an example of the people of the town, when the messengers came to it.

14. When We sent to them two, they rejected both of them, then We strengthened (them) with a third, so they said: Surely we are messengers to you.

15. They said: You are naught but mortals like ourselves, nor has the Beneficent God revealed anything; you only lie.

16. They said: Our Lord knows that we are most surely messengers to you.

17. And nothing devolves on us but a clear deliverance (of the message).

18. They said: Surely we augur evil from you; if you do not desist, we will certainly stone you, and there shall certainly afflict you a painful chastisement from us.

19. They said: Your evil fortune is with you; what! if you are reminded! Nay, you are an extravagant people.

20. And from the remote part of the city there came a man running; he said: O my people! follow the messengers;

21. Follow him who does not ask you for reward, and they are the followers of the right course;

22. And what reason have I that I should not serve Him Who brought me into existence? And to Him you shall be brought back;

23. What! shall I take besides Him gods whose intercession, if the Beneficent God should desire to afflict me with a harm, shall not avail me aught, nor shall they be able to deliver me?

24. In that case I shall most surely be in clear error:

25. Surely I believe in your Lord, therefore hear me.

26. It was said: Enter the garden. He said: O would that my people had known

27. Of that on account of which my Lord has forgiven me and made me of the honored ones!

28. And We did not send down upon his people after him any hosts from heaven, nor do We ever send down.

29. It was naught but a single cry, and lo! they were still.

30. Alas for the servants! there comes not to them an apostle but they mock at him.

31. Do they not consider how many of the generations have We destroyed before them, because they do not turn to them?

32. And all of them shall surely be brought before Us.

33. And a sign to them is the dead earth: We give life to it and bring forth from it grain so they eat of it.

34. And We make therein gardens of palms and grapevines, and We make springs to flow forth in it,

35. That they may eat of the fruit thereof, and their hands did not make it; will they not then be grateful?

36. Glory be to Him Who created pairs of all things, of what the earth grows, and of their kind and of what they do not know.

37. And a sign to them is the night: We draw forth from it the day, then lo! they are in the dark;

38. And the sun runs on to a term appointed for it; that is the ordinance of the Mighty, the Knowing.

39. And (as for) the moon, We have ordained for it stages till it becomes again as an old dry palm branch.

40. Neither is it allowable to the sun that it should overtake the moon, nor can the night outstrip the day; and all float on in a sphere.

41. And a sign to them is that We bear their offspring in the laden ship.

42. And We have created for them the like of it, what they will ride on.

43. And if We please, We can drown them, then there shall be no succorer for them, nor shall they be rescued,

44. But (by) mercy from Us and for enjoyment till a time.

45. And when it is said to them: Guard against what is before you and what is behind you, that mercy may be on you.

46. And there comes not to them a communication of the communications of their Lord but they turn aside from it.

47. And when it is said to them: Spend out of what Allah has given you, those who disbelieve say to those who believe: Shall we feed him whom, if Allah please, He could feed? You are in naught but clear error.

48. And they say: When will this threat come to pass, if you are truthful?

49. They wait not for aught but a single cry which will overtake them while they yet contend with one another.

50. So they shall not be able to make a bequest, nor shall they return to their families.

51. And the trumpet shall be blown, when lo! from their graves they shall hasten on to their Lord.

52. They shall say: O woe to us! who has raised us up from our sleeping-place? This is what the Beneficent God promised and the apostles told the truth.

53. There would be naught but a single cry, when lo! they shall all be brought before Us.

54. So this day no soul shall be dealt with unjustly in the least; and you shall not be rewarded aught but that which you did.

55. Surely the dwellers of the garden shall on that day be in an occupation quite happy.

56. They and their wives shall be in shades, reclining on raised couches.

57. They shall have fruits therein, and they shall have whatever they desire.

58. Peace: a word from a Merciful Lord.

59. And get aside today, O guilty ones!

60. Did I not charge you, O children of Adam! that you should not serve the Shaitan? Surely he is your open enemy,

61. And that you should serve Me; this is the right way.

62. And certainly he led astray numerous people from among you. What! could you not then understand?

63. This is the hell with which you were threatened.

64. Enter into it this day because you disbelieved.

65. On that day We will set a seal upon their mouths, and their hands shall speak to Us, and their feet shall bear witness of what they earned.

66. And if We please We would certainly put out their eyes, then they would run about groping for the way, but how should they see?

67. And if We please We would surely transform them in their place, then they would not be able to go on, nor will they return.

68. And whomsoever We cause to live long, We reduce (him) to an abject state in constitution; do they not then understand?

69. And We have not taught him poetry, nor is it meet for him; it is nothing but a reminder and a plain Quran,

70. That it may warn him who would have life, and (that) the word may prove true against the unbelievers.

71. Do they not see that We have created cattle for them, out of what Our hands have wrought, so they are their masters?

72. And We have subjected them to them, so some of them they have to ride upon, and some of them they eat.

73. And therein they have advantages and drinks; will they not then be grateful?

74. And they have taken gods besides Allah that they may be helped.

75. (But) they shall not be able to assist them, and they shall be a host brought up before them.

76. Therefore let not their speech grieve you; surely We know what they do in secret and what they do openly.

77. Does not man see that We have created him from the small seed? Then lo! he is an open disputant.

78. And he strikes out a likeness for Us and forgets his own creation. Says he: Who will give life to the bones when they are rotten?

79. Say: He will give life to them Who brought them into existence at first, and He is Cognizant of all creation,

80. He Who has made for you the fire (to burn) from the green tree, so that with it you kindle (fire).

81. Is not He Who created the heavens and the earth able to create the like of them? Yea! and He is the Creator (of all), the Knower.

82. His command, when He intends anything, is only to say to it: Be, so it is.

83. Therefore glory be to Him in Whose hand is the kingdom of all things, and to Him you shall be brought back.

THE RANGERS

In the name of Allah, the Beneficent, the Merciful.

1. I swear by those who draw themselves out in ranks,
2. Then those who drive away with reproof,
3. Then those who recite, being mindful,
4. Most surely your God is One:
5. The Lord of the heavens and the earth and what is between them, and Lord of the easts.

6. Surely We have adorned the nearest heaven with an adornment, the stars,

7. And (there is) a safeguard against every rebellious Shaitan.

8. They cannot listen to the exalted assembly and they are thrown at from every side,

9. Being driven off, and for them is a perpetual chastisement,

10. Except him who snatches off but once, then there follows him a brightly shining flame.

11. Then ask them whether they are stronger in creation or those (others) whom We have created. Surely We created them of firm clay.

12. Nay! you wonder while they mock,

13. And when they are reminded, they mind not,

14. And when they see a sign they incite one another to scoff,

15. And they say: This is nothing but clear magic:

16. What! when we are dead and have become dust and bones, shall we then certainly be raised,

17. Or our fathers of yore?

18. Say: Aye! and you shall be abject.

19. So it shall only be a single cry, when lo! they shall see.

20. And they shall say: O woe to us! this is the day of requital.

21. This is the day of the judgment which you called a lie.

22. Gather together those who were unjust and their associates, and what they used to worship

23. Besides Allah, then lead them to the way to hell.

24. And stop them, for they shall be questioned:

25. What is the matter with you that you do not help each other?

26. Nay! on that day they shall be submissive.

27. And some of them shall advance towards others, questioning each other.

28. They shall say: Surely you used to come to us from the right side.

29. They shall say: Nay, you (yourselves) were not believers;

30. And we had no authority over you, but you were an inordinate people;

31. So the sentence of our Lord has come to pass against us: (now) we shall surely taste;

32. So we led you astray, for we ourselves were erring.

33. So they shall on that day be sharers in the chastisement one with another.

34. Surely thus do We deal with the guilty.

35. Surely they used to behave proudly when it was said to them: There is no god but Allah;

36. And to say: What! shall we indeed give up our gods for the sake of a mad poet?

37. Nay: he has come with the truth and verified the apostles.

38. Most surely you will taste the painful punishment.

39. And you shall not be rewarded except (for) what you did.

40. Save the servants of Allah, the purified ones.

41. For them is a known sustenance,

42. Fruits, and they shall be highly honored,

43. In gardens of pleasure,

44. On thrones, facing each other.

45. A bowl shall be made to go round them from water running out of springs,

46. White, delicious to those who drink.

47. There shall be no trouble in it, nor shall they be exhausted therewith.

48. And with them shall be those who restrain the eyes, having beautiful eyes;

49. As if they were eggs carefully protected.

50. Then shall some of them advance to others, questioning each other.

51. A speaker from among them shall say: Surely I had a comrade of mine,

52. Who said: What! are you indeed of those who accept (the truth)?

53. What! when we are dead and have become dust and bones, shall we then be certainly brought to judgment?

54. He shall say: Will you look on?

55. Then he looked down and saw him in the midst of hell.

56. He shall say: By Allah! you had almost caused me to perish;

57. And had it not been for the favor of my Lord, I would certainly have been among those brought up.

58. Is it then that we are not going to die,

59. Except our previous death? And we shall not be chastised?

60. Most surely this is the mighty achievement.

61. For the like of this then let the workers work.

62. Is this better as an entertainment or the tree of Zaqqum?

63. Surely We have made it to be a trial to the unjust.

64. Surely it is a tree that grows in the bottom of the hell;

65. Its produce is as it were the heads of the serpents.

66. Then most surely they shall eat of it and fill (their) bellies with it.

67. Then most surely they shall have after it to drink of a mixture prepared in boiling water.

68. Then most surely their return shall be to hell.

69. Surely they found their fathers going astray,

70. So in their footsteps they are being hastened on.

71. And certainly most of the ancients went astray before them,

72. And certainly We sent among them warners.

73. Then see how was the end of those warned,

74. Except the servants of Allah, the purified ones.

75. And Nuh did certainly call upon Us, and most excellent answerer of prayer are We.

76. And We delivered him and his followers from the mighty distress.

77. And We made his offspring the survivors.

78. And We perpetuated to him (praise) among the later generations.

79. Peace and salutation to Nuh among the nations.

80. Thus do We surely reward the doers of good.

81. Surely he was of Our believing servants.

82. Then We drowned the others.

83. And most surely Ibrahim followed his way.

84. When he came to his Lord with a free heart,

85. When he said to his father and his people: What is it that you worship?

86. A lie—gods besides Allah—do you desire?

87. What is then your idea about the Lord of the worlds?

88. Then he looked at the stars, looking up once,

89. Then he said: Surely I am sick (of your worshipping these).

90. So they went away from him, turning back.

91. Then he turned aside to their gods secretly and said: What! do you not eat?

92. What is the matter with you that you do not speak?

93. Then he turned against them secretly, smiting them with the right hand.

94. So they (people) advanced towards him, hastening.

95. Said he: What! do you worship what you hew out?

96. And Allah has created you and what you make.

97. They said: Build for him a furnace, then cast him into the burning fire.

98. And they desired a war against him, but We brought them low.

99. And he said: Surely I fly to my lord; He will guide me.

100. My Lord! grant me of the doers of good deeds.

101. So We gave him the good news of a boy, possessing forbearance.

102. And when he attained to working with him, he said: O my son! surely I have seen in a dream that I should sacrifice you; consider then what you see. He said: O my father! do what you are commanded; if Allah please, you will find me of the patient ones.

103. So when they both submitted and he threw him down upon his forehead,

104. And We called out to him saying: O Ibrahim!

105. You have indeed shown the truth of the vision; surely thus do We reward the doers of good:

106. Most surely this is a manifest trial.

107. And We ransomed him with a great sacrifice.

108. And We perpetuated (praise) to him among the later generations.

109. Peace be on Ibrahim.

110. Thus do We reward the doers of good.

111. Surely he was one of Our believing servants.

112. And We gave him the good news of Ishaq, a prophet among the good ones.

113. And We showered Our blessings on him and on Ishaq; and of their offspring are the doers of good, and (also) those who are clearly unjust to their own souls.

114. And certainly We conferred a favor on Musa and Haroun.

115. And We delivered them both and their people from the mighty distress.

116. And We helped them, so they were the vanquishers.

117. And We gave them both the Book that made (things) clear.

118. And We guided them both on the right way.

119. And We perpetuated (praise) to them among the later generations.

120. Peace be on Musa and Haroun.

121. Even thus do We reward the doers of good.

122. Surely they were both of Our believing servants.

123. And Ilyas was most surely of the apostles.

124. When he said to his people: Do you not guard (against evil)?

125. What! do you call upon Ba'l and forsake the best of the creators,

126. Allah, your Lord and the Lord of your fathers of yore?

127. But they called him a liar, therefore they shall most surely be brought up.

128. But not the servants of Allah, the purified ones.

129. And We perpetuated to him (praise) among the later generations.

130. Peace be on Ilyas.

131. Even thus do We reward the doers of good.

132. Surely he was one of Our believing servants.

133. And Lut was most surely of the apostles.

134. When We delivered him and his followers, all—

135. Except an old woman (who was) amongst those who tarried.

136. Then We destroyed the others.

137. And most surely you pass by them in the morning,

138. And at night; do you not then understand?

139. And Yunus was most surely of the apostles.

140. When he ran away to a ship completely laden,

141. So he shared (with them), but was of those who are cast off.

142. So the fish swallowed him while he did that for which he blamed himself.

143. But had it not been that he was of those who glorify (Us),

144. He would certainly have tarried in its belly to the day when they are raised.

145. Then We cast him on to the vacant surface of the earth while he was sick.

146. And We caused to grow up for him a gourdplant.

147. And We sent him to a hundred thousand, rather they exceeded.

148. And they believed, so We gave them provision till a time.

149. Then ask them whether your Lord has daughters and they have sons.

150. Or did We create the angels females while they were witnesses?

151. Now surely it is of their own lie that they say:

152. Allah has begotten; and most surely they are liars.

153. Has He chosen daughters in preference to sons?

154. What is the matter with you, how is it that you judge?

155. Will you not then mind?

156. Or have you a clear authority?

157. Then bring your book, if you are truthful.

158. And they assert a relationship between Him and the jinn; and certainly the jinn do know that they shall surely be brought up;

159. Glory be to Allah (for freedom) from what they describe;

160. But not so the servants of Allah, the purified ones.

161. So surely you and what you worship,

162. Not against Him can you cause (any) to fall into trial,

163. Save him who will go to hell.

164. And there is none of us but has an assigned place,

165. And most surely we are they who draw themselves out in ranks,

166. And we are most surely they who declare the glory (of Allah).

167. And surely they used to say:

168. Had we a reminder from those of yore,

169. We would certainly have been the servants of Allah—the purified ones.

170. But (now) they disbelieve in it, so they will come to know.

171. And certainly Our word has already gone forth in respect of Our servants, the apostles:

172. Most surely they shall be the assisted ones,

173. And most surely Our host alone shall be the victorious ones.

174. Therefore turn away from them till a time,

175. And (then) see them, so they too shall see.

176. What! would they then hasten on Our chastisement?

177. But when it shall descend in their court, evil shall then be the morning of the warned ones.

178. And turn away from them till a time,

179. And (then) see, for they too shall see.

180. Glory be to your Lord, the Lord of Honor, above what they dsecribe.

181. And peace be on the apostles.

182. And all praise is due to Allah, the Lord of the worlds.

SUAD

In the name of Allah, the Beneficent, the Merciful.

1. Suad, I swear by the Quran, full of admonition.

2. Nay! those who disbelieve are in self-exaltation and opposition.

3. How many did We destroy before them of the generations, then they cried while the time of escaping had passed away.

4. And they wonder that there has come to them a warner from among themselves, and the disbelievers say: This is an enchanter, a liar.

5. What! makes he the gods a single God? A strange thing is this, to be sure!

6. And the chief persons of them break forth, saying: Go and steadily adhere to your gods; this is most surely a thing sought after.

7. We never heard of this in the former faith; this is nothing but a forgery:

8. Has the reminder been revealed to him from among us?. Nay! they are in doubt as to My reminder. Nay! they have not yet tasted My chastisement!

9. Or is it that they have the treasures of the mercy of your Lord, the Mighty, the great Giver?

10. Or is it that theirs is the kingdom of the heavens and the earth and what is between them? Then let them ascend by any means.

11. A host of deserters of the allies shall be here put to flight.

12. The people of Nuh and Ad, and Firon, the lord of spikes, rejected (apostles) before them.

13. And Samood and the people of Lut and the dwellers of the thicket; these were the parties.

14. There was none of them but called the apostles liars, so just was My retribution.

15. Nor do these await aught but a single cry, there being no delay in it.

16. And they say: O our Lord! hasten on to us our portion before the day of reckoning.

17. Bear patiently what they say, and remember Our servant Dawood, the possessor of power; surely he was frequent in returning (to Allah).

18. Surely We made the mountains to sing the glory (of Allah) in unison with him at the evening and the sunrise,

19. And the birds gathered together; all joined in singing with him.

20. And We strengthened his kingdom and We gave him wisdom and a clear judgment.

21. And has there come to you the story of the litigants, when they made an entry into the private chamber by ascending over the walls?

22. When they entered in upon Dawood and he was frightened at them, they said: Fear not; two litigants, of whom one has acted wrongfully towards the other, therefore decide between us with justice, and do not act unjustly, and guide us to the right way.

23. Surely this is my brother; he has ninety-nine ewes and I have a single ewe; but he said: Make it over to me, and he has prevailed against me in discourse.

24. He said: Surely he has been unjust to you in demanding your ewe (to add) to his own ewes; and most surely most of the partners act wrongfully towards one another, save those who believe and do good, and very few are they; and Dawood was sure that We had tried him, so he sought the protection of his Lord, and he fell down bowing and turned time after time (to Him).

25. Therefore We rectified for him this, and most surely he had a nearness to Us and an excellent resort.

26. O Dawood! surely We have made you a ruler in the land; so judge between men with justice and do not follow desire, lest it should lead you astray from the path of Allah; (as for) those who go astray from the path of Allah, they shall surely have a severe punishment because they forgot the day of reckoning.

27. And We did not create the heaven and the earth and what is between them in vain; that is the opinion of those who disbelieve; then woe to those who disbelieve on account of the fire.

28. Shall We treat those who believe and do good like the mischief-makers in the earth? Or shall We make those who guard (against evil) like the wicked?

29. (It is) a Book We have revealed to you abounding in good, that they may ponder over its verses, and that those endowed with understanding may be mindful.

30. And We gave to Dawood Sulaiman; most excellent the servant! Surely he was frequent in returning (to Allah).

31. When there were brought to him in the evening (horses) still when standing, swift when running—

32. Then he said: Surely I preferred the good things to the remembrance of my Lord—until the sun set and time for Asr prayer was over, (he said):

33. Bring them back to me; so he began to slash (their) legs and necks.

34. And certainly We tried Sulaiman, and We put on his throne a (mere) body, so he turned (to Allah).

35. He said: My Lord! do Thou forgive me and grant me a kingdom which is not fit for (being inherited by) anyone after me; nations;

36. Then We made the wind subservient to him; it made his command to run gently wherever he desired,

37. And the shaitans, every builder and diver,

38. And others fettered in chains.

39. This is Our free gift, therefore give freely or withhold, without reckoning.

40. And most surely he had a nearness to Us and an excellent resort.

41. And remember Our servant Ayyub, when he called upon his Lord: The Shaitan has afflicted me with toil and torment.

42. Urge with your foot; here is a cool washing-place and a drink.

43. And We gave him his family and the like of them with them, as a mercy from Us, and as a reminder to those possessed of understanding.

44. And take in your hand a green branch and beat her with it and do not break your oath; surely We found him patient; most excellent the servant! Surely he was frequent in returning (to Allah).

45. And remember Our servants Ibrahim and Ishaq and Yaqoub, men of power and insight.

46. Surely We purified them by a pure quality, the keeping in mind of the (final) abode.

47. And most surely they were with Us, of the elect, the best.

48. And remember Ismail and Al-Yasha and Zulkifl; and they were all of the best.

49. This is a reminder; and most surely there is an excellent resort for those who guard (against evil),

50. The gardens of perpetuity, the doors are opened for them.

51. Reclining therein, calling therein for many fruits and drink.

52. And with them shall be those restraining their eyes, equals in age.

53. This is what you are promised for the day of reckoning.

54. Most surely this is Our sustenance; it shall never come to an end;

55. This (shall be so); and most surely there is an evil resort for the inordinate ones;

56. Hell; they shall enter it, so evil is the resting-place.

57. This (shall be so); so let them taste it, boiling and intensely cold (drink).

58. And other (punishment) of the same kind—of various sorts.

59. This is an army plunging in without consideration along with you; no welcome for them, surely they shall enter fire.

60. They shall say: Nay! you—no welcome to you: you did proffer it to us, so evil is the resting-place.

61. They shall say: Our Lord! whoever prepared it first for us, add Thou to him a double chastisement in the fire.

62. And they shall say: What is the matter with us that we do not see men whom we used to count among the vicious?

63. Was it that we (only) took them in scorn, or have our eyes (now) turned aside from them?

64. That most surely is the truth: the contending one with another of the inmates of the fire.

65. Say: I am only a warner, and there is no god but Allah, the One, the Subduer (of all):

66. The Lord of the heavens and the earth and what is between them, the Mighty, the most Forgiving.

67. Say: It is a message of importance,

68. (And) you are turning aside from it:

69. I had no knowledge of the exalted chiefs when they contended:

70. Naught is revealed to me save that I am a plain warner.

71. When your Lord said to the angels; Surely I am going to create a mortal from dust:

72. So when I have made him complete and breathed into him of My spirit, then fall down making obeisance to him.

73. And the angels did obeisance, all of them,

74. But not Iblis: he was proud and he was one of the unbelievers.

75. He said: O Iblis! what prevented you that you should do obeisance to him whom I created with My two hands? Are you proud or are you of the exalted ones?

76. He said: I am better than he; Thou hast created me of fire, and him Thou didst create of dust.

77. He said: Then get out of it, for surely you are driven away:

78. And surely My curse is on you to the day of judgment.

79. He said: My Lord! then respite me to the day that they are raised.

80. He said: Surely you are of the respited ones,

81. Till the period of the time made known.

82. He said: Then by Thy Might I will surely make them live an evil life, all,

83. Except Thy servants from among them, the purified ones.

84. He said: The truth then is and the truth do I speak:

85. That I will most certainly fill hell with you and with those among them who follow you, all.

86. Say: I do not ask you for any reward for it; nor am I of those who affect:

87. It is nothing but a reminder to the nations;

88. And most certainly you will come to know about it after a time.

THE COMPANIES

In the name of Allah, the Beneficent, the Merciful.

1. The revelation of the Book is from Allah, the Mighty, the Wise.

2. Surely We have revealed to you the Book with the truth, therefore serve Allah, being sincere to Him in obedience.

3. Now, surely, sincere obedience is due to Allah (alone) and (as for) those who take guardians besides Him, (saying), We do not serve them save that they may make us nearer to Allah, surely Allah will judge between them in that in which they differ; surely Allah does not guide him aright who is a liar, ungrateful.

4. If Allah desire to take a son to Himself, He will surely choose those He pleases from what He has created. Glory be to Him: He is Allah, the One, the Subduer (of all).

5. He has created the heavens and the earth with the truth; He makes the night cover the day and makes the day overtake the night, and He has made the sun and the moon subservient; each one runs on to an assigned term; now surely He is the Mighty, the great Forgiver.

6. He has created you from a single being, then made its mate of the same (kind), and He has made for you eight of the cattle in pairs. He creates you in the wombs of your mothers—a creation after a creation—in triple darkness; that is Allah your Lord, His is the kingdom; there is no god but He; whence are you then turned away?

7. If you are ungrateful, then surely Allah is Self-sufficient, above all need of you; and He does not like ungratefulness in His servants; and if you are grateful, He likes it in you; and no bearer of burden shall bear the burden of another; then to your Lord is your return, then will He inform you of what you did; surely He is Cognizant of what is in the breasts.

8. And when distress afflicts a man he calls upon his Lord, turning to Him frequently; then when He makes him possess a favor from Him, he forgets that for which he called upon Him before, and sets up rivals to Allah that he may cause (men) to stray off from His path. Say: Enjoy yourself in your ungratefulness a little, surely you are of the inmates of the fire.

9. What! he who is obedient during hours of the night, prostrating himself and standing, takes care of the hereafter and hopes for the mercy of his Lord! Say: Are those who know and those who do not know alike? Only the men of understanding are mindful.

10. Say: O my servants who believe! be careful of (your duty to) your Lord; for those who do good in this world is good, and Allah's earth is spacious; only the patient will be paid back their reward in full without measure.

11. Say: I am commanded that I should serve Allah, being sincere to Him in obedience.

12. And I am commanded that I shall be the first of those who submit.

13. Say: I fear, if I disobey my Lord, the chastisement of a grievous day.

14. Say: Allah (it is Whom) I serve, being sincere to Him in my obedience:

15. Serve then what you like besides Him. Say: The losers surely are those who shall have lost themselves and their families on the day of resurrection; now surely that is the clear loss.

16. They shall have coverings of fire above them and coverings beneath them; with that Allah makes His servants to fear; so be careful of (your duty to) Me, O My servants!

17. And (as for) those who keep off from the worship of the

idols and turn to Allah, they shall have good news, therefore give good news to My servants,

18. Those who listen to the word, then follow the best of it; those are they whom Allah has guided, and those it is who are the men of understanding.

19. What! as for him then against whom the sentence of chastisement is due: What! can you save him who is in the fire?

20. But (as for) those who are careful of (their duty to) their Lord, they shall have high places, above them higher places, built (for them), beneath which flow rivers; (this is) the promise of Allah: Allah will not fail in (His) promise.

21. Do you not see that Allah sends down water from the cloud, then makes it go along in the earth in springs, then brings forth therewith herbage of various colors, then it withers so that you see it becoming yellow, then He makes it a thing crushed and broken into pieces? Most surely there is a reminder in this for the men of understanding.

22. What! is he whose heart Allah has opened for Islam so that he is in a light from his Lord (like the hard-hearted)? Nay, woe to those whose hearts are hard against the remembrance of Allah; those are in clear error.

23. Allah has revealed the best announcement, a book comformable in its various parts, repeating, whereat do shudder the skins of those who fear their Lord, then their skins and their hearts become pliant to the remembrance of Allah; this is Allah's guidance, He guides with it whom He pleases; and (as for) him whom Allah makes err, there is no guide for him.

24. Is he then who has to guard himself with his own person against the evil chastisement on the resurrection day? And it will be said to the unjust: Taste what you earned.

25. Those before them rejected (prophets), therefore there came to them the chastisement from whence they perceived not.

26. So Allah made them taste the disgrace in this world's life, and certainly the punishment of the hereafter is greater; did they but know!

27. And certainly We have set forth to men in this Quran similitudes of every sort that they may mind.

28. An Arabic Quran without any crookedness, that they may guard (against evil).

29. Allah sets forth an example: There is a slave in whom are (several) partners differing with one another, and there is another

slave wholly owned by one man. Are the two alike in condition? (All) praise is due to Allah. Nay! most of them do not know.

30. Surely you shall die and they (too) shall surely die.

31. Then surely on the day of resurrection you will contend one with another before your Lord.

32. Who is then more unjust than he who utters a lie against Allah and (he who) gives the lie to the truth when it comes to him; is there not in hell an abode for the unbelievers?

33. And he who brings the truth and (he who) accepts it as the truth—these are they that guard (against evil).

34. They shall have with their Lord what they please; that is the reward of the doers of good;

35. So that Allah will do away with the worst of what they did and give them their reward for the best of what they do.

36. Is not Allah sufficient for His servant? And they seek to frighten you with those besides Him; and whomsoever Allah makes err, there is no guide for him.

37. And whom Allah guides, there is none that can lead him astray; is not Allah Mighty, the Lord of retribution?

38. And should you ask them, Who created the heavens and the earth? They would most certainly say: Allah. Say: Have you then considered that what you call upon besides Allah, would they, if Allah desire to afflict me with harm, be the removers of His harm, or (would they), if Allah desire to show me mercy, be the withholders of His mercy? Say: Allah is sufficient for me; on Him do the reliant rely.

39. Say: O my people! work in your place, surely I am a worker, so you will come to know.

40. Who it is to whom there shall come a punishment which will disgrace him and to whom will be due a lasting punishment.

41. Surely We have revealed to you the Book with the truth for the sake of men; so whoever follows the right way, it is for his own soul and whoever errs, he errs only to its detriment; and you are not a custodian over them.

42. Allah takes the souls at the time of their death, and those that die not during their sleep; then He withholds those on whom He has passed the decree of death and sends the others back till an appointed term; most surely there are signs in this for a people who reflect.

43. Or have they taken intercessors besides Allah? Say: what! even though they did not ever have control over anything, nor do they understand.

44. Say: Allah's is the intercession altogether; His is the kingdom of the heavens and the earth, then to Him you shall be brought back.

45. And when Allah alone is mentioned, the hearts of those who do not believe in the hereafter shrink, and when those besides Him are mentioned, lo! they are joyful.

46. Say: O Allah! Originator of the heavens and the earth, Knower of the unseen and the seen! Thou (only) judgest between Thy servants as to that wherein they differ.

47. And had those who are unjust all that is in the earth and the like of it with it, they would certainly offer it as ransom (to be saved) from the evil of the punishment on the day of resurrection; and what they never thought of shall become plain to them from Allah.

48. And the evil (consequences) of what they wrought shall become plain to them, and the very thing they mocked at shall beset them.

49. So when harm afflicts a man he calls upon Us; then, when We give him a favor from Us, he says: I have been given it only by means of knowledge. Nay, it is a trial, but most of them do not know.

50. Those before them did say it indeed, but what they earned availed them not.

51. So there befell them the evil (consequences) of what they earned; and (as for) those who are unjust from among these, there shall befall them the evil (consequences) of what they earn, and they shall not escape.

52. Do they not know that Allah makes ample the means of subsistence to whom He pleases, and He straitens; most surely there are signs in this for a people who believe.

53. Say: O my servants! who have acted extravagantly against their own souls, do not despair of the mercy of Allah; surely Allah forgives the faults altogether; surely He is the Forgiving, the Merciful.

54. And return to your Lord time after time and submit to Him before there comes to you the punishment, then you shall not be helped.

55. And follow the best that has been revealed to you from your Lord before there comes to you the punishment all of a sudden while you do not even perceive;

56. Lest a soul should say: O woe to me! for what I fell short of my duty to Allah, and most surely I was of those who laughed to scorn;

57. Or it should say: Had Allah guided me, I would certainly have been of those who guard (against evil);

58. Or it should say when it sees the punishment: Were there only a returning for me, I should be of the doers of good.

59. Aye! My communications came to you, but you rejected them, and you were proud and you were one of the unbelievers.

60. And on the day of resurrection you shall see those who lied against Allah; their faces shall be blackened. Is there not in hell an abode for the proud?

61. And Allah shall deliver those who guard (against evil) with their achievement; evil shall not touch them, nor shall they grieve.

62. Allah is the Creator of every thing and He has charge over every thing.

63. His are the treasures of the heavens and the earth; and (as for) those who disbelieve in the communications of Allah, these it is that are the losers.

64. Say: What! Do you then bid me serve others than Allah, O ignorant men?

65. And certainly, it has been revealed to you and to those before you: Surely if you associate (with Allah), your work would certainly come to naught and you would certainly be of the losers.

66. Nay! but serve Allah alone and be of the thankful.

67. And they have not honored Allah with the honor that is due to Him; and the whole earth shall be in His grip on the day of resurrection and the heavens rolled up in His right hand; glory be to Him, and may He be exalted above what they associate (with Him).

68. And the trumpet shall be blown, so all those that are in the heavens and all those that are in the earth shall swoon, except such as Allah please; then it shall be blown again, then lo! they shall stand up awaiting.

69. And the earth shall beam with the light of its Lord, and the Book shall be laid down, and the prophets and the witnesses shall be brought up, and judgment shall be given between them with justice, and they shall not be dealt with unjustly.

70. And every soul shall be paid back fully what it has done, and He knows best what they do.

71. And those who disbelieve shall be driven to hell in companies; until, when they come to it, its doors shall be opened, and the keepers of it shall say to them: Did not there come to

you apostles from among you reciting to you the communications of your Lord and warning you of the meeting of this day of yours? They shall say: Yea! But the sentence of punishment was due against the unbelievers.

72. It shall be said: Enter the gates of hell to abide therein; so evil is the abode of the proud.

73. And those who are careful of (their duty to) their Lord shall be conveyed to the garden in companies; until when they come to it, and its doors shall be opened, and the keepers of it shall say to them: Peace be on you, you shall be happy; therefore enter it to abide.

74. And they shall say: (All) praise is due to Allah, Who has made good to us His promise, and He has made us inherit the land; we may abide in the garden where we please; so goodly is the reward of the workers.

75. And you shall see the angels going round about the throne glorifying the praise of their Lord; and judgment shall be given between them with justice, and it shall be said: All praise is due to Allah, the Lord of the worlds.

THE BELIEVER

In the name of Allah, the Beneficent, the Merciful.

1. Ha Mim.

2. The revelation of the Book is from Allah, the Mighty, the Knowing.

3. The Forgiver of the faults and the Acceptor of repentance, Severe to punish, Lord of bounty; there is no god but He; to Him is the eventual coming.

4. None dispute concerning the communications of Allah but those who disbelieve, therefore let not their going to and fro in the cities deceive you.

5. The people of Nuh and the parties after them rejected (prophets) before them, and every nation purposed against their apostle to destroy him, and they disputed by means of the falsehood that they might thereby render null the truth, therefore I destroyed them; how was then My retribution!

6. And thus did the word of your Lord prove true against those who disbelieved that they are the inmates of the fire.

7. Those who bear the power and those around Him celebrate the praise of their Lord and believe in Him and ask protection for those who believe: Our Lord! Thou embracest all things in mercy and knowledge, therefore grant protection to those who turn (to Thee) and follow Thy way, and save them from the punishment of the hell:

8. Our Lord! and make them enter the gardens of perpetuity which Thou hast promised to them and those who do good of their fathers and their wives and their offspring, surely Thou are the Mighty, the Wise.

9. And keep them from evil deeds, and whom Thou keepest from evil deeds this day, indeed Thou hast mercy on him, and that is the mighty achievement.

10. Surely those who disbelieve shall be cried out to: Certainly Allah's hatred (of you) when you were called upon to the faith and you rejected, is much greater than your hatred of yourselves.

11. They shall say: Our Lord! twice didst Thou make us subject to death, and twice hast Thou given us life, so we do confess our faults; is there then a way to get out?

12. That is because when Allah alone was called upon, you disbelieved, and when associates were given to Him, you believed; so judgment belongs to Allah, the High, the Great.

13. He it is Who shows you His signs and sends down for you sustenance from heaven, and none minds but he who turns (to Him) again and again.

14. Therefore call upon Allah, being sincere to Him in obedience, though the unbelievers are averse:

15. Possessor of the highest rank, Lord of power: He makes the inspiration to light by His command upon whom He pleases of His servants, that he may warn (men) of the day of meeting.

16. (Of) the day when they shall come forth; nothing concerning them remains hidden to Allah. To whom belongs the kingdom this day? To Allah, the One, the Subduer (of all).

17. This day every soul shall be rewarded for what it has earned; no injustice (shall be done) this day; surely Allah is quick in reckoning.

18. And warn them of the day that draws near, when hearts shall rise up to the throats, grieving inwardly; the unjust shall not have any compassionate friend nor any intercessor who should be obeyed.

19. He knows the stealthy looks and that which the breasts conceal.

20. And Allah judges with the truth; and those whom they call upon besides Him cannot judge aught; surely Allah is the Hearing, the Seeing.

21. Have they not travelled in the earth and seen how was the end of those who were before them? Mightier than these were they in strength and in fortifications in the land, but Allah destroyed them for their sins; and there was not for them any defender against Allah.

22. That was because there came to them their apostles with clear arguments, but they rejected (them), therefore Allah destroyed them; surely He is Strong, Severe in retribution.

23. And certainly We sent Musa with Our communications and clear authority,

24. To Firon and Haman and Qaroun, but they said: A lying magician.

25. So when he brought to them the truth from Us, they said: Slay the sons of those who believe with him and keep their women alive; and the struggle of the unbelievers will only come to a state of perdition.

26. And Firon said: Let me alone that I may slay Musa and let him call upon his Lord; surely I fear that he will change your religion or that he will make mischief to appear in the land.

27. And Musa said: Surely I take refuge with my Lord and your Lord from every proud one who does not believe in the day of reckoning.

28. And a believing man of Firon's people who hid his faith said: What! will you slay a man because he says: My Lord is Allah, and indeed he has brought to you clear arguments from your Lord? And if he be a liar, on him will be his lie, and if he be truthful, there will befall you some of that which he threatens you (with); surely Allah does not guide him who is extravagant, a liar:

29. O my people! yours is the kingdom this day, being masters in the land, but who will help us against the punishment of Allah if it come to us? Firon said: I do not show you aught but that which I see (myself), and I do not make you follow any but the right way.

30. And he who believed said: O my people! surely I fear for you the like of what befell the parties:

31. The like of what befell the people of Nuh and Ad and

Samood and those after them, and Allah does not desire injustice for (His) servants;

32. And, O my people! I fear for you the day of calling out,

33. The day on which you will turn back retreating; there shall be no savior for you from Allah, and whomsoever Allah causes to err, there is no guide for him:

34. And certainly Yusuf came to you before with clear arguments, but you ever remained in doubt as to what he brought; until when he died, you said: Allah will never raise an apostle after him. Thus does Allah cause him to err who is extravagant, a doubter,

35. Those who dispute concerning the communications of Allah without any authority that He has given them; greatly hated is it by Allah and by those who believe. Thus does Allah set a seal over the heart of every proud, haughty one.

36. And Firon said: O Haman! build for me a tower that I may attain the means of access,

37. The means of access to the heavens, then reach the God of Musa, and I surely think him to be a liar. And thus the evil of his deed was made fairseeming to Firon, and he was turned away from the way; and the struggle of Firon was not (to end) in aught but destruction.

38. And he who believed said: O my people! follow me, I will guide you to the right course;

39. O my people! this life of the world is only a (passing) enjoyment, and surely the hereafter is the abode to settle;

40. Whoever does an evil, he shall not be recompensed (with aught) but the like of it, and whoever does good, whether male or female, and he is a believer, these shall enter the garden, in which they shall be given sustenance without measure.

41. And, O my people! how is it that I call you to salvation and you call me to the fire?

42. You call on me that I should disbelieve in Allah and associate with Him that of which I have no knowledge, and I call you to the Mighty, the most Forgiving;

43. No doubt that what you call me to has no title to be called to in this world, nor in the hereafter, and that our turning back is to Allah, and that the extravagant are the inmates of the fire;

44. So you shall remember what I say to you, and I entrust my affair to Allah, Surely Allah sees the servants.

45. So Allah protected him from the evil (consequences) of

what they planned, and the most evil punishment overtook Firon's people:

46. The fire; they shall be brought before it (every) morning and evening and on the day when the hour shall come to pass: Make Firon's people enter the severest chastisement.

47. And when they shall contend one with another in the fire, then the weak shall say to those who were proud: Surely we were your followers; will you then avert from us a portion of the fire?

48. Those who were proud shall say: Surely we are all in it: surely Allah has judged between the servants.

49. And those who are in the fire shall say to the keepers of hell: Call upon your Lord that He may lighten to us one day of the punishment.

50. They shall say: Did not your apostles come to you with clear arguments? They shall say: Yea. They shall say: Then call. And the call of the unbelievers is only in error.

51. Most surely We help Our apostles, and those who believe, in this world's life and on the day when the witnesses shall stand up,

52. The day on which their excuse shall not benefit the unjust, and for them is curse and for them is the evil abode.

53. And certainly We gave Musa the guidance, and We made the children of Israel inherit the Book,

54. A guidance and a reminder to the men of understanding.

55. Therefore be patient; surely the promise of Allah is true; and ask protection for your fault and sing the praise of your Lord in the evening and the morning.

56. Surely (as for) those who dispute about the communications of Allah without any authority that has come to them, there is naught in their breasts but (a desire) to become great which they shall never attain to; therefore seek refuge in Allah, surely He is the Hearing, the Seeing.

57. Certainly the creation of the heavens and the earth is greater than the creation of the men, but most people do not know.

58. And the blind and the seeing are not alike, nor those who believe and do good and the evil-doer; little is it that you are mindful.

59. Most surely the hour is coming, there is no doubt therein, but most people do not believe.

60. And your Lord says: Call upon Me, I will answer you;

surely those who are too proud for My service shall soon enter hell abased.

61. Allah is He Who made for you the night that you may rest therein and the day to see; most surely Allah is Gracious to men, but most men do not give thanks.

62. That is Allah, your Lord, the Creator of everything; there is no God but He; whence are you then turned away?

63. Thus were turned away those who denied the communications of Allah.

64. Allah is He Who made the earth a resting-place for you and the heaven a canopy, and He formed you, then made goodly your forms, and He provided you with goodly things; that is Allah, your Lord; blessed then is Allah, the Lord of the worlds.

65. He is the Living, there is no god but He, therefore call on Him, being sincere to Him in obedience; (all) praise is due to Allah, the Lord of the worlds.

66. Say: I am forbidden to serve those whom you call upon besides Allah when clear arguments have come to me from my Lord, and I am commanded that I should submit to the Lord of the worlds.

67. He it is Who created you from dust, then from a small life-germ, then from a clot, then He brings you forth as a child, then that you may attain your maturity, then that you may be old— and of you there are some who are caused to die before—and that you may reach an appointed term, and that you may understand.

68. He it is Who gives life and brings death, so when He decrees an affair, He only says to it: Be, and it is.

69. Have you not seen those who dispute with respect to the communications of Allah: how are they turned away?

70. Those who reject the Book and that with which We have sent Our Apostle; but they shall soon come to know,

71. When the fetters and the chains shall be on their necks; they shall be dragged

72. Into boiling water, then in the fire shall they be burned;

73. Then shall it be said to them: Where is that which you used to set up

74. Besides Allah? They shall say: They are gone away from us, nay, we used not to call upon anything before. Thus does Allah confound the unbelievers.

75. That is because you exulted in the land unjustly and because you behaved insolently.

76. Enter the gates of hell to abide therein; evil then is the abode of the proud.

77. So be patient, surely the promise of Allah is true. So should We make you see part of what We threaten them with, or should We cause you to die, to Us shall they be returned.

78. And certainly We sent apostles before you: there are some of them that We have mentioned to you and there are others whom We have not mentioned to you; and it was not meet for an apostle that he should bring a sign except with Allah's permission, but when the command of Allah came, judgment was given with truth, and those who treated (it) as a lie were lost.

79. Allah is He Who made the cattle for you that you may ride on some of them, and some of them you eat.

80. And there are advantages for you in them, and that you may attain thereon a want which is in your breasts, and upon them and upon the ships you are borne.

81. And He shows you His signs: which then of Allah's signs will you deny?

82. Have they not then journeyed in the land and seen how was the end of those before them? They were more (in numbers) than these and greater in strength and in fortifications in the land, but what they earned did not avail them.

83. Then when their apostles came to them with clear arguments, they exulted in what they had with them of knowledge, and there beset them that which they used to mock.

84. But when they saw Our punishment, they said: We believe in Allah alone and we deny what we used to associate with Him.

85. But their belief was not going to profit them when they had seen Our punishment; (this is) Allah's law, which has indeed obtained in the matter of His servants, and there the unbelievers are lost.

HA MIM

In the name of Allah, the Beneficent, the Merciful.

1. Ha Mim!
2. A revelation from the Beneficent, the Merciful God:

3. A Book of which the verses are made plain, an Arabic Quran for a people who know:

4. A herald of good news and a warner, but most of them turn aside so they hear not.

5. And they say: Our hearts are under coverings from that to which you call us, and there is a heaviness in our ears, and a veil hangs between us and you, so work, we too are working.

6. Say: I am only a mortal like you; it is revealed to me that your God is one God, therefore follow the right way to Him and ask His forgiveness; and woe to the polytheists;

7. (To) those who do not give poor-rate and they are unbelievers in the hereafter.

8. (As for) those who believe and do good, they shall surely have a reward never to be cut off.

9. Say: What! do you indeed disbelieve in Him Who created the earth in two periods, and do you set up equals with Him? That is the Lord of the Worlds.

10. And He made in it mountains above its surface, and He blessed therein and made therein its foods, in four periods: alike for the seekers.

11. Then He directed Himself to the heaven and it is a vapor, so He said to it and to the earth: Come both, willingly or unwillingly. They both said: We come willingly.

12. So He ordained them seven heavens in two periods, and revealed in every heaven its affair; and We adorned the lower heaven with brilliant stars and (made it) to guard; that is the decree of the Mighty, the Knowing.

13. But if they turn aside, then say: I have warned you of a scourge like the scourge of Ad and Samood.

14. When their apostles came to them from before them and from behind them, saying, Serve nothing but Allah, they said: If our Lord had pleased He would certainly have sent down angels, so we are surely unbelievers in that with which you are sent.

15. Then as to Ad, they were unjustly proud in the land, and they said: Who is mightier in strength than we? Did they not see that Allah Who created them was mightier than they in strength, and they denied Our communications?

16. So We sent on them a furious wind in unlucky days, that We may make them taste the chastisement of abasement in this world's life; and certainly the chastisement of the hereafter is much more abasing, and they shall not be helped.

17. And as to Samood, We showed them the right way, but they chose error above guidance, so there overtook them the scourge of an abasing chastisement for what they earned.

18. And We delivered those who believed and guarded (against evil).

19. And on the day that the enemies of Allah shall be brought together to the fire, then they shall be formed into groups.

20. Until when they come to it, their ears and their eyes and their skins shall bear witness against them as to what they did.

21. And they shall say to their skins: Why have you borne witness against us? They shall say: Allah Who makes everything speak has made us speak, and He created you at first, and to Him you shall be brought back.

22. And you did not veil yourselves lest your ears and your eyes and your skins should bear witness against you, but you thought that Allah did not know most of what you did.

23. And that was your (evil) thought which you entertained about your Lord that has tumbled you down into perdition, so are you become of the lost ones.

24. Then if they will endure, still the fire is their abode, and if they ask for goodwill, then are they not of those who shall be granted goodwill.

25. And We have appointed for them comrades so they have made fair-seeming to them what is before them and what is behind them, and the word proved true against them—among the nations of the jinn and the men that have passed away before them—that they shall surely be losers.

26. And those who disbelieve say: Do not listen to this Quran and make noise therein, perhaps you may overcome.

27. Therefore We will most certainly make those who disbelieve taste a severe punishment, and We will most certainly reward them for the evil deeds they used to do.

28. That is the reward of the enemies of Allah—the fire; for them therein shall be the house of long abiding; a reward for their denying Our communications.

29. And those who disbelieve will say: Our Lord! show us those who led us astray from among the jinn and the men that we may trample them under our feet so that they may be of the lowest.

30. (As for) those who say: Our Lord is Allah, then continue in the right way, the angels descend upon them, saying: Fear not,

nor be grieved, and receive good news of the garden which you were promised.

31. We are your guardians in this world's life and in the hereafter, and you shall have therein what your souls desire and you shall have therein what you ask for:

32. A provision from the Forgiving, the Merciful.

33. And who speaks better than he who calls to Allah while he himself does good, and says: I am surely of those who submit?

34. And not alike are the good and the evil. Repel (evil) with what is best, when lo! he between whom and you was enmity would be as if he were a warm friend.

35. And none are made to receive it but those who are patient, and none are made to receive it but those who have a mighty good fortune.

36. And if an interference of the Shaitan should cause you mischief, seek refuge in Allah; surely He is the Hearing, the Knowing.

37. And among His signs are the night and the day and the sun and the moon; do not make obeisance to the sun nor to the moon; and make obeisance to Allah Who created them, if Him it is that you serve.

38. But if they are proud, yet those with your Lord glorify Him during the night and the day, and they are not tired.

39. And among His signs is this, that you see the earth still, but when We send down on it the water, it stirs and swells: most surely He Who gives it life is the Giver of life to the dead; surely He has power over all things.

40. Surely they who deviate from the right way concerning Our communications are not hidden from Us. What! is he then who is cast into the fire better, or he who comes safe on the day of resurrection? Do what you like, surely He sees what you do.

41. Surely those who disbelieve in the reminder when it comes to them, and most surely it is a Mighty Book:

42. Falsehood shall not come to it from before it nor from behind it; a revelation from the Wise, the Praised One.

43. Naught is said to you but what was said indeed to the apostles before you; surely your Lord is the Lord of forgiveness and the Lord of painful retribution.

44. And if We had made it a Quran in a foreign tongue, they would certainly have said: Why have not its communications

been made clear? What! a foreign (tongue) and an Arabian! Say: It is to those who believe a guidance and a healing; and (as for) those who do not believe, there is a heaviness in their ears and it is obscure to them; these shall be called to from a far-off place.

45. And certainly We gave the Book to Musa, but it has been differed about; and had not a word already gone forth from your Lord, judgment would certainly have been given between them; and most surely they are in a disquieting doubt about it.

46. Whoever does good, it is for his own soul, and whoever does evil, it is against it; and your Lord is not in the least unjust to the servants.

47. To Him is referred the knowledge of the hour, and there come not forth any of the fruits from their coverings, nor does a female bear, nor does she give birth, but with His knowledge; and on the day when He shall call out to them, Where are (those whom you called) My associates? They shall say: We declare to Thee, none of us is a witness.

48. And away from them shall go what they called upon before, and they shall know for certain that there is no escape for them.

49. Man is never tired of praying for good, and if evil touch him, then he is despairing, hopeless.

50. And if We make him taste mercy from Us after distress that has touched him, he would most certainly say: This is of me, and I do not think the hour will come to pass, and if I am sent back to my Lord, I shall have with Him sure good; but We will most certainly inform those who disbelieved of what they did, and We will most certainly make them taste of hard chastisement.

51. And when We show favor to man, he turns aside and withdraws himself; and when evil touches him, he makes lengthy supplications.

52. Say: Tell me if it is from Allah; then you disbelieve in it, who is in greater error than he who is in a prolonged opposition?

53. We will soon show them Our signs in the Universe and in their own souls, until it will become quite clear to them that it is the truth. Is it not sufficient as regards your Lord that He is a witness over all things?

54. Now surely they are in doubt as to the meeting of their Lord; now surely He encompasses all things.

THE COUNSEL

In the name of Allah, the Beneficent, the Merciful.

1. Ha Mim.
2. Ain Sin Qaf.
3. Thus does Allah, the Mighty, the Wise, reveal to you, and (thus He revealed) to those before you.
4. His is what is in the heavens and what is in the earth, and He is the High, the Great.
5. The heavens may almost rend asunder from above them and the angels sing the praise of their Lord and ask forgiveness for those on earth; now surely Allah is the Forgiving, the Merciful.
6. And (as for) those who take guardians besides Him, Allah watches over them, and you have not charge over them.
7. And thus have We revealed to you an Arabic Quran, that you may warn the mother city and those around it, and that you may give warning of the day of gathering together wherein is no doubt; a party shall be in the garden and (another) party in the burning fire.
8. And if Allah had pleased He would surely have made them a single community, but He makes whom He pleases enter into His mercy, and the unjust it is that shall have no guardian or helper.
9. Or have they taken guardians besides Him? But Allah is the Guardian, and He gives life to the dead, and He has power over all things.
10. And in whatever thing you disagree, the judgment thereof is (in) Allah's (hand); that is Allah, my Lord, on Him do I rely and to Him do I turn time after time.
11. The Originator of the heavens and the earth; He made mates for you from among yourselves, and mates of the cattle too, multiplying you thereby; nothing like a likeness of Him; and He is the Hearing, the Seeing.
12. His are the treasures of the heavens and the earth; He makes ample and straitens the means of subsistence for whom He pleases; surely He is Cognizant of all things.
13. He has made plain to you of the religion what He enjoined upon Nuh and that which We have revealed to you, and that which We enjoined upon Ibrahim and Musa and Isa, that keep

to obedience and be not divided therein; hard to the unbelievers is that which you call them to; Allah chooses for Himself whom He pleases, and guides to Himself him who turns (to Him) frequently.

14. And they did not become divided until after knowledge had come to them out of envy among themselves; and had not a word gone forth from your Lord till an appointed term, certainly judgment would have been given between them; and those who were made to inherit the Book after them are most surely in disquieting doubt concerning it.

15. To this then go on inviting, and go on steadfastly on the right way as you are commanded, and do not follow their low desires, and say: I believe in what Allah has revealed of the Book, and I am commanded to do justice between you: Allah is our Lord and your Lord; we shall have our deeds and you shall have your deeds; no plea need there be (now) between us and you: Allah will gather us together, and to Him is the return.

16. And (as for) those who dispute about Allah after that obedience has been rendered to Him, their plea is null with their Lord, and upon them is wrath, and for them is severe punishment.

17. Allah it is Who revealed the Book with truth, and the balance, and what shall make you know that haply the hour be nigh?

18. Those who do not believe in it would hasten it on, and those who believe are in fear from it, and they know that it is the truth. Now most surely those who dispute obstinately concerning the hour are in a great error.

19. Allah is Benignant to His servants; He gives sustenance to whom He pleases; and He is the Strong, the Mighty.

20. Whoever desires the gain of the hereafter, We will give him more of that again; and whoever desires the gain of this world, We give him of it, and in the hereafter he has no portion.

21. Or have they associates who have prescribed for them any religion that Allah does not sanction? And were it not for the word of judgment, decision would have certainly been given between them; and surely the unjust shall have a painful punishment.

22. You will see the unjust fearing on account of what they have earned, and it must befall them; and those who believe and do good shall be in the meadows of the gardens; they shall have what they please with their Lord: that is the great grace.

23. That is of which Allah gives the good news to His servants, (to) those who believe and do good deeds. Say: I do not ask of you any reward for it but love for my near relatives; and whoever earns good, We give him more of good therein; surely Allah is Forgiving, Grateful.

24. Or do they say: He has forged a lie against Allah? But if Allah pleased, He would seal your heart; and Allah will blot out the falsehood and confirm the truth with His words; surely He is Cognizant of what is in the breasts.

25. And He it is Who accepts repentance from His servants and pardons the evil deeds and He knows what you do;

26. And He answers those who believe and do good deeds, and gives them more out of His grace; and (as for) the unbelievers, they shall have a severe punishment.

27. And if Allah should amplify the provision for His servants they would certainly revolt in the earth; but He sends it down according to a measure as He pleases; surely He is Aware of, Seeing, His servants.

28. And He it is Who sends down the rain after they have despaired, and He unfolds His mercy; and He is the Guardian, the Praised One.

29. And one of His signs is the creation of the heavens and the earth and what He has spread forth in both of them of living beings; and when He pleases He is all-powerful to gather them together.

30. And whatever affliction befalls you, it is on account of what your hands have wrought, and (yet) He pardons most (of your faults).

31. And you cannot escape in the earth, and you shall not have a guardian or a helper besides Allah.

32. And among His signs are the ships in the sea like mountains.

33. If He pleases, He causes the wind to become still so that they lie motionless on its back; most surely there are signs in this for every patient, grateful one,

34. Or He may make them founder for what they have earned, and (even then) pardon most;

35. And (that) those who dispute about Our communications may know; there is no place of refuge for them.

36. So whatever thing you are given, that is only a provision of this world's life, and what is with Allah is better and more lasting for those who believe and rely on their Lord.

37. And those who shun the great sins and indecencies, and whenever they are angry they forgive.

38. And those who respond to their Lord and keep up prayer, and their rule is to take counsel among themselves, and who spend out of what We have given them.

39. And those who, when great wrong afflicts them, defend themselves.

40. And the recompense of evil is punishment like it, but whoever forgives and amends, he shall have his reward from Allah; surely He does not love the unjust.

41. And whoever defends himself after his being oppressed, these it is against whom there is no way (to blame).

42. The way (to blame) is only against those who oppress men and revolt in the earth unjustly; these shall have a painful punishment.

43. And whoever is patient and forgiving, these most surely are actions due to courage.

44. And whomsoever Allah makes err, he has no guardian after Him; and you shall see the unjust, when they see the punishment, saying: Is there any way to return?

45. And you shall see them brought before it humbling themselves because of the abasements, looking with a faint glance. And those who believe shall say: Surely the losers are they who have lost themselves and their followers on the resurrection day. Now surely the iniquitous shall remain in lasting chastisement.

46. And they shall have no friends to help them besides Allah; and whomsoever Allah makes err, he shall have no way.

47. Hearken to your Lord before there comes the day from Allah for which there shall be no averting; you shall have no refuge on that day, nor shall it be yours to make a denial.

48. But if they turn aside, We have not sent you as a watcher over them; on you is only to deliver (the message); and surely when We make man taste mercy from Us, he rejoices thereat; and if an evil afflicts them on account of what their hands have already done, then surely man is ungrateful.

49. Allah's is the kingdom of the heavens and the earth; He creates what He pleases; He grants to whom He pleases daughters and grants to whom He pleases sons.

50. Or He makes them of both sorts, male and female; and He makes whom He pleases barren; surely He is the Knowing, the Powerful.

51. And it is not for any mortal that Allah should speak to

him except by revelation or from behind a veil, or by sending a messenger and revealing by His permission what He pleases; surely He is High, Wise.

52. And thus did We reveal to you an inspired book by Our command. You did not know what the Book was, nor (what) the faith (was), but We made it a light, guiding thereby whom We please of Our servants; and most surely you show the way to the right path:

53. The path of Allah, Whose is whatsoever is in the heavens and whatsoever is in the earth; now surely to Allah do all affairs eventually come.

THE EMBELLISHMENT

In the name of Allah, the Beneficent, the Merciful.

1. Ha Mim.

2. I swear by the Book that makes things clear:

3. Surely We have made it an Arabic Quran that you may understand.

4. And surely it is in the original of the Book with Us, truly elevated, full of wisdom.

5. What! shall We then turn away the reminder from you altogether because you are an extravagant people?

6. And how many a prophet have We sent among the ancients.

7. And there came not to them a prophet but they mocked at him.

8. Then We destroyed those who were stronger than these in prowess, and the case of the ancients has gone before,

9. And if you should ask them, Who created the heavens and the earth? they would most certainly say: The Mighty, the Knowing One, has created them;

10. He Who made the earth a resting-place for you, and made in it ways for you that you may go aright;

11. And He Who sends down water from the cloud according to a measure, then We raise to life thereby a dead country; even thus shall you be brought forth;

12. And He Who created pairs of all things, and made for you of the ships and the cattle what you ride on,

13. That you may firmly sit on their backs, then remember the favor of your Lord when you are firmly seated thereon, and say: Glory be to Him Who made this subservient to us and we were not able to do it,

14. And surely to our Lord we must return.

15. And they assign to Him a part of His servants; man, to be sure, is clearly ungrateful.

16. What! has He taken daughters to Himself of what He Himself creates and chosen you to have sons?

17. And when one of them is given news of that of which he sets up as a likeness for the Beneficent God, his face becomes black and he is full of rage.

18. What! that which is made in ornaments and which in contention is unable to make plain speech!

19. And they make the angels—them who are the servants of the Beneficent God—female (divinities). What! did they witness their creation? Their evidence shall be written down and they shall be questioned.

20. And they say: If the Beneficent God had pleased, we should never have worshipped them. They have no knowledge of this; they only lie.

21. Or have We given them a book before it so that they hold fast to it?

22. Nay! they say: We found our fathers on a course, and surely we are guided by their footsteps.

23. And thus, We did not send before you any warner in a town, but those who led easy lives in it said: Surely we found our fathers on a course, and surely we are followers of their footsteps.

24. (The warner) said: What! even if I bring to you a better guide than that on which you found your fathers? They said: Surely we are unbelievers in that with which you are sent.

25. So We inflicted retribution on them, then see how was the end of the rejecters.

26. And when Ibrahim said to his father and his people: Surely I am clear of what you worship,

27. Save Him Who created me, for surely He will guide me.

28. And he made it a word to continue in his posterity that they may return.

29. Nay! I gave them and their fathers to enjoy until there came to them the truth and an Apostle making manifest (the truth).

30. And when there came to them the truth they said: This is magic, and surely we are disbelievers in it.

31. And they say: Why was not this Quran revealed to a man of importance in the two towns?

32. Will they distribute the mercy of your Lord? We distribute among them their livelihood in the life of this world, and We have exalted some of them above others in degrees, that some of them may take others in subjection; and the mercy of your Lord is better than what they amass.

33. And were it not that all people had been a single nation, We would certainly have assigned to those who disbelieve in the Beneficent God (to make) of silver the roofs of their houses and the stairs by which they ascend.

34. And the doors of their houses and the couches on which they recline,

35. And (other) embellishments of gold; and all this is naught but provision of this world's life, and the hereafter is with your Lord only for those who guard (against evil).

36. And whoever turns himself away from the remembrance of the Beneficent God, We appoint for him a Shaitan, so he becomes his associate.

37. And most surely they turn them away from the path, and they think that they are guided aright:

38. Until when he comes to Us, he says: O would that between me and you there were the distance of the East and the West; so evil is the associate!

39. And since you were unjust, it will not profit you this day that you are sharers in the chastisement.

40. What! can you then make the deaf to hear or guide the blind and him who is in clear error?

41. But if We should take you away, still We shall inflict retribution on them;

42. Rather We will certainly show you that which We have promised them; for surely We are the possessors of full power over them.

43. Therefore hold fast to that which has been revealed to you; surely you are on the right path.

44. And most surely it is a reminder for you and your people, and you shall soon be questioned.

45. And ask those of Our apostles whom We sent before you: Did We ever appoint gods to be worshipped besides the Beneficent God?

46. And certainly We sent Musa with Our communications to Firon and his chiefs, so he said: Surely I am the apostle of the Lord of the worlds.

47. But when he came to them with Our signs, lo! they laughed at them.

48. And We did not show them a sign but it was greater than its like, and We overtook them with chastisement that they may turn.

49. And they said: O magician! call on your Lord for our sake, as He has made the covenant with you; we shall surely be the followers of the right way.

50. But when We removed from them the chastisement, lo! they broke the pledge.

51. And Firon proclaimed amongst his people: O my people! is not the kingdom of Egypt mine? And these rivers flow beneath me; do you not then see?

52. Nay! I am better than this fellow, who is contemptible, and who can hardly speak distinctly:

53. But why have not bracelets of gold been put upon him, or why have there not come with him angels as companions?

54. So he incited his people to levity and they obeyed him: surely they were a transgressing people.

55. Then when they displeased Us, We inflicted retribution on them, so We drowned them all together,

56. And We made them a precedent and example to the later generations.

57. And when a description of the son of Marium is given, lo! your people raise a clamor thereat.

58. And they say: Are our gods better, or is he? They do not set it forth to you save by way of disputation; nay, they are a contentious people.

59. He was naught but a servant on whom We bestowed favor, and We made him an example for the children of Israel.

60. And if We please, We could make among you angels to be successors in the land.

61. And most surely it is a knowledge of the hour, therefore have no doubt about it and follow me: this is the right path.

62. And let not the Shaitan prevent you; surely he is your open enemy.

63. And when Isa came with clear arguments, he said: I have

come to you indeed with wisdom, and that I may make clear to you part of what you differ in; so be careful of (your duty to) Allah and obey me:

64. Surely Allah is my Lord and your Lord, therefore serve Him; this is the right path:

65. But parties from among them differed, so woe to those who were unjust because of the chastisement of a painful day.

66. Do they wait for aught but the hour, that it should come upon them all of a sudden while they do not perceive?

67. The friends shall on that day be enemies one to another, except those who guard (against evil).

68. O My servants! there is no fear for you this day, nor shall you grieve.

69. Those who believed in Our communications and were submissive:

70. Enter the garden, you and your wives; you shall be made happy.

71. There shall be sent round to them golden bowls and drinking-cups and therein shall be what their souls yearn after and (wherein) the eyes shall delight, and you shall abide therein.

72. And this is the garden which you are given as an inheritance on account of what you did.

73. For you therein are many fruits of which you shall eat.

74. Surely the guilty shall abide in the chastisement of hell.

75. It shall not be abated from them and they shall therein be despairing.

76. And We are not unjust to them, but they themselves were unjust.

77. And they shall call out: O Malik! let your Lord make an end of us. He shall say: Surely you shall tarry.

78. Certainly We have brought you the truth, but most of you are averse to the truth.

79. Or have they settled an affair? Then surely We are the settlers.

80. Or do they think that We do not hear what they conceal and their secret discourses? Aye! and Our messengers with them write down.

81. Say: If the Beneficent God has a son, I am the foremost of those who serve.

82. Glory to the Lord of the heavens and the earth, the Lord of power, from what they describe.

83. So leave them plunging into false discourses and sporting until they meet their day which they are threatened with.

84. And He it is Who is God in the heavens and God in the earth; and He is the Wise, the Knowing.

85. And blessed is He Whose is the kingdom of the heavens and the earth and what is between them, and with Him is the knowledge of the hour, and to Him shall you be brought back.

86. And those whom they call upon besides Him have no authority for intercession, but he who bears witness of the truth and they know (him).

87. And if you should ask them who created them, they would certainly say: Allah. Whence are they then turned back?

88. Consider his cry: O my Lord! surely they are a people who do not believe.

89. So turn away from them and say, Peace, for they shall soon come to know.

THE EVIDENT SMOKE

In the name of Allah, the Beneficent, the Merciful.

1. Ha Mim!

2. I swear by the Book that makes manifest (the truth).

3. Surely We revealed it on a blessed night—surely We are ever warning—

4. Therein every wise affair is made distinct,

5. A command from Us; surely We are the senders (of apostles),

6. A mercy from your Lord, surely He is the Hearing, the Knowing,

7. The Lord of the heavens and the earth and what is between them, if you would be sure.

8. There is no god but He; He gives life and causes death, your Lord and the Lord of your fathers of yore.

9. Nay, they are in doubt, they sport.

10. Therefore keep waiting for the day when the heaven shall bring an evident smoke,

11. That shall overtake men; this is a painful punishment.

12. Our Lord! remove from us the punishment; surely we are believers.

13. How shall they be reminded, and there came to them an Apostle making clear (the truth),

14. Yet they turned their backs on him and said: One taught (by others), a madman.

15. Surely We will remove the punishment a little, (but) you will surely return (to evil).

16. On the day when We will seize (them) with the most violent seizing; surely We will inflict retribution.

17. And certainly We tried before them the people of Firon, and there came to them a noble apostle,

18. Saying: Deliver to me the servants of Allah, surely I am a faithful apostle to you,

19. And that do not exalt yourselves against Allah, surely I will bring to you a clear authority:

20. And surely I take refuge with my Lord and your Lord that you should stone me to death:

21. And if you do not believe in me, then leave me alone.

22. Then he called upon his Lord: These are a guilty people.

23. So go forth with My servants by night; surely you will be pursued:

24. And leave the sea intervening; surely they are a host that shall be drowned.

25. How many of the gardens and fountains have they left!

26. And cornfields and noble places!

27. And goodly things wherein they rejoiced;

28. Thus (it was), and We gave them as a heritage to another people.

29. So the heaven and the earth did not weep for them, nor were they respited.

30. And certainly We delivered the children of Israel from the abasing chastisement,

31. From Firon; surely he was haughty, (and) one of the extravagant.

32. And certainly We chose them, having knowledge, above the nations.

33. And We gave them of the communications wherein was clear blessing.

34. Most surely these do say:

35. There is naught but our first death and we shall not be raised again.

36. So bring our fathers (back), if you are truthful.

37. Are they better or the people of Tubba and those before them? We destroyed them, for surely they were guilty.

38. And We did not create the heavens and the earth and what is between them in sport.

39. We did not create them both but with the truth, but most of them do not know.

40. Surely the day of separation is their appointed term, of all of them;

41. The day on which a friend shall not avail (his) friend aught, nor shall they be helped,

42. Save those on whom Allah shall have mercy; surely He is the Mighty, the Merciful.

43. Surely the tree of the Zaqqum,

44. Is the food of the sinful,

45. Like dregs of oil; it shall boil in (their) bellies,

46. Like the boiling of hot water.

47. Seize him, then drag him down into the middle of the hell;

48. Then pour above his head of the torment of the boiling water:

49. Taste; you forsooth are the mighty, the honorable:

50. Surely this is what you disputed about.

51. Surely those who guard (against evil) are in a secure place,

52. In gardens and springs;

53. They shall wear of fine and thick silk, (sitting) face to face;

54. Thus (shall it be), and We will wed them with Houris pure, beautiful ones.

55. They shall call therein for every fruit in security;

56. They shall not taste therein death except the first death, and He will save them from the punishment of the hell,

57. A grace from your Lord; this is the great achievement.

58. So have We made it easy in your tongue that they may be mindful.

59. Therefore wait; surely they are waiting.

THE KNEELING

In the name of Allah, the Beneficent, the Merciful.

1. Ha Mim.

2. The revelation of the Book is from Allah, the Mighty, the Wise.

3. Most surely in the heavens and the earth there are signs for the believers.

4. And in your (own) creation and in what He spreads abroad of animals there are signs for a people that are sure;

5. And (in) the variation of the night and the day, and (in) what Allah sends down of sustenance from the cloud, then gives life thereby to the earth after its death, and (in) the changing of the winds, there are signs for a people who understand.

6. These are the communications of Allah which We recite to you with truth; then in what announcement would they believe after Allah and His communications?

7. Woe to every sinful liar,

8. Who hears the communications of Allah recited to him, then persists proudly as though he had not heard them; so announce to him a painful punishment.

9. And when he comes to know of any of Our communications, he takes it for a jest; these it is that shall have abasing chastisement.

10. Before them is hell, and there shall not avail them aught of what they earned, nor those whom they took for guardians besides Allah, and they shall have a grievous punishment.

11. This is guidance; and (as for) those who disbelieve in the communications of their Lord, they shall have a painful punishment on account of uncleanness.

12. Allah is He Who made subservient to you the sea that the ships may run therein by His command, and that you may seek of His grace, and that you may give thanks.

13. And He has made subservient to you whatsoever is in the heavens and whatsoever is in the earth, all, from Himself; most surely there are signs in this for a people who reflect.

14. Say to those who believe (that) they forgive those who do not fear the days of Allah that He may reward a people for what they earn.

15. Whoever does good, it is for his own soul, and whoever does evil, it is against himself; then you shall be brought back to your Lord.

16. And certainly We gave the Book and the wisdom and the prophecy to the children of Israel, and We gave them of the goodly things, and We made them excel the nations.

17. And We gave them clear arguments in the affair, but they did not differ until after knowledge had come to them out of envy among themselves; surely your Lord will judge between them on the day of resurrection concerning that wherein they differed.

18. Then We have made you follow a course in the affair, therefore follow it, and do not follow the low desires of those who do not know.

19. Surely they shall not avail you in the least against Allah; and surely the unjust are friends of each other, and Allah is the guardian of those who guard (against evil).

20. These are clear proofs for men, and a guidance and a mercy for a people who are sure.

21. Nay! do those who have wrought evil deeds think that We will make them like those who believe and do good—that their life and their death shall be equal? Evil it is that they judge.

22. And Allah created the heavens and the earth with truth and that every soul may be rewarded for what it has earned and they shall not be wronged.

23. Have you then considered him who takes his low desire for his god, and Allah has made him err having knowledge and has set a seal upon his ear and his heart and put a covering upon his eye. Who can then guide him after Allah? Will you not then be mindful?

24. And they say: There is nothing but our life in this world; we live and die and nothing destroys us but time, and they have no knowledge of that; they only conjecture.

25. And when Our clear communications are recited to them, their argument is no other than that they say: Bring our fathers (back) if you are truthful.

26. Say: Allah gives you life, then He makes you die, then will He gather you to the day of resurrection wherein is no doubt, but most people do not know.

27. And Allah's is the kingdom of the heavens and the earth; and on the day when the hour shall come to pass, on that day shall they perish who say false things.

28. And you shall see every nation kneeling down; every nation shall be called to its book: today you shall be rewarded for what you did.

29. This is Our book that speaks against you with justice; surely We wrote what you did,

30. Then as to those who believed and did good, their Lord will make them enter into His mercy; that is the manifest achievement.

31. As to those who disbelieved: What! were not My communications recited to you? But you were proud and you were a guilty people.

32. And when it was said, Surely the promise of Allah is true and as for the hour, there is no doubt about it, you said: We do not know what the hour is; we do not think (that it will come to pass) save a passing thought, and we are not at all sure.

33. And the evil (consequences) of what they did shall become manifest to them and that which they mocked shall encompass them.

34. And it shall be said: Today We forsake you as you neglected the meeting of this day of yours and your abode is the fire, and there are not for you any helpers:

35. That is because you took the communications of Allah for a jest and the life of this world deceived you. So on that day they shall not be brought forth from it, nor shall they be granted goodwill.

36. Therefore to Allah is due (all) praise, the Lord of the heavens and the Lord of the earth, the Lord of the worlds.

37. And to Him belongs greatness in the heavens and the earth, and He is the Mighty, the Wise.

THE SANDHILLS

In the name of Allah, the Beneficent, the Merciful.

1. Ha Mim.

2. The revelation of the Book is from Allah, the Mighty, the Wise.

3. We did not create the heavens and the earth and what is between them two save with truth and (for) an appointed term; and those who disbelieve turn aside from what they are warned of.

4. Say: Have you considered what you call upon besides Allah? Show me what they have created of the earth, or have they a share in the heavens? Bring me a book before this or traces of knowledge, if you are truthful.

5. And who is in greater error than he who calls besides Allah upon those that will not answer him till the day of resurrection and they are heedless of their call?

6. And when men are gathered together they shall be their enemies, and shall be deniers of their worshipping (them).

7. And when Our clear communications are recited to them, those who disbelieve say with regard to the truth when it comes to them: This is clear magic.

8. Nay! they say: He has forged it. Say: If I have forged it, you do not control anything for me from Allah; He knows best what you utter concerning it; He is enough as a witness between me and you, and He is the Forgiving, the Merciful.

9. Say: I am not the first of the apostles, and I do not know what will be done with me or with you: I do not follow anything but that which is revealed to me, and I am nothing but a plain warner.

10. Say: Have you considered if it is from Allah, and you disbelieve in it, and a witness from among the children of Israel has borne witness of one like it, so he believed, while you are big with pride; surely Allah does not guide the unjust people.

11. And those who disbelieve say concerning those who believe: If it had been a good, they would not have gone ahead of us therein. And as they do not seek to be rightly directed thereby, they say: It is an old lie.

12. And before it the Book of Musa was a guide and a mercy: and this is a Book verifying (it) in the Arabic language that it may warn those who are unjust and as good news for the doers of good.

13. Surely those who say, Our Lord is Allah, then they continue on the right way, they shall have no fear nor shall they grieve.

14. These are the dwellers of the garden, abiding therein: a reward for what they did.

15. And We have enjoined on man doing of good to his parents; with trouble did his mother bear him and with trouble did she bring him forth; and the bearing of him and the weaning of him was thirty months; until when he attains his maturity and reaches forty years, he says: My Lord! grant me that I may give thanks for Thy favor which Thou hast bestowed on me and on my parents, and that I may do good which pleases Thee and do good to me in respect of my offspring; surely I turn to Thee, and surely I am of those who submit.

16. These are they from whom We accept the best of what they have done and pass over their evil deeds, among the dwellers of the garden; the promise of truth which they were promised.

17. And he who says to his parents: Fie on you! do you threaten me that I shall be brought forth when generations have

already passed away before me? And they both call for Allah's aid: Woe to you! believe, surely the promise of Allah is true. But he says: This is nothing but stories of the ancients.

18. These are they against whom the word has proved true among nations of the jinn and the men that have already passed away before them; surely they are losers.

19. And for all are degrees according to what they did, and that He may pay them back fully their deeds and they shall not be wronged.

20. And on the day when those who disbelieve shall be brought before the fire: You did away with your good things in your life of the world and you enjoyed them for a while, so today you shall be rewarded with the punishment of abasement because you were unjustly proud in the land and because you transgressed.

21. And mention the brother of Ad; when he warned his people in the sandy plains,—and indeed warners came before him and after him—saying: Serve none but Allah; surely I fear for you the punishment of a grievous day.

22. They said: Have you come to us to turn us away from our gods; then bring us what you threaten us with, if you are of the truthful ones.

23. He said: The knowledge is only with Allah, and I deliver to you the message with which I am sent, but I see you are a people who are ignorant.

24. So when they saw it as a cloud appearing in the sky advancing towards their valleys, they said: This is a cloud which will give us rain. Nay! it is what you sought to hasten on, a blast of wind in which is a painful punishment,

25. Destroying everything by the command of its Lord; so they became such that naught could be seen except their dwellings. Thus do We reward the guilty people.

26. And certainly We had established them in what We have not established you in, and We had given them ears and eyes and hearts, but neither their ears, nor their eyes, nor their hearts availed them aught, since they denied the communications of Allah, and that which they mocked encompassed them.

27. And certainly We destroyed the towns which are around you, and We repeat the communications that they might turn.

28. Why did not then those help them whom they took for gods besides Allah to draw (them) nigh (to Him)? Nay! they were lost to them; and this was their lie and what they forged.

29. And when We turned towards you a party of the jinn who listened to the Quran; so when they came to it, they said: Be silent; then when it was finished, they turned back to their people warning (them).

30. They said: O our people! we have listened to a Book revealed after Musa verifying that which is before it, guiding to the truth and to a right path:

31. O our people! accept the Divine caller and believe in Him, He will forgive you of your faults and protect you from a painful punishment.

32. And whoever does not accept the Divine caller, he shall not escape in the earth and he shall not have guardians besides Him; these are in manifest error.

33. Have they not considered that Allah, Who created the heavens and the earth and was not tired by their creation, is able to give life to the dead? Aye! He has surely power over all things.

34. And on the day when those who disbelieve shall be brought before the fire: Is it not true? They shall say: Aye! by our Lord! He will say: Then taste the punishment, because you disbelieved.

35. Therefore bear up patiently as did the apostles endowed with constancy bear up with patience and do not seek to hasten for them (their doom). On the day that they shall see what they are promised they shall be as if they had not tarried save an hour of the day. A sufficient exposition! Shall then any be destroyed save the transgressing people?

MUHAMMAD

In the name of Allah, the Beneficent, the Merciful.

1. (As for) those who disbelieve and turn away from Allah's way, He shall render their works ineffective.

2. And (as for) those who believe and do good, and believe in what has been revealed to Muhammad, and it is the very truth from their Lord, He will remove their evil from them and improve their condition.

3. That is because those who disbelieve follow falsehood, and

those who believe follow the truth from their Lord; thus does Allah set forth to men their examples.

4. So when you meet in battle those who disbelieve, then smite the necks until when you have overcome them, then make (them) prisoners, and afterwards either set them free as a favor or let them ransom (themselves) until the war terminates. That (shall be so); and if Allah had pleased He would certainly have exacted what is due from them, but that He may try some of you by means of others; and (as for) those who are slain in the way of Allah, He will by no means allow their deeds to perish.

5. He will guide them and improve their condition.

6. And cause them to enter the garden which He has made known to them.

7. O you who believe! if you help (the cause of) Allah, He will help you and make firm your feet.

8. And (as for) those who disbelieve, for them is destruction, and He has made their deeds ineffective.

9. That is because they hated what Allah revealed, so He rendered their deeds null.

10. Have they not then journeyed in the land and seen how was the end of those before them: Allah brought down destruction upon them, and the unbelievers shall have the like of it.

11. That is because Allah is the Protector of those who believe, and because the unbelievers shall have no protector for them.

12. Surely Allah will make those who believe and do good enter gardens beneath which rivers flow; and those who disbelieve enjoy themselves and eat as the beasts eat, and the fire is their abode.

13. And how many a town which was far more powerful than the town of yours which has driven you out: We destroyed them so there was no helper for them.

14. What! is he who has a clear argument from his Lord like him to whom the evil of his work is made fairseeming: and they follow their low desires.

15. A parable of the garden which those guarding (against evil) are promised: Therein are rivers of water that does not alter, and rivers of milk the taste whereof does not change, and rivers of drink delicious to those who drink, and rivers of honey clarified; and for them therein are all fruits and protection from their Lord. (Are these) like those who abide in the fire and who are made to drink boiling water so it rends their bowels asunder.

16. And there are those of them who seek to listen to you, until

when they go forth from you, they say to those who have been given the knowledge: What was it that he said just now? These are they upon whose hearts Allah has set a seal and they follow their low desires.

17. And (as for) those who follow the right direction, He increases them in guidance and gives them their guarding (against evil).

18. Do they then wait for aught but the hour that it should come to them all of a sudden? Now indeed the tokens of it have (already) come, but how shall they have their reminder when it comes on them?

19. So know that there is no god but Allah, and, ask protection for your fault and for the believing men and the believing women; and Allah knows the place of your returning and the place of your abiding.

20. And those who believe say: Why has not a chapter been revealed? But when a decisive chapter is revealed, and fighting is mentioned therein you see those in whose hearts is a disease look to you with the look of one fainting because of death. Woe to them then!

21. Obedience and a gentle word (was proper); but when the affair becomes settled, then if they remain true to Allah it would certainly be better for them.

22. But if you held command, you were sure to make mischief in the land and cut off the ties of kinship!

23. Those it is whom Allah has cursed so He has made them deaf and blinded their eyes.

24. Do they not then reflect on the Quran? Nay, on the hearts there are locks.

25. Surely (as for) those who return on their backs after that guidance has become manifest to them, the Shaitan has made it a light matter to them; and He gives them respite.

26. That is because they say to those who hate what Allah has revealed: We will obey you in some of the affairs; and Allah knows their secrets.

27. But how will it be when the angels cause them to die smiting their backs.

28. That is because they follow what is displeasing to Allah and are averse to His pleasure, therefore He has made null their deeds.

29. Or do those in whose hearts is a disease think that Allah will not bring forth their spite?

30. And if We please We would have made you know them so

that you would certainly have recognized them by their marks; and most certainly you can recognize them by the intent of (their) speech; and Allah knows your deeds.

31. And most certainly We will try you until We have known those among you who exert themselves hard, and the patient, and made your case manifest.

32. Surely those who disbelieve and turn away from Allah's way and oppose the Apostle after that guidance has become clear to them cannot harm Allah in any way, and He will make null their deeds.

33. O you who believe! obey Allah and obey the Apostle, and do not make your deeds of no effect.

34. Surely those who disbelieve and turn away from Allah's way, then they die while they are unbelievers, Allah will by no means forgive them.

35. And be not slack so as to cry for peace and you have the upper hand, and Allah is with you, and He will not bring your deeds to naught.

36. The life of this world is only idle sport and play, and if you believe and guard (against evil) He will give you your rewards, and will not ask of you your possessions.

37. If He should ask you for it and urge you, you will be miserly, and He will bring forth your malice.

38. Behold! you are those who are called upon to spend in Allah's way, but among you are those who are miserly, and whoever is miserly is miserly against his own soul; and Allah is Self-sufficient and you have need (of Him), and if you turn back He will bring in your place another people, then they will not be like you.

THE VICTORY

In the name of Allah, the Beneficent, the Merciful.

1. Surely We have given to you a clear victory,

2. That Allah may forgive your community their past faults and those to follow and complete His favor to you and keep you on a right way,

3. And that Allah might help you with a mighty help.

4. He it is Who sent down tranquillity into the hearts of the believers that they might have more of faith added to their faith—and Allah's are the hosts of the heavens and the earth, and Allah is Knowing, Wise—

5. That He may cause the believing men and the believing women to enter gardens beneath which rivers flow to abide therein and remove from them their evil; and that is a grand achievement with Allah;

6. And (that) He may punish the hypocritical men and the hypocritical women, and the polytheistic men and the polytheistic women, the entertainers of evil thoughts about Allah. On them is the evil turn, and Allah is wroth with them and has cursed them and prepared hell for them, and evil is the resort.

7. And Allah's are the hosts of the heavens and the earth; and Allah is Mighty, Wise.

8. Surely We have sent you as a witness and as a bearer of good news and as a warner,

9. That you may believe in Allah and His Apostle and may aid him and revere him; and (that) you may declare His glory, morning and evening.

10. Surely those who swear allegiance to you do but swear allegiance to Allah; the hand of Allah is above their hands. Therefore whoever breaks (his faith), he breaks it only to the injury of his own soul, and whoever fulfills what he has covenanted with Allah, He will grant him a mighty reward.

11. Those of the dwellers of the desert who were left behind will say to you: Our property and our families kept us busy, so ask forgiveness for us. They say with their tongues what is not in their hearts. Say: Then who can control anything for you from Allah if He intends to do you harm or if He intends to do you good; nay, Allah is Aware of what you do:

12. Nay! you rather thought that the Apostle and the believers would not return to their families ever, and that was made fairseeming to your hearts and you thought an evil thought and you were a people doomed to perish.

13. And whoever does not believe in Allah and His Apostle, then surely We have prepared burning fire for the unbelievers.

14. And Allah's is the kingdom of the heavens and the earth; He forgives whom He pleases and punishes whom He pleases, and Allah is Forgiving, Merciful.

15. Those who are left behind will say when you set forth for

the gaining of acquisitions: Allow us (that) we may follow you. They desire to change the word of Allah. Say: By no means shall you follow us; thus did Allah say before. But they will say: Nay! you are jealous of us. Nay! they do not understand but a little.

16. Say to those of the dwellers of the desert who were left behind: You shall soon be invited (to fight) against a people possessing mighty prowess; you will fight against them until they submit; then if you obey, Allah will grant you a good reward; and if you turn back as you turned back before, He will punish you with a painful punishment.

17. There is no harm in the blind, nor is there any harm in the lame, nor is there any harm in the sick (if they do not go forth); and whoever obeys Allah and His Apostle, He will cause him to enter gardens beneath which rivers flow, and whoever turns back, He will punish him with a painful punishment.

18. Certainly Allah was well pleased with the believers when they swore allegiance to you under the tree, and He knew what was in their hearts, so He sent down tranquillity on them and rewarded them with a near victory,

19. And many acquisitions which they will take; and Allah is Mighty, Wise.

20. Allah promised you many acquisitions which you will take, then He hastened on this one for you and held back the hands of men from you, and that it may be a sign for the believers and that He may guide you on a right path.

21. And others which you have not yet been able to achieve Allah has surely encompassed them, and Allah has power over all things.

22. And if those who disbelieve fight with you, they would certainly turn (their) backs, then they would not find any protector or a helper.

23. Such has been the course of Allah that has indeed run before, and you shall not find a change in Allah's course.

24. And He it is Who held back their hands from you and your hands from them in the valley of Mecca after He had given you victory over them; and Allah is Seeing what you do.

25. It is they who disbelieved and turned you away from the Sacred Mosque and (turned off) the offering withheld from arriving at its destined place; and were it not for the believing men and the believing women, whom, not having known, you might have trodden down, and thus something hateful might have afflicted you on their account without knowledge—so that Allah

may cause to enter into His mercy whomsoever He pleases; had they been widely separated one from another, We would surely have punished those who disbelieved from among them with a painful punishment.

26. When those who disbelieved harbored in their hearts (feelings of) disdain, the disdain of (the days of) ignorance, but Allah sent down His tranquillity on His Apostle and on the believers, and made them keep the word of guarding (against evil), and they were entitled to it and worthy of it; and Allah is Cognizant of all things.

27. Certainly Allah had shown to His Apostle the vision with truth: you shall most certainly enter the Sacred Mosque, if Allah pleases, in security, (some) having their heads shaved and (others) having their hair cut, you shall not fear, but He knows what you do not know, so He brought about a near victory before that.

28. He it is Who sent His Apostle with the guidance and the true religion that He may make it prevail over all the religions; and Allah is enough for a witness.

29. Muhammad is the Apostle of Allah, and those with him are firm of heart against the unbelievers, compassionate among themselves; you will see them bowing down, prostrating themselves, seeking grace from Allah and pleasure; their marks are in their faces because of the effect of prostration; that is their description in the Taurat and their description in the Injeel; like as seed-produce that puts forth its sprout, then strengthens it, so it becomes stout and stands firmly on its stem, delighting the sowers that He may enrage the unbelievers on account of them; Allah has promised those among them who believe and do good, forgiveness and a great reward.

SURAH XLIX   *The Chambers*

THE CHAMBERS

In the name of Allah, the Beneficent, the Merciful.

1. O you who believe! be not forward in the presence of Allah and His Apostle, and be careful of (your duty to) Allah; surely Allah is Hearing, Knowing.

2. O you who believe! do not raise your voices above the voice

of the Prophet, and do not speak loud to him as you speak loud to one another, lest your deeds become null while you do not perceive.

3. Surely those who lower their voices before Allah's Apostle are they whose hearts Allah has proved for guarding (against evil); they shall have forgiveness and a great reward.

4. (As for) those who call out to you from behind the private chambers, surely most of them do not understand.

5. And if they wait patiently until you come out to them, it would certainly be better for them, and Allah is Forgiving, Merciful.

6. O you who believe! if an evil-doer comes to you with a report, look carefully into it, lest you harm a people in ignorance, then be sorry for what you have done.

7. And know that among you is Allah's Apostle; should he obey you in many a matter, you would surely fall into distress, but Allah has endeared the faith to you and has made it seemly in your hearts, and He has made hateful to you unbelief and transgression and disobedience; these it is that are the followers of a right way.

8. By grace from Allah and as a favor; and Allah is Knowing, Wise.

9. And if two parties of the believers quarrel, make peace between them; but if one of them acts wrongfully towards the other, fight that which acts wrongfully until it returns to Allah's command; then if it returns, make peace between them with justice and act equitably; surely Allah loves those who act equitably.

10. The believers are but brethren, therefore make peace between your brethren and be careful of (your duty to) Allah that mercy may be had on you.

11. O you who believe! let not (one) people laugh at (another) people perchance they may be better than they, nor let women (laugh) at (other) women, perchance they may be better than they; and do not find fault with your own people nor call one another by nicknames; evil is a bad name after faith, and whoever does not turn, these it is that are the unjust.

12. O you who believe! avoid most of suspicion, for surely suspicion in some cases is a sin, and do not spy nor let some of you backbite others. Does one of you like to eat the flesh of his dead brother? But you abhor it; and be careful of (your duty to) Allah, surely Allah is Oft-returning (to mercy), Merciful.

13. O you men! surely We have created you of a male and a female, and made you tribes and families that you may know each

other; surely the most honorable of you with Allah is the one among you most careful (of his duty); surely Allah is Knowing, Aware.

14. The dwellers of the desert say: We believe. Say: You do not believe but say, We submit; and faith has not yet entered into your hearts; and if you obey Allah and His Apostle, He will not diminish aught of your deeds; surely Allah is Forgiving, Merciful.

15. The believers are only those who believe in Allah and His Apostle then they doubt not and struggle hard with their wealth and their lives in the way of Allah; they are the truthful ones.

16. Say: Do you apprise Allah of your religion, and Allah knows what is in the heavens and what is in the earth; and Allah is Cognizant of all things.

17. They think that they lay you under an obligation by becoming Muslims. Say: Lay me not under obligation by your Islam: rather Allah lays you under an obligation by guiding you to the faith if you are truthful.

18. Surely Allah knows the unseen things of the heavens and the earth; and Allah sees what you do.

SURAH L *Qaf*

QAF

In the name of Allah, the Beneficent, the Merciful.

1. Qaf. I swear by the glorious Quran (that Muhammad is the Apostle of Allah.)

2. Nay! they wonder that there has come to them a warner from among themselves, so the unbelievers say: This is a wonderful thing:

3. What! when we are dead and have become dust? That is a far (from probable) return.

4. We know indeed what the earth diminishes of them, and with Us is a writing that preserves.

5. Nay, they rejected the truth when it came to them, so they are (now) in a state of confusion.

6. Do they not then look up to heaven above them how We have made it and adorned it and it has no gaps?

7. And the earth, We have made it plain and cast in it mountains and We have made to grow therein of all beautiful kinds,

8. To give sight and as a reminder to every servant who turns frequently (to Allah).

9. And We send down from the cloud water abounding in good, then We cause to grow thereby gardens and the grain that is reaped,

10. And the tall palm-trees having spadices closely set one above another,

11. A sustenance for the servants, and We give life thereby to a dead land; thus is the rising.

12. (Others) before them rejected (prophets): the people of Nuh and the dwellers of Ar-Rass and Samood,

13. And Ad and Firon and Lut's brethren,

14. And the dwellers of the grove and the people of Tuba; all rejected the apostles, so My threat came to pass.

15. Were We then fatigued with the first creation? Yet are they in doubt with regard to a new creation.

16. And certainly We created man, and We know what his mind suggests to him, and We are nearer to him than his life-vein.

17. When the two receivers receive, sitting on the right and on the left.

18. He utters not a word but there is by him a watcher at hand.

19. And the stupor of death will come in truth; that is what you were trying to escape.

20. And the trumpet shall be blown; that is the day of the threatening.

21. And every soul shall come, with it a driver and a witness.

22. Certainly you were heedless of it, but now We have removed from you your veil, so your sight today is sharp.

23. And his companions shall say: This is what is ready with me.

24. Do cast into hell every ungrateful, rebellious one,

25. Forbidder of good, exceeder of limits, doubter,

26. Who sets up another god with Allah, so do cast him into severe chastisement.

27. His companion will say: Our Lord! I did not lead him into inordinacy but he himself was in a great error.

28. He will say: Do not quarrel in My presence, and indeed I gave you the threatening beforehand:

29. My word shall not be changed, nor am I in the least unjust to the servants.

30. On the day that We will say to hell: Are you filled up? And it will say: Are there any more?

31. And the garden shall be brought near to those who guard (against evil), not far off:

32. This is what you were promised, (it is) for every one who turns frequently (to Allah), keeps (His limits);

33. Who fears the Beneficent God in secret and comes with a penitent heart:

34. Enter it in peace, that is the day of abiding.

35. They have therein what they wish and with Us is more yet.

36. And how many a generation did We destroy before them who were mightier in prowess than they, so they went about and about in the lands. Is there a place of refuge?

37. Most surely there is a reminder in this for him who has a heart or he gives ear and is a witness.

38. And certainly We created the heavens and the earth and what is between them in six periods and there touched Us not any fatigue.

39. Therefore be patient of what they say, and sing the praise of your Lord before the rising of the sun and before the setting.

40. And glorify Him in the night and after the prayers.

41. And listen on the day when the crier shall cry from a near place,

42. The day when they shall hear the cry in truth; that is the day of coming forth.

43. Surely We give life and cause to die, and to Us is the eventual coming;

44. The day on which the earth shall cleave asunder under them, they will make haste; that is a gathering together easy to Us.

45. We know best what they say, and you are not one to compel them; therefore remind him by means of the Quran who fears My threat.

SURAH LI   *The Scatterers*

THE SCATTERERS

In the name of Allah, the Beneficent, the Merciful.

1. I swear by the wind that scatters far and wide,

2. Then those clouds bearing the load (of minute things in space).

3. Then those (ships) that glide easily,

4. Then those (angels who) distribute blessings by Our command;

5. What you are threatened with is most surely true,

6. And the judgment must most surely come about.

7. I swear by the heaven full of ways.

8. Most surely you are at variance with each other in what you say,

9. He is turned away from it who would be turned away.

10. Cursed be the liars,

11. Who are in a gulf (of ignorance) neglectful;

12. They ask: When is the day of judgment?

13. (It is) the day on which they shall be tried at the fire.

14. Taste your persecution! this is what you would hasten on.

15. Surely those who guard (against evil) shall be in gardens and fountains.

16. Taking what their Lord gives them; surely they were before that, the doers of good.

17. They used to sleep but little in the night.

18. And in the morning they asked forgiveness.

19. And in their property was a portion due to him who begs and to him who is denied (good).

20. And in the earth there are signs for those who are sure,

21. And in your own souls (too); will you not then see?

22. And in the heaven is your sustenance and what you are threatened with.

23. And by the Lord of the heavens and the earth! it is most surely the truth, just as you do speak.

24. Has there come to you information about the honored guests of Ibrahim?

25. When they entered upon him, they said: Peace. Peace, said he, a strange people.

26. Then he turned aside to his family secretly and brought a fat (roasted) calf,

27. So he brought it near them. He said: What! will you not eat?

28. So he conceived in his mind a fear on account of them. They said: Fear not. And they gave him the good news of a boy possessing knowledge.

29. Then his wife came up in great grief, and she struck her face and said: An old barren woman!

30. They said: Thus says your Lord: Surely He is the Wise, the Knowing.

31. He said: What is your affair then, O messengers!

32. They said: Surely we are sent to a guilty people,

33. That we may send down upon them stone of clay,

34. Sent forth from your Lord for the extravagant.

35. Then We brought forth such as were therein of the believers.

36. But We did not find therein save a (single) house of those who submitted (the Muslims).

37. And We left therein a sign for those who fear the painful punishment.

38. And in Musa: When We sent him to Firon with clear authority.

39. But he turned away with his forces and said: A magician or a mad man.

40. So We seized him and his hosts and hurled them into the sea, and he was blamable.

41. And in Ad: When We sent upon them the destructive wind.

42. It did not leave aught on which it blew, but it made it like ashes.

43. And in Samood: When it was said to them: Enjoy yourselves for a while.

44. But they revolted against the commandment of their Lord, so the rumbling overtook them while they saw.

45. So they were not able to rise up, nor could they defend themselves;

46. And the people of Nuh before, surely they were a transgressing people.

47. And the heaven, We raised it high with power, and most surely We are the makers of things ample.

48. And the earth, We have made it a wide extent; how well have We then spread (it) out.

49. And of everything We have created pairs that you may be mindful.

50. Therefore fly to Allah, surely I am a plain warner to you from Him.

51. And do not set up with Allah another god: surely I am a plain warner to you from Him.

52. Thus there did not come to those before them an apostle but they said: A magician or a mad man.

53. Have they charged each other with this? Nay! they are an inordinate people.

54. Then turn your back upon them for you are not to blame;

55. And continue to remind, for surely the reminder profits the believers.

56. And I have not created the jinn and the men except that they should serve Me.

57. I do not desire from them any sustenance and I do not desire that they should feed Me.

58. Surely Allah is the Bestower of sustenance, the Lord of Power, the Strong.

59. So surely those who are unjust shall have a portion like the portion of their companions, therefore let them not ask Me to hasten on.

60. Therefore woe to those who disbelieve because of their day which they are threatened with.

THE MOUNTAIN

In the name of Allah, the Beneficient, the Merciful.

1. I swear by the Mountain,

2. And the Book written

3. In an outstretched fine parchment,

4. And the House (Kaaba) that is visited,

5. And the elevated canopy,

6. And the swollen sea;

7. Most surely the punishment of your Lord will come to pass;

8. There shall be none to avert it;

9. On the day when the heaven shall move from side to side,

10. And the mountains shall pass away passing away (altogether).

11. So woe on that day to those who reject (the truth),

12. Those who sport entering into vain discourses.

13. The day on which they shall be driven away to the fire of hell with violence.

14. This is the fire which you used to give the lie to.

15. Is it magic then or do you not see?

16. Enter into it, then bear (it) patiently, or do not bear (it) patiently, it is the same to you; you shall be requited only (for) what you did.

17. Surely those who guard (against evil) shall be in gardens and bliss,

18. Rejoicing because of what their Lord gave them, and their Lord saved them from the punishment of the burning fire.

19. Eat and drink pleasantly for what you did,

20. Reclining on thrones set in lines, and We will unite them to large-eyed beautiful ones.

21. And (as for) those who believe and their offspring follow them in faith, We will unite with them their offspring and We will not diminish to them aught of their work; every man is responsible for what he shall have wrought.

22. And We will aid them with fruit and flesh such as they desire.

23. They shall pass therein from one to another a cup wherein there shall be nothing vain nor any sin.

24. And round them shall go boys of theirs as if they were hidden pearls.

25. And some of them shall advance towards others questioning each other.

26. Saying: Surely we feared before on account of our families:

27. But Allah has been gracious to us and He has saved us from the punishment of the hot wind:

28. Surely we called upon Him before: Surely He is the Benign, the Merciful.

29. Therefore continue to remind, for by the grace of your Lord, you are not a soothsayer, or a madman.

30. Or do they say: A poet, we wait for him the evil accidents of time.

31. Say: Wait, for surely I too with you am of those who wait.

32. Nay! do their understandings bid them this? Or are they an inordinate people?

33. Or do they say: He has forged it. Nay! they do not believe.

34. Then let them bring an announcement like it if they are truthful.

35. Or were they created without there being anything, or are they the creators?

36. Or did they create the heavens and the earth? Nay! they have no certainty.

37. Or have they the treasures of your Lord with them? Or have they been set in absolute authority?

38. Or have they the means by which they listen? Then let their listener bring a clear authority.

39. Or has He daughters while you have sons?

40. Or do you ask them for a reward, so that they are over-burdened by a debt?

41. Or have they the unseen so that they write (it) down?

42. Or do they desire a war? But those who disbelieve shall be the vanquished ones in war.

43. Or have they a god other than Allah? Glory be to Allah from what they set up (with Him).

44. And if they should see a portion of the heaven coming down, they would say: Piled up clouds.

45. Leave them then till they meet that day of theirs wherein they shall be made to swoon (with terror):

46. The day on which their struggle shall not avail them aught, nor shall they be helped.

47. And surely those who are unjust shall have a punishment besides that (in the world), but most of them do not know.

48. And wait patiently for the judgment of your Lord, for surely you are before Our eyes, and sing the praise of your Lord when you rise;

49. And in the night, give Him glory too, and at the setting of the stars.

THE STAR

In the name of Allah, the Beneficent, the Merciful.

1. I swear by the star when it goes down.

2. Your companion does not err, nor does he go astray;

3. Nor does he speak out of desire.

4. It is naught but revelation that is revealed,

5. The Lord of Mighty Power has taught him,

6. The Lord of Strength; so he attained completion,

7. And he is in the highest part of the horizon.

8. Then he drew near, then he bowed,

9. So he was the measure of two bows or closer still.

10. And He revealed to His servant what He revealed.

11. The heart was not untrue in (making him see) what he saw.

12. What! do you then dispute with him as to what he saw?

13. And certainly he saw him in another descent,

14. At the farthest lote-tree;

15. Near which is the garden, the place to be resorted to.

16. When that which covers covered the lote-tree;

17. The eye did not turn aside, nor did it exceed the limit.

18. Certainly he saw of the greatest signs of his Lord.

19. Have you then considered the Lat and the Uzza,

20. And Manat, the third, the last?

21. What! for you the males and for Him the females!

22. This indeed is an unjust division!

23. They are naught but names which you have named, you and your fathers; Allah has not sent for them any authority. They follow naught but conjecture and the low desires which (their) souls incline to; and certainly the guidance has come to them from their Lord.

24. Or shall man have what he wishes?

25. Nay! for Allah is the hereafter and the former (life).

26. And how many an angel is there in the heavens whose intercession does not avail at all except after Allah has given permission to whom He pleases and chooses.

27. Most surely they who do not believe in the hereafter name the angels with female names.

28. And they have no knowledge of it; they do not follow anything but conjecture, and surely conjecture does not avail against the truth at all.

29. Therefore turn aside from him who turns his back upon Our reminder and does not desire anything but this world's life.

30. That is their goal of knowledge; surely your Lord knows best him who goes astray from His path and He knows best him who follows the right direction.

31. And Allah's is what is in the heavens and what is in the earth, that He may reward those who do evil according to what they do, and (that) He may reward those who do good with goodness.

32. Those who keep aloof from the great sins and the indecencies but the passing idea; surely your Lord is liberal in forgiving. He knows you best when He brings you forth from the earth and when you are embryos in the wombs of your mothers; therefore do not attribute purity to your souls; He knows him best who guards (against evil).

33. Have you then seen him who turns his back?

34. And gives a little and (then) withholds.

35. Has he the knowledge of the unseen so that he can see?

36. Or, has he not been informed of what is in the scriptures of Musa?

37. And (of) Ibrahim who fulfilled (the commandments):

38. That no bearer of burden shall bear the burden of another;

39. And that man shall have nothing but what he strives for;

40. And that his striving shall soon be seen;

41. Then shall he be rewarded for it with the fullest reward;

42. And that to your Lord is the goal;

43. And that He it is Who makes (men) laugh and makes (them) weep;

44. And that He it is Who causes death and gives life;

45. And that He created pairs, the male and the female,

46. From the small seed when it is adapted;

47. And that on Him is the bringing forth a second time;

48. And that He it is Who enriches and gives to hold;

49. And that He is the Lord of the Sirius;

50. And that He did destroy the Ad of old,

51. And Samood, so He spared not,

52. And the people of Nuh before; surely they were most unjust and inordinate;

53. And the overthrown cities did He overthrow,

54. So there covered them that which covered.

55. Which of your Lord's benefits will you then dispute about?

56. This is a warner of the warners of old.

57. The near event draws nigh.

58. There shall be none besides Allah to remove it.

59. Do you then wonder at this announcement?

60. And will you laugh and not weep?

61. While you are indulging in varieties.

62. So make obeisance to Allah and serve (Him).

SURAH LIV   *The Moon*

THE MOON

In the name of Allah, the Beneficent the Merciful.

1. The hour drew nigh and the moon did rend asunder.

2. And if they see a miracle they turn aside and say: Transient magic.

3. And they call (it) a lie, and follow their low desires; and every affair has its appointed term.

4. And certainly some narratives have come to them wherein is prevention—

5. Consummate wisdom—but warnings do not avail;

6. So turn (your) back on them (for) the day when the inviter shall invite them to a hard task,

7. Their eyes cast down, going forth from their graves as if they were scattered locusts,

8. Hastening to the inviter. The unbelievers shall say: This is a hard day.

9. Before them the people of Nuh rejected, so they rejected Our servant and called (him) mad, and he was driven away.

10. Therefore he called upon his Lord: I am overcome, come Thou then to help.

11. So We opened the gates of the cloud with water pouring down,

12. And We made water to flow forth in the land in springs, so the water gathered together according to a measure already ordained.

13. And We bore him on that which was made of planks and nails,

14. Sailing, before Our eyes, a reward for him who was denied.

15. And certainly We left it as a sign, but is there anyone who will mind?

16. How (great) was then My punishment and My warning!

17. And certainly We have made the Quran easy for remembrance, but is there anyone who will mind?

18. Ad treated (the truth) as a lie, so how (great) was My punishment and My warning!

19. Surely We sent on them a tornado in a day of bitter ill-luck,

20. Tearing men away as if they were the trunks of palm-trees torn up.

21. How (great) was then My punishment and My warning!

22. And certainly We have made the Quran easy for remembrance, but is there anyone who will mind?

23. Samood rejected the warning.

24. So they said: What! a single mortal from among us! Shall we follow him? Most surely we shall in that case be in sure error and distress:

25. Has the reminder been made to light upon him from among us? Nay! he is an insolent liar!

26. Tomorrow shall they know who is the liar, the insolent one.

27. Surely We are going to send the she-camel as a trial for them; therefore watch them and have patience.

28. And inform them that the water is shared between them; every share of the water shall be regulated.

29. But they called their companion, so he took (the sword) and slew (her).

30. How (great) was then My punishment and My warning!

31. Surely We sent upon them a single cry, so they were like the dry fragments of trees which the maker of an enclosure collects.

32. And certainly We have made the Quran easy for remembrance, but is there anyone who will mind?

33. The people of Lut treated the warning as a lie.

34. Surely We sent upon them a stonestorm, except Lut's followers; We saved them a little before daybreak,

35. A favor from Us; thus do We reward him who gives thanks.

36. And certainly he warned them of Our violent seizure, but they obstinately disputed the warning.

37. And certainly they endeavored to turn him from his guests, but We blinded their eyes; so taste My chastisement and My warning.

38. And certainly a lasting chastisement overtook them in the morning.

39. So taste My chastisement and My warning.

40. And certainly We have made the Quran easy for remembrance, but is there anyone who will mind?

41. And certainly the warning came to Firon's people.

42. They rejected all Our communications, so We overtook them after the manner of a Mighty, Powerful One.

43. Are the unbelievers of yours better than these, or is there an exemption for you in the scriptures?

44. Or do they say: We are a host allied together to help each other?

45. Soon shall the hosts be routed, and they shall turn (their) backs.

46. Nay, the hour is their promised time, and the hour shall be most grievous and bitter.

47. Surely the guilty are in error and distress.

48. On the day when they shall be dragged upon their faces into the fire; taste the touch of hell.

49. Surely We have created everything according to a measure.

50. And Our command is but one, as the twinkling of an eye.

51. And certainly We have already destroyed the likes of you, but is there anyone who will mind?

52. And everything they have done is in the writings.

53. And everything small and great is written down.

54. Surely those who guard (against evil) shall be in gardens and rivers,

55. In the seat of honor with a most Powerful King.

THE BENEFICENT

In the name of Allah, the Beneficent, the Merciful.

1. The Beneficent God,

2. Taught the Quran.

3. He created man,

4. Taught him the mode of expression.

5. The sun and the moon follow a reckoning.

6. And the herbs and the trees do adore (Him).

7. And the heaven, He raised it high, and He made the balance,

8. That you may not be inordinate in respect of the measure.

9. And keep up the balance with equity and do not make the measure deficient.

10. And the earth, He has set it for living creatures;

11. Therein is fruit and palms having sheathed clusters,

12. And the grain with (its) husk and fragrance.

13. Which then of the bounties of your Lord will you deny?

14. He created man from dry clay like earthen vessels,

15. And He created the jinn of a flame of fire.

16. Which then of the bounties of your Lord will you deny?

17. Lord of the East and Lord of the West.

18. Which then of the bounties of your Lord will you deny?

19. He has made the two seas to flow freely (so that) they meet together:

20. Between them is a barrier which they cannot pass.

21. Which then of the bounties of your Lord will you deny?

22. There come forth from them pearls, both large and small.

23. Which then of the bounties of your Lord will you deny?

24. And His are the ships reared aloft in the sea like mountains.

25. Which then of the bounties of your Lord will you deny?

26. Everyone on it must pass away.

27. And there will endure for ever the person of your Lord, the Lord of glory and honor.

28. Which then of the bounties of your Lord will you deny?

29. All those who are in the heavens and the earth ask of Him; every moment He is in a state (of glory).

30. Which then of the bounties of your Lord will you deny?

31. Soon will We apply Ourselves to you, O you two armies.

32. Which then of the bounties of your Lord will you deny?

33. O assembly of the jinn and the men! If you are able to pass through the regions of the heavens and the earth, then pass through; you cannot pass through but with authority.

34. Which then of the bounties of your Lord will you deny?

35. The flames of fire and smoke will be sent on you two, then you will not be able to defend yourselves.

36. Which then of the bounties of your Lord will you deny?

37. And when the heaven is rent asunder, and then becomes red like red hide.

38. Which then of the bounties of your Lord will you deny?

39. So on that day neither man nor jinni shall be asked about his sin.

40. Which then of the bounties of your Lord will you deny?

41. The guilty shall be recognized by their marks, so they shall be seized by the forelocks and the feet.

42. Which then of the bounties of your Lord will you deny?

43. This is the hell which the guilty called a lie.

44. Round about shall they go between it and hot, boiling water.

45. Which then of the bounties of your Lord will you deny?

46. And for him who fears to stand before his Lord are two gardens.

47. Which then of the bounties of your Lord will you deny?

48. Having in them various kinds.

49. Which then of the bounties of your Lord will you deny?

50. In both of them are two fountains flowing.

51. Which then of the bounties of your Lord will you deny?

52. In both of them are two pairs of every fruit.

53. Which then of the bounties of your Lord will you deny?

54. Reclining on beds, the inner coverings of which arc of silk brocade; and the fruits of the two gardens shall be within reach.

55. Which then of the bounties of your Lord will you deny?

56. In them shall be those who restrained their eyes; before them neither man nor jinni shall have touched them.

57. Which then of the bounties of your Lord will you deny?

58. As though they were rubies and pearls.

59. Which then of the bounties of your Lord will you deny?

60. Is the reward of goodness aught but goodness?

61. Which then of the bounties of your Lord will you deny?

62. And besides these two are two (other) gardens:

63. Which then of the bounties of your Lord will you deny?

64. Both inclining to blackness.

65. Which then of the bounties of your Lord will you deny?

66. In both of them are two springs gushing forth.

67. Which then of the bounties of your Lord will you deny?

68. In both are fruits and palms and pomegranates.

69. Which then of the bounties of your Lord will you deny?

70. In them are goodly things, beautiful ones.

71. Which then of the bounties of your Lord will you deny?

72. Pure ones confined to the pavilions.

73. Which then of the bounties of your Lord will you deny?

74. Man has not touched them before them nor jinni.

75. Which then of the bounties of your Lord will you deny?

76. Reclining on green cushions and beautiful carpets.

77. Which then of the bounties of your Lord will you deny?

78. Blessed be the name of your Lord, the Lord of Glory and Honor!

SURAH LVI   *The Great Event*

THE GREAT EVENT

In the name of Allah, the Beneficent, the Merciful.

1. When the great event comes to pass,

2. There is no belying its coming to pass—

3. Abasing (one party), exalting (the other),

4. When the earth shall be shaken with a (severe) shaking,

5. And the mountains shall be made to crumble with (an awful) crumbling,

6. So that they shall be as scattered dust.

7. And you shall be three sorts.

8. Then (as to) the companions of the right hand; how happy are the companions of the right hand!

9. And (as to) the companions of the left hand; how wretched are the companions of the left hand!

10. And the foremost are the foremost,

11. These are they who are drawn nigh (to Allah),

12. In the gardens of bliss.

13. A numerous company from among the first,

14. And a few from among the latter.

15. On thrones decorated,

16. Reclining on them, facing one another.

17. Round about them shall go youths never altering in age,

18. With goblets and ewers and a cup of pure drink;

19. They shall not be affected with headache thereby, nor shall they get exhausted;

20. And fruits such as they choose,

21. And the flesh of fowl such as they desire.

22. And pure, beautiful ones,

23. The like of the hidden pearls:

24. A reward for what they used to do.

25. They shall not hear therein vain or sinful discourse,

26. Except the word peace, peace.

27. And the companions of the right hand; how happy are the companions of the right hand!

28. Amid thornless lote-trees,

29. And banana-trees (with fruits), one above another.

30. And extended shade,

31. And water flowing constantly,

32. And abundant fruit,

33. Neither intercepted nor forbidden,

34. And exalted thrones.

35. Surely We have made them to grow into a (new) growth,

36. Then We have made them virgins,

37. Loving, equals in age,

38. For the sake of the companions of the right hand.

39. A numerous company from among the first,

40. And a numerous company from among the last.

41. And those of the left hand, how wretched are those of the left hand!

42. In hot wind and boiling water,

43. And the shade of black smoke,

44. Neither cool nor honorable.

45. Surely they were before that made to live in ease and plenty.

46. And they persisted in the great violation.

47. And they used to say: What! when we die and have become dust and bones, shall we then indeed be raised?

48. Or our fathers of yore?

49. Say: The first and the last,

50. Shall most surely be gathered together for the appointed hour of a known day.

51. Then shall you, O you who err and call it a lie!

52. Most surely eat of a tree of Zaqqoom,

53. And fill (your) bellies with it;

54. Then drink over it of boiling water;

55. And drink as drinks the thirsty camel.

56. This is their entertainment on the day of requital.

57. We have created you, why do you not then assent?

58. Have you considered the seed?

59. Is it you that create it or are We the creators?

60. We have ordained death among you and We are not to be overcome,

61. In order that We may bring in your place the likes of you and make you grow into what you know not.

62. And certainly you know the first growth, why do you not then mind?

63. Have you considered what you sow?

64. Is it you that cause it to grow, or are We the causers of growth?

65. If We pleased, We should have certainly made it broken down into pieces, then would you begin to lament:

66. Surely we are burdened with debt:

67. Nay! we are deprived.

68. Have you considered the water which you drink?

69. Is it you that send it down from the clouds, or are We the senders?

70. If We pleased, We would have made it salty; why do you not then give thanks?

71. Have you considered the fire which you strike?

72. Is it you that produce the trees for it, or are We the producers?

73. We have made it a reminder and an advantage for the wayfarers of the desert.

74. Therefore glorify the name of your Lord, the Great.

75. But nay! I swear by the falling of stars;

76. And most surely it is a very great oath if you only knew;

77. Most surely it is an honored Quran,

78. In a book that is protected;

79. None shall touch it save the purified ones.

80. A revelation by the Lord of the worlds.

81. Do you then hold this announcement in contempt?

82. And to give (it) the lie you make your means of subsistence.

83. Why is it not then that when it (soul) comes up to the throat,

84. And you at that time look on—

85. And We are nearer to it than you, but you do not see—

86. Then why is it not—if you are not held under authority—

87. That you send it (not) back—if you are truthful?

88. Then if he is one of those drawn nigh (to Allah),

89. Then happiness and bounty and a garden of bliss.

90. And if he is one of those on the right hand,

91. Then peace to you from those on the right hand.

92. And if he is one of the rejecters, the erring ones,

93. He shall have an entertainment of boiling water,

94. And burning in hell.

95. Most surely this is a certain truth.

96. Therefore glorify the name of your Lord, the Great.

IRON

In the name of Allah, the Beneficent, the Merciful.

1. Whatever is in the heavens and the earth declares the glory of Allah, and He is the Mighty, the Wise.

2. His is the kingdom of the heavens and the earth; He gives life and causes death; and He has power over all things.

3. He is the First and the Last and the Ascendant (over all) and the Knower of hidden things, and He is Cognizant of all things.

4. He it is who created the heavens and the earth in six periods, and He is firm in power; He knows that which goes deep

down into the earth and that which comes forth out of it, and that which comes down from the heaven and that which goes up into it, and He is with you wherever you are; and Allah sees what you do.

5. His is the kingdom of the heavens and the earth; and to Allah are (all) affairs returned.

6. He causes the night to enter in upon the day, and causes the day to enter in upon the night, and He is Cognizant of what is in the hearts.

7. Believe in Allah and His Apostle, and spend out of what He has made you to be successors of; for those of you who believe and spend shall have a great reward.

8. And what reason have you that you should not believe in Allah? And the Apostle calls on you that you may believe in your Lord, and indeed He has made a covenant with you if you are believers.

9. He it is who sends down clear communications upon His servant, that he may bring you forth from utter darkness into light; and most surely Allah is Kind, Merciful to you.

10. And what reason have you that you should not spend in Allah's way? And Allah's is the inheritance of the heavens and the earth; not alike among you are those who spent before the victory and fought (and those who did not): they are more exalted in rank than those who spent and fought afterwards; and Allah has promised good to all; and Allah is Aware of what you do.

11. Who is there that will offer to Allah a good gift so He will double it for him, and he shall have an excellent reward.

12. On that day you will see the faithful men and the faithful women—their light running before them and on their right hand—good news for you today: gardens beneath which rivers flow, to abide therein, that is the grand achievement.

13. On the day when the hypocritical men and the hypocritical women will say to those who believe: Wait for us, that we may have light from your light; it shall be said: Turn back and seek a light. Then separation would be brought about between them, with a wall having a door in it; (as for) the inside of it, there shall be mercy in it, and (as for) the outside of it, before it there shall be punishment.

14. They will cry out to them: Were we not with you? They shall say: Yea! but you caused yourselves to fall into temptation, and you waited and doubted, and vain desires deceived you till

the threatened punishment of Allah came, while the arch-deceiver deceived you about Allah.

15. So today ransom shall not be accepted from you nor from those who disbelieved; your abode is the fire; it is your friend, and evil is the resort.

16. Has not the time yet come for those who believe that their hearts should be humble for the remembrance of Allah and what has come down of the truth? And (that) they should not be like those who were given the Book before, but the time became prolonged to them, so their hearts hardened, and most of them are transgressors.

17. Know that Allah gives life to the earth after its death; indeed, We have made the communications clear to you that you may understand.

18. Surely (as for) the charitable men and the charitable women and (those who) set apart for Allah a goodly portion, it shall be doubled for them and they shall have a noble reward.

19. And (as for) those who believe in Allah and His apostles, these it is that are the truthful and the faithful ones in the sight of their Lord: they shall have their reward and their light; and (as for) those who disbelieve and reject Our communications, these are the inmates of the hell.

20. Know that this world's life is only sport and play and gaiety and boasting among yourselves, and a vying in the multiplication of wealth and children, like the rain, whose causing the vegetation to grow, pleases the husbandmen; then it withers away so that you will see it become yellow, then it becomes dried up and broken down; and in the hereafter is a severe chastisement and (also) forgiveness from Allah and (His) pleasure; and this world's life is naught but means of deception.

21. Hasten to forgiveness from your Lord and to a garden the extensiveness of which is as the extensiveness of the heaven and the earth; it is prepared for those who believe in Allah and His apostles; that is the grace of Allah: He gives it to whom He pleases, and Allah is the Lord of mighty grace.

22. No evil befalls on the earth nor in your own souls, but it is in a book before We bring it into existence; surely that is easy to Allah:

23. So that you may not grieve for what has escaped you, nor be exultant at what He has given you; and Allah does not love any arrogant boaster:

24. Those who are niggardly and enjoin niggardliness on men;

and whoever turns back, then surely Allah is He Who is the Self-sufficient, the Praised.

25. Certainly We sent Our apostles with clear arguments, and sent down with them the Book and the balance that men may conduct themselves with equity; and We have made the iron, wherein is great violence and advantages to men, and that Allah may know who helps Him and His apostles in the secret; surely Allah is Strong, Mighty.

26. And certainly We sent Nuh and Ibrahim and We gave to their offspring the (gift of) prophecy and the Book; so there are among them those who go aright, and most of them are transgressors.

27. Then We made Our apostles to follow in their footsteps, and We sent Isa son of Marium afterwards, and We gave him the Injeel; and We put in the hearts of those who followed him kindness and mercy; and (as for) monkery, they innovated it— We did not prescribe it to them—only to seek Allah's pleasure, but they did not observe it with its due observance; so We gave to those of them who believed their reward, and most of them are transgressors.

28. O you who believe! be careful of (your duty to) Allah and believe in His Apostle: He will give you two portions of His mercy, and make for you a light with which you will walk, and forgive you, and Allah is Forgiving, Merciful;

29. So that the followers of the Book may know that they do not control aught of the grace of Allah, and that grace is in Allah's hand, He gives it to whom He pleases; and Allah is the Lord of mighty grace.

SURAH LVIII   *The Pleading One*

THE PLEADING ONE

In the name of Allah, the Beneficent, the Merciful.

1. Allah indeed knows the plea of her who pleads with you about her husband and complains to Allah, and Allah knows the contentions of both of you; surely Allah is Hearing, Seeing.

2. (As for) those of you who put away their wives by likening their backs to the backs of their mothers, they are not their mothers; their mothers are no others than those who gave them

birth; and most surely they utter a hateful word and a falsehood; and most surely Allah is Pardoning, Forgiving.

3. And (as for) those who put away their wives by likening their backs to the backs of their mothers then would recall what they said, they should free a captive before they touch each other; to that you are admonished (to conform); and Allah is Aware of what you do.

4. But whoever has not the means, let him fast for two months successively before they touch each other; then as for him who is not able, let him feed sixty needy ones; that is in order that you may have faith in Allah and His Apostle, and these are Allah's limits, and the unbelievers shall have a painful punishment.

5. Surely those who act in opposition to Allah and His Apostle shall be laid down prostrate as those before them were laid down prostrate; and indeed We have revealed clear communications, and the unbelievers shall have an abasing chastisement.

6. On the day when Allah will raise them up all together, then inform them of what they did: Allah has recorded it while they have forgotten it; and Allah is a witness of all things.

7. Do you not see that Allah knows whatever is in the heavens and whatever is in the earth? Nowhere is there a secret counsel between three persons but He is the fourth of them, nor (between) five but He is the sixth of them, nor less than that nor more but He is with them wheresoever they are; then He will inform them of what they did on the day of resurrection: surely Allah is Cognizant of all things.

8. Have you not seen those who are forbidden secret counsels, then they return to what they are forbidden, and they hold secret counsels for sin and revolt and disobedience to the Apostle; and when they come to you they greet you with a greeting with which Allah does not greet you, and they say in themselves: Why does not Allah punish us for what we say? Hell is enough for them; they shall enter it, and evil is the resort.

9. O you who believe! when you confer together in private, do not give to each other counsel of sin and revolt and disobedience to the Apostle, and give to each other counsel of goodness and guarding (against evil); and be careful of (your duty to) Allah, to Whom you shall be gathered together.

10. Secret counsels are only (the work) of the Shaitan that he may cause to grieve those who believe, and he cannot hurt them in the least except with Allah's permission; and on Allah let the believers rely.

11. O you who believe! when it is said to you, Make room in (your) assemblies, then make ample room, Allah will give you ample; and when it is said: Rise up, then rise up. Allah will exalt those of you who believe, and those who are given knowledge, in high degrees; and Allah is Aware of what you do.

12. O you who believe! when you consult the Apostle, then offer something in charity before your consultation; that is better for you and purer; but if you do not find, then surely Allah is Forgiving, Merciful.

13. Do you fear that you will not (be able to) give in charity before your consultation? So when you do not do it and Allah has turned to you (mercifully), then keep up prayer and pay the poor-rate and obey Allah and His Apostle; and Allah is Aware of what you do.

14. Have you not seen those who befriend a people with whom Allah is wroth? They are neither of you nor of them, and they swear falsely while they know.

15. Allah has prepared for them a severe punishment; surely what they do is evil.

16. They make their oaths to serve as a cover so they turn away from Allah's way; therefore they shall have an abasing chastisement.

17. Neither their wealth nor their children shall avail them aught against Allah; they are the inmates of the fire, therein they shall abide.

18. On the day that Allah will raise them up all, then they will swear to Him as they swear to you, and they think that they have something; now surely they are the liars.

19. The Shaitan has gained the mastery over them, so he has made them forget the remembrance of Allah; they are the Shaitan's party; now surely the Shaitan's party are the losers.

20. Surely (as for) those who act in opposition to Allah and His Apostle; they shall be among the most abased.

21. Allah has written down: I will most certainly prevail, I and My apostles; surely Allah is Strong, Mighty.

22. You shall not find a people who believe in Allah and the latter day befriending those who act in opposition to Allah and His Apostle, even though they were their (own) fathers, or their sons, or their brothers, or their kinsfolk; these are they into whose hearts He has impressed faith, and whom He has strengthened with an inspiration from Him: and He will cause them to enter gardens beneath which rivers flow, abiding therein; Allah

is well-pleased with them and they are well-pleased with Him; these are Allah's party: now surely the party of Allah are the successful ones.

THE BANISHMENT

In the name of Allah, the Beneficent, the Merciful.

1. Whatever is in the heavens and whatever is in the earth declares the glory of Allah, and He is the Mighty, the Wise.

2. He it is Who caused those who disbelieved of the followers of the Book to go forth from their homes at the first banishment; you did not think that they would go forth, while they were certain that their fortresses would defend them against Allah; but Allah came to them whence they did not expect, and cast terror into their hearts; they demolished their houses with their own hands and the hands of the believers; therefore take a lesson, O you who have eyes!

3. And had it not been that Allah had decreed for them the exile, He would certainly have punished them in this world, and in the hereafter they shall have chastisement of the fire.

4. That is because they acted in opposition to Allah and His Apostle, and whoever acts in opposition to Allah, then surely Allah is severe in retributing (evil).

5. Whatever palm-tree you cut down or leave standing upon its roots, it is by Allah's command, and that He may abase the transgressors.

6. And whatever Allah restored to His Apostle from them, you did not press forward against it any horse or a riding camel, but Allah gives authority to His apostles against whom He pleases, and Allah has power over all things.

7. Whatever Allah has restored to His Apostle from the people of the towns, it is for Allah and for the Apostle, and for the near of kin and the orphans and the needy and the wayfarer, so that it may not be a thing taken by turns among the rich of you, and whatever the Apostle gives you, accept it, and from whatever he forbids you, keep back, and be careful of (your duty to) Allah; surely Allah is severe in retributing (evil):

8. (It is) for the poor who fled, those who were driven from their homes and their possessions, seeking grace of Allah and (His) pleasure, and assisting Allah and His Apostle: these it is that are the truthful.

9. And those who made their abode in the city and in the faith before them love those who have fled to them, and do not find in their hearts a need of what they are given, and prefer (them) before themselves though poverty may afflict them, and whoever is preserved from the niggardliness of his soul, these it is that are the successful ones.

10. And those who come after them say: Our Lord! forgive us and those of our brethren who had precedence of us in faith, and do not allow any spite to remain in our hearts towards those who believe; our Lord! surely Thou art Kind, Merciful.

11. Have you not seen those who have become hypocrites? They say to those of their brethren who disbelieve from among the followers of the Book: If you are driven forth, we shall certainly go forth with you, and we will never obey any one concerning you, and if you are fought against, we will certainly help you; and Allah bears witness that they are most surely liars.

12. Certainly if these are driven forth, they will not go forth with them, and if they are fought against, they will not help them, and even if they help them, they will certainly turn (their) backs, then they shall not be helped.

13. You are certainly greater in being feared in their hearts than Allah; that is because they are a people who do not understand.

14. They will not fight against you in a body save in fortified towns or from behind walls; their fighting between them is severe; you may think them as one body, and their hearts are disunited; that is because they are a people who have no sense.

15. Like those before them shortly; they tasted the evil result of their affair, and they shall have a painful punishment.

16. Like the Shaitan when he says to man: Disbelieve, but when he disbelieves, he says: I am surely clear of you; surely I fear Allah, the Lord of the worlds.

17. Therefore the end of both of them is that they are both in the fire to abide therein, and that is the reward of the unjust.

18. O you who believe! be careful of (your duty to) Allah, and let every soul consider what it has sent on for the morrow, and be careful of (your duty to) Allah; surely Allah is Aware of what you do.

19. And be not like those who forsook Allah, so He made them forsake their own souls: these it is that are the transgressors.

20. Not alike are the inmates of the fire and the dwellers of the garden: the dwellers of the garden are they that are the achievers.

21. Had We sent down this Quran on a mountain, you would certainly have seen it falling down, splitting asunder because of the fear of Allah, and We set forth these parables to men that they may reflect.

22. He is Allah besides Whom there is no god; the Knower of the unseen and the seen; He is the Beneficent, the Merciful.

23. He is Allah, besides Whom there is no god; the King, the Holy, the Giver of peace, the Granter of security, Guardian over all, the Mighty, the Supreme, the Possessor of every greatness; Glory be to Allah from what they set up (with Him).

24. He is Allah the Creator, the Maker, the Fashioner; His are the most excellent names; whatever is in the heavens and the earth declares His glory; and He is the Mighty, the Wise.

THE EXAMINED ONE

In the name of Allah, the Beneficent, the Merciful.

1. O you who believe! do not take My enemy and your enemy for friends: would you offer them love while they deny what has come to you of the truth, driving out the Apostle and yourselves because you believe in Allah, your Lord? If you go forth struggling hard in My path and seeking My pleasure, would you manifest love to them? And I know what you conceal and what you manifest; and whoever of you does this, he indeed has gone astray from the straight path.

2. If they find you, they will be your enemies, and will stretch forth towards you their hands and their tongues with evil, and they ardently desire that you may disbelieve.

3. Your relationship would not profit you, nor your children, on the day of resurrection; He will decide between you; and Allah sees what you do.

4. Indeed, there is for you a good example in Ibrahim and those with him when they said to their people: Surely we are

clear of you and of what you serve besides Allah; we declare ourselves to be clear of you, and enmity and hatred have appeared between us and you forever until you believe in Allah alone—but not in what Ibrahim said to his father: I would certainly ask forgiveness for you, and I do not control for you aught from Allah—Our Lord! on Thee do we rely, and to Thee do we turn, and to Thee is the eventual coming:

5. Our Lord! do not make us a trial for those who disbelieve, and forgive us, our Lord! surely Thou art the Mighty, the Wise.

6. Certainly there is for you in them a good example, for him who fears Allah and the last day; and whoever turns back, then surely Allah is the Self-sufficient, the Praised.

7. It may be that Allah will bring about friendship between you and those whom you hold to be your enemies among them; and Allah is Powerful; and Allah is Forgiving, Merciful.

8. Allah does not forbid you respecting those who have not made war against you on account of (your) religion, and have not driven you forth from your homes, that you show them kindness and deal with them justly; surely Allah loves the doers of justice.

9. Allah only forbids you respecting those who made war upon you on account of (your) religion, and drove you forth from your homes and backed up (others) in your expulsion, that you make friends with them, and whoever makes friends with them, these are the unjust.

10. O you who believe! when believing women come to you flying, then examine them; Allah knows best their faith; then if you find them to be believing women, do not send them back to the unbelievers; neither are these (women) lawful for them, nor are those (men) lawful for them, and give them what they have spent; and no blame attaches to you in marrying them when you give them their dowries; and hold not to the ties of marriage of unbelieving women, and ask for what you have spent, and let them ask for what they have spent. That is Allah's judgment; He judges between you; and Allah is Knowing, Wise.

11. And if anything (out of the dowries) of your wives has passed away from you to the unbelievers, then your turn comes, give to those whose wives have gone away the like of what they have spent, and be careful of (your duty to) Allah in Whom you believe.

12. O Prophet! when believing women come to you giving you a pledge that they will not associate aught with Allah, and

will not steal, and will not commit fornication, and will not kill their children, and will not bring a calumny which they have forged of themselves, and will not disobey you in what is good, accept their pledge, and ask forgiveness for them from Allah; surely Allah is Forgiving, Merciful.

13. O you who believe! do not make friends with a people with whom Allah is wroth; indeed they despair of the hereafter as the unbelievers despair of those in tombs.

THE RANKS

In the name of Allah, the Beneficent, the Merciful.

1. Whatever is in the heavens and whatever is in the earth declares the glory of Allah; and He is the Mighty, the Wise.

2. O you who believe! why do you say that which you do not do?

3. It is most hateful to Allah that you should say that which you do not do.

4. Surely Allah loves those who fight in His way in ranks as if they were a firm and compact wall.

5. And when Musa said to his people: O my people! why do you give me trouble? And you know indeed that I am Allah's apostle to you; but when they turned aside, Allah made their hearts turn aside, and Allah does not guide the transgressing people.

6. And when Isa son of Marium said: O children of Israel! surely I am the apostle of Allah to you, verifying that which is before me of the Taurat and giving the good news of an Apostle who will come after me, his name being Ahmad; but when he came to them with clear arguments they said: This is clear magic.

7. And who is more unjust than he who forges a lie against Allah and he is invited to Islam, and Allah does not guide the unjust people.

8. They desire to put out the light of Allah with their mouths, but Allah will perfect His light, though the unbelievers may be averse.

9. He it is Who sent His Apostle with the guidance and the true religion, that He may make it overcome the religions, all of them, though the polytheists may be averse.

10. O you who believe! shall I lead you to a merchandise which may deliver you from a painful chastisement?

11. You shall believe in Allah and His Apostle, and struggle hard in Allah's way with your property and your lives; that is better for you, did you but know!

12. He will forgive you your faults and cause you to enter into gardens, beneath which rivers flow, and goodly dwellings in gardens of perpetuity; that is the mighty achievement;

13. And yet another (blessing) that you love: help from Allah and a victory near at hand; and give good news to the believers.

14. O you who believe! be helpers (in the cause) of Allah, as Isa son of Marium said to (his) disciples: Who are my helpers in the cause of Allah? The disciples said: We are helpers (in the cause) of Allah. So a party of the children of Israel believed and another party disbelieved; then We aided those who believed against their enemy, and they became uppermost.

FRIDAY

In the name of Allah, the Beneficent, the Merciful.

1. Whatever is in the heavens and whatever is in the earth declares the glory of Allah, the King, the Holy, the Mighty, the Wise.

2. He it is Who raised among the inhabitants of Mecca an Apostle from among themselves, who recites to them His communications and purifies them, and teaches them the Book and the Wisdom, although they were before certainly in clear error,

3. And others from among them who have not yet joined them; and He is the Mighty, the Wise.

4. That is Allah's grace; He grants it to whom He pleases, and Allah is the Lord of mighty grace.

5. The likeness of those who were charged with the Taurat, then they did not observe it, is as the likeness of the ass bearing

books, evil is the likeness of the people who reject the communications of Allah; and Allah does not guide the unjust people.

6. Say: O you who are Jews, if you think that you are the favorites of Allah to the exclusion of other people, then invoke death if you are truthful.

7. And they will never invoke it because of what their hands have sent before; and Allah is Cognizant of the unjust.

8. Say: (As for) the death from which you flee, that will surely overtake you, then you shall be sent back to the Knower of the unseen and the seen, and He will inform you of that which you did.

9. O you who believe! when the call is made for prayer on Friday, then hasten to the remembrance of Allah and leave off trading; that is better for you, if you know.

10. But when the prayer is ended, then disperse abroad in the land and seek of Allah's grace, and remember Allah much, that you may be successful.

11. And when they see merchandise or sport they break up for it, and leave you standing. Say: What is with Allah is better than sport and (better) than merchandise, and Allah is the best of Sustainers.

THE HYPOCRITES

In the name of Allah, the Beneficent, the Merciful.

1. When the hypocrites come to you, they say: We bear witness that you are most surely Allah's Apostle; and Allah knows that you are most surely His Apostle, and Allah bears witness that the hypocrites are surely liars.

2. They make their oaths a shelter, and thus turn away from Allah's way; surely evil is that which they do.

3. That is because they believe, then disbelieve, so a seal is set upon their hearts so that they do not understand.

4. And when you see them, their persons will please you, and if they speak, you will listen to their speech; (they are) as if they were big pieces of wood clad with garments; they think every cry

to be against them. They are the enemy, therefore beware of them; may Allah destroy them, whence are they turned back?

5. And when it is said to them: Come, the Apostle of Allah will ask forgiveness for you, they turn back their heads and you may see them turning away while they are big with pride.

6. It is alike to them whether you beg forgiveness for them or do not beg forgiveness for them; Allah will never forgive them; surely Allah does not guide the transgressing people.

7. They it is who say: Do not spend upon those who are with the Apostle of Allah until they break up. And Allah's are the treasures of the heavens and the earth, but the hypocrites do not understand.

8. They say: If we return to Medina, the mighty will surely drive out the meaner therefrom; and to Allah belongs the might and to His Apostle and to the believers, but the hypocrites do not know.

9. O you who believe! let not your wealth, or your children, divert you from the remembrance of Allah; and whoever does that, these are the losers.

10. And spend out of what We have given you before death comes to one of you, so that he should say: My Lord! why didst Thou not respite me to a near term, so that I should have given alms and been of the doers of good deeds?

11. And Allah does not respite a soul when its appointed term has come, and Allah is Aware of what you do.

LOSS AND GAIN

In the name of Allah, the Beneficent, the Merciful.

1 Whatever is in the heavens and whatever is in the earth declares the glory of Allah; to Him belongs the kingdom, and to Him is due (all) praise, and He has power over all things.

2. He it is Who created you, but one of you is an unbeliever and another of you is a believer; and Allah sees what you do.

3. He created the heavens and the earth with truth, and He formed you, then made goodly your forms, and to Him is the ultimate resort.

4. He knows what is in the heavens and the earth, and He knows what you hide and what you manifest; and Allah is Cognizant of what is in the hearts.

5. Has there not come to you the story of those who disbelieved before, then tasted the evil result of their conduct, and they had a painful punishment?

6. That is because there came to them their apostles with clear arguments, but they said: Shall mortals guide us? So they disbelieved and turned back, and Allah does not stand in need (of anything), and Allah is Self-sufficient, Praised.

7. Those who disbelieve think that they shall never be raised. Say: Aye! by my Lord! you shall most certainly be raised, then you shall most certainly be informed of what you did; and that is easy to Allah.

8. Therefore believe in Allah and His Apostle and the Light which We have revealed; and Allah is Aware of what you do.

9. On the day that He will gather you for the day of gathering, that is the day of loss and gain; and whoever believes in Allah and does good, He will remove from him his evil and cause him to enter gardens beneath which rivers flow, to abide therein forever; that is the great achievement.

10. And (as for) those who disbelieve and reject Our communications, they are the inmates of the fire, to abide therein, and evil is the resort.

11. No affliction comes about but by Allah's permission; and whoever believes in Allah, He guides aright his heart; and Allah is Cognizant of all things.

12. And obey Allah and obey the Apostle, but if you turn back, then upon Our Apostle devolves only the clear delivery (of the message).

13. Allah, there is no god but He; and upon Allah, then, let the believers rely.

14. O you who believe! surely from among your wives and your children there is an enemy to you; therefore beware of them; and if you pardon and forbear and forgive, then surely Allah is Forgiving, Merciful.

15. Your possessions and your children are only a trial, and Allah it is with Whom is a great reward.

16. Therefore be careful of (your duty to) Allah as much as you can, and hear and obey and spend, it is better for your souls; and whoever is saved from the greediness of his soul, these it is that are the successful.

17. If you set apart for Allah a goodly portion, He will double it for you and forgive you; and Allah is the Multiplier (of rewards), Forbearing,

18. The Knower of the unseen and the seen, the Mighty, the Wise.

THE DIVORCE

In the name of Allah, the Beneficent, the Merciful.

1. O Prophet! when you divorce women, divorce them for their prescribed time, and calculate the number of the days prescribed, and be careful of (your duty to) Allah, your Lord. Do not drive them out of their houses, nor should they themselves go forth, unless they commit an open indecency; and these are the limits of Allah, and whoever goes beyond the limits of Allah, he indeed does injustice to his own soul. You do not know that Allah may after that bring about reunion.

2. So when they have reached their prescribed time, then retain them with kindness or separate them with kindness, and call to witness two men of justice from among you, and give upright testimony for Allah. With that is admonished he who believes in Allah and the latter day; and whoever is careful of (his duty to) Allah, He will make for him an outlet,

3. And give him sustenance from whence he thinks not; and whoever trusts in Allah, He is sufficient for him; surely Allah attains His purpose; Allah indeed has appointed a measure for everything.

4. And (as for) those of your women who have despaired of menstruation, if you have a doubt, their prescribed time shall be three months, and of those too who have not had their courses; and (as for) the pregnant women, their prescribed time is that they lay down their burden; and whoever is careful of (his duty to) Allah He will make easy for him his affair.

5. That is the command of Allah which He has revealed to you, and whoever is careful of (his duty to) Allah, He will remove from him his evil and give him a big reward.

6. Lodge them where you lodge according to your means, and do not injure them in order that you may straiten them; and if they are pregnant, spend on them until they lay down their burden; then if they suckle for you, give them their recompense, and enjoin one another among you to do good; and if you disagree, another (woman) shall suckle for him.

7. Let him who has abundance spend out of his abundance, and whoever has his means of subsistence straitened to him, let him spend out of that which Allah has given him; Allah does not lay on any soul a burden except to the extent to which He has granted it; Allah brings about ease after difficulty.

8. And how many a town which rebelled against the commandment of its Lord and His apostles, so We called it to account severely and We chastised it (with) a stern chastisement.

9. So it tasted the evil result of its conduct, and the end of its affair was perdition.

10. Allah has prepared for them severe chastisement, therefore be careful of (your duty to) Allah, O men of understanding who believe! Allah has indeed revealed to you a reminder,

11. An Apostle who recites to you the clear communications of Allah so that he may bring forth those who believe and do good deeds from darkness into light; and whoever believes in Allah and does good deeds, He will cause him to enter gardens beneath which rivers flow, to abide therein forever; Allah has indeed given him a goodly sustenance.

12. Allah is He Who created seven heavens, and of the earth the like of them; the decree continues to descend among them, that you may know that Allah has power over all things and that Allah indeed encompasses all things in (His) knowledge.

THE PROHIBITION

In the Name of Allah, the Beneficent, the Merciful.

1. O Prophet! why do you forbid (yourself) that which Allah has made lawful for you; you seek to please your wives; and Allah is Forgiving, Merciful.

2. Allah indeed has sanctioned for you the expiation of your

oaths and Allah is your Protector, and He is the Knowing, the Wise.

3. And when the prophet secretly communicated a piece of information to one of his wives—but when she informed (others) of it, and Allah made him to know it, he made known part of it and avoided part; so when he informed her of it, she said: Who informed you of this? He said: The Knowing, the one Aware, informed me.

4. If you both turn to Allah, then indeed your hearts are already inclined (to this); and if you back up each other against him, then surely Allah it is Who is his Guardian, and Jibreel and the believers that do good, and the angels after that are the aiders.

5. Maybe, his Lord, if he divorce you, will give him in your place wives better than you, submissive, faithful, obedient, penitent, adorers, fasters, widows and virgins.

6. O you who believe! save yourselves and your families from a fire whose fuel is men and stones; over it are angels stern and strong, they do not disobey Allah in what He commands them, and do as they are commanded.

7. O you who disbelieve! do not urge excuses today; you shall be rewarded only according to what you did.

8. O you who believe! turn to Allah a sincere turning; maybe your Lord will remove from you your evil and cause you to enter gardens beneath which rivers flow, on the day on which Allah will not abase the Prophet and those who believe with him; their light shall run on before them and on their right hands; they shall say: Our Lord! make perfect for us our light, and grant us protection, surely Thou hast power over all things.

9. O Prophet! strive hard against the unbelievers and the hypocrites, and be hard against them; and their abode is hell; and evil is the resort.

10. Allah sets forth an example to those who disbelieve the wife of Nuh and the wife of Lut: they were both under two of Our righteous servants, but they acted treacherously towards them so they availed them naught against Allah, and it was said: Enter both the fire with those who enter.

11. And Allah sets forth an example to those who believe the wife of Firon when she said: My Lord! build for me a house with Thee in the garden and deliver me from Firon and his doing, and deliver me from the unjust people:

12. And Marium, the daughter of Imran, who guarded her

chastity, so We breathed into her of Our inspiration and she accepted the truth of the words of her Lord and His books, and she was of the obedient ones.

THE KINGDOM

In the name of Allah, the Beneficent, the Merciful.

1. Blessed is He in Whose hand is the kingdom, and He has power over all things,

2. Who created death and life that He may try you—which of you is best in deeds; and He is the Mighty, the Forgiving,

3. Who created the seven heavens one above another; you see no incongruity in the creation of the Beneficent God; then look again, can you see any disorder?

4. Then turn back the eye again and again; your look shall come back to you confused while it is fatigued.

5. And certainly We have adorned this lower heaven with lamps and We have made these missiles for the Shaitans, and We have prepared for them the chastisement of burning.

6. And for those who disbelieve in their Lord is the punishment of hell, and evil is the resort.

7. When they shall be cast therein, they shall hear a loud moaning of it as it heaves,

8. Almost bursting for fury. Whenever a group is cast into it, its keeper shall ask them: Did there not come to you a warner?

9. They shall say: Yea! indeed there came to us a warner, but we rejected (him) and said: Allah has not revealed anything; you are only in a great error.

10. And they shall say: Had we but listened or pondered, we should not have been among the inmates of the burning fire.

11. So they shall acknowledge their sins, but far will be (forgiveness) from the inmates of the burning fire.

12. (As for) those who fear their Lord in secret, they shall surely have forgiveness and a great reward.

13. And conceal your word or manifest it; surely He is Cognizant of what is in the hearts.

14. Does He not know, Who created? And He is the Knower of the subtleties, the Aware.

15. He it is Who made the earth smooth for you, therefore go about in the spacious sides thereof, and eat of His sustenance, and to Him is the return after death.

16. Are you secure of those in the heaven that He should not make the earth to swallow you up? Then lo! it shall be in a state of commotion.

17. Or are you secure of those in the heaven that He should not send down upon you a punishment? Then shall you know how was My warning.

18. And certainly those before them rejected (the truth), then how was My disapproval.

19. Have they not seen the birds above them expanding (their wings) and contracting (them)? What is it that withholds them save the Beneficent God? Surely He sees everything.

20. Or who is it that will be a host for you to assist you besides the Beneficent God? The unbelievers are only in deception.

21. Or who is it that will give you sustenance if He should withhold His sustenance? Nay! they persist in disdain and aversion.

22. What! is he who goes prone upon his face better guided or he who walks upright upon a straight path?

23. Say: He it is Who brought you into being and made for you the ears and the eyes and the hearts: little is it that you give thanks.

24. Say: He it is Who multiplied you in the earth and to Him you shall be gathered.

25. And they say: When shall this threat be (executed) if you are truthful?

26. Say: The knowledge (thereof) is only with Allah and I am only a plain warner.

27. But when they shall see it nigh, the faces of those who disbelieve shall be sorry, and it shall be said; This is that which you used to call for.

28. Say: Have you considered if Allah should destroy me and those with me—rather He will have mercy on us; yet who will protect the unbelievers from a painful punishment?

29. Say: He is the Beneficent God, we believe in Him and on Him do we rely, so you shall come to know who it is that is in clear error.

30. Say: Have you considered if your water should go down, who is it then that will bring you flowing water?

THE PEN

In the name of Allah, the Beneficent, the Merciful.

1. Noon. I swear by the pen and what the angels write,

2. By the grace of your Lord you are not mad.

3. And most surely you shall have a reward never to be cut off.

4. And most surely you conform (yourself) to sublime morality.

5. So you shall see, and they (too) shall see,

6. Which of you is afflicted with madness.

7. Surely your Lord best knows him who errs from His way, and He best knows the followers of the right course.

8. So do not yield to the rejecters.

9. They wish that you should be pliant so they (too) would be pliant.

10. And yield not to any mean swearer,

11. Defamer, going about with slander,

12. Forbidder of good, outstepping the limits, sinful,

13. Ignoble, besides all that, base-born;

14. Because he possesses wealth and sons.

15. When Our communications are recited to him, he says: Stories of those of yore.

16. We will brand him on the nose.

17. Surely We will try them as We tried the owners of the garden, when they swore that they would certainly cut off the produce in the morning,

18. And were not willing to set aside a portion (for the poor).

19. Then there encompassed it a visitation from your Lord while they were sleeping.

20. So it became as black, barren land.

21. And they called out to each other in the morning,

22. Saying: Go early to your tilth if you would cut (the produce).

23. So they went, while they consulted together secretly,

24. Saying: No poor man shall enter it today upon you.

25. And in the morning they went, having the power to prevent.

26. But when they saw it, they said: Most surely we have gone astray.

27. Nay! we are made to suffer privation.

28. The best of them said: Did I not say to you, Why do you not glorify (Allah)?

29. They said: Glory be to our Lord, surely we were unjust.

30. Then some of them advanced against others, blaming each other.

31. Said they: O woe to us! surely we were inordinate:

32. Maybe, our Lord will give us instead one better than it; surely to our Lord do we make our humble petition.

33. Such is the chastisement, and certainly the chastisement of the hereafter is greater, did they but know!

34. Surely those who guard (against evil) shall have with their Lord gardens of bliss.

35. What! shall We then make (i.e. treat) those who submit as the guilty?

36. What has happened to you? How do you judge?

37. Or have you a book wherein you read,

38. That you have surely therein what you choose?

39. Or have you received from Us an agreement confirmed by an oath extending to the day of resurrection that you shall surely have what you demand?

40. Ask them which of them will vouch for that,

41. Or have they associates if they are truthful.

42. On the day when there shall be a severe affliction, and they shall be called upon to make obeisance, but they shall not be able,

43. Their looks cast down, abasement shall overtake them; and they were called upon to make obeisance indeed while yet they were safe.

44. So leave Me and him who rejects this announcement; We will overtake them by degrees, from whence they perceive not:

45. And I do bear with them, surely My plan is firm.

46. Or do you ask from them a reward, so that they are burdened with debt?

47. Or have they (the knowledge of) the unseen, so that they write (it) down?

48. So wait patiently for the judgment of your Lord, and be not like the companion of the fish, when he cried while he was in distress.

49. Were it not that favor from his Lord had overtaken him, he would certainly have been cast down upon the naked ground while he was blamed.

50. Then his Lord chose him, and He made him of the good.

51. And those who disbelieve would almost smite you with their eyes when they hear the reminder, and they say: Most surely he is mad.

52. And it is naught but a reminder to the nations.

THE SURE CALAMITY

In the name of Allah, the Beneficent, the Merciful.

1. The sure calamity!

2. What is the sure calamity!

3. And what would make you realize what the sure calamity is!

4. Samood and Ad called the striking calamity a lie.

5. Then as to Samood, they were destroyed by an excessively severe punishment.

6. And as to Ad, they were destroyed by a roaring, violent blast.

7. Which He made to prevail against them for seven nights and eight days unremittingly, so that you might have seen the people therein prostrate as if they were the trunks of hollow palms.

8. Do you then see of them one remaining?

9. And Firon and those before him and the overthrown cities continuously committed sins.

10. And they disobeyed the Apostle of their Lord, so He punished them with a vehement punishment.

11. Surely We bore you up in the ship when the water rose high,

12. So that We may make it a reminder to you, and that the retaining ear might retain it.

13. And when the trumpet is blown with a single blast,

14. And the earth and the mountains are borne away and crushed with a single crushing.

15. On that day shall the great event come to pass,

16. And the heaven shall cleave asunder, so that on that day it shall be frail,

17. And the angels shall be on the sides thereof; and above them eight shall bear on that day your Lord's power.

18. On that day you shall be exposed to view—no secret of yours shall remain hidden.

19. Then as for him who is given his book in his right hand, he will say: Lo! read my book:

20. Surely I knew that I shall meet my account.

21. So he shall be in a life of pleasure,

22. In a lofty garden,

23. The fruits of which are near at hand:

24. Eat and drink pleasantly for what you did beforehand in the days gone by.

25. And as for him who is given his book in his left hand he shall say: O would that my book had never been given me:

26. And I had not known what my account was:

27. O would that it had made an end (of me):

28. My wealth has availed me nothing:

29. My authority is gone away from me.

30. Lay hold on him, then put a chain on him,

31. Then cast him into the burning fire;

32. Then thrust him into a chain the length of which is seventy cubits.

33. Surely he did not believe in Allah, the Great,

34. Nor did he urge the feeding of the poor.

35. Therefore he has not here today a true friend,

36. Nor any food except refuse,

37. Which none but the wrongdoers eat.

38. But nay! I swear by that which you see,

39. And that which you do not see.

40. Most surely, it is the Word brought by an honored Apostle,

41. And it is not the word of a poet; little is it that you believe;

42. Nor the word of a soothsayer; little is it that you mind.

43. It is a revelation from the Lord of the worlds.

44. And if he had fabricated against Us some of the sayings,

45. We would certainly have seized him by the right hand,

46. Then We would certainly have cut off his aorta.

47. And not one of you could have withheld Us from him.

48. And most surely it is a reminder for those who guard (against evil).

49. And most surely We know that some of you are rejecters.

50. And most surely it is a great grief to the unbelievers.

51. And most surely it is the true certainty.
52. Therefore glorify the name of your Lord, the Great.

THE WAYS OF ASCENT

In the name of Allah, the Beneficent, the Merciful.

1. One demanding, demanded the chastisement which must befall

2. The unbelievers—there is none to avert it—

3. From Allah, the Lord of the ways of Ascent.

4. To Him ascend the angels and the Spirit in a day the measure of which is fifty thousand years.

5. Therefore endure with a goodly patience.

6. Surely they think it to be far off,

7. And We see it nigh.

8. On the day when the heaven shall be as molten copper,

9. And the mountains shall be as tufts of wool;

10. And friend shall not ask of friend,

11. (Though) they shall be made to see each other. The guilty one would fain redeem himself from the chastisement of that day by (sacrificing) his children,

12. And his wife and his brother,

13. And the nearest of his kinsfolk who gave him shelter,

14. And all those that are in the earth, (wishing) then (that) this might deliver him.

15. By no means! Surely it is a flaming fire,

16. Dragging by the head,

17. It shall claim him who turned and fled (from truth),

18. And amasses (wealth) then shuts it up.

19. Surely man is created of a hasty temperament;

20. Being greatly grieved when evil afflicts him,

21. And miserly when good befalls him,

22. Except those who pray,

23. Those who are constant at their prayer,

24. And those in whose wealth there is a fixed portion.

25. For him who begs and for him who is denied (good),

26. And those who accept the truth of the judgment day,

27. And those who are fearful of the chastisement of their Lord—

28. Surely the chastisement of their Lord is (a thing) not to be felt secure of—

29. And those who guard their private parts,

30. Except in the case of their wives or those whom their right hands possess—for these surely are not to be blamed,

31. But he who seeks to go beyond this, these it is that go beyond the limits—

32. And those who are faithful to their trusts and their covenant,

33. And those who are upright in their testimonies,

34. And those who keep a guard on their prayer,

35. Those shall be in gardens, honored.

36. But what is the matter with those who disbelieve that they hasten on around you,

37. On the right hand and on the left, in sundry parties?

38. Does every man of them desire that he should be made to enter the garden of bliss?

39. By no means! Surely We have created them of what they know.

40. But nay! I swear by the Lord of the Easts and the Wests that We are certainly able

41. To bring instead (others) better than them, and We shall not be overcome.

42. Therefore leave them alone to go on with the false discourses and to sport until they come face to face with that day of theirs with which they are threatened;

43. The day on which they shall come forth from their graves in haste, as if they were hastening on to a goal,

44. Their eyes cast down; disgrace shall overtake them; that is the day which they were threatened with.

NUH

In the name of Allah, the Beneficent, the Merciful.

1. Surely We sent Nuh to his people, saying: Warn your people before there come upon them a painful chastisement.

2. He said: O my people! Surely I am a plain warner to you:

3. That you should serve Allah and be careful of (your duty to) Him and obey me:

4. He will forgive you some of your faults and grant you a delay to an appointed term; surely the term of Allah when it comes is not postponed; did you but know!

5. He said: O my Lord! surely I have called my people by night and by day!

6. But my call has only made them flee the more:

7. And whenever I have called them that Thou mayest forgive them, they put their fingers in their ears, cover themselves with their garments, and persist and are puffed up with pride:

8. Then surely I called to them aloud:

9. Then surely I spoke to them in public and I spoke to them in secret:

10. Then I said, Ask forgiveness of your Lord, surely He is the most Forgiving:

11. He will send down upon you the cloud, pouring down abundance of rain:

12. And help you with wealth and sons, and make for you gardens, and make for you rivers.

13. What is the matter with you that you fear not the greatness of Allah?

14. And indeed He has created you through various grades:

15. Do you not see how Allah has created the seven heavens one above another,

16. And made the moon therein a light, and made the sun a lamp?

17. And Allah has made you grow out of the earth as a growth:

18. Then He returns you to it, then will He bring you forth a (new) bringing forth:

19. And Allah has made for you the earth a wide expanse,

20. That you may go along therein in wide paths.

21. Nuh said: My Lord! surely they have disobeyed me and followed him whose wealth and children have added to him nothing but loss.

22. And they have planned a very great plan.

23. And they say: By no means leave your gods, nor leave Wadd, nor Suwa; nor Yaghus, and Yauq and Nasr.

24. And indeed they have led astray many, and do not increase the unjust in aught but error.

25. Because of their wrongs they were drowned, then made to enter fire, so they did not find any helpers besides Allah.

26. And Nuh said: My Lord! leave not upon the land any dweller from among the unbelievers:

27. For surely if Thou leave them they will lead astray Thy servants, and will not beget any but immoral, ungrateful (children);

28. My Lord! forgive me and my parents and him who enters my house believing, and the believing men and the believing women; and do not increase the unjust in aught but destruction!

SURAH LXXII　　　　　　　　　　　　*The Jinn*

THE JINN

In the name of Allah, the Beneficent, the Merciful.

1. Say: It has been revealed to me that a party of the jinn listened, and they said: Surely we have heard a wonderful Quran,

2. Guiding to the right way, so we believe in it, and we will not set up any one with our Lord:

3. And that He—exalted be the majesty of our Lord—has not taken a consort, nor a son:

4. And that the foolish amongst us used to forge extravagant things against Allah:

5. And that we thought that men and jinn did not utter a lie against Allah:

6. And that persons from among men used to seek refuge with persons from among jinn, so they increased them in wrongdoing:

7. And that they thought as you think, that Allah would not raise anyone:

8. And that we sought to reach heaven, but we found it filled with strong guards and flaming stars.

9. And that we used to sit in some of the sitting-places thereof to steal a hearing, but he who would (try to) listen now would find a flame lying in wait for him:

10. And that we know not whether evil is meant for those who are on earth or whether their Lord means to bring them good:

11. And that some of us are good and others of us are below that: we are sects following different ways:

12. And that we know that we cannot escape Allah in the earth, nor can we escape Him by flight:

13. And that when we heard the guidance, we believed in it; so whoever believes in his Lord, he should neither fear loss nor being overtaken (by disgrace):

14. And that some of us are those who submit, and some of us are the deviators; so whoever submits, these aim at the right way:

15. And as to the deviators, they are fuel of hell:

16. And that if they should keep to the (right) way, We would certainly give them to drink of abundant water,

17. So that We might try them with respect to it; and whoever turns aside from the reminder of his Lord, He will make him enter into an afflicting chastisement:

18. And that the mosques are Allah's, therefore call not upon any one with Allah:

19. And that when the servant of Allah stood up calling upon Him, they wellnigh crowded him (to death).

20. Say: I only call upon my Lord, and I do not associate any one with Him.

21. Say: I do not control for you evil or good.

22. Say: Surely no one can protect me against Allah, nor can I find besides Him any place of refuge:

23. (It is) only a delivering (of communications) from Allah and His messages; and whoever disobeys Allah and His Apostle, surely he shall have the fire of hell to abide therein for a long time.

24. Until when they see what they are threatened with, then shall they know who is weaker in helpers and fewer in number.

25. Say: I do not know whether that with which you are threatened be nigh or whether my Lord will appoint for it a term:

26. The Knower of the unseen! so He does not reveal His secrets to any,

27. Except to him whom He chooses as an apostle; for surely He makes a guard to march before him and after him,

28. So that He may know that they have truly delivered the messages of their Lord, and He encompasses what is with them, and He records the number of all things.

THE WRAPPED UP

In the name of Allah, the Beneficent, the Merciful.

1. O you who have wrapped up in your garments!

2. Rise to pray in the night except a little,

3. Half of it, or lessen it a little,

4. Or add to it, and recite the Quran as it ought to be recited.

5. Surely We will make to light upon you a weighty Word.

6. Surely the rising by night is the firmest way to tread and the best corrective of speech.

7. Surely you have in the day time a long occupation.

8. And remember the name of your Lord and devote yourself to Him with (exclusive) devotion.

9. The Lord of the East and the West—there is no god but He—therefore take Him for a protector.

10. And bear patiently what they say and avoid them with a becoming avoidance.

11. And leave Me and the rejecters, the possessors of ease and plenty, and respite them a little.

12. Surely with Us are heavy fetters and a flaming fire,

13. And food that chokes and a painful punishment,

14. On the day when the earth and the mountains shall quake and the mountains shall become (as) heaps of sand let loose.

15. Surely We have sent to you an Apostle, a witness against you, as We sent an apostle to Firon.

16. But Firon disobeyed the apostle, so We laid on him a violent hold.

17. How, then, will you guard yourselves, if you disbelieve, on the day which shall make children grey-headed?

18. The heaven shall rend asunder thereby; His promise is ever brought to fulfillment.

19. Surely this is a reminder, then let him, who will take the way to his Lord.

20. Surely your Lord knows that you pass in prayer nearly two-thirds of the night, and (sometimes) half of it, and (sometimes) a third of it, and (also) a party of those with you; and Allah measures the night and the day. He knows that you are not able to do it, so He has turned to you (mercifully), therefore read what is easy of the Quran. He knows that there must be among you sick, and others who travel in the land seeking of the bounty of Allah, and others who fight in Allah's way, therefore read as much of it as is easy (to you), and keep up prayer and pay the poor-rate and offer to Allah a goodly gift, and whatever of good you send on beforehand for yourselves, you will find it with Allah; that is best and greatest in reward; and ask forgiveness of Allah; surely Allah is Forgiving, Merciful.

THE CLOTHED ONE

In the name of Allah, the Beneficent, the Merciful.

1. O you who are clothed!
2. Arise and warn,
3. And your Lord do magnify,
4. And your garments do purify,
5. And uncleanness do shun,
6. And bestow not favors that you may receive again with increase,
7. And for the sake of your Lord, be patient.
8. For when the trumpet is sounded,
9. That, at that time, shall be a difficult day,
10. For the unbelievers, anything but easy.
11. Leave Me and him whom I created alone,
12. And give him vast riches,
13. And sons dwelling in his presence,
14. And I adjusted affairs for him adjustably;
15. And yet he desires that I should add more!
16. By no means! surely he offers opposition to Our communications.
17. I will make a distressing punishment overtake him.
18. Surely he reflected and guessed,
19. But may he be cursed how he plotted;
20. Again, may he be cursed how he plotted;
21. Then he looked,
22. Then he frowned and scowled,
23. Then he turned back and was big with pride,
24. Then he said: This is naught but enchantment, narrated (from others);
25. This is naught but the word of a mortal.
26. I will cast him into hell.
27. And what will make you realize what hell is?
28. It leaves naught nor does it spare aught.
29. It scorches the mortal.
30. Over it are nineteen.
31. And We have not made the wardens of the fire others than angels, and We have not made their number but as a trial for those who disbelieve, that those who have been given the book may be certain and those who believe may increase in faith, and

those who have been given the book and the believers may not
doubt, and that those in whose hearts is a disease and the
unbelievers may say: What does Allah mean by this parable?
Thus does Allah make err whom He pleases, and He guides
whom He pleases, and none knows the hosts of your Lord but
He Himself; and this is naught but a reminder to the mortals.

32. Nay; I swear by the moon,

33. And the night when it departs,

34. And the daybreak when it shines;

35. Surely it (hell) is one of the gravest (misfortunes),

36. A warning to mortals,

37. To him among you who wishes to go forward or remain
behind.

38. Every soul is held in pledge for what it earns,

39. Except the people of the right hand,

40. In gardens, they shall ask each other

41. About the guilty:

42. What has brought you into hell?

43. They shall say: We were not of those who prayed;

44. And we used not to feed the poor;

45. And we used to enter into vain discourse with those who
entered into vain discourses.

46. And we used to call the day of judgment a lie;

47. Till death overtook us.

48. So the intercession of intercessors shall not avail them.

49. What is then the matter with them, that they turn away
from the admonition,

50. As if they were asses taking fright

51. That had fled from a lion?

52. Nay; every one of them desires that he may be given pages
spread out;

53. Nay! but they do not fear the hereafter.

54. Nay! it is surely an admonition.

55. So whoever pleases may mind it.

56. And they will not mind unless Allah please. He is worthy
to be feared and worthy to forgive.

THE RESURRECTION

In the name of Allah, the Beneficent, the Merciful.

1. Nay! I swear by the day of resurrection.
2. Nay! I swear by the self-accusing soul.
3. Does man think that We shall not gather his bones?
4. Yea! We are able to make complete his very fingertips,
5. Nay! man desires to give the lie to what is before him.
6. He asks: When is the day of resurrection?
7. So when the sight becomes dazed,
8. And the moon becomes dark,
9. And the sun and the moon are brought together,
10. Man shall say on that day: Whither to fly to?
11. By no means! there shall be no place of refuge!
12. With your Lord alone shall on that day be the place of rest.
13. Man shall on that day be informed of what he sent before and (what he) put off.
14. Nay! man is evidence against himself,
15. Though he puts forth his excuses.
16. Do not move your tongue with it to make haste with it,
17. Surely on Us (devolves) the collecting of it and the reciting of it.
18. Therefore when We have recited it, follow its recitation.
19. Again on Us (devolves) the explaining of it.
20. Nay! But you love the present life,
21. And neglect the hereafter.
22. (Some) faces on that day shall be bright,
23. Looking to their Lord.
24. And (other) faces on that day shall be gloomy,
25. Knowing that there will be made to befall them some great calamity.
26. Nay! When it comes up to the throat,
27. And it is said: Who will be a magician?
28. And he is sure that it is the (hour of) parting,
29. And affliction is combined with affliction;
30. To your Lord on that day shall be the driving.
31. So he did not accept the truth, nor did he pray,
32. But called the truth a lie and turned back,

33. Then he went to his followers, walking away in haughtiness.

34. Nearer to you (is destruction) and nearer,

35. Again (consider how) nearer to you and nearer.

36. Does man think that he is to be left to wander without an aim?

37. Was he not a small seed in the seminal elements,

38. Then he was a clot of blood, so He created (him) then made (him) perfect.

39. Then He made of him two kinds, the male and the female.

40. Is not He able to give life to the dead?

THE MAN

In the name of Allah, the Beneficent, the Merciful.

1. There surely came over man a period of time when he was a thing not worth mentioning.

2. Surely We have created man from a small life-germ uniting (itself): We mean to try him, so We have made him hearing, seeing.

3. Surely We have shown him the way: he may be thankful or unthankful.

4. Surely We have prepared for the unbelievers chains and shackles and a burning fire.

5. Surely the righteous shall drink of a cup the admixture of which is camphor,

6. A fountain from which the servants of Allah shall drink; they make it to flow a (goodly) flowing forth.

7. They fulfill vows and fear a day the evil of which shall be spreading far and wide.

8. And they give food out of love for Him to the poor and the orphan and the captive:

9. We only feed you for Allah's sake; we desire from you neither reward nor thanks:

10. Surely we fear from our Lord a stern, distressful day.

11. Therefore Allah will guard them from the evil of that day and cause them to meet with ease and happiness;

12. And reward them, because they were patient, with garden and silk,

13. Reclining therein on raised couches, they shall find therein neither (the severe heat of) the sun nor intense cold.

14. And close down upon them (shall be) its shadows, and its fruits shall be made near (to them), being easy to reach.

15. And there shall be made to go round about them vessels of silver and goblets which are of glass,

16. (Transparent as) glass, made of silver; they have measured them according to a measure.

17. And they shall be made to drink therein a cup the admixture of which shall be ginger,

18. (Of) a fountain therein which is named Salsabil.

19. And round about them shall go youths never altering in age; when you see them you will think them to be scattered pearls.

20. And when you see there, you shall see blessings and a great kingdom.

21. Upon them shall be garments of fine green silk and thick silk interwoven with gold, and they shall be adorned with bracelets of silver, and their Lord shall make them drink a pure drink.

22. Surely this is a reward for you, and your striving shall be recompensed.

23. Surely We Ourselves have revealed the Quran to you, revealing (it) in portions.

24. Therefore wait patiently for the command of your Lord, and obey not from among them a sinner or an ungrateful one.

25. And glorify the name of your Lord morning and evening.

26. And during part of the night adore Him, and give glory to Him (a) long (part of the) night.

27. Surely these love the transitory and neglect a grievous day before them.

28. We created them and made firm their make, and when We please We will bring in their place the likes of them by a change.

29. Surely this is a reminder, so whoever pleases takes to his Lord a way.

30. And you do not please except that Allah please; surely Allah is Knowing, Wise;

31. He makes whom He pleases to enter into His mercy; and (as for) the unjust, He has prepared for them a painful chastisement.

THE EMISSARIES

In the name of Allah, the Beneficent, the Merciful.

1. I swear by the emissary winds, sent one after another (for men's benefit),

2. By the raging hurricanes,

3. Which scatter clouds to their destined places,

4. Then separate them one from another,

5. Then I swear by the angels who bring down the revelation,

6. To clear or to warn.

7. Most surely what you are threatened with must come to pass.

8. So when the stars are made to lose their light,

9. And when the heaven is rent asunder,

10. And when the mountains are carried away as dust,

11. And when the apostles are gathered at their appointed time,

12. To what day is the doom fixed?

13. To the day of decision.

14. And what will make you comprehend what the day of decision is?

15. Woe on that day to the rejecters.

16. Did We not destroy the former generations?

17. Then did We follow them up with later ones.

18. Even thus shall We deal with the guilty.

19. Woe on that day to the rejecters.

20. Did We not create you from contemptible water?

21. Then We placed it in a secure resting-place,

22. Till an appointed term,

23. So We proportion it—how well are We at proportioning (things).

24. Woe on that day to the rejecters.

25. Have We not made the earth to draw together to itself,

26. The living and the dead,

27. And made therein lofty mountains, and given you to drink of sweet water?

28. Woe on that day to the rejecters.

29. Walk on to that which you called a lie.

30. Walk on to the covering having three branches,

31. Neither having the coolness of the shade nor availing against the flame.

32. Surely it sends up sparks like palaces,

33. As if they were tawny camels.

34. Woe on that day to the rejecters.

35. This is the day on which they shall not speak,

36. And permission shall not be given to them so that they should offer excuses.

37. Woe on that day to the rejecters.

38. This is the day of decision: We have gathered you and those of yore.

39. So if you have a plan, plan against Me (now).

40. Woe on that day to the rejecters.

41. Surely those who guard (against evil) shall be amid shades and fountains,

42. And fruits such as they desire.

43. Eat and drink pleasantly because of what you did.

44. Surely thus do We reward the doers of good.

45. Woe on that day to the rejecters.

46. Eat and enjoy yourselves for a little; surely you are guilty.

47. Woe on that day to the rejecters.

48. And when it is said to them: Bow down, they do not bow down.

49. Woe on that day to the rejecters.

50. In what announcement, then, after it, will they believe?

THE GREAT EVENT

In the name of Allah, the Beneficent, the Merciful.

1. Of what do they ask one another?

2. About the great event,

3. About which they differ?

4. Nay! they shall soon come to know;

5. Nay! Nay! they shall soon know.

6. Have We not made the earth an even expanse?

7. And the mountains as projections (thereon)?

8. And We created you in pairs,

9. And We made your sleep to be rest (to you),

10. And We made the night to be a covering,

11. And We made the day for seeking livelihood.

12. And We made above you seven strong ones,

13. And We made a shining lamp,

14. And We send down from the clouds water pouring forth abundantly,

15. That We may bring forth thereby corn and herbs,

16. And gardens dense and luxuriant.

17. Surely the day of decision is (a day) appointed:

18. The day on which the trumpet shall be blown so you shall come forth in hosts,

19. And the heaven shall be opened so that it shall be all openings,

20. And the mountains shall be moved off so that they shall remain a mere semblance.

21. Surely hell lies in wait,

22. A place of resort for the inordinate,

23. Living therein for ages.

24. They shall not taste therein cool nor drink

25. But boiling and intensely cold water,

26. Requital corresponding.

27. Surely they feared not the account,

28. And called Our communications a lie, giving the lie (to the truth).

29. And We have recorded everything in a book,

30. So taste! for We will not add to you aught but chastisement.

31. Surely for those who guard (against evil) is achievement,

32. Gardens and vineyards,

33. And those showing freshness of youth, equals in age,

34. And a pure cup.

35. They shall not hear therein any vain words nor lying.

36. A reward from your Lord, a gift according to a reckoning:

37. The Lord of the heavens and the earth and what is between them, the Beneficent God, they shall not be able to address Him.

38. The day on which the spirit and the angels shall stand in ranks; they shall not speak except he whom the Beneficent God permits and who speaks the right thing.

39. That is the sure day, so whoever desires may take refuge with his Lord.

40. Surely We have warned you of a chastisement near at hand: the day when man shall see what his two hands have sent before, and the unbeliever shall say: O! would that I were dust!

THOSE WHO PULL OUT

In the name of Allah, the Beneficent, the Merciful.

1. I swear by the angels who violently pull out the souls of the wicked,

2. And by those who gently draw out the souls of the blessed,

3. And by those who float in space,

4. Then those who are foremost going ahead,

5. Then those who regulate the affair.

6. The day on which the quaking one shall quake,

7. What must happen afterwards shall follow it.

8. Hearts on that day shall palpitate,

9. Their eyes cast down.

10. They say: Shall we indeed be restored to (our) first state?

11. What! when we are rotten bones?

12. They said: That then would be a return occasioning loss.

13. But it shall be only a single cry,

14. When lo! they shall be wakeful.

15. Has not there come to you the story of Musa?

16. When his Lord called upon him in the holy valley, twice,

17. Go to Firon, surely he has become inordinate.

18. Then say: Have you (a desire) to purify yourself:

19. And I will guide you to your Lord so that you should fear.

20. So he showed him the mighty sign.

21. But he rejected (the truth) and disobeyed.

22. Then he went back hastily.

23. Then he gathered (men) and called out.

24. Then he said: I am your lord, the most high.

25. So Allah seized him with the punishment of the hereafter and the former life.

26. Most surely there is in this a lesson to him who fears.

27. Are you the harder to create or the heaven? He made it.

28. He raised high its height, then put it into a right good state.

29. And He made dark its night and brought out its light.

30. And the earth, He expanded it after that.

31. He brought forth from it its water and its pasturage.

32. And the mountains, He made them firm,

33. A provision for you and for your cattle.

34. But when the great predominating calamity comes;

35. The day on which man shall recollect what he strove after,

36. And the hell shall be made manifest to him who sees

37. Then as for him who is inordinate,

38. And prefers the life of this world,

39. Then surely the hell, that is the abode.

40. And as for him who fears to stand in the presence of his Lord and forbids the soul from low desires,

41. Then surely the garden—that is the abode.

42. They ask you about the hour, when it will come.

43. About what! You are one to remind of it.

44. To your Lord is the goal of it.

45. You are only a warner to him who would fear it.

46. On the day that they see it, it will be as though they had not tarried but the latter part of a day or the early part of it.

HE FROWNED

In the name of Allah, the Beneficent, the Merciful.

1. He frowned and turned (his) back,

2. Because there came to him the blind man.

3. And what would make you know that he would purify himself,

4. Or become reminded so that the reminder should profit him?

5. As for him who considers himself free from need (of you),

6. To him do you address yourself.

7. And no blame is on you if he would not purify himself.

8. And as to him who comes to you striving hard,

9. And he fears,

10. From him will you divert yourself.

11. Nay! surely it is an admonishment.

12. So let him who pleases mind it.

13. In honored books,

14. Exalted, purified,

15. In the hands of scribes,

16. Noble, virtuous.

17. Cursed be man! how ungrateful is he!

18. Of what thing did He create him?

19. Of a small seed; He created him, then He made him according to a measure,

20. Then (as for) the way—He has made it easy (for him),

21. Then He causes him to die, then assigns to him a grave,

22. Then when He pleases, He will raise him to life again.

23. Nay; but he has not done what He bade him.

24. Then let man look to his food,

25. That We pour down the water, pouring (it) down in abundance,

26. Then We cleave the earth, cleaving (it) asunder,

27. Then We cause to grow therein the grain,

28. And grapes and clover,

29. And the olive and the palm,

30. And thick gardens,

31. And fruits and herbage,

32. A provision for you and for your cattle.

33. But when the deafening cry comes,

34. The day on which a man shall fly from his brother,

35. And his mother and his father,

36. And his spouse and his son—

37. Every man of them shall on that day have an affair which will occupy him.

38. (Many) faces on that day shall be bright,

39. Laughing, joyous.

40. And (many) faces on that day, on them shall be dust,

41. Darkness shall cover them.

42. These are they who are unbelievers, the wicked.

THE COVERING UP

In the name of Allah, the Beneficent, the Merciful.

1. When the sun is covered,

2. And when the stars darken,

3. And when the mountains are made to pass away,

4. And when the camels are left untended,

5. And when the wild animals are made to go forth,

6. And when the seas are set on fire,

7. And when souls are united,

8. And when the female infant buried alive is asked

9. For what sin she was killed,

10. And when the books are spread,

11. And when the heaven has its covering removed,

12. And when the hell is kindled up,

13. And when the garden is brought nigh,

14. Every soul shall (then) know what it has prepared.

15. But nay! I swear by the stars,

16. That run their course (and) hide themselves,

17. And the night when it departs,

18. And the morning when it brightens,

19. Most surely it is the Word of an honored messenger,

20. The processor of strength, having an honorable place with the Lord of the Dominion,

21. One (to be) obeyed, and faithful in trust.

22. And your companion is not gone mad.

23. And of a truth he saw himself on the clear horizon.

24. Nor of the unseen is he a tenacious concealer.

25. Nor is it the word of the cursed Shaitan,

26. Whither then will you go?

27. It is naught but a reminder for the nations,

28. For him among you who pleases to go straight.

29. And you do not please except that Allah please, the Lord of the worlds.

THE CLEAVING ASUNDER

In the name of Allah, the Beneficent, the Merciful.

1. When the heaven becomes cleft asunder,

2. And when the stars become dispersed,

3. And when the seas are made to flow forth,

4. And when the graves are laid open,

5. Every soul shall know what it has sent before and held back.

6. O man! what has beguiled you from your Lord, the Gracious one,

7. Who created you, then made you complete, then made you symmetrical?

8. Into whatever form He pleased He constituted you.

9. Nay! but you give the lie to the judgment day,

10. And most surely there are keepers over you,

11. Honorable recorders,

12. They know what you do.

13. Most surely the righteous are in bliss,

14. And most surely the wicked are in burning fire,

15. They shall enter it on the day of judgment.

16. And they shall by no means be absent from it.

17. And what will make you realize what the day of judgment is?

18. Again, what will make you realize what the day of judgment is?

19. The day on which no soul shall control anything for (another) soul; and the command on that day shall be entirely Allah's.

THE DEFRAUDERS

In the name of Allah, the Beneficent, the Merciful.

1. Woe to the defrauders,

2. Who, when they take the measure (of their dues) from men, take it fully,

3. But when they measure out to others or weigh out for them, they are deficient.

4. Do not these think that they shall be raised again,

5. For a mighty day,

6. The day on which men shall stand before the Lord of the worlds?

7. Nay! most surely the record of the wicked is in the Sijjin.

8. And what will make you know what the Sijjin is?

9. It is a written book.

10. Woe on that day to the rejecters,

11. Who give the lie to the day of judgment.

12. And none gives the lie to it but every exceeder of limits, sinful one;

13. When Our communications are recited to him, he says: Stories of those of yore.

14. Nay! rather, what they used to do has become like rust upon their hearts.

15. Nay! most surely they shall on that day be debarred from their Lord.

16. Then most surely they shall enter the burning fire.

17. Then shall it be said: This is what you gave the lie to.

18. Nay! Most surely the record of the righteous shall be in the Iliyin.

19. And what will make you know what the highest Iliyin is?

20. It is a written book,

21. Those who are drawn near (to Allah) shall witness it.

22. Most surely the righteous shall be in bliss,

23. On thrones, they shall gaze;

24. You will recognize in their faces the brightness of bliss.

25. They are made to quaff of a pure drink that is sealed (to others).

26. The sealing of it is (with) musk; and for that let the aspirers aspire.

27. And the admixture of it is a water of Tasnim,

28. A fountain from which drink they who are drawn near (to Allah).

29. Surely they who are guilty used to laugh at those who believe.

30. And when they passed by them, they winked at one another.

31. And when they returned to their own followers they returned exulting.

32. And when they saw them, they said: Most surely these are in error;

33. And they were not sent to be keepers over them.

34. So today those who believe shall laugh at the unbelievers;

35. On thrones, they will look.

36. Surely the disbelievers are rewarded as they did.

THE BURSTING ASUNDER

In the name of Allah, the Beneficent, the Merciful.

1. When the heaven bursts asunder,
2. And obeys its Lord and it must.
3. And when the earth is stretched,
4. And casts forth what is in it and becomes empty,
5. And obeys its Lord and it must.
6. O man! surely you must strive (to attain) to your Lord, a hard striving until you meet Him.
7. Then as to him who is given his book in his right hand,
8. He shall be reckoned with by an easy reckoning,
9. And he shall go back to his people joyful.
10. And as to him who is given his book behind his back,
11. He shall call for perdition,
12. And enter into burning fire.
13. Surely he was (erstwhile) joyful among his followers.
14. Surely he thought that he would never return.
15. Yea! surely his Lord does ever see him.
16. But nay! I swear by the sunset redness,
17. And the night and that which it drives on,
18. And the moon when it grows full,
19. That you shall most certainly enter one state after another.
20. But what is the matter with them that they do not believe,
21. And when the Quran is recited to them they do not make obeisance?
22. Nay! those who disbelieve give the lie to the truth.
23. And Allah knows best what they hide,
24. So announce to them a painful punishment,
25. Except those who believe and do good; for them is a reward that shall never be cut off.

THE MANSIONS OF THE STARS

In the name of Allah, the Beneficent, the Merciful.

1. I swear by the mansions of the stars,
2. And the promised day,

3. And the bearer of witness and those against whom the witness is borne.

4. Cursed be the makers of the pit,

5. Of the fire (kept burning) with fuel,

6. When they sat by it,

7. And they were witnesses of what they did with the believers.

8. And they did not take vengeance on them for aught except that they believed in Allah, the Mighty, the Praised,

9. Whose is the kingdom of the heavens and the earth; and Allah is a Witness of all things.

10. Surely (as for) those who persecute the believing men and the believing women, then do not repent, they shall have the chastisement of hell, and they shall have the chastisement of burning.

11. Surely (as for) those who believe and do good, they shall have gardens beneath which rivers flow, that is the great achievement.

12. Surely the might of your Lord is great.

13. Surely He it is Who originates and reproduces,

14. And He is the Forgiving, the Loving,

15. Lord of the Arsh, the Glorious,

16. The great doer of what He will.

17. Has not there come to you the story of the hosts,

18. Of Firon and Samood?

19. Nay! those who disbelieve are in (the act of) giving the lie to the truth.

20. And Allah encompasses them on every side.

21. Nay! it is a glorious Quran,

22. In a guarded tablet.

THE NIGHT-COMER

In the name of Allah, the Beneficent, the Merciful.

1. I swear by the heaven and the comer by night;

2. And what will make you know what the comer by night is?

3. The star of piercing brightness;

4. There is not a soul but over it is a keeper.

5. So let man consider of what he is created:

6. He is created of water pouring forth,

7. Coming from between the back and the ribs.

8. Most surely He is able to return him (to life).

9. On the day when hidden things shall be made manifest,

10. He shall have neither strength nor helper.

11. I swear by the raingiving heavens,

12. And the earth splitting (with plants);

13. Most surely it is a decisive word,

14. And it is no joke.

15. Surely they will make a scheme,

16. And I (too) will make a scheme.

17. So grant the unbelievers a respite: let them alone for a while.

THE MOST HIGH

In the name of Allah, the Beneficent, the Merciful.

1. Glorify the name of your Lord, the Most High,

2. Who creates, then makes complete,

3. And Who makes (things) according to a measure, then guides (them to their goal),

4. And Who brings forth herbage,

5. Then makes it dried up, dust-colored.

6. We will make you recite so you shall not forget,

7. Except what Allah pleases, surely He knows the manifest, and what is hidden.

8. And We will make your way smooth to a state of ease.

9. Therefore do remind, surely reminding does profit.

10. He who fears will mind,

11. And the most unfortunate one will avoid it,

12. Who shall enter the great fire;

13. Then therein he shall neither live nor die.

14. He indeed shall be successful who purifies himself,

15. And magnifies the name of his Lord and prays.

16. Nay! you prefer the life of this world,

17. While the hereafter is better and more lasting.

18. Most surely this is in the earlier scriptures,

19. The scriptures of Ibrahim and Musa.

THE OVERWHELMING CALAMITY

In the name of Allah, the Beneficent, the Merciful.

1. Has not there come to you the news of the overwhelming calamity?
2. (Some) faces on that day shall be downcast,
3. Laboring, toiling,
4. Entering into burning fire,
5. Made to drink from a boiling spring.
6. They shall have no food but of thorns,
7. Which will neither fatten nor avail against hunger.
8. (Other) faces on that day shall be happy,
9. Well-pleased because of their striving,
10. In a lofty garden,
11. Wherein you shall not hear vain talk.
12. Therein is a fountain flowing,
13. Therein are thrones raised high,
14. And drinking-cups ready placed,
15. And cushions set in a row,
16. And carpets spread out.
17. Will they not then consider the camels, how they are created?
18. And the heaven, how it is reared aloft,
19. And the mountains, how they are firmly fixed,
20. And the earth, how it is made a vast expanse?
21. Therefore do remind, for you are only a reminder.
22. You are not a watcher over them;
23. But whoever turns back and disbelieves,
24. Allah will chastise him with the greatest chastisement.
25. Surely to Us is their turning back,
26. Then surely upon Us is the taking of their account.

THE DAYBREAK

In the name of Allah, the Beneficent, the Merciful.

1. I swear by the daybreak,
2. And the ten nights,

3. And the even and the odd,

4. And the night when it departs.

5. Truly in that there is an oath for those who possess understanding.

6. Have you not considered how your Lord dealt with Ad,

7. (The people of) Aram, possessors of lofty buildings,

8. The like of which were not created in the (other) cities;

9. And (with) Samood, who hewed out the rocks in the valley,

10. And (with) Firon, the lord of hosts,

11. Who committed inordinacy in the cities,

12. So they made great mischief therein?

13. Therefore your Lord let down upon them a portion of the chastisement.

14. Most surely your Lord is watching.

15. And as for man, when his Lord tries him, then treats him with honor and makes him lead an easy life, he says: My Lord honors me.

16. But when He tries him (differently), then straitens to him his means of subsistence, he says: My Lord has disgraced me.

17. Nay! but you do not honor the orphan,

18. Nor do you urge one another to feed the poor,

19. And you eat away the heritage, devouring (everything) indiscriminately,

20. And you love wealth with exceeding love.

21. Nay! when the earth is made to crumble to pieces,

22. And your Lord comes and (also) the angels in ranks,

23. And hell is made to appear on that day. On that day shall man be mindful, and what shall being mindful (then) avail him?

24. He shall say: O! would that I had sent before for (this) my life!

25. But on that day shall no one chastise with (anything like) His chastisement,

26. And no one shall bind with (anything like) His binding.

27. O soul that art at rest!

28. Return to your Lord, well-pleased (with him), well-pleasing (Him),

29. So enter among My servants,

30. And enter into My garden.

THE CITY

In the name of Allah, the Beneficent, the Merciful.

1. Nay! I swear by this city.
2. And you shall be made free from obligation in this city—
3. And the begetter and whom he begot.
4. Certainly We have created man to be in distress.
5. Does he think that no one has power over him?
6. He shall say: I have wasted much wealth.
7. Does he think that no one sees him?
8. Have We not given him two eyes,
9. And a tongue and two lips,
10. And pointed out to him the two conspicuous ways?
11. But he would not attempt the uphill road,
12. And what will make you comprehend what the uphill road is?
13. (It is) the setting free of a slave,
14. Or the giving of food in a day of hunger
15. To an orphan, having relationship,
16. Or to the poor man lying in the dust.
17. Then he is of those who believe and charge one another to show patience, and charge one another to show compassion.
18. These are the people of the right hand.
19. And (as for) those who disbelieve in our communications, they are the people of the left hand.
20. On them is fire closed over.

THE SUN

In the name of Allah, the Beneficent, the Merciful.

1. I swear by the sun and its brilliance,
2. And the moon when it follows the sun,
3. And the day when it shows it,
4. And the night when it draws a veil over it,
5. And the heaven and Him Who made it,
6. And the earth and Him Who extended it,

7. And the soul and Him Who made it perfect,

8. Then He inspired it to understand what is right and wrong for it;

9. He will indeed be successful who purifies it,

10. And he will indeed fail who corrupts it.

11. Samood gave the lie (to the truth) in their inordinacy,

12. When the most unfortunate of them broke forth with mischief,

13. So Allah's apostle said to them: (Leave alone) Allah's she-camel, and (give) her (to) drink.

14. But they called him a liar and slaughtered her, therefore their Lord crushed them for their sin and levelled them (with the ground).

15. And He fears not its consequence.

THE NIGHT

In the name of Allah, the Beneficent, the Merciful.

1. I swear by the night when it draws a veil,

2. And the day when it shines in brightness,

3. And the creating of the male and the female,

4. Your striving is most surely (directed to) various (ends).

5. Then as for him who gives away and guards (against evil),

6. And accepts the best,

7. We will facilitate for him the easy end.

8. And as for him who is parsimonious and considers himself free from need (of Allah),

9. And rejects the best,

10. We will facilitate for him the difficult end.

11. And his wealth will not avail him when he perishes.

12. Surely Ours is it to show the way,

13. And most surely Ours is the hereafter and the former.

14. Therefore I warn you of the fire that flames:

15. None shall enter it but the most unhappy,

16. Who gives the lie (to the truth) and turns (his) back.

17. And away from it shall be kept the one who guards most (against evil),

18. Who gives away his wealth, purifying himself.

19. And no one has with him any boon for which he should be rewarded,

20. Except the seeking of the pleasure of his Lord, the Most High.

21. And he shall soon be well-pleased.

THE EARLY HOURS

In the name of Allah, the Beneficent, the Merciful.

1. I swear by the early hours of the day,

2. And the night when it covers with darkness.

3. Your Lord has not forsaken you, nor has He become displeased,

4. And surely what comes after is better for you than that which has gone before.

5. And soon will your Lord give you so that you shall be well pleased.

6. Did He not find you an orphan and give you shelter?

7. And find you lost (i.e. unrecognized by men) and guide (them to you)?

8. And find you in want and make you to be free from want?

9. Therefore, as for the orphan, do not oppress (him).

10. And as for him who asks, do not chide (him),

11. And as for the favor of your Lord, do announce (it).

THE EXPANSION

In the name of Allah, the Beneficent, the Merciful.

1. Have We not expanded for you your breast,

2. And taken off from you your burden,

3. Which pressed heavily upon your back,

4. And exalted for you your esteem?

5. Surely with difficulty is ease.
6. With difficulty is surely ease.
7. So when you are free, nominate.
8. And make your Lord your exclusive object.

THE FIG

In the name of Allah, the Beneficent, the Merciful.

1. I swear by the fig and the olive,
2. And mount Sinai,
3. And this city made secure,
4. Certainly We created man in the best make.
5. Then We render him the lowest of the low.
6. Except those who believe and do good, so they shall have a reward never to be cut off.
7. Then who can give you the lie after (this) about the judgment?
8. Is not Allah the best of the Judges?

THE CLOT

In the name of Allah, the Beneficent, the Merciful.

1. Read in the name of your Lord Who created.
2. He created man from a clot.
3. Read and your Lord is Most Honorable,
4. Who taught (to write) with the pen,
5. Taught man what he knew not.
6. Nay! man is most surely inordinate,
7. Because he sees himself free from want.
8. Surely to your Lord is the return.
9. Have you seen him who forbids
10. A servant when he prays?
11. Have you considered if he were on the right way,

12. Or enjoined guarding (against evil)?

13. Have you considered if he gives the lie to the truth and turns (his) back?

14. Does he not know that Allah does see?

15. Nay! if he desist not, We would certainly smite his forehead,

16. A lying, sinful forehead.

17. Then let him summon his council,

18. We too would summon the braves of the army.

19. Nay! obey him not, and make obeisance and draw nigh (to Allah).

THE MAJESTY

In the name of Allah, the Beneficent, the Merciful.

1. Surely We revealed it on the grand night.

2. And what will make you comprehend what the grand night is?

3. The grand night is better than a thousand months.

4. The angels and Gibreel descend in it by the permission of their Lord for every affair,

5. Peace! it is till the break of the morning.

THE CLEAR EVIDENCE

In the name of Allah, the Beneficent, the Merciful.

1. Those who disbelieved from among the followers of the Book and the polytheists could not have separated (from the faithful) until there had come to them the clear evidence:

2. An apostle from Allah, reciting pure pages,

3. Wherein are all the right ordinances.

4. And those who were given the Book did not become divided except after clear evidence had come to them.

5. And they were not enjoined anything except that they should serve Allah, being sincere to Him in obedience, upright, and keep up prayer and pay the poor-rate, and that is the right religion.

6. Surely those who disbelieve from among the followers of the Book and the polytheists shall be in the fire of hell, abiding therein; they are the worst of men.

7. (As for) those who believe and do good, surely they are the best of men.

8. Their reward with their Lord is gardens of perpetuity beneath which rivers flow, abiding therein for ever; Allah is well pleased with them and they are well pleased with Him; that is for him who fears his Lord.

THE SHAKING

In the name of Allah, the Beneficent, the Merciful.

1. When the earth is shaken with her (violent) shaking,
2. And the earth brings forth her burdens,
3. And man says: What has befallen her?
4. On that day she shall tell her news,
5. Because your Lord had inspired her.
6. On that day men shall come forth in sundry bodies that they may be shown their works.
7. So. he who has done an atom's weight of good shall see it.
8. And he who has done an atom's weight of evil shall see it.

THE ASSAULTERS

In the name of Allah, the Beneficent, the Merciful.

1. I swear by the runners breathing pantingly,
2. Then those that produce fire striking,
3. Then those that make raids at morn,

4. Then thereby raise dust,
5. Then rush thereby upon an assembly:
6. Most surely man is ungrateful to his Lord.
7. And most surely he is a witness of that.
8. And most surely he is tenacious in the love of wealth.
9. Does he not then know when what is in the graves is raised,
10. And what is in the breasts is made apparent?
11. Most surely their Lord that day shall be fully aware of them.

THE TERRIBLE CALAMITY

In the Name of Allah, the Beneficent, the Merciful.

1. The terrible calamity!
2. What is the terrible calamity!
3. And what will make you comprehend what the terrible calamity is?
4. The day on which men shall be as scattered moths,
5. And the mountains shall be as loosened wool.
6. Then as for him whose measure of good deeds is heavy,
7. He shall live a pleasant life.
8. And as for him whose measure of good deeds is light,
9. His abode shall be the abyss.
10. And what will make you know what it is?
11. A burning fire.

THE MULTIPLICATION OF WEALTH AND CHILDREN

In the name of Allah, the Beneficent, the Merciful.

1. Abundance diverts you,
2. Until you come to the graves.

3. Nay! you shall soon know,

4. Nay! Nay! you shall soon know.

5. Nay! if you had known with a certain knowledge,   •

6. You should most certainly have seen the hell;

7. Then you shall most certainly see it with the eye of certainty;

8. Then on that day you shall most certainly be questioned about the boons.

TIME

In the name of Allah, the Beneficent, the Merciful.

1. I swear by the time,

2. Most surely man is in loss,

3. Except those who believe and do good, and enjoin on each other truth, and enjoin on each other patience.

THE SLANDERER

In the name of Allah, the Beneficent, the Merciful.

1. Woe to every slanderer, defamer,

2. Who amasses wealth and considers it a provision (against mishap);

3. He thinks that his wealth will make him immortal.

4. Nay! he shall most certainly be hurled into the crushing disaster,

5. And what will make you realize what the crushing disaster is?

6. It is the fire kindled by Allah,

7. Which rises above the hearts.

8. Surely it shall be closed over upon them,

9. In extended columns.

THE ELEPHANT

In the name of Allah, the Beneficent, the Merciful.

1. Have you not considered how your Lord dealt with the possessors of the elephant?
2. Did He not cause their war to end in confusion,
3. And send down (to prey) upon them birds in flocks,
4. Casting against them stones of baked clay,
5. So He rendered them like straw eaten up?

THE QUREAISH

In the name of Allah, the Beneficent, the Merciful.

1. For the protection of the Qureaish—
2. Their protection during their trading caravans in the winter and the summer—
3. So let them serve the Lord of this House,
4. Who feeds them against hunger and gives them security against fear.

THE DAILY NECESSARIES

In the name of Allah, the Beneficent, the Merciful.

1. Have you considered him who calls the judgment a lie?
2. That is the one who treats the orphan with harshness,
3. And does not urge (others) to feed the poor.
4. So woe to the praying ones,
5. Who are unmindful of their prayers,
6. Who do (good) to be seen,
7. And withhold the necessaries of life.

THE HEAVENLY FOUNTAIN

In the name of Allah, the Beneficent, the Merciful.

1. Surely We have given you Kausar,
2. Therefore pray to your Lord and make a sacrifice.
3. Surely your enemy is the one who shall be without posterity.

THE UNBELIEVERS

In the name of Allah, the Beneficent, the Merciful.

1. Say: O unbelievers!
2. I do not serve that which you serve,
3. Nor do you serve Him Whom I serve:
4. Nor am I going to serve that which you serve,
5. Nor are you going to serve Him Whom I serve:
6. You shall have your religion and I shall have my religion.

THE HELP

In the name of Allah, the Beneficent, the Merciful.

1. When there comes the help of Allah and the victory,
2. And you see men entering the religion of Allah in companies,
3. Then celebrate the praise of your Lord, and ask His forgiveness; surely He is oft-returning (to mercy).

THE FLAME

In the name of Allah, the Beneficent, the Merciful.

1. Perdition overtake both hands of Abu Lahab, and he will perish.
2. His wealth and what he earns will not avail him.
3. He shall soon burn in fire that flames,
4. And his wife, the bearer of fuel,
5. Upon her neck a halter of strongly twisted rope.

THE UNITY

In the name of Allah, the Beneficent, the Merciful.

1. Say: He, Allah, is One.
2. Allah is He on Whom all depend.
3. He begets not, nor is He begotten.
4. And none is like Him.

THE DAWN

In the name of Allah, the Beneficent, the Merciful.

1. Say: I seek refuge in the Lord of the dawn,
2. From the evil of what He has created,
3. And from the evil of the utterly dark night when it comes,
4. And from the evil of those who blow on knots,
5. And from the evil of the envious when he envies.

THE MEN

In the name of Allah, the Beneficent, the Merciful.

1. Say: I seek refuge in the Lord of men,
2. The King of men,
3. The God of men,
4. From the evil of the whisperings of the slinking (Shaitan),
5. Who whispers into the hearts of men,
6. From among the jinn and the men.

PRAYER

To be used after reading the Holy Qur'an

O Allah! change my fear in my grave into love! O Allah! have mercy on me in the name of the Great Qur'an; and make it for me a Guide and Light and Guidance and Mercy; O Allah! Make me remember what of it I have forgotten; make me know of it that which I have become ignorant of; and make me recite it in the hours of the night and the day; and make it an argument for me O Thou Sustainer of (all) the worlds! Ameen!

INDEX

comes in between a man and his heart, 8:24

created things in due proportion and Truth (for just ends), 6:73; 14:19; 15:29, 85; 16:3; 25:2; 29:44; 30:8; 32:9; 39:5; 44:38-39; 45:22; 46:3; 54:49; 64:3; 79:28; 82:7; 87:2; 91:7

creates what He wills, 3:47; 5:17; 24:45; 28:68; 30:54; 35:1; 42:49; 82:8

does what He wills, 2:253; 3:40; 11:107; 14:27; 22:14-18; 85:16

encompasses all things, 4:126; 17:60; 40:7; 41:54; 65:12; 72:28

encompasses unbelievers, 2:19; 3:120; 4:108; 8:47; 11:92; 85:20

enlarges the provision and restricts it, 2:245; 13:26; 17:30; 28:82; 29:62; 30:37; 34:36, 39; 39:52; 42:12, 27; 89:15-16

established (istiwa) on the Throne of Authority, 7:54; 10:3; 13:2; 20:5; 25:59; 32:4; 57:4

exalted above what they ascribe to Him, 6:100; 7:190; 10:18; 16:1, 3; 17:43; 20:114; 21:22; 23:91-92; 23:116; 27:63; 28:68; 30:40; 37:180; 39:67; 43:82; 52:43; 59:23; 72:3

feeds but is not fed, 6:14; 51:57-58

for all things He has appointed a due proportion, 13:8; 17:30; 65:3

forgives sins, 2:284; 3:31, 195; 4:48, 116; 5:18, 39-40; 7:161; 8:29, 70; 12:92; 13:6; 14:10; 26:82; 28:16; 33:71; 36:27; 39:53; 40:3; 42:25; 42:30, 34; 46:31; 48:14; 57:28; 58:13; 61:12; 64:17; 71:4

gives life and death, 2:258; 3:156; 7:158; 9:116; 10:56; 15:23; 22:66; 23:80; 26:81; 40:68; 44:8; 45:26; 50:43; 53:44; 57:2

gives life to the dead. 1:57; 2:28, 243, 259-260; 3:27; 6:36; 7:57; 10:31; 22:6; 30:19, 40, 50; 36:12, 79; 41:39; 42:9; 46:33; 50:11; 75:40; 80:22; 86:8

gives sustenance, 2:57, 126, 172, 212; 3:27, 37, 169; 5:114; 6:151; 7:50, 160; 8:26; 10:31, 93; 11:88; 14:37; 16:72, 75; 17:31, 70; 20:81, 132; 24:38; 27:64; 29:60; 30:40; 34:24; 35:3; 40:13, 40, 64; 42:19; 45:5, 16; 50:11; 65:3; 67:15, 21; 106:4

gives wealth, 4:130; 24:32; 53:48; 93:5-8

gives without measure, 2:212; 3:27, 37; 24:38; 40:40

gives you shape, and makes your shapes beautiful, 3:6; 7:11; 15:28-29; 38:72; 40:64; 64:3; 82:8   Glory be to Him, 2:32, 116; 3:191; 4:171; 5:116; 6:100; 7:143; 9:31; 10:10, 18, 68; 12:108; 16:1; 17:43-44, 94, 108; 21:22, 26, 87; 24:16, 36; 25:18; 27:8; 28:68; 30:17, 40; 33:42; 34:41; 36:83; 37:159, 180; 39:4, 67; 40:64; 43:13, 82; 56:74, 96; 59:23; 68:28-29; 69:52; 76:26; 87:1; 110:3

God in heaven and God on earth, 43:84

God of Mankind, 114:3

grants Laughter and Tears, 53:43

guides to Himself those who turn to Him, 42:13

guides whom He will, 2:213, 272; 7:155; 10:25; 13:27; 13:31; 14:4; 16:9, 93; 22:16; 24:35, 46; 28:56; 35:8; 39:23; 42:52; 74:31

has grasp of every creature's forelock, 11:56; 96:15-16

has no partner, 6:163; 7:190-198; 9:31; 10:66; 17:111; 23:91; 25:2; 34:27; 35:40; 42:21; 68:41; 72:3

has no son, 2:116; 4:171; 6:101; 9:30; 10:68; 17:111; 18:4; 19:35, 88-92; 21:26; 23:91; 25:2; 37:152; 39:4; 43:81-82; 72:3

has subjected to you all things, 31:20; 45:12-13

hasten you to Him, 51:50

hears the arguments from both husband and wife, 58:1

helping Him, 57:25; 59:8; 61:14

His Hand is over their hands, 48:10

in His presence are those who celebrate His praises, 41:38

hope in, 33:21; 39:9; 60:6

is not unjust, 3:108, 117, 182; 4:40; 8:51; 9:70; 10:44; 18:49; 22:10; 41:46; 43:76; 50:29

is not unmindful of what you do, 2:74, 85, 140, 144, 149; 3:99; 6:132; 11:123; 14:42; 16:91; 22:68; 23:17; 27:93;

is sufficient, 2:137; 3:173; 4:6, 45, 70, 79, 81, 132, 166, 171; 8:62, 64; 9:59, 129; 10:29; 13:43; 15:95; 17:17, 65, 96; 25:31, 58; 29:52; 33:3, 25, 39, 48; 39:36, 38; 46:8; 48:28; 65:3

is the best of planners, 3:54; 8:30; 13:42

is with you wheresoever you may be, 57:4; 58:7

knowledge of the heavens and the earth, 3:29; 5:97; 6:59; 11:123; 14:38; 16:77; 17:55; 18:26; 21:4; 22:70; 25:6; 27:65; 29:52; 34:2; 35:38; 49:16, 18; 57:4; 58:7; 64:4

knows all you reveal and conceal, 2:77, 284; 3:29; 5:99; 6:2; 11:5;

14:38; 16:19, 23; 27:25, 74; 28:69; 33:54; 36:76; 53:32; 60:1; 64:4

knows best who is guided, 6:117; 16:125; 17:84; 28:56; 53:30; 68:7

knows the secrets of hearts, 3:29, 119, 154; 5:7; 8:43; 11:5; 28:69; 29:10; 33:51, 35:38; 39:7; 40:19; 42:24; 50:16; 57:6; 64:4; 67:13-14; 84:23

knows what is hidden (the Unseen), 2:33; 5:109, 116; 6:59, 73; 9:78, 94, 105; 10:20; 11:123; 13:9-10; 16:77; 18:26; 20:7; 21:110; 23:92; 25:6; 27:65; 32:6; 34:3, 48; 49:18; 72:26; 84:23; 87:7

listens to the distressed, 27:62

listens to those who believe and do deeds of righteousness, 42:26

love for Him, 2:165, 177; 3:31; 5:54; 21:90; 76:8

loves the righteous, 9:4, 7; 19:96

loves those who are kind and do good, 2:195; 3:134, 148; 5:13, 93

loves those who are just, 4:42; 49:9; 60:8

loves those who fight in His Cause, 61:4

loves those who make themselves pure, 2:222; 9:108

loves those who put their trust in Him, 3:159

made everything He created good, 32:7

magnify Him, 2:185; 17:111; 22:37; 74:3

manifests His glory (tajalla), 7:143

meeting with Him, 2:46, 223, 249; 6:154; 10:11, 15, 45; 13:2; 18:48, 110; 25:21; 29:5, 23; 30:8; 32:10, 14; 33:44; 41:54; 84:6

splits and sprouts the seeds, 6:95

sustains the heavens and the earth, 30:25; 35:41

takes account of every single thing, 2:284; 72:28

takes your souls by night, 6:60

taught man, 2:31; 55:2, 4; 96:4-5

there is none like unto Him, 42:11; 112:4

to Him all questions go back, 2:210; 3:109; 8:44; 11:123; 22:41, 76; 42:53; 57:5

to Him applies the highest similitude, 16:60; 30:27

to Him belong all glory and power, 4:139; 10:65; 35:10; 37:180; 63:8

to Him belong the East and the west, 2:115, 142; 26:28; 55:17; 70:40; 73:9

to Him belong the End and the Beginning, 53:25; 92:13

to Him belong the Forces of the heavens and the earth, 48:4; 48:7

to Him belong the keys of the heavens and the earth, 39:63; 42:12

to Him belong the Most Beautiful Names, 7:180;17:110;, 20:8; 59:24

to Him belong the treasures of the heavens and the earth, 63:7

to Him belongs all in the heavens and on earth, 2:225, 284; 3:109, 129; 4:126, 131-132, 170-171; 6:12; 10:66, 68; 14:2; 16:52; 20:6; 21:19; 22:64; 23:84-85; 24:64; 27:91; 30:26; 31:26; 34:1; 42:4, 53; 53:31

to Him belongs the dominion of the heavens and the earth, 2:107, 116; 3:109, 189; 4:126, 131, 132, 170-171; 5:17, 18, 40, 120, 181; 6:12; 7:158; 9:116; 10:55; 11:123; 13:15-16; 14:2; 16:49, 52, 77;

19:65; 20:6; 21:19; 22:64; 24:42, 64; 25:2; 26:24; 30:26; 31:26; 35:13; 36:83; 37:5; 38:6; 39:38, 44; 42:4; 42:49; 43:85; 45:27; 48:14; 53:31; 57:2, 5; 64:1, 4; 67:1; 78:37; 85:9

to Him belongs the heritage of the heavens and the earth, 3:180; 15:23; 57:10

to Him is the final goal, 2:285; 5:18, 105; 6:164; 22:48; 24:42; 35:18; 40:3; 42:15; 50:43; 53:42; 60:4; 64:3

to Him you shall be brought (gathered) back, 2:28, 46, 156, 281; 3:158; 5:48, 96; 6:12, 36, 38, 60, 164; 8:24; 10:4, 23, 45, 56; 11:3, 4; 15:25; 19:40; 21:35; 23:79, 115; 24:64; 28:70, 88; 29:8, 57; 30:11; 31:15; 32:11; 36:22, 32, 83; 39:44; 43:85; 45:15; 67:24; 96:8

towards Him you are turned, 7:125; 26:50; 26:227; 29:21; 43:14

trust in, 3:159-160, 173; 4:81; 5:11, 23; 7:89; 8:2, 61; 9:51, 129; 10:71, 84-85; 11:56, 88, 123; 12:67; 13:30; 14:11-12; 16:42, 99; 17:65; 25:58; 26:217; 27:79; 29:59; 33:3, 48; 39:38; 42:10, 36; 58:10; 60:4; 64:13; 65:3; 67:29

turn all your attention to Him, 94:8

watchtower, 89:14

what is with Him will endure, 16:96; 28:60; 42:36; 55:27

will change evil into good, 25:70

will gather you together, 3:9; 45:26

will not change the condition of a people until they change, 13:11

will not suffer the reward to be lost, 3:195; 9:120; 12:56, 90; 18:30; 21:94; 52:21

will prevail, 12:21; 58:21

with Him is the outcome of all affairs, 31:22

worship Him (alone), 1:5; 3:64; 6:56, 102; 7:59, 65, 85, 206; 11:2, 26, 50, 61, 84, 123; 12:40; 13:36; 17:23; 19:65; 21:25; 22:77; 23:23, 32; 24:55; 25:60; 26:61; 39:66; 41:37; 46:21; 53:62; 71:3; 98:5; 106:3

Allah's artistry, 27:88;

Allah's attributes, 7:180; 17:110; 20:8; 59:24

All-Embracing (cares for al) *[Al Wasi7*, 2:115, 247, 261, 268; 3:73; 4:130; 5:54; 24:32; 53:32

answers petitions [Al Mujib], 11:61; 37:75

Aware (Well-acquainted) *[Al Khabir]*, 2:234, 271; 3:153, 180; 4:35, 94, 128, 135, 5:8; 6:18, 73, 103; 9:16; 11:1, 111; 17:17, 30, 96; 22:63; 24:30, 53; 25:58-59; 27:88; 31:16, 29, 34; 33:2, 34; 34:1; 35:14, 31; 42:27; 48:11; 49:13; 57:10; 58:3, 11, 13; 59:18; 63:11; 64:8; 66:3; 67:14; 100:11

Beneficent [Al Barr], 52:28

Best of judges *[Al Khayr al Fasilin]*, 6:57

Best of those who show mercy *[Arham ar Rahimin]*, 7:151; 12:64, 92; 21:83

[Khayr al Rahimin], 23:109, 118

Bestower of Forms and Colours *[Al Musawwir]*, 59:24

Best to decide

[Ahkam al Hakimin], 11:45; 95:8

[Khayr al Hakimin], 7:87; 10:109; 11:45; 12:80

Blots out sins *[Al 'Afu]*, 4:43, 99, 149; 22:60; 58:2

Calls to account *[Al Hasib]*, 4:6, 86; 6:62; 17:14; 21:47; 33:39

Cherisher and Sustainer *[Al Rabb]*, 1:2; 6:45, 162-163; 7:54, 58, 61, 67; 10:10, 32; 13:16, 18:42; 21:92; 23:52; 26:16, 23-28, 77; 29:59; 37:126, 182; 39:6; 44:8; 45:36; 81:29; 96:1; 98:8; 114:1; etc.

Creator *[Al Khaliq; Al Khallaq]*, 6:102; 13:16; 15:28, 86; 35:3; 36:81; 37:125; 38:71; 39:62; 40:62; 59:24

Disposer of affairs *[Al Wakil]*, 4:171; 6:102; 17:65; 28:28; 33:3, 48; 39:62; 73:9

Eternal, Absolute *[Al Samad]*, 112:2

Evident *[Al Zahirl]*, 57:3

Evolver *[Al Bari']*, 59:24

Exalted in Power and Might *[Al 'Aziz]*, 2:209, 220, 228, 240; 3:6, 18, 62, 126; 4:56, 158, 165; 5:38, 118; 6.96; 8:10, 63; 9:71, 40, 128, 129; 11:66; 14:14, 47; 16:60; 22:40, 74; 26:9, 104, 122, 140, 159, 175, 191, 217; 27:9, 78; 29:26, 42; 30:27; 31:9, 27; 32:6; 33:25; 34:6, 27; 35:2, 28; 36:5; 38:9, 66; 39:1, 5, 37; 40:2, 42; 41:12; 42:3, 19; 43:9; 44:42; 45:2, 37; 46:2; 48:7, 19; 54:42; 57:1, 25; 58:21; 59:1, 23-24; 60:5; 61:1; 62:1, 3; 64:18; 67:2; 85:8

First *[Al Awwal]*, 57:3

Forbearing *[Al Halim]*, 2:225, 235, 263; 3:155; 4:12; 5:101; 17:44; 22:59; 33:51; 35:41; 64:17

forgives again and again *[Al Ghaffar]*, 20:82; 38:66; 39:5; 40:42; 71:10

Free of all wants *[Al Ghani]*, 4:131; 6:133; 10:68; 14:8; 22:64; 27:40; 29:6; 31:12; 31:26; 35:15; 39:7; 47:38; 57:24; 60:6; 64:6

Caller will call out from a place quite near, the, 50:41; 54:6

Camels, 5:103; 6:144; 7:40, 73, 77; 11:64-65; 12:65; 17:59; 22:27, 36-37; 26:155-157; 54:27-29; 59:6; 77:33; 81:4; 88:17; 91:13

Captives, 2:85; 8:67, 70; 33:26; 76:8

Cattle, 3:14; 4:119; 6:136, 138-139, 142-144; 7:179; 12:43, 46; 16:5-7, 10, 66; 20:54; 23:21-22; 25:44, 49; 26:133; 32:27; 36:71-73; 39:6; 40:79-80; 42:11; 43:12-14; 47:12; 79:33; 80:32

Cave, Companions of the, 18:9-22, 25-26

Cave of Thawr, 9:40,

Certainty, 56:95

Its three kinds, 69:51, 102:5,

Charity [zakah], 2:43, 83, 110, 177, 270-274, 277; 4:77, 162; 5:12, 55; 7:156; 9:71; 19:31, 55; 21:73; 22:41, 78; 23:4; 23:60; 24:37, 56; 27:3; 28:54; 30:39; 32:16; 33:33, 35; 35:29; 36:47; 41:7; 57:7; 57:10; 58:13; 63:10; 64:16; 70:24-25; 93:10; 98:5

a beautiful loan to Allah, 2:245; 5:12; 57:11, 18; 64:17; 73:20

Children, 7:189-190; 8:28; 13:38; 16:72; 17:64; 24:31; 25:58-59; 42:49-50; 46:15; 60:3; 63:9; 64:14-15; 71:12; 90:3

after divorce, 2:233; 65:6

and inheritance, 4:11

do not kill, 6:137, 140, 151; 17:31; 60:12

see also Daughters; Sons.

Children of Israel, 2:211, 246-252; 3:49, 93; 5:12, 32; 7:159-171; 10:93; 17:2; 17:101; 19:58; 20:80; 26:17, 22; 32:23-24; 40:53

and Jesus, 3:49-51; 5:46; 5:72, 110; 61:14

and the calf, 2:51-54, 93; 4:153; 7:148, 152; 20:87-97

and the Qur'an, 26:197; 27:76; 46:10

deliverance from Pharaoh, 2:48-49; 7:136-141; 10:90; 14:6; 20:77-80; 26:60-67; 44:30-33

forty years in the wilderness, 5:26

distort the Book, 3:78; 5:14; 7:162

dwellings in Egypt, 10:87; 26:57-59

granted Prophethood, 45:16

hearts went wrong, 61:5

like a donkey carrying books, 62:5

told to remember Allah's favours, 2:40, 47, 122; 5:20

warning given to them, 17:4-8, 104

see also Jews; Tribes; People of the Book; Covenant

Christ, see Jesus

Christians, 2:111, 113, 120, 135; 5:14, 18; 22:17;

believers rewarded, 2:62; 5:69, 85; 57:27-29

Compassion and Mercy in their hearts, 57:27

love for the Believers, 5:82

recognize the truth, 5:83-84

see also People of the Book

Cities overthrown, 69:9

Cleanliness, 4:43; 5:6

Clothing, 7:22, 31; 16:81; 24:31, 58; 60; 33:59

of Paradise, 18:31; 35:33; 44:53; 76:12, 21

Clouds, 2:57, 164; 7:57, 160; 13:12; 24:43; 30:48; 35:9; 46:24-25; 52:44; 56:69

Colors,

of animals, 2:69; 35:27

of Gardens of Paradise, 55:64, 76

of honey, 16:69

of mountains, 35:28

of people, 30:22; 35:28

of plants, 35:27; 39:21

see also Ka'bah.

Mother of Cities, see Makkah.

Mother of the Book, see Qur'an.

Mothers, 2:233; 4:1; 16:78 22:2;
24:61; 31:14; 39:6; 46:15; 58:2

see also Parents; Wombs.

Mothers of the Believers, see Wives
of the Prophet.

Mountains, 13:3, 31; 15:19, 82;
16:15, 81; 17:36; 21:31, 79;
22:18; 26:149; 31:10; 33:72;
38:18; 50:7; 7:27; 78:7; 79:32;
88:19

destroyed, made into dust, 7:143;
18:47; 19:90; 20:105- 107; 27:88;
52:10; 56:5-6; 59:21; 69:14; 70:9;
73:14; 77:10; 78:20; 81:3; 101:5

Mount Sinai, 19:52; 23:20; 28:46;
52:1; 95:2

Mubahalah,

Muddaththir, al, S. 74

Muhajirs, 9:117; 16:41-42, 110;
22:58; 24:22; 29:26: 59:8-10

Muhammad, S. 47, see also Ahmad

Allahs favours to, 9:117; 48:2; 68:2;
93:3-8; 94:1-6; 108:1

in Allahs eyes, 52:48

in battle, 3:153

a beautiful pattern of conduct, 33:21

belief in, 4:136, 170; 7:158; 13:43;
24:62; 46:31; 48:9, 13; 49:15;
57:7, 28; 58:4; 61:11; 64:8

blessings and peace upon him, 33:56

and the blind man, 80:1-10

a bringer of glad tidings and a
warner, 5:19; 7:184, 188; 11:2;
13:7; 15:84; 17:105; 19:97; 21:45;
22:49; 25:56; 27:92; 28:46; 29:50;
32:3; 33:45; 34:28, 46; 35:23-24;
36:6; 38:65-70; 46:9; 48:8;
51:50-51; 61:13; 67:86; 74:2;
79:45

brings no new doctrine among the
messengers, 46:9

brought back to the Place of Return,
28:85

closer to the Believers then their own
selves, 33:6

confirms the Messengers before him,
37:37

confronts the Hypocrites, 33:12-20;
63:1-8; 66:9

consultation with, 58:12-13

cry of, 43:88

devotion to Allah, 73:7-8

did not fabricate the Message,
10:37-39; 52:33; 69:41-47

does not ask rewards of people,
12:104; 25:57; 34:47; 38:86;
42:23; 34:47; 38:86; 42:23; 52:40;
68:46

does not speak of his own desire,
53:3

duty to proclaim the message, 5:67,
92, 99; 9:33; 13:40; 15:94; 16:82;
24:54; 42:48; 46:35; 64:12; 72:23

enfolded, wrapped up in garments,
73:1; 74:1

exalted standard of character, 68:4

faith of, 2:285; 42:15; 109:6

family of, purified, 33:33

foretold in Scripture, 3:81; 7:157

a freeman of Makkah, 90:2

given the revelation, 8:41; 10:2;
12:3; 13:30; 14:1; 15:87; 16:44,
64, 89; 25:1; 27:6; 29:47; 34:50;
41:6; 42:3; 42:7, 52; 47:2;
53:4-11; 57:9; 73:5

granted Victory, 48:1-3, 18, 24, 27;
61:13; 110:1

grieve not, 15:88; 16:127; 18:6; 26:3;
27:70; 31:23; 35:8; 36:76

has no power except as Allah wills,
7:188; 10:49; 72:21- 22

better than deed deserves, 27:84; 30:39

according to best of deeds and more, 24:38; 29:7; 39:35

for good, no reward other than good, 55:60 righteous, company of the, 4:69

shall inherit the earth, 21:105

described, 51:15-19; 76:5-12.

R*iba* see Usury

Righteous, the, 3:15-17; 4:69; 6:69, 85; 7:35, 128, 169-170; 13:23, 35; 16:30, 97, 122; 21:72, 75, 105; 25:74; 26:83; 27:19; 28:27; 29:9, 27; 37:112; 43:35, 67; 44:51-57; 45:19; 49:7; 50:31-35; 51:15-19; 52:17-28; 54:34; 66:4; 68:34, 50; 76:5-22; 77:41-44; 78:31-36; 82:13; 83:18-28; 92:17-21

loved by Allah, 9:4, 7; 19:96

Righteousness, 2:177; 3:92; 5:93; 6:153, 155, 158; 7:26; 10:5; 11:11; 23:100; 27:19; 28:67; 32:12; 34:11; 41:18, 46; 42:26; 47:2; 49:13; 57:9; 65:11; 74:56; 96:12; 98:7; 103:3

exalted by Allah, 35:10

Right Hand, Companions of, 56:8, 27-40, 90-91; 74:39-42; 90:18

Right hands possess, those whom, see Handmaidens.

Rivers, 13:3, 17; 14:32; 16:15; 18:33; 19:24; 27:61; 43:51; 47:15; 71:12
Rocks, parable of, 2:74, 264

Rocky Tract, Companions of the, 15:80-84

see also Thamid.

Roman Empire, 30:2-6;

R*um, al,* S. 30

S*aba;* S. 34; 27:22-35; 34:15-21

Sabbath, transgressed, 2:65; 4:47, 154; 7:163; 16:124;

Sabians, 2:62; 5:69; 22:17

Sacred Mosque, see Ka'bah.

Sacrifice, 2:67-71; 6:162; 22:28; 22:32-34, 36-37; 48:25; 108:2

of Abraham, 37:102-107

S*ad,* S. 38

Safa and Marwah, 2:158;

S*aff, al,* S. 61

S*affat, al,* S. 37

S*ajdah, al,* S. 32

Salah, see Prayer

Salih, 7:73-79; 11:61-66; 26:142-158; 27:45-53; 54:27; 91:13

S*alsabil;* 76:18

Salutation, see Greeting.

Samiri, 20:85, 87-88, 95-97

Samuel, 2:246-248

Sanctification, 2:129; 3:164; 62:2

see also Purification of the soul.

Satan, 2:268, 275; 3:155, 175; 4:38, 60, 83; 6:68; 12:42; 22:52-53; 31:21; 47:25

cannot harm the Believers, 58:10

do not follow or obey or worship, 2:168, 208; 6:142; 19:44-45; 22:3-4; 24:21; 36:60

enemy of man, 12:5, 100; 17:53; 18:50; 20:117; 25:29; 35:5; 36:60; 43:62

fails in his promise, 14:22

fears Allah, 8:48; 59:16

has no authority over Allah's servants, 15:42; 16:99-100; 17:65; 34:21

makes sins fair-seeming, 6:43; 8:48; 15:39; 16:63; 27:24; 29:38

misleads and deceives, 4:117-121; 15:39; 17:62-68; 20:120; 34:20; 36:62; 57:14; 59:16

Party of, will perish, 58:19

seek refuge with Allah from, 7:200-201; 16:98; 41:36